The Libyan Novel

Edinburgh Studies in Modern Arabic Literature
Series Editor: Rasheed El-Enany

Writing Beirut: Mappings of the City in the Modern Arabic Novel
Samira Aghacy

Autobiographical Identities in Contemporary Arab Literature
Valerie Anishchenkova

The Iraqi Novel: Key Writers, Key Texts
Fabio Caiani and Catherine Cobham

Sufism in the Contemporary Arabic Novel
Ziad Elmarsafy

Gender, Nation, and the Arabic Novel: Egypt 1892–2008
Hoda Elsadda

The Unmaking of the Arab Intellectual: Prophecy, Exile and the Nation
Zeina G. Halabi

Egypt 1919: The Revolution in Literature and Film
Dina Heshmat

Post-War Anglophone Lebanese Fiction: Home Matters in the Diaspora
Syrine Hout

Prophetic Translation: the Making of Modern Egyptian Literature
Maya I. Kesrouany

Nasser in the Egyptian Imaginary
Omar Khalifah

Conspiracy in Modern Egyptian Literature
Benjamin Koerber

War and Occupation in Iraqi Fiction
Ikram Masmoudi

Literary Autobiography and Arab National Struggles
Tahia Abdel Nasser

The Libyan Novel: Humans, Animals and the Poetics of Vulnerability
Charis Olszok

The Arab Nahdah*: The Making of the Intellectual and Humanist Movement*
Abdulrazzak Patel

Blogging from Egypt: Digital Literature, 2005–2016
Teresa Pepe

Religion in the Egyptian Novel
Christina Phillips

Space in Modern Egyptian Fiction
Yasmine Ramadan

Occidentalism: Literary Representations of the Maghrebi Experience of the East-West Encounter
Zahia Smail Salhi

Sonallah Ibrahim: Rebel with a Pen
Paul Starkey

Minorities in the Contemporary Egyptian Novel
Mary Youssef

www.edinburghuniversitypress.com/series/smal

The Libyan Novel

Humans, Animals and the Poetics of Vulnerability

Charis Olszok

EDINBURGH
University Press

Edinburgh University Press is one of the leading university presses in the UK. We publish academic books and journals in our selected subject areas across the humanities and social sciences, combining cutting-edge scholarship with high editorial and production values to produce academic works of lasting importance. For more information visit our website: edinburghuniversitypress.com

First published in hardback by Edinburgh University Press 2020

Edinburgh University Press Ltd
The Tun – Holyrood Road
12(2f) Jackson's Entry
Edinburgh EH8 8PJ

Typeset in 11/15 Adobe Garamond by
IDSUK (DataConnection) Ltd

A CIP record for this book is available from the British Library

ISBN 978 1 4744 5745 3 (hardback)
ISBN 978 1 4744 5746 0 (paperback)
ISBN 978 1 4744 5747 7 (webready PDF)
ISBN 978 1 4744 5748 4 (epub)

Contents

Series Editor's Foreword vi
Acknowledgements ix
Note on Translation and Transliteration xi

Introduction: A Nation of Others 1

Part I Survival

1 Animal Fable in Novels of Survival 35
2 The Primordial Turn 64

Part II Signs and Cityscapes

3 God's Wide Land: War, Melancholy and the Camel 95
4 Absent Stories in the Urban Novel 126

Part III Children of the Land

5 Too-Long-a-Tale 171
6 *'Une histoire de mouche'*: The Libyan Novel in Other Voices 198

Afterword: Breaking Fevers and Strange Metamorphoses 226

Notes 237
Bibliography 277
Index 300

Series Editor's Foreword

Edinburgh Studies in Modern Arabic Literature is a new and unique series that will, it is hoped, fill in a glaring gap in scholarship in the field of modern Arabic literature. Its dedication to Arabic literature in the modern period (that is, from the nineteenth century onwards) is what makes it unique among series undertaken by academic publishers in the English-speaking world. Individual books on modern Arabic literature in general or aspects of it have been and continue to be published sporadically. Series on Islamic studies and Arab/Islamic thought and civilisation are not in short supply either in the academic world, but these are far removed from the study of Arabic literature qua literature, that is, imaginative, creative literature as we understand the term when, for instance, we speak of English literature or French literature. Even series labelled 'Arabic/Middle Eastern Literature' make no period distinction, extending their purview from the sixth century to the present, and often including non-Arabic literatures of the region. This series aims to redress the situation by focusing on the Arabic literature and criticism of today, stretching its interest to the earliest beginnings of Arab modernity in the nineteenth century.

The need for such a dedicated series, and generally for the redoubling of scholarly endeavour in researching and introducing modern Arabic literature to the Western reader, has never been stronger. Among activities and events heightening public, let alone academic, interest in all things Arab, and not least Arabic literature, are the significant growth in the last decades of the translation of contemporary Arab authors from all genres, especially fiction, into English; the higher profile of Arabic literature internationally since the award of the Nobel Prize in Literature to Naguib Mahfouz in 1988; the growing number of Arab authors living in the Western diaspora and writing both in English and Arabic; the adoption of such authors and others by mainstream, high-circulation publishers, as opposed to the academic publishers of the past; the establishment of prestigious prizes, such as the International Prize for Arabic Fiction (IPAF; the Arabic Booker), run by the Man Booker Foundation, which brings huge publicity to the shortlist and winner every year, as well as translation contracts into English and other languages; and, very recently, the events of the Arab Spring. It is therefore part of the ambition of this series that it will increasingly address a wider reading public beyond its natural territory of students and researchers in Arabic and world literature. Nor indeed is the academic readership of the series expected to be confined to specialists in literature in the light of the growing trend for interdisciplinarity, which increasingly sees scholars crossing field boundaries in their research tools and coming up with findings that equally cross discipline borders in their appeal.

The novel genre in Arabic generally is sometimes described as 'young' because it entered a language reputed for its age-old tradition of poetry mainly through European literary influence and can only be dated back to the 1870s in its earliest enunciations. However, this happened only in the relatively developed cultural centres at the time of Cairo and Beirut. It took much longer for the genre to evolve in other parts of the Arabic-speaking world, and in the case of Libya, it was to make its tentative appearance only a hundred years later in the 1970s. But it was not perhaps until the 1990s that some mature works began to attract attention in literary circles, while some individual writers with exceptional talent, well ahead of cultural development within Libya as a whole, began to come to the fore and attract attention with the quality of their work beyond Libya and the Arab world, for example Ibrahim al-Koni and Ahmad Ibrahim al-Faqih, now translated into many European languages. Not only that but there are now some Anglophone Libyans writing in the diaspora having fled Gaddafi's repression, such as Hisham Matar, one of the authors studied in this monograph.

While the Libyan novel has made admirable progress in just a few decades, scholarship has lagged behind badly. You will find an article here or a chapter there looking at limited parts of the picture, but no systematic study of the emergence and development of the genre as a whole in Libya, no examination of the major exponents and themes in the context of the despotic regime of Gaddafi who came to power in 1969, around the time of the nascence of the genre in the country. This unsatisfactory condition is what the current monograph, the first in English about the Libyan novel, proffers to correct. Charis Olszok does not only provide a survey of the evolution of the genre in the Libyan context but also goes on to focus on its major writers and analyse in detail some of their salient works. Perhaps one of the most exciting elements in the author's approach is her focus on the poetics of creaturely vulnerability, an approach rarely used in the study of Arabic fiction, but one to which the Libyan novel freely and rewardingly lends itself, as this study shows.

Professor Rasheed El-Enany, Series Editor,
Emeritus Professor of Modern Arabic Literature,
University of Exeter

Acknowledgements

My sincere gratitude goes to Professor Rasheed El-Enany for his invaluable advice in adapting my PhD into the current monograph and widening the scope of its creaturely imaginings. The patient support of the editorial and production teams at Edinburgh University Press greatly smoothed the process of bringing it to publication. Special thanks also go to my PhD supervisor, Professor Wen-chin Ouyang, for her tireless support during the first stage of this project and for her continued friendship. For providing the first inspiration, I am grateful to Margaret Obank and Samuel Shimon, and all the incredible work they do at *Banipal Magazine of Modern Arab Literature*. With the generous funding of the Wolfson Foundation, I was able to run with this inspiration and lay the groundwork for a project that has continued to fascinate and challenge me. I would also like to thank Ghassan Fergiani and Ghazi Gheblawi for supplying me with books, information and contacts. Thanks to Muhammad Bin Lamin for generously allowing me to use his beautiful artwork for the cover of this book, as well as providing food for thought for the analyses within it.

At the Faculty of Asian and Middle Eastern Studies, I am especially indebted to Professor Amira Bennison who, as my first Head of Department, has been an unfailing fount of calm and reason during the last years. I would also like to thank colleagues James Montgomery, Yaron Peleg, Andrew Marsham, Christine van Ruymbeke, Khaled Fahmy, Assef Ashraf, Nathan Miller and Vicky Young. Special thanks to Basim Musallam for his wisdom and humour. Lastly, this book owes much to my fantastic students, who have had me thinking about literature in the most unexpected ways from day one.

Thanks also to friends and family for support and cheer. Special thanks to my mum, Fran, an impossible wonder of peace and pottering, and to my Dad, Mark, for his brilliant madness. Thanks to Hannah, for forest runs, chats, jokes and the fabulous Madlet. Thanks to Ewa and Wiesław for boundless hospitality, and to Sean and Rosemary for many fine evenings. A final thanks to my husband, Alek, for perennial love and laughter.

Note on Translation and Transliteration

I have followed the transliteration guidelines of the *International Journal of Middle Eastern Studies*. For readability, names of major authors are given with full diacritics only upon first mention. In more minor references to authors and historical figures not widely known in English names are given in full transliteration. Where a published translation exists, I have generally used this. In other cases, I indicate in the notes when the translation is my own and, if a published English translation exists, I also reference this when citing substantial passages of text.

Introduction: A Nation of Others

There is no creature that crawls on the face of the earth, no bird on the wing, but they are nations like you. We have not neglected any matter in this Book, and then to God they shall be mustered. (Qur᾿an 6:38)[1]

In 2010, Libyan author ᶜUmar al-Kiddi (al-Kiddī, b.1959) published a short story, 'al-Hayah al-Qasira al-ᶜAjiba li-l-Kalb Ramadan' (2010; 'The Wonderful Short Life of the Dog Ramadan', 2011). In it, a wily stray dog, escaped from neglectful owners, is adopted by Mrs de Vries, the wife of an engineer in a Dutch irrigation project in the Libyan desert. Luring Ramadan with treats, Mrs de Vries secures his affection, and, when it is time for her to return to Holland, is distraught to learn that obtaining him a passport will not be as straightforward as she had at first thought. In a country where humans cannot leave, dogs have little chance. In desperation, Mrs de Vries pays for Ramadan's passage aboard an illegal migrant crossing to Lampedusa, where she breathlessly awaits his arrival some weeks later. Having safely arrived in Holland, Ramadan's story then goes viral, prompting audiences to weep at the suffering of 'animals in the Third World', and transform him into a national treasure, championed by animal rights activists.[2] Toys are made in his image, and a biopic filmed of his life, with the proviso that, while in Libya, the crew are to film nothing but Ramadan and the events strictly related to his life. After several happy years in Holland, Ramadan dies peacefully, mourned with a state funeral and buried in a Protestant grave.

Al-Kiddi's sharply satirical story holds several narratives in uncomfortable tension. On the one hand, its affectionate portrayal of Ramadan renders it a rare iteration of 'happily ever after' in Libyan fiction and a whimsical take on the popular 'dog's journey home' genre. On the other, the invisibility of all but Ramadan, both in Libya and his migrant crossing, speaks to the country's long cultural and political marginalisation under Muᶜammar al-Qadhafi (al-Qadhdhāfī, 1942–2011), from 1969 until 2011. From the barriers surrounding the irrigation project to the selective filming of Ramadan's life, to cursory mention of a 'boat full of Africans', the story is traversed by fault lines, determining who can be seen, and who is free to move.[3] Blithely unaware of the geopolitical circumstances, in which his 'wonderful' journey unfolds, Ramadan casts humans' contrasting imperceptibility into bitter relief. As a stray dog, he clearly alludes to al-Qadhafi's 1980s' 'Stray Dog' campaign (*ᶜamaliyyat al-kilāb al-ḍālla*), rounding up and assassinating Libyan dissidents abroad. Simultaneously, he points to the double standards of the West, lamenting the treatment of 'animals in the Third World', and echoing the suspicions and stereotypes in which Libya has long been shrouded, while ignoring the wider circumstances of Ramadan's home country, and making his welcome contingent on his transformation into toy, film and national hero.

Through these tensions, Ramadan resists straightforward symbolic analysis, satirising the Dutch whims through which his 'wonderful life' is permitted, while also representing an unassuming creature, attempting to survive within the Jamahiriyya ('People's Republic'). Within al-Kiddi's wider literary *oeuvre*, he also demonstrates the dictates of censorship, as, following the 17th February Revolution and subsequent collapse of the Qadhafi regime in 2011, the author reworked his story as a novel, *Hurub Marish wa-Thawratuha al-Thalath* (2013, The Wars and Three Revolutions of Marish). Supplemented by various *human* characters who help him escape, as well as a drama involving al-Qadhafi himself and his determination to reclaim the Libyan dog, the novel suggests the tantalising possibilities for Libyans to enter the realms of fiction, after decades of existing on its margins, in allegorical, veiled narrative.

From its first flourishing in the 1980s, the Libyan novel has but rarely described contemporary life in direct, realist terms. Overwhelmingly, it has turned to the past, whether Italian colonisation (1911–43), British Military Administration (1943–51) or the Senusi Monarchy (1951–69). From popular resistance to Italian rule to the 1960s oil boom, this fiction strives to recover neglected memories, and digest disorienting social transformations. It also, however, indicates the impossibility of speaking openly of anything beyond 1969. In a literary tradition where every story is problematic, both through the horror of telling it, and the danger that telling it brings, narrative becomes necessarily allusive. Stories conceal other stories, striving to express human experience in a country that has moved, within a few decades, from nomadic to urban, and from colonisation to dictatorship, in a nation both rentier and 'rogue', stateless and authoritarian, and, since 2014, caught in the throes of civil war.

This narrative fragility, or what I term 'difficulty of story', is reflected in the very genesis of Libyan fiction, in a land which, as author Ibrahim al-Kuni (al-Kūnī, b.1948) puts it, has suffered 'isolation inherited from isolation'.[4] In 1911, Italy began its military incursion into the Ottoman provinces of Fezzan, Cyrenaica and Tripolitania, inaugurating decades of bitter fighting, until its declaration of dominion over the newly designated 'Libya' in 1934. Under the Italians, Libyans were designated as second-class citizens, barred from education and employment, and submitted to a long-standing 'cultural embargo'.[5] At Independence, in 1951, illiteracy remained at 94 per cent and the demands of survival, against starvation, disease and genocide, were foremost.[6] With the country's intellectuals exiled abroad, in Tunisia, Egypt and Syria, the literary scene remained limited, with the first short stories published in the 1930s, by Wahbī al-Būrī (1916–2010), in the Tripoli journal *Libya al-Musawwara*.

Beyond al-Būrī, fiction did not flourish in earnest until the 1960s, in the wake of the Second World War and the struggle for Independence, when Cyrenaica, Tripolitania and Fezzan were brought together by the United Nations General Assembly as the United Kingdom of Libya, under the rule of King Idris al-Sanusi (al-Sanūsī, 1889–1983). Through this rather haphazard process, regional tensions became swiftly apparent. After the Italians' summary destruction of local political administration and identity, people fell back on tribe and kinship ties, haunted by an abiding distrust of centralised bureaucracy, cemented by colonial rule.[7] With the arrival of oil, corrupt and nepotistic practices spread, leading to growing social inequalities, as Idris remained firmly biased towards his native region of Cyrenaica.[8] Ongoing affiliations with the West further set the country against wider Pan-Arab currents.

Out of this turbulent context came both a pioneering literary generation, and the young officer, al-Qadhafi, whose sudden and comprehensive assumption of power relegated literature, once again, to the margins. Until today, the

Libyan novel has a limited readership in Libya, the wider Arab world and the West, where, even within academic research, it is virtually unknown. From 1970 to 2011, I therefore examine how the novel is haunted by marginality, as characters transform into 'footnotes' (*hawāmish*), and speech resonates with the 'unsaid' (*al-maskūt ᶜanhu*), expressing a population 'othered' within its own land, whether as second-class citizens under the Italians, or as the 'stray dogs', 'rats' and 'cockroaches', which al-Qadhafi labelled them.[9] Focusing on images of vulnerability, to both environmental and political precarity, I draw on the concept of 'creatureliness' to theorise how depictions of realist human relationships shift to the melancholy, heterotopic worlds of desert, coastline and neglected city park, exploring the boundaries of humanness, and extending attention to paradigmatically excluded forms of being. This poetics, I argue, represents a specificity of the Libyan novel, expressing the ontological, ethical and epistemological uncertainties of existing within a hazardous world.

While representing an evident response to censorship, resonant with wider political meaning, this poetics is further rooted in a melancholy vision of history, informed by Libya's centuries of outside occupation, and the culminating horrors of Italian colonisation. So, too, does it resonate with the country's folkloric and Sufi legacies, anchored in lost ways of relating to the land and relaying experience. Extreme geographies, of vast desert, rugged coastline and seasonal sandstorms, as well as sporadic flooding and drought, represent a final dimension, whether dramatising the material difficulty of survival or inflected with unease over urbanisation and environmental degradation. Together, these dimensions come together in narratives of vulnerability, resistance and solidarity, underpinned by images of flight, homelessness and exposure. In a 1977 article, at the height of al-Qadhafi's 'Cultural Revolution', Libya's celebrated critic, Muḥammad al-Faqīh Ṣāliḥ (1953–2017) thus declares that writing must derive from '*qaswa*' (harshness, austerity, cruelty), as well as from 'conscious integration into the unfolding of creation' (*istighrāq wāᶜin fī ṣayrūrat al-khalq*).[10] Such writing, he declares, must not be predicated on straightforward prose, mimicking reality and putting its readers at ease, but rather on 'chiselling' (*naḥt*) and 'bleeding' (*nazf*), combining the sublime and vulnerable, as it draws on the 'rhythms of labour, the birth of the Universe, and the dance of humans, rising from their pent up suffering and pain'.[11]

In my examination of this poetics, non-human animals represent a specific, but not exclusive, focus of my analyses, whether as a tool of political allegory, reminder of former pastoralism or focal point for exploring the boundaries of humanness.[12] Above all, animals emerge as a means of rethinking both political and cosmological hierarchies, and thereby subverting those who dictate life, meaning and value. As I argue, creatureliness emerges not just as an expression of vulnerability, but a way of rethinking ethics and forging affiliations beyond monolithic ideology and political oppression. Charting the transformations to Libyan land, society and politics, animals embody both paradigmatically excluded forms of being and forms of being that exist beyond the established hierarchies and totalising discourses that have long dominated Libya's political system. Together, animals and humans become 'creatures' (*makhlūqāt*), and I explore them as such, drawing on perspectives from both Ecocriticism and Animal Studies, in which thinking on creatureliness has been fostered.

In recent decades, both interdisciplinary fields have grown in prominence, exploring, within literary studies, how narrative might be read for non-human presences and the land, paying attention to the human value systems with which they are loaded and the material exploitation to which they are exposed, as well as how they unsettle human ethics, ontologies and epistemologies.[13] Coming together with the concerns of postcolonial thought, the 'animalising' rhetoric and environmentally appropriative practices of imperialism have become a particular focus, explored in authors such as the Nigerian Ken Saro-Wiwa (1941–95) and Indian Arundhati Roy (b.1961).[14] Neither field has, however, engaged much with modern Arabic literature, while scholars of Arabic literature have also tended to focus more on the political, national and social than the ecological.[15] In the Libyan novel, however, the political and ecological have always been entangled, through depictions of the changing landscape of an oil state, and allusions to the advent of al-Qadhafi, metamorphosing the nation into a land of 'others', and predicating his power on the management and control of natural resources. Steeped in the wider tradition of animal imagery, in classical Arabic and Islamic literature and popular folklore, the Libyan novel therefore provides a vital case study for thinking about human–animal bonds within the material landscape, beyond the European tradition to which Animal Studies has been largely limited. Specifically, it encourages a focus on creatureliness as an ethical and epistemological endeavour and literary poetics. For a field concerned with animals as the 'limit case for theories of difference, otherness and power', it is certainly imperative that Animal Studies moves into such contexts, and explores the kind of attention extended to creatures within them, countering suggestions that concern for 'animal victims' is limited to the rich West.[16] In the following sections of this introduction, I therefore explore creatureliness more fully, after first tracing central components of the Libyan literary and novelistic tradition.

Writing under Dictatorship

Libya's first wave of pioneering authors were recognised as the 'sixties generation', emerging during a time of shifting literary sensibilities and increasingly experimental poetics within Arabic literature more broadly. As literacy grew and newspapers and printing presses flourished, these authors addressed growing economic inequalities, abiding patriarchy and encroaching American interference, combining realism with forays into symbolism, surrealism and stream-of-consciousness.[17] Celebrated at the First Libyan Writers Conference in 1968, a vibrant community developed, with none more popular than essayist and novelist al-Sadiq al-Nayhum (al-Nayhūm, 1937–92), at the centre of a new generation of fiction writers, from Kāmil Ḥasan al-Maqhūr (1935–2002) to al-Kuni and Ahmad Ibrahim al-Faqih (al-Faqīh, 1942–2019), and poets, from Khalīfa al-Tilīsī (1930–2010) to al-Jīlānī Ṭuraybshān (1944–2001).

A decade of both hope and anxiety, the 1960s concluded with al-Qadhafi's September 1st al-Fatih Revolution. Facilitated by oil money, al-Qadhafi's initial drive to improve healthcare, housing and education prompted some early optimism, but his crackdown on free speech was immediately apparent, as were the paradoxes of his erratic governance. Espousing a 'direct democracy', outlined in his *Green Book* (1975, *al-Kitāb al-Akhḍar*), his 'Revolutionary Decade' of the 1970s led to the creation of both a 'stateless' society, for which he coined the term 'Jamahiriyya' in 1977, and a society of omnipresent surveillance. Both were operated through 'Popular' and 'Revolutionary' Committees (*Lijān shaᶜbiyya wa-thawriyya*), supposedly encouraging political participation, while really acting as mechanisms of surveillance.

Infiltrating every aspect of society, these committees created an atmosphere of universal fear, in which any comment could be deadly. 'Anecdotally',

Ethan Chorin writes, 'by the mid-1980s, an estimated 10 percent of the population had been incorporated through the Revolutionary Committees into a web of informants that frequently spied and reported on family members and each other.'[18] Through the spectacles of torture and execution, broadcast on TV and radio, all lives were incorporated within a national 'state of exception'. While al-Qadhafi had initially enriched the country through renegotiation of oil prices, the 1980s then brought drastic economic decline, with falling oil revenues compounded by lavish spending on military campaigns, administrative chaos, the outlawing of commerce and seizing of private assets, and imposition of US sanctions. By 1982, between fifty and one hundred thousand Libyans – the 'stray dogs' of al-Qadhafi's campaign – are believed to have fled abroad.[19]

Simultaneously, Libya became more ethnically homogenous and internally divided. After the 1967 June War, the last of the Jewish population were expelled, while, in 1970, al-Qadhafi ousted all remaining Italians. Announcing the pre-eminence of Arabic language and Islamic culture, he denied the rights of Amazigh, Tuareg, Tebu and black minorities and did little to protect the growing population of migrant workers. Throughout, he nevertheless remained willing to exploit tribal tensions and ethnic differences for his own gain, setting one group against the other, and creating a society of mutual suspicion.

Authors were specifically targeted as 'enemies of the revolution', and receptacles of foreign ideas. As novelist Hisham Matar (b.1970) comments: 'Dictatorship by its essence is interested in one narrative, an intolerant narrative, and writers are interested in a multiplicity of narratives and conflicting empathies and what the other is thinking and feeling. And that completely unsettles the dictatorial project.'[20] In 1970, clashes between government forces and students led to the first large-scale arrests, while the Seminar on Revolutionary Thought (*Nadwat al-fikr al-thawrī*) confirmed the hostile stance of the Revolutionary Command Council (RCC) towards all other 'stories'. Having clashed with one of the Council's founding members, ᶜUmar al-Muḥayshī, al-Nayhum was termed a 'reactionary element' and swiftly silenced.[21] Al-Kuni's written riposte to the seminar, *Naqd al-Fikr al-Thawri* (1970, A Critique of Revolutionary Thought), was allegedly the first book to be banned by the regime, while its author left for Moscow and a life outside the country.[22]

Following al-Qadhafi's announcement of the Cultural Revolution (*al-Thawra al-thaqāfiyya*) in Zuwara, 1973, aiming to purge the country of 'political illnesses' and 'deviations', books with 'imported ideas' were burnt and libraries and bookshops emptied.[23] Private newspapers were replaced with government publications, *al-Fajr al-Jadid* and *al-Usbu*ᶜ *al-Thaqafi*, while publishers were combined into a single government-owned entity. As the 'ideological bible of Libya', the *Green Book* came to dominate the country's intellectual scene, while, with the publication of al-Qadhafi's 'short stories' in 1993, he completed his dominion over intellectual and cultural expression.[24] Founded in 1976, the Union of Libyan Writers (*Rābiṭa al-udabāʾ wa-l-kuttāb al-libiyyīn*) was immediately subject to government control, followed, in 1978, by a mass imprisonment of authors for over a decade. Executions and televised trials became a daily occurrence, while, in the 1990s, amid the growth of popular unrest and Islamist opposition, the massacre of Abu Salim Prison (April 1996) left an estimated 1,200 people dead, with their families left for years with no news of their fate. Summing up the regime's many abuses, an Amnesty International Report states:

> Routine abuses committed in the 1970s, 1980s and 1990s included arbitrary detentions, enforced disappearances, torture and other ill-treatment, extrajudicial executions and deaths in custody. Victims ranged from political dissidents living in Libya or abroad to suspected members or supporters of armed Islamist groups.[25]

Author Muhammad al-Asfar (al-Aṣfar, b.1960) has written about these circumstances in more personal terms: 'For decades, we lived in terror, surrounded by spies and informants, facing the risk of imprisonment or "disappearance" at any moment. No one could intervene on your behalf; there were no real courts, no human rights, nothing.'[26]

Almost all writers positioned themselves at either the centre or periphery of what Rita Sakr calls the 'anti-Qaddafi cultural and political imaginary'.[27] Many fell silent or retreated abroad, whether seeking asylum or sent on diplomatic missions. All developed a 'disciplined sense of self-censorship'.[28] Citing al-Faqih, Chorin writes that 'Libya under Gaddafi was one of the few dictatorial regimes to maintain a government unit specifically dedicated to repressing innovation and artistic creation in all forms.'[29] Some authors, like al-Faqih himself, trod an outwardly conciliatory path, accepting state prizes, and honing a style that mixed critique and caution. As Suha Taji-Farouki comments, they were inevitably tainted by the 'uncompromising yardstick [. . .] according to which any relationship with the authorities, regardless of its nature, was considered deplorable', in a country riven by suspicion and fear.[30]

While caution remained rife, the 2000s represented a second golden age for Libyan literature, aided by the arrival of the internet in 1998 and popularity of foreign-based websites such as *Balad al-Tuyub* and *Libya al-Mustaqbal.* Freedoms were seemingly also increased by al-Qadhafi's improved relations with the West, officially inaugurated by the 2003 weapons of mass destruction (WMD) deal, and championed by the outwardly reform-minded Sayf al-Islam (b.1972). With the end of international sanctions and the reopening of diplomatic relations, glimpses of change could be felt, though many dreaded the possibility that al-Qadhafi might achieve his rehabilitation without true accountability. Censorship also remained tight. Author Wafāʾ al-Būʿīssī (b.1973) describes a harrowing encounter with al-Qadhafi in 2007: 'In veiled terms, he told me that there was a report, which would unfortunately prevent my novel's publication, and, because of this "security reading" (*al-qirāʾa al-amniyya*), I risked paying the highest price.'[31] In a small nation, connected by vast tribal networks, al-Qadhafi had easy access to authors, who could be whisked into his presence at a moment's notice. As Sakr comments, the Jamahiriyya transformed into Foucault's panoptic state, a 'faceless gaze that transformed the whole social body into a field of perception: thousands of eyes posted everywhere, mobile attentions ever on the alert, a long, hierarchized network'.[32]

Within this climate, the Libyan novel, from the 1970s to 2011, presents a melancholy world, in which fragile human relationships and visceral images of stasis, hunger and pain evoke the country's 'starving out' (*tajwīʿ*), 'marginalisation' (*tahmīsh*) and 'stultification' (*tajhīl*) during the 'lean years' (*al-sanawāt al-ʿijāf*) of al-Qadhafi's rule.[33] Born from precarity, the Libyan novel poignantly demonstrates how a genre, celebrated for polyphony, democratic modernity and 'imagining nation', is shaped by oppression, and how a disparate corpus, written from exile and imprisonment, addresses historically distinct regions, and extreme geographies.[34] As I explore, the state's 'faceless gaze' is countered by transgressive affiliations under the radar, contesting the society's 'forced love' for al-Qadhafi as alternative passions and obsessions come to the fore.[35]

The Libyan Novel

From its beginnings, the Libyan novel has struggled against censorship and neglect, coming to prominence only in the 1980s, following several earlier works in the 1960s and 1970s. Oral poetry and the folkloric *khurāfa* (fantastical tale) represent the country's principal literary heritage, while the short story flourished in the 1960s, becoming, as al-Maqhūr comments, 'a symbol of Libyan culture, and reflection of our people's struggles, compelling new authors to make their mark upon it'.[36] Despite the popularity of neighbouring Egyptian authors, al-Maqhūr insists on the shaping influence of folklore, particularly as composed under Italian occupation, when people were constantly on the move, and in need of succinct narrative forms to convey fleeting moments of heroism or tragedy.[37] During the 1960s, this shifted to the upheavals of the oil boom, influencing the 'committed short story', in which, as Tetz Rooke suggests, 'young people found inspiration for change, images that moved them to action and imaginative texts that welded the nation together in the narrow territorial sense'.[38]

From the 1980s, many authors transitioned to the novel, embracing the polyphony and structural openness of the longer form. Growing in prominence throughout the 1990s and 2000s, this openness prompts my focus. While the Libyan short story conveys sudden acts of transformation and rebellion, the novel opens onto a broad, creaturely totality, juxtaposing the official, and giving voice to the marginal and silenced. Intertextuality with the short story, folklore and poetry further produces an experimental generic hybridity, entangling histories, species and geographies, and exemplifying the hospitality with which Waïl Hassan associates the novel:

> The novel is worldly but not necessarily or exclusively secular, prosaic yet open to poetic and myriad other styles, potentially encyclopaedic but potentially also (auto)biographical, open to individualistic as well as social panoramic vistas. It was born in the city but it travels through the countryside and the desert – by land, at sea, and in outer space. In short, the novel is a hospitable genre defined by a constitutive otherness, but it is also alive to the frequent violence of encounter.[39]

As such a hospitable, open space, the novel in Libya has provided a valuable, if fragile, antidote to overarching social and political stasis, while its hospitality, as I suggest, is rooted in its creaturely imaginary, opening up to encounter with the vulnerability of the absolute, non-human other.

To date, critical attention to the Libyan novel has been limited. In Arabic, the 1980s saw the first overviews, by Syrian critic Samar Rūḥī al-Fayṣal, alongside a scattering of articles in *al-Fusul al-Arbaᶜa*, journal of the Libyan Writers' Union.[40] The late 1990s and 2000s brought an increase in coverage: Fāṭima al-Hājī focuses on the theme of time; Maḥmūd Amlūda offers a comparative study of the intellectual; ᶜAbd al-Ḥakīm al-Mālikī focuses on symbolism and narratology; and Aḥmad al-Shaylābī studies social issues.[41] 'Maktabat al-Nayhum', a series by Dar Tala, has further reprinted articles by and about al-Nayhum. Most critics, however, are markedly restricted by censorship, limited, like the novels of which they write, to allusion. Since 2011, this has somewhat shifted, with a flourishing of personal memoirs shedding light on intellectual life within the Jamahiriyya, alongside online articles and interviews, referenced throughout my analyses.

In European languages, Elvira Diana's overview of modern Libyan poetry and prose represents the most comprehensive work to date.[42] With a few exceptions, English-language scholarship has, however, primarily devoted itself to al-Kuni, most often seen apart from his Libyan roots, and recognised as a 'different voice' in Arabic literature due to his Tuareg heritage and mythic, desert writing.[43] Matar has also grown in prominence through his writing in English, resulting in the Libyan novel's recognition through authors who, linguistically and culturally, fall on its outer edges. Al-Kuni and Matar are, however, not the outliers they might first appear. Despite the evident distinctiveness of their writing, I suggest that they share certain themes and aesthetics, anchored in the breakdown of family relationships under political and social pressure and the opening of the human onto a wider ecological whole, evident in the Libyan novel from its beginnings.[44]

Self-published in his Syrian exile, Ḥusayn Ibn Mūsā's (1892–1952) *Mabruka* (1937) is regarded as the first Libyan novel. Depicting anti-colonial resistance in the verdant region of Jabal Akhdar, it was banned by the French at the Italians' request and, with no copies remaining, is prescient of the novel's censored fate in the ensuing decades.[45] Anti-colonial struggle further dominates novels from the 1960s and 1970s, serialised in newspapers and celebrating historical figures such as Tripolitanian nationalist

Ramaḍān al-Suwayḥilī (1872–1940) and national hero, ᶜUmar al-Mukhtar (al-Mukhtār, 1858–1931).[46] Social critique, in the guise of romance, also features prominently, concerning gender and generational tensions and, as Sulaymān Kashlāf indicates, influenced by the melodramas of Egyptian cinema and the novels of Iḥsān ᶜAbd al-Quddūs (1919–90).[47]

In all these novels, the nation, its past and present, is a central concern. Aida Bamia phrases it succinctly: 'Most (Libyan) writers seemed torn between three worlds – the world they lived in, which was undergoing profound change, the Western, modern, industrialized world, and the world they dreamed of.'[48] In a particularly fascinating iteration of these 'worlds', Yūsuf al-Quwayrī's (1938–2018) *Min Mufakkirat Rajul lam Yulad* (1972, Diaries of an Unborn Man) is a series of interconnected anecdotes and dialogues, set in Libya between the years 2565 and 2567, and first published serially between 1966 and 1968.[49] While not widely recognised as a novel, it may certainly be read as such, focusing on a family of three, composed of the narrating father and his wife and daughter. In an often pedagogical tone, *Min Mufakkirat* features imaginative visions of the future, in a desert nation become verdant, fuelled by the sun, and harnessing the precarity of earthquakes, floods and sandstorms. While al-Quwayrī's overall optimism contrasts the Libyan novel's more prominent turn to lament for the past, and anxiety over the future, the novel's narrator admits that there have been some causalities of the forward march of humanity, that 'wonderful, awesome creature' (*al-makhlūq al-ᶜajīb al-rāʾiᶜ*).[50] Birds have gone extinct, as have palm trees, an exemplary symbol of Libya's traditional ecology.[51] Between an orderly future, free from political and environmental precarity, and the loss of visceral connections to land and past, the novel thus fits within a broader focus on the land, as a central domain for thinking about the nation, in haunting visions of political, social and ecological fertility, whether lost to history, regained in the future or a dreamed-of absence.

Following al-Qadhafi's coup, the range of permitted topics grew slowly more restricted, until, from 1975 to 1980, no new novels were published at all, while emerging novelists such as Muḥammad Ṣāliḥ al-Qammūdī (b.1943) and Muḥammad Farīd Siyāla (1928–2008) retreated into silence. In none is this retreat more poignant than in al-Nayhum. While Libyan critics indicate the stylistic faults of many early novels, all recognise the merits of his *Min*

Makka ila Huna (1970, From Mecca to Here), as what many call the first cohesive Libyan novel, a lasting and hugely influential pillar of the national imaginary.[52] Begun in 1966, it was published to widespread acclaim and, in its juxtaposition of realism, fable and Sufi symbolism, ranks among the wider pioneering and experimental Arabic fiction of the 1960s. Al-Nayhum was also, however, a decidedly local writer.[53] Living abroad in Finland, his satirical writing for the Benghazi weekly, *al-Haqiqa*, launched him to literary stardom and, as Taji-Farouki suggests, 'his writings were unique in their impact, and were indeed instrumental, according to some assessments, in encouraging Libyans to read and to take an interest in literary matters.'[54] Allegedly, queues would form on the day his column appeared and, despite being accused by some of writing with a 'tourist's mentality', he was deeply invested in Libya and its changing social realities.[55]

Set in the 1930s, *Min Makka* depicts Mas^cud al-Tabbal, an elderly black fisherman, struggling against the prejudice of both Italians and local religious elites. Isolated from his community, he retreats to the coastline, engaging in heated debates with turtles, rats and seagulls. As they answer back, *Min Makka* departs from realism into a poetics embedded in the land, combining fantasy and spiritual reflection, and evoking what, in a 1969 interview with al-Kuni, al-Nayhum describes as a kind of 'simple-minded Sufism' (*al-ṣūfiyya al-balhā*ʾ), underlying his social critique.[56] This departure both distinguishes *Min Makka* from other early Libyan novels and introduces a poetics characteristic of later work, as human relationships collapse and affiliations are sought beyond their realms.

Exemplifying the frustrated potential of the Libyan novel, al-Nayhum went on to write only two more fictional works, *al-Hayawanat* (1974, The Animals) and *al-Qurud* (1984, The Primates). Bleak fables, they abandon the human world altogether, allegorising political oppression through jungle kingdoms and, in their despairing narrative voice, inaugurating the novel's 'difficulty of story'. Through his complicated relationship with the regime, al-Nayhum found himself clouded in suspicion and condemned to a life in voluntary exile, while, in stark contrast to the flourishing of the 1960s, other new writers of the 'seventies generation' faded into silence.[57]

When novels reappeared in the 1980s, almost all were published through the government-controlled press, al-Dar al-Jamahiriyya. If expressed, criticism was obliquely allegorical, while most shifted to themes of environmental transformation and social alienation, focusing on the hinterland's takeover by oil companies, the loss of traditional community and growing social inequalities.[58] Khalīfa Ḥusayn Muṣṭafā (1944–2008) was particularly prolific, depicting the results of the oil boom through empty villages, growing slums and a new class of rich, exploitative oilmen. In his writing and that of others, nagging anxiety is expressed over Libya's transformation into a 'consumerist culture' (*thaqāfat al-istihlāk*) in which, as critic Ṣāliḥ writes in 1976, society submits to 'stagnation' (*jumūd*) and 'laxity' (*istirkhāʾ*), severed from the dynamic movement between past and future, and closed to 'innovation' (*ibdāʿ*).[59] In the Jamahiriyya, this was, of course, primarily a result of political stagnation while, through experimental and hybrid novels, predicated on *qaswa* (harshness) and *nazf* (bleeding), al-Faqih and al-Kuni are two authors whose literary aesthetics have struggled against it.

From his first novel, *Huqul al-Ramad* (1985; *Valley of Ashes*, 2008), al-Faqih interweaves political and environmental themes, depicting the transformation of local communities as, with the arrival of western companies, people abandon their traditional date palms (*nakhīl*) for life in city and factory. In his later fiction, this ecological focus continues, interweaving political and ecological critique through primordial images of displacement, homelessness and appropriation. With over twenty works to his name, his *oeuvre* spans theatre, short story and a twelve-volume historical saga *Kharaʾit al-Ruh* (2008; *Maps of the Soul*, 2015). His most celebrated work, the trilogy *Hadaʾiq al-Layl* (1991; *Gardens of the Night*, 1995) juxtaposes contemporary Edinburgh and Tripoli to the fantastical city of ʿIqd al-Murjan, a utopia run according to an imagined natural law, inspired by Sufi contemplation. *Fiʾran bila Juhur* (2000; *Homeless Rats*, 2011) further juxtaposes animal fable to realism, providing striking crossovers to both *Min Makka* and the ecological poetics of al-Kuni who, like al-Faqih, came to international attention at the end of the 1990s.

In many ways, it is understandable that al-Kuni is often seen apart from broader Libyan fiction. From the Tuareg tribes of the southern Sahara, he began learning Arabic only at the age of twelve, after settling in an oasis town for school, and identifies as equally Saharan, Tuareg and Libyan. Intellectually, however, he belongs firmly to the Libyan literary community. It was there, during the 1960s, that he began writing for local newspapers, inspired by the thriving literary community as he moved first to Sabha and then Tripoli. His four-volume autobiography, *ᶜUdus al-Sura* (2012, Night Wanderer) further testifies to his intimate friendships with many of the country's foremost authors during his and their years abroad, in his case in Russia, Poland and Switzerland. Above all, he describes al-Nayhum as a 'legendary figure' (*shakhṣīyya usṭūriyya*), whose writing he followed 'ardently' (*bi-shaghaf*), and with whom he forged a lifelong friendship, until al-Nayhum's death, when al-Kuni escorted his body back to Benghazi.[60]

Like many of his contemporaries, al-Kuni's early writing is further anchored in anxiety over the rise of urban 'satiation' (*shabᶜ*) and 'addiction' (*idmān*), and coinciding loss of 'nobility' (*nubl*) and 'endurance' (*ṣabr*).[61] His first novel-quartet, *al-Khusuf* (1988, The Lunar Eclipse), thus critiques the emerging authority of the Senusi monarchy in manners similar to fellow Libyan authors. For al-Kuni, however, a radical turning point, and what he calls his literary 'rebirth' (*mīlādī al-thānī*), came at the end of the 1980s, prompting his turn to what Roger Allen calls less 'immediately approachable' fiction.[62] Dwelling on desert flora and fauna, he departs into metaphysical exploration of diverse spiritual traditions, and, inspired by the likes of Kafka and Marquez, embraces the magical and mystical in a parallel rejection of the 'demon of ideology' (*al-ghūl al-īdiyūlūjī*).[63] His 'twin' novels, *Nazif al-Hajar* (1990; *The Bleeding of the Stone*, 2002) and *al-Tibr* (1990; *Gold Dust*, 2008), tell respectively of human relationships with wild and domestic species, opening up, through animal fable and Sufi imagery, to a literary domain both apart from, and entangled in, the contexts of the Libyan desert in the early twentieth century. During the 1990s, when al-Kuni dominated Libyan literary output, this poetics continues through increasingly experimental novels such as *Anubis* (2002; *Anubis*, 2005), the final quarter of which consists solely of Tuareg 'aphorisms' (*waṣāyā*).

This shift has led in part to al-Kuni's decontextualisation as a Libyan intellectual.[64] Caught between the monolithic ideologies of the Jamahiriyya and the Soviet Union, where he lived for two decades, his depictions of lone nomads and prophetic *waddān* (moufflons/Barbary sheep) nevertheless resonate with creaturely vulnerability within the land, and faced with political censorship and oppression. Libyan critics and authors further embrace al-Kuni as a major player on the literary scene, while recognising the distinctive poetics of his Tuareg desert fiction.[65] Above all, and despite this distinctiveness, he represents part of a broader turn to what Bamia describes as the Libyan novel's 'special spirituality and symbolism'.[66]

Ahmad Yusuf ᶜAqila (ᶜAqīla, b.1955) represents another significant figure within this turn. From the 1990s, his numerous short story collections, set in Jabal Akhdar, combine intimate portraits of human, animal and land. His sole novel, *al-Jirab: Hikayat al-Najᶜ* (2000, A Sack of Village Tales), is based on his childhood under the open sky and infused with local folklore and geography. Like him, ᶜAbdallah al-Ghazal (al-Ghazāl, b.1961), from the new generation of the 2000s, also expands from detailed attention to the land and its creatures into contemplation of nation and creation. His writing is also, however, marked by a greater sense of psychological malaise and more explicit political critique, from Libya's 1980s war with Chad in *al-Tabut* (2004, The Coffin) to literary censorship and social instability. Fragmented, melancholy and elusive, his haunting depiction of Misrata in *al-Khawf Abqani Hayyan* (2008, Fear Kept Me Breathing) is one of several striking depictions of contemporary urban Libya, breaking with the historical turn of preceding decades.

Among others, Ahmad al-Fayturi (al-Faytūrī, b.1954), Mansur Bushnaf (Būshnāf, b.1954) and al-Asfar have all returned to writing in the 2000s, after the curtailment of their promising literary careers in the 1970s. Al-Asfar is most prolific, through chaotic, vibrant depictions of Benghazi that flout literary conventions and expectations. After twelve years in prison, *al-ᶜIlka* (2008; *Chewing Gum*, 2014) is Bushnaf's sole novel, a darkly satirical evocation of 1980s Tripoli. Imprisoned alongside Bushnaf, al-Fayturi also has only one novel to his name, *Sarib* (2000, A Long Story), which, like ᶜAqila's *al-Jirab*, returns to his childhood, in 1960s Benghazi. Together with the diasporic writing of Matar in English and Kamal Ben Hameda (b.1954) in French, they represent an important strand of childhood *Bildungsroman*, portraying memories of disorientation and vulnerability, and imaginative dialogues with land and animals. While in *Sarib* and *al-Jirab*, childhood geographies are mourned through the lens of urbanisation and dictatorship, in Matar's *In the Country of Men* (2006) and Ben Hameda's *La compagnie des Tripolitaines* (2011; *Under the Tripoli Sky*, 2013) they resonate with the distance of exile.

Finally, authors Razzan Naᶜim al-Maghrabi (al-Maghrabī, b.1961), Najwa Bin Shatwan (Bin Shatwān, b.1969) and Wafāʾ al-Būᶜissī (b.1973) have brought women's fiction to the fore. From pioneering figures such as Marḍiyya al-Naᶜās (b.1949) and Nādira al-ᶜUwaytī (1949–2015) in the 1970s and 1980s, writing by women has struggled against both patriarchy and political oppression. Most prominently, it has emerged through coming-of-age narratives concerning women's journey to find a literary and social voice. In the 2000s, al-Maghrabi continues this tradition through her 2011 IPAF-shortlisted *Nisaᵓ al-Rih* (2010, Women of the Wind). Bin Shatwan, meanwhile, has shifted into experimental, elliptical and defamiliarising writing, exemplified by her first novel, *Wabr al-Ahsina* (2003, The Horse's Hair). Narrated by an unborn foetus, it takes the childhood *Bildungsroman* into the domain of the pre-human world and, like Bin Shatwan's wider writing, represents a creative response to censorship through attentiveness to traditionally imperceptible layers of being.

From al-Nayhum to Bin Shatwan, this elusive, densely symbolic style has, inevitably, led some to observe, if not bemoan, the Libyan novel's departure from recognisable contexts into heterotopic margins. In the 1990s, critic Salīm Hābīl argues that, 'There is still no true novelistic tradition in Libya. We are still awaiting the birth of the Libyan novel, diverging from what has gone before and baring a loving portrait of the nation within it.'[67] Similarly, Chorin remarks on the absence of concrete 'places' in Libyan fiction, replaced by 'a kind of anodyne universe where allegory and alternate realities predominate'.[68] This 'universe', I suggest, is best read through a poetics of creaturely vulnerability, fleeing censorship in defamiliarising, fragmented poetics. In this light, the Libyan novel, as national tradition, might be understood, as a whole, through Deleuze and Guattari's 'minor writing', though this term is usually applied only to linguistically and culturally marginal groups within broader national traditions.[69] Incorporating both the founding poetics of al-Nayhum and al-Faqih, and the culturally and linguistically outlying figures of al-Kuni and Matar, Libyan minor writing counters the oppressive rhetoric of the *Green Book*, and the authors' wider marginality within Arabic and world literary circles. Expressing what Deleuze and Guattari term a politically charged 'potential' community, bound by creative endeavour, authors imagine an alternative wholeness to nation, through the land and its creatures, and through outcast figures and deterritorializing 'lines of flight'.[70]

Humans as *makhlūqāt*: Creaturely Vulnerability in the Libyan Novel

Derived from the fundamental nexus of creation and creator, the English 'creature' tends to be associated with strange, monstrous forms of being, outside human 'norms' and often subjected to another's control.[71] In Arabic, contrastingly, the passive participle *makhlūq* conveys an abidingly powerful notion of 'createdness', rooted in the Qur'an and evoking the shared status of material beings, before their creator and prior to species, ethnic and social hierarchies. Occurring frequently in classical and modern literature, it suggests the shared needs of 'sustenance' (*rizq*) and 'shelter' (*mustaqarr*), emphasised in the Qur'an.[72] Even in evidently secular texts, it, alongside description of humans and animals as *kāʾināt* (beings), grounds relationality within the plight of different species upon the land. Within the Libyan novel, specifically, animals, as *makhlūqāt*, emerge both as symbols of paradigmatic *human* political exclusion, and as embodiments of an existence beyond political demarcations. As such, they suggest rich intersections with the recent turn to creatureliness in European and North American thought, theorised as a condition of exposure to sovereign power, as well as of shared human and non-human vulnerability, and closely associated with German-Jewish thinkers of the interwar and post-Second World War period.

Most prominently, Walter Benjamin (1892–1940) shifts the dynamics of 'creature' (*kreatur*) and creator to that of creature and 'sovereign', positing the creature, within secular modernity, as an embodiment of abandonment to the force of law and states of exception.[73] Stripped of the symbolic systems that once granted it meaning and exposed to the 'animal life' from which it was formally sheltered, humanity is envisioned as an 'excessive bodily and fleshy substance that continues to be solicited by a divine force that has become powerless to shelter it'.[74] In the short stories of Franz Kafka (1883–1924), Benjamin finds an exemplar of this condition, through hybrid beings struggling for shelter and blurring the boundaries of human and animal.[75]

Within literary criticism and philosophy, and particularly within Ecocriticism and Animal Studies, the 'creature' has since been adopted as a means of expressing bodily and psychological exposure across species lines and of theorising life within the Anthropocene. Derived from the Latin *vulnus* (wound), 'vulnerability', connoting both fragility and openness, is frequently associated with it, theorising human life beyond the law, stripped of agency, and exposed to the mercy of others. For Eric Santner, the creaturely marks a specifically *human* vulnerability to the transient ideological systems that both define and exclude individual lives, opening a 'new way of understanding how human bodies and psyches register the "states of exception" that punctuate the "normal" run of social and political life'.[76] As his words suggest, Agamben's understanding of 'bare life' and 'states of exception', and the Foucauldian 'biopower' on which they are based, underpin his thinking.[77] All are centred on the control of biological life within modernity, alongside its simultaneous exclusion, as foundational to the operation of power. Ultimately, for Santner, humans 'are in some sense *more creaturely* than other creatures by virtue of an excess that is produced in the space of the political and that, paradoxically, accounts for their "humanity"'.[78]

Anat Pick, on the other hand, emphasises the shared vulnerability of *human* and *animal* as the starting point for creaturely poetics and ethics.[79] Foundational to her work, as to the broader field of Animal Studies, Derrida's 'The Animal that Therefore I Am' evokes this 'proto-ethics' through the unknowable gaze of the animal, collapsing established systems of politics and law before the paramount need to respond to the absolute other.[80] For Pick, creatureliness becomes the means of doing so, moving beyond otherness to shared vulnerability, and, rather than ascribing particular rights to one creature and not another, extending 'attention' to the 'materiality and vulnerability of all'.[81] Drawing on philosopher Cora Diamond, she further posits creatureliness as a dispelling of 'comfort-thinking', perceiving the body without 'consolatory illusions', in all its physicality and transience, in order to reframe truth not as a 'terminus of thought or a resting place of concepts but the site of encounter with reality that rattles concepts and confounds thought'.[82]

Haunted by a time when human and animal coexisted in harsh but self-sufficient freedom, sundered by war, urbanisation and dictatorship, Libya's *makhlūqāt* bind Santner and Pick's understandings of the creaturely as animals emerge both as allegories of specifically *human* suffering and as embodiments of shared precarity. In a striking number of novels, whether set in wilderness or city, characters are defined by homelessness and wandering, with vulnerability dramatised through life 'in the open' (*fī al-ʿarāʾ*), under the fearsome sun and the panoptic gaze, and undergoing states of fever, hallucination and transformation, often channelled through non-human beings. As what I call 'creaturely signs', shifting between political, social and environmental import, human and animal characters are further vulnerable to the semiotic tyranny of censorship, as al-Asfar mockingly demonstrates in his depiction of 'Revolutionary Men', wrangling over a poem about a bird and a trap:

> 'This text must not be published', declared Mr Finger (*Abū Iṣbaᶜ*), 'it is full of symbols and symbolism (*bihi ramziyya murammaza*). What is this "worm"? And this "trap"? He's attacking you, my dear Starling (*al-Zarzūr*), insulting you and all you represent. Consider, for example, the relationship between starlings and worms and think of what is then signified by this "trap".'[83]

Following al-Asfar, I explore how depictions of vulnerability move beyond vehicles of fixed, political meaning into nuanced explorations of oppression on multiple symbolic and spiritual layers. Beyond the coincidence of animal allegory and national allegory, I suggest that the creaturely is naturally productive of investigations that transcend nation. Contrary to the traditional realist novel, which, as Anderson suggests, obscures the notion of 'mankind' behind the 'deep horizontal comradeship' of nation, encounters with 'creaturely signs' prove eminently disruptive, producing an 'unimagining' of nation, undermining straightforward notions of citizenship, identity, possession and power.[84] As Dominik Ohrem puts it, 'creaturely life seeks to move beyond the narrative of Man to rethink the human as a specific expression of the broader currents of life that both constitute and exceed it.'[85]

Al-Faqih's short story, 'Masraᶜ al-Naml' ('Fall of the Ants') demonstrates these dynamics. From his collection *Fi Hijaʾ al-Bashar wa-Madih al-Bahaʾim wa-l-Hasharat* (2010, In Praise of Beasts and Censure of Humankind), it invites a political reading, symbolising human injustice towards humans through human injustice towards animals. At the same time, the collection is prefaced by Qurʾan 6:38, evoking animals as 'nations like you' (*umamun amthālukum*).[86] Each story is then based on the recurring motif of 'praise' (*madīḥ*) of animals and 'mockery' (*hijāʾ*) of humans, echoing the famous litterateur al-Jahiz's (al-Jāḥiẓ, 776–868) *Kitab al-Hayawan*, and shifting its encyclopaedic celebration of God's creation into a damning portrait of humanity's place within it. From the first, this double perspective, of nation and species, complicates and nuances al-Faqih's allegorical critique. In the case of 'Masraᶜ al-Naml', the brutality of two 'interrogator ants' (*namlatā al-taḥqīq*) towards a worker ant is immediately evocative of military dictatorship, while, overarching all, the scene is prompted by the boredom of the human narrator, idly toying with the ant society and becoming complicit in its injustices.[87] Through this encounter, the local and specific are addressed in covert terms, within a deeper exploration of dark human impulses.

Such sustained literary attention to animals is, arguably, surprising. In a country deprived of basic human rights, those of animals might be expected to lose priority. As al-Kiddi's 'al-Hayah al-Qasira al-ᶜAjiba' shows, however, animals particularly well emphasise the fault lines that traverse human societies, and, through their simple striving for life, counter human systems of exclusion through a creaturely 'proto-ethics', extending attention to all living beings. In the spirit of this 'attention', my own analyses also extend beyond animals to a broader spectrum of land, cityscapes and non-human characters. Statues, artworks and ruins are, for example, frequently imagined into melancholy being, evocative of mortality, transience and al-Qadhafi's relegation of every meaningful 'symbol' (*ramz*) to the margins of signification. In a striking parallel to the dog Ramadan, Miftāḥ Qanāw's (b.1958) 'ᶜAwdat al-Qaysar' (2004; 'The Return of Caesar', 2008) animates two of Libya's most famous statues, an ancient bronze of the Roman Emperor, Septimius Severus (145–211), and the Italian-era 'Girl and Gazelle', long occupying a roundabout in central Tripoli.[88] Regardless of the differing ideologies that forged them and the centuries that separate them, the statues become united in solidarity against neglect and, in the case of Severus, al-Qadhafi's literal removal of him from Martyr's Square to Leptis Magna in the late 1970s. Joining a queue, the statues wait to leave for Malta, expelled from the symbolic systems that once granted them meaning and mirroring the parallel exclusion of humans, who, beyond reference to the taxi driver who takes Septimius to Tripoli and the waiting queue, are absent from the narrative and its derelict political landscape.

Infused with a melancholy, yet playful, historical consciousness, Qanāw's story encapsulates the turn within Libyan fiction to subversive and genre-defying affiliations, characteristic of creatureliness as openness. Beyond the 'hopeless closure of creaturely life', Santner suggests the '"ensoulment," of the creature by acts of neighbour-love – small miracles, as it were, performed *one by one*, moving from one neighbour to the next (rather than by way of a love directed immediately to *all* humankind)'.[89] Pick similarly speaks of 'a creaturely fellowship by default, self-evident and undeniable, in a world of imbalance and injustice'.[90] In the Libyan novel, such small acts of kindness within the totality of dictatorship are central, as poet Khaled Mattawa (b. 1964) notes:

> Ill-educated, confined, dependent, most citizens felt that any escape from the Leader's dystopian Jamahiriya (people's democracy) would be akin to drifting into the vast desert that surrounded them. Yet in such a stale, agonizingly uneventful, dread-filled atmosphere, acts of kindness [. . .] can and do arise. Small hopes bud and leaf in cornered bits of Libya's harsh sunshine.[91]

In tracing these acts of kindness, rooted in the recognition of otherness, I suggest an animating impulse as central to the Libyan novel's creaturely imaginary, binding animals and humans, natural landscapes and urban architecture. For Ohrem, the extent to which we perceive animacy amid our surroundings says much about 'our ways of perceiving and storying and making sense of the living world of which we are a part'.[92] Rooted in a poetics of 'close listening' (*inṣāt*) and 'interrogation' (*istinṭāq*), this impulse in the Libyan novel elicits both the eloquence of fable and wordlessness of 'lament' (*nuwāḥ*), expressing the traumas that resist telling and the censorship that threatens speech. Projecting life onto humans' others, it contests Libya's fate as a nation of 'others', challenging the de-animation, or 'making killable', of humans within bare life and the hierarchy that dictates who can speak, move and survive. As author ᶜAqila puts it:

> When we humanise or spiritualise objects, we widen the horizons of place, movement, shape and relationships. The humanisation of objects (*ansanat al-ashyāʾ*) further counters the objectification of humans (*tashayyuʾ al-insān*). We do not merely need to humanise objects. We need to humanise humans.[93]

Opening new horizons for places stifled by surveillance, those who animate in the Libyan novel tend to be outsiders to the category of 'Man', from children to the elderly to the outcast, surveying, in their dialogue with land, animals and ruins, the passage of oppressive ideologies. In all, this dialogue moves through memories of Italian colonisation, political oppression and the slow encroachment of environmental ruin, looking to the Qurʾan, Sufism and literary tradition as a means of imagining them otherwise. In concluding this introduction, I thus focus on each of these contexts, tying the creaturely to the postcolonial, ecocritical, and broader intertextuality of the Arabic novel.

'No Illness But . . .'

Libya's brutal colonial experience was exemplary of bare life. In the most violent years of fascist military occupation, led by Marshal Rodolfo Graziani (1882–1955), Cyrenaica's nomadic population was rounded up and interned in concentration camps, suddenly subject to borders and curfews.[94] Designed to suppress the guerrilla resistance of ᶜUmar al-Mukhtar, the camps held an estimated 100,000 people, along with their 600,000 livestock. From 1928 to 1930, most died from disease, starvation or execution in an act of genocide ended only in 1931, with Mukhtar's public hanging and the quelling of the resistance.[95] Followed by the large-scale settlement of the 1930s, the camps resonate in Libyan consciousness as a pivotal breaking point, sundering ties to land and past. Matar thus describes how, 'Stories of torture, humiliation and famine have filtered down through the generations.'[96]

As Libya's principal literary heritage, poems and folktales represent a central store of this memory, with none more famous than Rajab Buhwaysh al-Minifi's (al-Minifi, d.1950) oral qasida, 'Ma bi Marad . . .' ('No Illness But . . .'), recited at the ᶜAqila Camp.[97] Through the refrain of its opening words, it dwells on the tribe's torture, rape and deprivation, travelling across adjoining camps as an expression of suffering and resistance. Widely taught in Libyan schools, its opening stanzas encapsulate themes that have migrated across the short story and novel, from evocation of the 'tribe's imprisonment' to 'lack of sustenance', 'distance from home' and the suddenly curtailed movement of a proud steed:

> No illness but endless grief
> meagre provisions
> and the loss of my black red-spotted steed
>
> who, when strife broke, stretched her solid-flesh neck,
> impossible to describe,
> her peer does not exist.[98]

For al-Minifi, Italian occupation is indelibly entangled in the loss of land and bonds to its animal inhabitants in the fertile Jabal Akhdar, where the population had subsisted on herding and seasonal agriculture. Similar lamentations resonate across modern fiction, with authors citing al-Minifi's verses or depicting elderly relatives telling their descendants of similar horrors.[99] In them, literal hunger and displacement are echoed in visions of life under al-Qadhafi, in different forms of exile, imprisonment and starvation, weaving together citizens of the Jamahiriyya with those of the 'fourth shore', haunted by 'illnesses' enumerated, but not overcome, as, from what the Italians declared a 'big box of sand' (*scatolone di sabia*), Libya became coveted instead as a 'barrel of oil'.

The Curse of Oil

From the earliest novels, Libyan fiction resonates with what Patricia Yaeger calls energy 'unconscious' or 'anxiety', as, through the nation's transformation into rentier state, its fiction is formed, shaped and underpinned by oil.[100] From al-Nayhum's satirical articles to caricaturist Muḥammad al-Zawāwī's (1936–2011) famous illustrations, the 1960s saw a marked antipathy to sudden excesses, carnivorousness and environmental imbalance. Discussing al-Zawāwī's characteristic 'picnic' scenes, in which Libyans arrive in trucks and speedboats, on beaches and in forests, to roast sheep on open fires and guzzle fizzy drinks, al-Kuni evokes how *nuzha* (picnic) turns to *ghazwa* (invasion), as the artist conveys the misguided attempts of a newly urban population to re-establish connections to the land.[101]

In much fiction, oil is seen as an outright curse, fuelling al-Qadhafi's tyrannical reign and shifting swiftly from 'populist fairy tales of sudden bounty' to the 'disenchantments of a ruined environment'.[102] Devoid of the 'page-turning power' of burning towers, avalanches and tsunamis, environmental degradation represents what Rob Nixon calls 'slow violence', requiring a 'different kind of witnessing: of sights unseen'.[103] Often, it is conveyed through animation of the land, whether as a powerful, mythic expanse upon which human and animal must struggle for survival, or as a victim of appropriation whose fragile ecology is neglected by those who would seize its subterranean 'black gold'. Expressive of what Terry Gifford calls the 'post-pastoral', the land is seen through both its wild, natural shifts – from the power of the famed and dreaded Qibli wind, blowing hot desert dust, to flash floods, earthquakes and drought – and through its human invasion, drained of life and stripped of memory.[104] Encroaching barrenness represents a particularly prominent image, contrasted to the Sahara's pluvial past, and to myths of the Hesperides' Garden and of lost Atlantis, conveying both literal environmental lament and figurative political critique for a lost plenty, ease and harmony.

It is worth noting that al-Qadhafi himself also espoused a marked environmental rhetoric. Alongside his grandiose but misguided Great Manmade River and desert farms, his short stories 'al-Madina', 'al-Qarya' and 'al-Ard' idealise desert and village, and depict the city as a 'graveyard of social interaction' in which people are no different from 'rats', 'slugs' and 'snails', and the earth is slowly suffocated beneath concrete.[105] In response, authors depict the city, like the desert, as vulnerable, overwhelmed by smoke, ruins and rubbish, and exposed to omnipresent surveillance. In these neglected urban spaces, as in the wilderness, unofficial bonds form between human, land and animal, reclaiming the labels of 'rats', 'slugs' and 'snails', and rooting ethics in an interconnected ecological vision steeped in Qurʾanic and Sufi imagery.

The Vulnerability-of-Being

Ecocriticism and Animal Studies have increasingly drawn on indigenous spiritual traditions to theorise relations between human, animal and land, beyond the Cartesian equation of animals as unthinking, unfeeling automata and the land as exploitable resource.[106] In the Libyan novel, the central influence of the Qurʾan, alongside popular folklore and Sufi belief, suggests a reading of animals as *āyāt*, signifying 'signs' of divine creation that invite human contemplation, as well as warnings against human hubris. As Sarra Tlili demonstrates, the Qurʾan grants animals a significant share of divine attention, with seven surahs named after different species, and one after the jinn.[107] Drawing on reference to animals as 'nations like you' (*umamun amthālukum*), on their engagement in 'praise of God' (*tasbīḥ*), and on the portrayal of Solomon's conversations with hoopoe and ant, Tlili concludes that 'even though the Qurʾan, being "guidance for humankind", focuses on humans, a number of its themes and stylistic features indicate that all species have an ample share in divine attention'.[108] Picked up by different authors, these and other Qurʾanic terms are used to endow animals with agency and emotion, as fellow creatures sharing in 'God's wide land' (*arḍ Allāh al-wāsiʿa*).[109]

Sufi motifs deepen this ecological interconnection, reflecting the influence of brotherhoods (*ṭuruq*) across the Sahara from the fourteenth century, as the melding of orthodox beliefs and local folklore produced orders ranging from the ascetic rigour of the Sanusiyya to the popular ʿAysawiyya, animating the streets with spectacular ceremonies and festivals. In the novel, popular practice and orthodox belief come together as a powerful 'relational epistemology', eradicating barriers between self and other, whether through strange metamorphoses or meditations on the shared 'origin' (*aṣl*) of all.[110] In many respects, this is in keeping with the role of Sufism in broader Arabic literature, as a counter-narrative to secular modernity, reaction to political hegemony and embrace of otherness.[111] In the Libyan novel, however, the creaturely and ecological become central, as, through the fundamental concept of *waḥdat al-wujūd* (oneness-of-being), a communion of beings is imagined, gravitating from disparate 'nations' into a holistic unity.

Often, *waḥda* is further envisioned on an uncomfortably organic level through entangled visions of human and animal flesh, echoing al-Kuni's observation in *Nazif al-Hajar* that 'it was the Maghreb that had brought Sufism down from its throne of heavenly philosophy, to the common soil of everyday life'.[112] Through harsh existence in the open, and the often literal baring of flesh and blood, this visceral poetics is channelled through the mad, outcast and non-human, discarding the shackles of reason.[113] Combining the wonder, warning and unknowability of the Qurʾanic *āya* and Sufi *sirr* (secret), these marginal characters become creaturely signs, leading to the fundamental, shared truths of physicality, stripped of 'consolatory thinking' and evoking 'openness' (*futūḥ*) as both Sufi revelation and a vision of the world as 'vulnerability of being'.[114]

Animal Worlds in Arabic Literature

Many of these Qurʾanic and Sufi motifs echo across wider Arabic literature, with the Libyan novel certainly not alone in its ecological poetics, and with its animals steeped in pre-existing literary traditions, from fable to qasida. In the course of my analyses, these influences are discussed in further detail but, briefly, I review animals' abiding centrality in Arabic literature, encoding social structures and values, on the one hand, and, on the other, embodying peace, wisdom and restraint, as they take narrative into the wild, heterotopic and spiritual.[115]

From the first, this is exemplified in the pre-Islamic qasida, in which man and camel embark upon a desert journey (*raḥīl*), exemplifying heroic endurance (*ṣabr*) and often likened to onagers and oryx, struggling through the wilderness and grieving the loss of young. Upon the poet's return to the tribe, the camel is often then slaughtered in an act of self-sacrifice for the collective, and celebration of tribe and culture.[116]

In contrast, animal struggle replaces tribal kinship altogether in the 'perpetual liminality' of al-Shanfarā and the 'brigand poets' (*ṣaᶜālīk*).[117] In animals, the poet identifies fidelity, discretion and restraint, depicting, as Moneera al-Ghadeer observes, an 'oppositional world of ethics, responsibility and hospitality'.[118] Famous ᶜUdhri poet Majnūn Laylā similarly attributes moral values to the 'wild animals' (*al-waḥsh*) with which he roams after his love is refused, expressing jealousy at their harmonious existence in 'couples' (*alīfayn*) and thus bemoaning the harshness of human social customs.[119] In later poetry, from *ghazal* to elegy and Sufi mystical verse, animals continue to embody love, longing and vulnerable suffering. The eleventh-century poet Abū al-ᶜAlāᵓ al-Maᶜarrī (973–1057) even points to this prominent depiction as justification for his abstention from meat and dairy, observing the 'suffering of the wild beasts, and the pining of the wild cow for her calf' as a 'commonplace' in Arabic poetry (*taraddada fi kalām al-ᶜarab*).[120] In the Libyan novel too, evocation of animal suffering from literary tradition goes alongside frequent expressions of aversion to the eating of meat.

As in poetry, animals are formative to prose *adab* and, particularly, to allegory.[121] Ibn al-Muqaffaᶜ's (d. circa 759) foundational eight-century version of the Bidpai fables, *Kalila wa-Dimna*, dramatises the virtues of fidelity, wit and wiles in a court of animals, serving as a 'mirror for princes' for rulers and their entourage.[122] Inspired by it, the Ikhwan al-Safaᵓ's twenty-second *Risala*, the 'Case of the Animals Against Man before the King of the Jinn' (*c.* tenth century) shifts its ethical focus to animals themselves. Taking men to trial for their appropriation of a once harmonious island, animals, as Robert Irwin observes, argue for their own survival, while the inclusion of 'realistic zoological detail' moves beyond symbolism into reflection on animals in and of themselves.[123] In more playful fashion, Ibn al-Marzuban's (d. 921) *Kitab Tafdil al-Kilab ᶜala Kathir mimman Labisa al-Thiyab* (The Book of the Superiority of Dogs to Many of Those Who Wear Clothes) comments on the declining standards of human society through anecdotes and poems in praise of canines' greater fidelity and trustworthiness. Another classic, Ibn Tufayl's (d. circa 1185) *Hayy Ibn Yaqzan* ('Alive, Son of Awakening'), turns again to a desert island on which the baby Hayy is stranded. Hearing his cries, a gazelle adopts him and through the nurturing kindness of this 'mother', he grows to maturity, while, upon her death, he is driven by love to dissect her body, hoping to revive her and, in the process, opening his mind to the first levels of intellectual discovery.

As spiritual and ethical enquiry, these allegories return to the Qurʾanic injunction to meditate upon animals as *āyāt*, clarifying humans' place within a greater whole. So, too, does the established tradition of *ᶜajāʾib* (mirabilia), incorporating travel accounts and encyclopaedias of real and mythic creatures. None, however, goes further than al-Jahiz's (776–868) *Kitab al-Hayawan*. As James Montgomery observes, it is a 'totalising' work, attempting to capture existence in all its magnificent diversity, driven by a sense of 'the need to express gratitude to God for His creation by producing a comprehensive inventory of it'.[124] A sprawling, unfinished collection of animal wisdom, derived from poetry, anecdotes and observations, its very incompleteness is suggestive of the limitations of human knowledge, setting them within a wider, creaturely whole.[125]

Within the realms of popular literature, *Alf Layla wa-layla* is similarly sprawling, exploiting 'all of the narrative possibilities of animals', from metamorphosis to bestiality to 'nations' of monkeys and snakes.[126] In 'Hasib Karim al-Din' and the framed stories of 'Buluqiyya' and 'Janshah', animals animate a vast, marvellous geography, prompting humans to continuous 'wonder' (*ᶜajab*).[127] With the orderly rule of King Solomon at an end, the stories open onto wild spaces in which humans test themselves, before returning to the security of kingdom and civilisation.

The Libyan novel, then, is by no means an outlier in the prominence it accords animals, with many modern Arabic literatures similarly drawing on the Qurʾan and premodern literary traditions, whether in social and political allegories in the *nahḍa*, Romantic natural imaginary, or environmental consciousness, most prominently associated with Saudi-Jordanian ᶜAbd al-Raḥmān Munīf (1933–2004).[128] As in the Libyan novel, animals emerge in reflections on political instability and violence, from the Lebanese Civil War to conflict in Iraq, as well as in Aesopic critique of despotic regimes.[129] Across North Africa, specifically, they are further animated through Sufi and folkloric sensibilities as part of a broader desert geography.[130]

Libya, nevertheless, presents a particularly intriguing case, due both to the prominence of animals in its most celebrated authors and to the dazzlingly diverse traditions upon which authors draw, whether anchored in Libyan, Arabic or more distant contexts and intertexts. Libyan folklore is the most evident of these sources, abounding in animals and fantastical creatures, and characterised by the close connection of people to 'land' (*turba*) and 'environment' (*bīʾa*).[131] Migrating into the novel, this folklore expresses lament for both lost nomadism and lost narrative forms, with animals often portrayed through the hybrid combination of folkloric tropes and realist detail. In an intriguing study of selected stories, Libyan critic, Sālim al-ᶜAbbār, further observes the prominent motif of celebration of animals and mockery of humans, which he interprets as a lasting legacy of Italian colonisation and its destruction of local communities.[132] 'Proving themselves superior to humans', al-ᶜAbbār writes, 'animals indicate the extremes of alienation and melancholy resulting from centuries of despotism', leading to 'humanity's displacement from the central place which God accorded it'.[133] Through broader folkloric motifs, celebrating the underdog, and reversing hierarchies of big and small, strong and weak, this upsetting of anthropocentrism represents a recurring, pessimistic critique in the Libyan novel, returning to primordial imaginings of humanity's tyranny in its dominion over other species.

Depiction of animals also opens onto a broader geographical and cultural conception of 'Libya', in its former meaning of wider North Africa, west of the Nile. Prehistoric cave art from the Akakus Mountains and Massak Satfat plateau is one such source, depicting frescoes of hunting alongside strange, theriomorphic creatures.[134] *The Histories* (440 BCE) of Herodotus and their account of ancient Libya, filled with 'dog-faced' and 'headless' creatures, is another.[135] From Roman times, Apuleius' *The Golden Ass* (*c.*170) is a third source. Translated into Arabic by Libyan historian ᶜAlī Fahmī Khushaym (1936–2011) in 1980, and running to a second edition in 1984, it is often seen as one of the world's first novels, while Khushaym emphasises Apuleius' belonging to the 'ancient Libyan Gaetulian tribe', anchoring the novel's foundational metamorphosis in a firmly local perspective.[136]

At the other end of the historical spectrum, Munīr al-Baᶜlbakī's translation of Ernest Hemingway's *The Old Man and the Sea* (1952) has been described as the 'gospel of al-Nayhum's generation', with its central drama of struggle between human, animal and sea. Al-Kuni further cites Kyrgyz author Chingiz Aitmatov's *The White Steamship* (*Belyĭ Parokhod*, 1970) as a central influence and pioneering environmentalist novel, featuring a mythical 'mother deer' protesting her treatment at human hands.[137] Final mention, however, must be made of Libyan authors' intertextual conversations with one another, within the close-knit community formed through wider isolation. In *Hiwar*, the published transcript of a 1978 discussion between al-Nayhum, al-Kuni and other authors, al-Kuni questions al-Nayhum about what drew him to sustained portrayals of animal characters, citing, in his opening, a tradition stretching from Ovid to Kafka.[138] Investigating the many possible answers to this question, I explore the multifaceted nature of Libyan animals, opening from the more familiar genealogy of Ovid, Kafka and Hemingway onto a diverse and unexpected literary diversity that nevertheless remains rooted in local, creaturely geographies.

Chapters

While this book provides overviews of some of Libya's best known but little studied authors, it is worth specifying that my analyses are by no means exhaustive. Prominent authors such as Muṣṭafā, Ṣāliḥ al-Sanūsī (b. 1949) and al-Būᶜissī have not received the coverage they perhaps should.[139] Primarily, I track the non-realist, structurally fragmented and hybrid novel, anchored in al-Nayhum's foundational *Min Makka* and concluding in 2011, beyond which the literary landscape has profoundly shifted. Including foundational novelists from the 1960s generation, writers who re-emerged from silence or prison in the 2000s, and a new generation that grew up within the Jamahiriyya, I combine those who stayed in Libya and those who left, those who portray coastal cities and those who evoke the Sahara. Drawing together the diverse and overlapping concerns that have marked the novel, different chapters emphasise the centrality of ecology, the Aesopic/symbolic and the Sufi. Some are centred on animals and intertextual engagement with qasida, fable and rock art, while others explore animated statues or human metamorphosis.

Part I addresses the pioneering writing of al-Nayhum, al-Faqih and al-Kuni as exemplars of the 1960s generation, from the respective regions of Cyrenaica, Tripolitania and Fezzan. Through parallels between their writing, I emphasise the central facets of 'survival' and 'primordiality' within creaturely consciousness. Chapter 1 focuses on the postcolonial ecocritical perspectives of *Min Makka*, *Fiʾran Bila Juhur* and *Nazif al-Hajar*. Through their strikingly similar juxtaposition of realism and animal fable, I explore how the novels convey social and environmental critique through images of violent appropriation and contrasting spiritual holism. Chapter 2 moves to *al-Qurud*, *Hadaʾiq al-Layl* and *Anubis*, shifting from the environmental to the political. Despite significant stylistic differences, all three are marked by an undercurrent of primordial imagery, of evolution and fall, through which they address the dilemma of the intellectual in exile, and express a broader sense of human existential alienation.

Part II bridges these authors to those of the 2000s, focusing on animals and statues as 'symbols' (*rumūz*), 'signs' (*āyāt*) and 'secrets' (*asrār*), in which a dense nexus of buried traumas, Sufi revelations and the political 'unsaid' are contained. In Chapter 3, I bring together al-Kuni's *al-Tibr*, as a pinnacle of Libyan creaturely poetics, and al-Ghazal's *al-Tabut* and *al-Khawf Abqani Hayyan*, suggesting the buried political dimensions of *al-Tibr* through al-Ghazal's more open depictions of modern Libya. Chapter 4 explores depictions of the city in Bushnaf's *al-ᶜIlka*, al-Asfar's *Sharmula* (2008, Sharmula Salad) and al-Maghrabi's *Nisaʾ al-Rih*. The heart of Libya's social and political transformations, the city stages emotional, rather than literal, hunger and homelessness, while the problematics of 'story' represent a defining struggle as, in both chapters, narratives and 'signs' break down into 'lines of flight', diverging into spiritual journey, traumatic remembering and Aesopic protest.

Part III examines childhood as a paradigmatic expression of vulnerability, bridging novels in Arabic, French and English. In Chapter 5, I explore hesitant narratives of self through al-Fayturi's *Sarib*, ᶜAqila's *al-Jirab* and Bin Shatwan's *Wabr al-Ahsina*. Focusing on Libyan dialect terms for oral narrative, '*sarīb*' (a long, rambling tale) and '*kharārīf*' (folk tales), I explore their entanglement in past ways of knowing and telling, and, ultimately, in primordial myth, based on the collective, creaturely experiences of flight and exposure. In Chapter 6, I conclude with a discussion of Matar's *In the Country of Men* and Ben Hameda's *La compagnie des Tripolitaines*, in which the distance of writing in English and French is countered by an intimate evocation of the child's sensorial and imaginative perceptions, bound into the natural world around them.

Part I

SURVIVAL

1

Animal Fable in Novels of Survival

No beast there is on earth but its livelihood rests with God. He knows its berth and its final resting place. All is in a manifest Book. (Qurʾan 11:6)[1]

There I sleep the sweet sleep of tranquillity, of satisfied desire, of achieved ambition: for I possess a house. (Kafka, 'The Burrow')[2]

A popular Libyan expression goes that 'the luckless finds bones in a stomach'.[3] The term for 'luckless', the idiomatic '*rāqid al-rīḥ*' – literally, 'the sleeper on the wind' – signifies someone with no family, home or possessions, and aptly evokes the characters that populate what I term the Libyan 'novel of survival'. Close to the English 'going from bad to worse', but more directly 'going from little to less', the expression evokes the empty-handedness of these novels, in which the complexities of existence shift to bare survival. Such narratives form a distinct canon in Libyan fiction, paralleling the prominent rural imaginary of neighbouring Egypt, where, as Samah Selim suggests, the figure of the *fallāḥ* (peasant) crystallises 'an ongoing social and textual dialogue'.[4] Across the border, the Libyan subsistence survivor, whether fisherman, water carrier or goatherd, is characterised by precarity, always hunting for the next 'crust of bread' (*kisrat al-khubz / luqmat al-ʿaysh*). The survivor is, furthermore, never far from animals, whether battling them or empathising with their similar struggle, while the environment exists in fragile harmony, demanding balance and restraint.

Most frequently, these dramas return to Italian occupation, or the aftermath of the Second World War, when Libya was recognised by the UN as the poorest nation in the world, with scant chance of development.[5] Through this pre-oil past, and the military and commercial forces that shaped it, writers reflect on the present building of nation, as the laws that codified human relationships to one another and the environment disintegrate, alongside the dividing line between need and desire, 'subsistence' (*rizq*) and 'satiation' (*shabᶜ*). Juxtaposing foreign invasion to the local allure of excess produced by the inrush of 'energy' (*ṭāqa*), they negotiate the troubled concepts of 'development' and 'entitlement' central to postcolonial and ecocritical thinking alike.[6]

Spanning 1970–2000, I examine three of Libya's most celebrated novels in which community and nation are negotiated through the most fundamental considerations of who deserves life and why. In al-Nayhum's *Min Makka ila Huna* (1970, From Mecca to Here),[7] al-Faqih's *Fiʾran bila Juhur* (2000; *Homeless Rats*, 2011) and al-Kuni's *Nazif al-Hajar* (1989; *The Bleeding of the Stone*, 2002), this exploration emerges through strikingly similar hybrid aesthetics, in which predominantly realist narratives are interrupted by fable, animating the marginalised subjectivities of the land's animal inhabitants. Combining Santner and Pick's conceptions of the creaturely, animals both allegorise specifically human exclusion and evoke an ethics of shared vulnerability across species lines.

Published serially from 1966, *Min Makka* portrays the competing powers of Italian settlers and the local *fgi*, a popular religious leader and Qurʾan teacher (from the MSA *faqīh*), in the north-eastern fishing town of Susa during the 1930s. Through the struggles of its black protagonist, Masᶜud, seeking his living on the stormy seas and resorting to conversations with rats, turtles and seagulls, it constructs an iconography of power, concerning the use and abuse of Libyan land and people. Like *Min Makka*, *Fiʾran* first appeared in instalments in 1966, but remained unfinished until 2000, bridging pre- and post-Qadhafi periods. Set in the 1950s, it depicts the starving tribe of Shaykh Abu Layla arriving in the western desert of Jandouba, where they hope to harvest barley, before discovering that it has already been hoarded by a colony of jerboas. Lastly, *Nazif* depicts a lone goatherd, Asuf, living peacefully with his herds, alongside the mysterious *waddān* (Barbary sheep) of Massak Satfat. With the arrival of the Libyan Cain (Qābīl) and American John Parker, this harmony is disrupted, as the men hunt the animals to near-extinction. The environmentalism of the ensuing drama, and its magical realist, animist and Sufi poetics, has garnered significant critical attention.[8]

There has, however, been little engagement with its intersections with wider Libyan fiction.[9]

Despite this, parallels between the three novels are striking. From the coast of Cyrenaica to the deserts of Tripolitania and Fezzan, they offer a panorama of survival struggles in the young nation. Set at around the time that each author was born – between the 1930s and 1950s – and in places close to where they grew up, they combine nostalgia with critique, moving from human communities to the animals that coexist with them, and, as Elmarsafy observes of al-Kuni's fiction, from historical wars to struggles both creaturely and spiritual:

> In his *oeuvre*, we are treated to tale upon tale of violent invasion and settlement but the actors are not (or very rarely) Western colonial powers versus indigenous Africans. Instead we have beings that are usually considered heterogeneous – human and nonhuman animals, deities and spirits, 'inorganic' beings such as earth, heaven and the law locked in a struggle for space and sovereignty.[10]

In each novel, community and individual are depicted in crisis, and animals become battlegrounds for these crises, during which human failure to respond is dramatised, alongside animals' stubborn demand for recognition. Through these struggles, and the creaturely ethics to which they point, animals, on one level, allegorise and emphasise the plight of the nation's minorities and marginalised, representing, the 'foundational example of all subsequent forms of human othering'.[11] They also, however, open onto a broader communion. Countering his derogatory labelling as 'beast' (*dābba*) and 'slave' (*ᶜabd*), Masᶜud embraces the animals of the coast as *ᶜibād Allāh* (God's worshippers), while both *Fiᵓran* and *Nazif* juxtapose the divisions of tribes and generations, as well as city and desert, to the founding binary of human and animal.

Prompting humans to step beyond their societies' accepted hierarchies and practices, animals lead them into the wilderness, where the narrative moves from harsh realism into playful, parabolic fable, and animals transform from suffering victims to ethical nations. Rooted in Qurᵓanic concepts of *arḍ Allāh* (God's land) and *rizq* (subsistence/sustenance), fable evokes, above all, the spirit of animals as *umamun amthālukum* (nations like you), used as an epigraph by both al-Kuni and al-Faqih.[12] Underlying all is a vision of Sufi 'oneness' (*waḥdat al-wujūd*), imagined in both spiritual and ecological terms, and upsetting the borders of colony and nation. Within this oneness, all elements of creation, however seemingly insignificant, must be accounted for, sharing an equal need for *rizq*.[13]

In each novel, this shift in perception emerges vividly, and often uncomfortably, through animals' fluctuation between speech and silence, symbolism and materiality, and nation and meat, infusing otherness with vitality and questioning every minute act of appropriation. Becoming both allegorical and literal battlegrounds for land and resources, symbolically central to narrative and materially central to the communities depicted, they dismantle the 'taxonomic certainties' of both literary and biological genre, challenging their figurative and literal appropriation.[14] In this sense, they speak to the central concerns of postcolonial ecocriticism, seeking 'another relationship to alterity itself'.[15] As DeLoughrey and Handley write, 'demanding an imagination of a totality and an otherness that nevertheless cannot be possessed marks the central common ground between ecocritical and postcolonial critique.'[16]

Fable, meanwhile, is exploited in its full force as ancient, veiled protest, harking back to the manumitted slave Aesop (d. 564 BCE), as it conveys moral precepts and ethical advice, and addresses unequal power dynamics.[17] As a genre defined by truth statements in symbolic guise, fable has tended to be treated with scepticism within Animal Studies, transforming animals into empty ciphers for human meaning.[18] Ursula Le Guin thus quips that, 'if you want to clear the room of derrideans, mention Beatrix Potter without sneering'.[19] For Naama Harel, however, fables which feature humans alongside animals are particularly productive of multiple meanings, both literal and allegorical.[20] Onno Oerlemans similarly argues that fable best demonstrates the conflicted way in which humans regard other animals, suggesting that they are 'the heart of the matter', but also revealing fundamental 'glimmers of likeness' between them and animals.[21] 'One origin of animal fables', he writes, 'is that the carefully observed behaviour of animals contains its own natural wisdom of survival, adaptation, and even community, codifying human *and* animal wisdom.'[22]

For Steve Baker, fable more radically exposes humanity to otherness through the 'disruptive animality' of anthropomorphised animals.[23] While the conventions of fable are supposed to serve as 'built-in safeguards', demarcating the human from 'that which is other', certain 'awkwardnesses' arise from the fact that the animality of literary animals can never be fully eliminated, particularly in texts where 'real' animals are contrasted to 'speaking' ones.[24] 'It is', Baker writes, 'the very instability of the anthropomorphized animal's identity which can make contact or even proximity with it so hazardous for those with an overblown sense of their own importance, power and identity.'[25]

In *Min Makka*, *Fiʾran* and *Nazif*, sections of fable create the expectation of a clear morality, and all three have been identified as modern parables.[26] Narrative 'awkwardnesses' arise, however, from the fact that some animals speak and some do not, some humans are receptive to them and others are not. Creating layers of dramatic irony and tension, these awkwardnesses exemplify the paradigmatic breakdown of communication within the Libyan 'difficulty of story', while battles for *rizq* compound 'glimmers of likeness', suggesting that, whether human, anthropomorphised animal or 'real' beast, all are struggling creatures.

The environmental, psychological and spiritual dimensions of these fables are, of course, further rooted in Arabic tradition, from the Qurʾan's reference to birds' 'speech' (*manṭiq*) and animals' 'praise of God' (*tasbīḥ*) to its depiction of a talking hoopoe and ant.[27] As Tlili suggests, the Qurʾan presents animals as 'moral beings capable of making choices' and offering a critical external view of humanity. Resonating across Arabic literature, this perspective is exemplified by the Ikhwan al-Safaʾ's aptly titled *Case of the Animals Against Man*. As Goodman observes, 'the personification of the animals by the Ikhwan points not to projected human motives but to the natural, God-given needs and strengths, zest, and élan of all animals, striving after life'.[28] In particular, the Ikhwan's repeated notion of all beings' 'pursuit of their own ends' (*al-taṣarraf fī maʾāribihā*), indicates the fable's emphasis on this 'striving after life', free from enslavement and appropriation.[29] In similar fashion, Libyan survival novels depict animals struggling for survival and forced into speech by the oppressiveness of human invaders, expressing, in *Min Makka*, an ethics of 'fishermen's struggle', in *Fiʾran* of 'self-preservation' and in *Nazif* of 'self-sacrifice'.

Juxtaposing this, sections of 'silence' further upset generic orders, reinforcing animals as what Pick terms 'creaturely witness' and 'embodied revelation', whereby 'inarticulacy' becomes a 'refusal to speak' and suffering becomes 'martyrdom'.[30] For Pick, animals' silence cuts through the 'allegorical paraphernalia' of film and literature, and, in *Min Makka*, *Fi'ran* and *Nazif*, this coincides with the novels' endings, in which land is reaffirmed beyond human discourses, and characters reduced to empty-handedness.[31] Water, in the form of storm, sea or flood, brings material and spiritual transformation, connoting purification, punishment and the unpredictable, visceral force of nature.

This poetics, I suggest, represents a founding pillar of the Libyan creaturely imaginary, returning to *Min Makka*, which, though not as explicitly environmental as *Fi'ran* and *Nazif*, resonates through them in the struggles of human and animal. Musing on the power of literary animals, in a 1978 discussion with al-Nayhum, al-Kuni thus quotes Hemingway's description of his desire to create 'a real sea, a real old man, and a real fish', which, through their materiality, would evoke 'many things'.[32] These words aptly convey the simultaneous materiality, symbolism and spirituality of animals in the Libyan novel, shifting attention to the margins of law and citizenship. Beginning with al-Nayhum, I move to al-Faqih and then al-Kuni, following the novels' movement further into the wilderness, from coastline to Sahara, and tracking dramas of *rizq*, in which animals become enmeshed in human discourses, before moving narrative to fable and silence.

Min Makka ila Huna: A Changing Bay

Born in 1937 in Italian-colonised Benghazi, al-Nayhum lived through turbulent times, from the bombing of his home city during the Second World War to Independence and oil. One of the first graduates in Arabic Language from the Libyan University in Benghazi, he left in 1963 to study in Cairo and Munich, before settling in Helsinki with his Finnish wife. While there, he began writing regularly for the Benghazi weekly, *al-Haqiqa*, and soon became wildly popular as its long-distance correspondent, with fans copying his sharp, satirical writing and even mimicking his casual dress sense, dubbing him the 'hippy in jeans'.[33] Equally urgent and amusing, his articles express an intimate desire to reconnect to a rapidly changing homeland and preserve it from harmful trends, whether religious superstition propagated by the *fgi* (local religious leader) or shiny cars, devouring dilapidated streets.[34] Ranging between literary criticism and social and religious reform, he avoids direct political stances, speaking to the daily lives of his readers.[35]

Oil was a particular bugbear, addressed in his articles, alluded to in his stories, and often entangled with critique of superstition through what Jennifer Wenzel elsewhere terms the 'trope of oil-as-magic', offering false promises of quick wealth.[36] In '^{c}An Marakib al-Sultan' (1969, 'About the Sultan's Ships'), for example, al-Nayhum depicts a corrupt *fgi* convincing the ruler and citizens of Jalo to abandon their land for fear of an apocalyptic storm, with a sole farmer remaining to tend his date palms.[37] While the story has been interpreted in political, religious and existential terms, oil represents its clearest subtext, with the date palm a pre-eminent symbol of Libya's neglected ecology.[38] Similar themes animate 'Ba$^{\circ}$i^{c} al-Milh al-Tayyib al-Qalb' (1969, 'The Good-Hearted Salt Seller'), in which a malevolent jinni tempts a salt seller to abandon the salt flats (*sabakhāt*) around Benghazi, luring him with diamonds.[39] In both, al-Nayhum encourages his readers not to abandon the land and to perceive the world beyond both religious superstition and the 'magic' of oil.[40]

As both stories demonstrate, al-Nayhum's writing is further marked by intricate symbolism, based in Libyan realities, and whose nuances his readers followed from week to week. According to al-Fayturi, people repeated his sentences like 'maxims' and 'riddles' to be solved.[41] In his highly controversial *al-Ramz fi al-Qur$^{\circ}$an* (1966, Symbolism in the Qur$^{\circ}$an), prompting his house arrest in 1968, and *al-^{c}Awda al-Muhzina ila al-Bahr* (1969, Sad Return to the Sea), he further flouts religious orthodoxy through idiosyncratic, metaphorical readings of sacred text. Interwoven with existentialist, Freudian and Darwinian ideas, *al-^{c}Awda*, in particular, is rooted in a drive towards social and ecological balance, rooted in reflection on evolution and mythic symbolism.[42] Following the Frankfurt School's Erich Fromm (1900–80), al-Nayhum links humanity's neuroses to its separation from the natural world and, like Fromm, suggests Adam and Eve's plight not as original sin but evolution, leading to self-consciousness, responsibility and choice.[43] If social relationships based on love and reason are not fostered to compensate, humans cannot relate to one another or to nature in a 'sane' manner.[44]

While humanity in general, and Libya specifically, drive al-Nayhum's thought, he thus connects them to a wider whole. As Abū Bakr al-Hūnī comments, his thinking is underpinned by 'self-denial' (*inkār li-l-dhāt*) for the 'whole' (*al-kull*), signifying not just 'all people' but the 'whole universe'.[45] Drawing on symbolic analysis of Qur$^{\circ}$anic 'creation' (*khalq*), al-Nayhum suggests that humanity, made from 'soil' (*turāb*), has an inherent potential for growth, while Satan, made of 'fire' (*nār*), symbolises consumption.[46] Since civilisation began with fire, however, it has proven innately destructive in its pursuit of 'ever more energy' (*al-mazīd min al-ṭāqa*).[47] Opposing 'ease' (*rakhāʾ*) and 'progress' (*taṭawwur*) to 'growth' (*numuww*), al-Nayhum emphasises altruism and restraint against heedless pursuit of 'material efficiency' (*al-kafāʾa al-māddiyya*) and 'mechanisation' (*al-āliyya*), threatening the 'original whole' (*al-kull al-aṣlī*), and resulting in mental illness and addiction.[48] *Al-ᶜAwda* thus evokes the 'return of life to its origin [the sea], burdened with disappointment in material efficiency'.[49] Through the symbolic dimensions of sea, soil and fire, al-Nayhum evokes a 'vulnerability-of-being' steeped in the paradoxes of Libya's ecology. Perceiving environmental threat as what Nixon calls a 'set of inhabited risks, some imminent, others obscurely long term', he speaks to the immediate, distressing transformations of childhood geographies.[50] As he writes: 'Everything is burning in our country [. . .] consuming fuel to produce energy and belch out smoke.'[51]

This, then, represents the immediate intellectual backdrop to *Min Makka*, depicting the Cyrenaican coast, clouded by various 'myths' from which Masᶜud must liberate them. While depicting a pre-oil Libya, the novel is riven by imbalance, experienced by those on its margins. Describing the novel, al-Faqih writes:

> Despite its realistic setting, filled with battles for sustenance, and where land and sea, black and white are all too concrete, a haze of mythology colours the novel, lifting it from the world of time, place and realistic characters into symbols and existential signs, mixed with a dose of playfulness and an astounding capacity to detect and depict life's hypocrisies. The novel may thus be considered one of the pioneering attempts to establish this literary genre (*hādhā al-jins al-adabī*) and implant it in the soil of Arabic literature in Libya.[52]

The 'genre' that al-Faqih refers to may be understood as the '*turāthī*' (heritage) trend of the 1960s, in which return to premodern literary traditions, within experimental, modernist narratives, reflected a growing disillusionment in former certainties. This 'new literary sensibility', Christina Phillips writes, is marked by a 'rejection of unitary meaning, reason and orthodoxy and tendency towards symbol, allusion, polyphony and fragmentation'.[53] In the Libyan novel, it is particularly marked by a focus on animals, land and the creaturely.

Often, too, it draws on Sufi imagery. As al-Faqih suggests, *Min Makka* is infused with 'symbols and existential signs' (*dalālāt ramziyya wa-wujūdiyya*), centred on Masᶜud, who, according to al-Nayhum, was written 'in the spirit' of Hemingway's *The Old Man and the Sea*.[54] While Masᶜud, like Santiago, engages the sea and its creatures in an ongoing dialogue, in *Min Makka*, the natural world also answers back, evoking both the popular tradition of fable, and the potency of Sufi 'signs'.[55] For al-Nayhum, Sufism is not the preserve of Shaykhs, but 'survivors', who, through their struggle, change perceptions of community and land.[56] This emerges in his writing through what he describes, in an interview with al-Kuni, as a 'simple-minded Sufism' (*al-ṣūfiyya al-balhāʾ*), opening onto encounter with otherness, and seeking what is shared.[57]

Turtle Tales

Masᶜud belongs neither with locals nor Italians, surrounded by rumours claiming he 'eats pork' and spies for the Italians, and Italians' labelling of him as a 'barbaric slave' (*al-zanjī al-damawī*) who 'carries a skull in his bag'.[58] Referred to throughout as '*al-zanjī*' – a derogatory term for those of African origins – Masᶜud calls himself a 'slave' (*ᶜabd*), 'coward', 'drunkard' and 'beast' (*dābba*), internalising the insults of others and, in his feverish stream-of-consciousness, envisioning the world as a battleground, constantly repeating the words 'enemy', 'defeat' and 'battle'.[59] While interpreted as the novel's enlightened hero, he thus becomes somewhat anti-heroic, lying and venting his frustration on his cloistered wife.

Through this striking and, in the 1960s, largely unprecedented depiction of a black protagonist, al-Nayhum anchors his narrative in social and racial exclusion, evoking the marginalisation of Libya's black population in the Benghazi suburb of al-Sabri, a shanty town of reed huts from which Masᶜud hails.[60] Nicknamed '*zarāʾib al-ᶜabīd*' (the slave pens), al-Sabri is the product of centuries of trans-Saharan trade, dwindling to a close by the 1930s but leaving many former slaves, or descendants of slaves, as impoverished labourers, with ethnic tensions compounded under the Italians, as Eritrean *ascari* were conscripted to quell the Libyan resistance and Libyans to fight in Ethiopia.[61] In the 1960s, when al-Nayhum conceived of Masᶜud, African migrants further arrived en masse to meet the oil-fuelled demand for low-skilled, low-paid labour, similarly remaining on the margins of the law.[62]

Struggling to purchase a motor for his boat, Masᶜud's economic plight is entangled with his religious and ethnic othering, dramatised through his pursuit of turtles around which the novel is structured. Offered three francs for every turtle he brings to a new Italian restaurant, he comes up against local belief in the turtles as enchanted, wrathful jinn, a superstition manipulated by the local *fgi* to maintain his power over the villagers and ruthlessly scapegoat Masᶜud. As different characters struggle over it, the turtle thus symbolises a battle for Libya itself, torn between the *fgi*, the Italian settlers and Masᶜud's attempts to eek a living.[63] Through references to Benghazi's new governor, Italo Balbo (d.1940), the Bank of Rome's appropriation of land, and the forced conscription of locals to fight in Ethiopia, local powers are further framed by broader systems of oppression, transforming the fishing communities in which al-Nayhum grew up, and his father served as union leader. Receptive to every current and gust of wind, Masᶜud and his 'two oars' embody self-sufficiency, 'crossing ports crowded with municipal guards, and Italian boats, equipped with engines and giant nets'.[64]

From this position of precarity, Masᶜud transfers his struggles onto the natural world, attempting to disentangle the sea turtle from the discourses that the *fgi* constructs around it, claiming that everything from storms at sea to Masᶜud's back pain represent divine revenge for hunting them.[65] Finally, as a male turtle enters the bay, the *fgi* claims that it has come to punish Masᶜud, necessitating his departure from Susa. The turtle is thus enmeshed in superstitious discourses to the extent that Masᶜud's exclusion is dictated by its movements, as he observes to his wife: 'The *fgi* wants me out of Susa so the turtles remain his commodity alone. I'm telling you. The turtles are part of his invisible tavern where he sells riddles and saints and godly wrath. And when someone eats his turtles, they're eating his divinity.'[66]

Alone at sea, Masᶜud's hunting expeditions become battles to relate to the turtle beyond fear and hatred as, caught by a storm, he is marooned overnight with the animal's gaze on him:

> Masᶜud sat on the edge of the boat in stony silence, watching the turtle's ugly eyes fixed sternly and unblinkingly upon him [. . .] She was hungry and her eyes were pleading with him for a crust of bread. He gazed at her, frozen with fear, before standing up so suddenly he almost toppled into the water. He

> began cursing her as loudly as he could. And then he did something terrible and childish that would haunt him for the rest of his days: he lifted his robe and urinated on her head in a miserable attempt to allay his fears by turning the whole thing into a joke.[67]

Even after killing the turtle, Masᶜud continues insulting her, describing her as the 'queen of the sea' (*sulṭānat al-baḥr*), 'upturned on her back' and 'following her slave'.[68] He cannot, however, shake the memory of her 'dignified gaze' (*ᶜaynayhā al-waqūratayn*) and how she died 'with head held high' while he behaved like a 'foolish child'.[69]Testifying to his senseless destruction, the turtle embodies the barriers of fear and hatred constructed by the *fgi*, distorting human relationships, as, haunted by the animal's suffering, Masᶜud begins to identify his own social exclusion with hers:

> He saw himself lying face down on the marble worktop where the turtles were to be butchered. Then he saw his turtle next to him, burying her head into her shell. He knew that they had finally reached the end of their journey, side by side, and that neither of them had anything to complain about anymore. So he lifted his head and, within full sight of the market boy, he winked at her.[70]

Awaking from the dream, Masᶜud is 'overcome by loneliness' (*waḥda*), longing to 'push his wife aside and return to the turtle'.[71] From exclusionary discourse and commodity, the turtle thus becomes creaturely companion, leading Masᶜud to his elaboration of a 'fishermen's ethics'. As Aḥmad ᶜAṭiyya remarks, the coastline and its wildlife represent the novel's 'second hero', animated in nostalgic detail, and becoming the domain in which Masᶜud locates community, as they increasingly disrupt his stream-of-consciousness.[72]

Fishermen's Struggle

While the sea turtle represents the novel's symbolic heart, a seagull and rat form its rebellious margins as Masᶜud spirals into hallucinations, forgetting 'the *fgi*, the Italians and the church', and 'conversing with the chill east wind blowing from behind the hills'.[73] As he departs from the human world, the reader is forced into the same liminal zone between fantasy, reality and hallucination as, on several occasions, the villagers catch Masᶜud debating with thin air, while the narrative voice declares 'it wasn't an illusion, it was really happening'.[74] In particular, a black-headed seagull becomes Masᶜud's doppelgänger, 'piercing through his loneliness', and declaring, 'We're not like the rest of the fishermen. We're just two ill-fated slaves.'[75]

On one level, Masᶜud's dialogue with nature appears narcissistic and hallucinatory, echoing Fromm's diagnosis of the 'insane person' who 'cannot experience reality, either physical or human reality *as it is*, but only as formed and determined by his own inner processes'.[76] Most critics duly interpret it as a symptom of his lack of human interlocutors.[77] Gradually, however, the coastal world gains autonomy, as the strands of human and animal, fantasy and reality, become entangled. At the novel's midpoint, for example, hallucinatory dialogue is supplemented by what might be called 'fable proper', from the perspective of a 'real' rat. Providing a momentary respite from Masᶜud's disturbed consciousness, the section shifts from the power games of Susa to the simple struggles of its non-human neighbours:

> The turtle, upturned on her back, twitched her neck nervously on the oars, swivelling her head despairingly towards the gulf as a yellow sand crab scuttled over her neck and across her belly, escaping the lapping sea [. . .] But just then a wave slapped him heavily, and threw a rusty can onto his head [. . .] The residents of the sandy dune were having a tough time of it.[78]

On this sandy dune, choked with 'trash', the rat searches for a 'scrap of bread' (*kisrat al-khubz*).[79] Anchored in the spirituality of *rizq*, his thoughts evoke a fully formed rat 'nation', complete with religious belief and elders, as, 'burying his face into the sand and feeling his abominable hunger, he remembered that one of the elders had once told him that God sometimes lowers a rope from the sky to feed his hungry slaves (*ᶜibādahu al-juyāᶜ*)'.[80]

Returning to Masᶜud, fable then merges with feverish dream, as he sees a phantom boy gnawing through his rope. Rushing to his boat, he spies only the rat, however, realising, in profound relief, that no supernatural forces are at work, just other hungry creatures. Masᶜud does not speak, and his encounter with the rat emerges solely through their shared gaze as, between hallucination and fable, al-Nayhum creates a moment of profound mutual understanding whose absence from the rest of the novel renders it all the more striking:

> When the rat raised his head, giving up all hope of escape, he found Mas^{c}ud observing him in stony silence from out of the fog. Their eyes met in a simple gaze, devoid of enmity. They both belonged to the same world (*kānā yantamiyān ilā ^{c}ālam wāḥid*).[81]

Throughout *Min Makka*, Mas^{c}ud is depicted 'observing' (*yurāqib*) others in 'stony silence' (*wājiman*). Unlike most of his judgmental 'observing', his contemplation of the rat leads to compassion, as he declares the animal to be 'his sole friend, united with him against the world'.[82] Thereafter, he is constantly reminded of him, making a wide berth of the mound to avoid frightening him, while, spying a pigeon, he similarly 'observes' it silently, 'remembering his friend, the rat, who did not possess wings, and to whom he had given his rope, so that he would not die of hunger'.[83] In language identical to that describing the seagull, the rat is said to 'pierce through his loneliness' (*yaqtaḥim waḥdatahu*), while mentioning him to his wife provides guilty pleasure and a 'secret feeling of intimacy'.[84] Described as his 'laughable secret', the animal adds a degree of humorous bathos to the novel.[85]

Both rat and seagull, alongside the silent turtle, are also central to Mas^{c}ud's formulation of a creaturely 'fishermen's ethics', expressing both a nostalgic idealisation of traditional fishing communities and a holistic communion of beings, beyond religious and racial othering.[86] 'The rat', Mas^{c}ud realises, 'was really a fisherman (*ṣayyād*) like him and had gone out to earn a scrap (*likay yaḥṣul ^{c}alā rizqihi*). The storm had united them on the hill, as two brother fishermen.'[87] Later, hearing a group of Italians discussing the invasion of Ethiopia, he further declares the Ethiopians to be '*zunūj* (pl. *zanjī*) like me', and Jesus to be a 'fisherman like me', cutting through the tensions of ethnic and religious divides.[88]

'Slave' (^{c}*abd*) is similarly transformed from a derogatory nickname into an expression of unity, extended to, and expressed through, animals. Commenting on the term in later writing, al-Nayhum argues that it signifies not the historical phenomenon of 'slavery' (*riqq*), but the relationship of all beings with God, synonymous with 'God's creatures' (*makhlūqāt Allāh*).[89] Tlili echoes this view, suggesting that, in contrast to the mostly negative connotations of '*insān*' (human), the root *ᶜ-b-d* denotes worshipful harmony, particularly when humans are referred to as 'My/Our subjects (*ᶜibādī*/*ᶜibāduna*)'.[90] While Masᶜud labels both the seagull and Jesus as 'slaves', the rat himself refers to 'God's hungry slaves'.[91]

Increasingly, spiritual encounter becomes central to *Min Makka*, as, from terrifying superstitions, Masᶜud moves to unmediated encounter with the divine, lying on the western rocks 'to observe God in stony silence'.[92] Similarly, the novel's imagery of 'storms', 'hunting' and 'battles' shifts to Masᶜud's realisation that God might even be on the same 'side' as an 'ignorant slave' (*ᶜabd jāhil*) and 'beast' (*dābba*).[93] This is culminated as the supposedly male turtle enters the bay, bobbing between the boats, and ironically described as 'carrying the full weight of God and the dark heavens on his shoulders'.[94] As the *fgi* immediately claims that the animal has come for Masᶜud, the turtle becomes the final 'battleground' (*masraḥ al-qitāl*) for their conflict, while the bay, where Masᶜud rows to meet him, shifts from the *fgi's* 'commodity' to a stage, both real and metaphoric, allowing him to rethink the world as *arḍ Allāh*.[95]

Finally, however, the novel turns, once again, from Masᶜud's perspective to the manoeuverings of the *fgi*, who also spends the night by the water, reciting the Qurᵓanic story of Jonah and the whale.[96] As he does so, the rocks, waves and seagulls 'listen' (*yunṣit*), while the North Star 'beckons from the Heavens' (*yūmiᵓ lahu min samawātihi*) and the mountains 'submit in silence' (*yakhshaᶜ ṣāmitan*).[97] Steeped in Qurᵓanic imagery, the passage, somewhat ironically, subsumes the *fgi* within the 'signs' (*āyāt*) of nature, just as Jonah is subsumed within the whale. It is not long, however, before this unity is disrupted as, glimpsing the turtle coming ashore, the *fgi* realises that, contrary to his myths, it is not a male, come to avenge Masᶜud, but a female, come to lay her eggs.[98] Despite being manipulated into his fallacious discourses, she is simply acting according to seasonal cycles, impassive to the human drama around her and seeking to protect her young. Unwilling to forsake his 'piece of divinity', the *fgi* casts her eggs into the sea, in a final act of injustice, to both Masᶜud and the turtles. While the natural world listens to the *fgi*, the *fgi* remains deaf, and, as Masᶜud drifts through the bay, he retains his grip over the village, leaving little room for the imagining of harmonious community, whether national, spiritual or ecological.

With this provocative image, al-Nayhum concludes his novel, opening uncertainly onto a future of social and political transformation in which the tensions of 1930s Susa would remain central, from environmental precarity to ethnic othering. *Min Makka* thus retains its foundational status as a searing social, political and ecological commentary, and forerunner of later aesthetic trends. Following al-Qadhafi's coup, its poetics of creaturely struggle and fear resonate through the writing of later authors, interwoven with increasingly extreme visions of human and non-human suffering and persecution.

Fi'ran bila Juhur: Nomadic Swansong and Species Critique

While *Min Makka* portrays an individual whose conflict with society is transferred onto nature, *Fi'ran* depicts an entire community in conflict with it. Begun in the 1960s, the novel was, al-Faqih states, postponed by his dismay at the 1967 June War, shifting his attention to more immediate political concerns.[99] It then took him thirty-three years to complete, with his return prompted, as he states, by guilt towards his family, whose 'struggles against the harshness of the environment' and 'difficulty of historical circumstance' had first inspired him to write it as a record of their 'human experience of great depth and fertility'.[100] Subtitled 'A Page from the Book of Hunger' (*ṣafḥa min kitāb al-jūʿ*), it offers a panorama of subsistence livelihoods in the pre-oil state as, facing starvation, the tribe are faced with various bleak choices: working on the coast as labourers, collecting scrap metal from the Second World War, felling trees for charcoal or picking grain from camel dung. Just as they despair, however, the Shaykh's grandson, ʿAli, digs up a jerboa hole filled with barley, and the tribe proceeds to amass it, while the jerboas organise their resistance. Matters are then complicated as a second tribe, Āl Jibrīl, arrives from the East, astounding them with their liberal ways as they drive cars, mix with women and even eat jerboas. Thereafter, the novel is divided between a realist human strand and an animal fable strand, with the first shifting to romantic plots, negotiating tradition and modernity, and the second remaining anchored in survival.

Given al-Faqih's desire to produce a 'human' record of a lost world, this animal strand is certainly intriguing. For Rita Sakr, the battle of humans and jerboas symbolises al-Qadhafi's oppression of his citizens, pre-empting his labelling of them as 'rats' and 'cockroaches' in 2011.[101] More explicitly, it echoes his description of city life as the 'existence of rats in holes' (*maʿīshat al-fi'rān wa-juḥūrihā*) in his own short stories.[102] This straightforward allegorical reading is, however, problematised by the novel's initial publication in 1966. Since the tribe is inspired by al-Faqih's family, it further seems unlikely that they should symbolise a brutal dictator. Like the jerboas, they are victims of circumstance and, while critique of al-Qadhafi is latent in some aspects of the novel, the initial seeds were planted by alternative reflection. Through each of its strands, *Fiʾran* represents both a swansong to nomadic life and an indictment of human divisiveness, bridging distinct phases of al-Faqih's writing.

Having moved to Tripoli from rural Mizda in the 1960s, al-Faqih's first stories were primarily social realist pieces, depicting entangled, human and animal communities in critical yet affectionate fashion. In 'al-Jarad' (1965, 'The Locusts'), he depicts a village struggling against locust invasion, united in heroic battle and joyful song.[103] Commenting on the story, al-Faqih insists on its real, historical dimensions rather than the symbolic dimensions of struggle against Italians allegedly read into it.[104] Three decades later, the motif of human versus animal reappears, but this time animals become the heroes, in more symbolic, experimental writing. In 'Khams Khanafis Tuhakim al-Shajara' (1999, 'Five Beetles Try the Tree'), for example, a village is dismayed by the sudden barrenness of their sacred olive tree.[105] Initially, they believe they are being punished for adopting western ways, but it transpires that vengeful beetles are punishing the tree itself for attracting humans to the land and disrupting its fragile ecosystem. Rather than the expected theme of tradition and modernity, the story highlights the beetles' imperceptible plight and, like *Fiʾran*, entwines environmental and political import, rooted in primordial images of appropriation, concerning the misuse of land and mistreatment of its inhabitants, and anchored, equally, in al-Faqih's earlier social realism, and later Aesopic critique.

'Umm Bsisi' Gone Wrong

In the tradition of folkloric influence, *Fiʾran* most clearly represents an unsettling engagement with the traditional tale of 'Umm Bsisi', told by Shaykh Abu Layla's wife Hajja Khadija to their grandson ʿAli as the tribe arrives in Jandouba to discover the barley's disappearance. As the story goes, a little mouse steals milk from Umm Bsisi, the sparrow, and in revenge she pecks off his tail, which he needs to dance at Eid. In order to earn it back, he must bring her milk from the nanny goat. The nanny goat, however, requires berries from the *nabk* tree while the tree requires water from the valley, and so on.[106] Animating the flow of life through the desert, the original tale concludes happily, as 'the Prophet's family' (*ahl al-bayt*) take pity on the mouse, allowing him to satisfy his creditors and dance at Eid.[107] In concluding her version of the tale, however, Khadija brings it to bear on the tribe's situation, observing how the mouse had, in fact, seized everything for himself and become 'master of the land'.[108] In response, the tribe proceed to seize it back, and traditional, folkloric harmony is thus juxtaposed to the novel's central drama of imbalance and appropriation.

As the novel opens, the tribe's position within a broader, creaturely whole is immediately emphasised. The jerboas are introduced first, while, as the tribe enter the valley, the 'forty human beings' are listed last, after 'five camels, three donkeys, four dogs and one horse'. Even then, they are recognised first as 'beings' (*kāʾin*) and then as 'human' (*basharī*).[109] Following this opening, the novel continues to shift from above to below, and from expansive panorama to the minute and imperceptible. While the sun glares down on all, an ant colony is destroyed underfoot, echoing Solomon's encounter with the 'valley of ants' in the Qurʾan, and contrasting the receptivity of the prophet-king to the oblivious tribe.[110]

As they set up camp, the people are, however, also depicted in affectionate terms, singing, joking and tending their animals. When forced to sacrifice his camel to feed the starving people, Shaykh Abu Layla is haunted by the loss of his 'friend', while ᶜAmma Maryuma, the tribe matriarch, gives her share of its meat to her dog, Maᶜruf.[111] As in 'al-Jarad', individual character development is replaced by animation of the tribe as community, through affectionate relationships between humans and with animals.

As the tribe transcribe their adventure into song and story, however, this harmony is again disrupted by uncomfortable reminders of the dispossessed jerboas. Composing a folksong in which they thank the jerboas, as 'neighbours', for harvesting the barley, they thereafter jokingly refer to it as the 'jerboas' barley' (*shaᶜīr al-jarābīᶜ*).[112] Depiction of the two tribes feasting on jerboa meat is similarly ambivalent, particularly as it provides a central means through which they overcome their cultural differences, prompted by the romance of Zahra of Āl Jibrīl and al-Rumani of Shaikh Abu Layla's tribe:

> When he'd declared he was ready to eat the roast jerboa meat (*al-jarābīᶜ al-mashwiyya*), she'd been filled with delight and offered it to him with her own hand. Then, when their hands touched, they'd stuck together because of the fatty meat, and he'd been filled with a passionate desire to hold her in his arms.[113]

As desire is laced with the smell, texture and taste of meat, it literally binds the lovers and, by extension, their tribes. At the same time, the scurrying of 'homeless jerboas' continues to disrupt both the narrative and its human characters, prompting questions, as with all the beetles, insects and creepy crawlies (*ḥasharāt*) of al-Faqih's work, as to what is perceptible within the literary, ecological and political space.

Self-Preservation

Unlike in *Min Makka*, sections of fable and realism are firmly distinguished in the novel, with humans entirely unable to hear animals speak. For this reason, the tribe's camel and donkey are never heard, while the jerboas alternate between silently scurrying forms and fully anthropomorphised characters. The lizard and hedgehog, Jandouba's 'wise ascetics', retain their voices throughout, never encountering the tribes and the novel's realist mode. Introduced at the novel's end, they peruse the valley below, where life forms intermingle, casting the human–animal drama into broad perspective:

> Between these motionless landmarks were to be found living creatures, which, from the high point of the plateau, could be seen going about their daily work. They included humans, dogs, donkeys and camels, all appearing as small dots against the vast expanse, and there were many other creatures too that couldn't be seen from the heights.[114]

As the wise animals survey the view, they recall 'the battles fought between the creatures of the valley', from the 1913 Battle of Jandouba, led by Berber statesman Sulaymān al-Bārūnī (*c.* 1870–1940) against the Italians, to the generational clashes between and within the tribes, and, finally, the jerboas' battle for survival.[115] Meditating on existence as 'conflict' (*ṣirāᶜ*) and 'self-preservation' (*ḥifẓ al-dhāt*), the friends themselves opt out, rarely moving, and consuming only the 'leftovers' (*mukhallafāt*) of other animals.[116] In contrast, humans embrace excess and devise 'weapons of annihilation' (*asliḥat al-ibāda*).[117] Echoing Qurᵓan 6:38, the comprehensiveness of their 'massacre' (*majzara*) of the valley insects is conveyed through description of how 'No insect that crawled or flew [. . .] could escape the weapon and live' (*mā min ḥashara, zāḥifa aw ṭāᵓira, yumkinuhā an tanjū min hādhā al-silāḥ*).[118]

Echoing the Ikhwan al-Safaᵓ's *Case of the Animals*, 'delegates' (*mūfadūn*) from the beleaguered animals arrive to consult the friends, who are shocked to hear that the jerboas are considering matching the humans' destructiveness through recruiting city mice to spread disease.[119] The lizard's response provides the novel's central ethics, to abandon revenge and focus on 'procreation and proliferation' (*al-ikhṣāb wa-l-tawālud*).[120] The central message of al-Faqih's fable, and its creaturely ethics of survival, is thus the natural fact of 'pursuing one's needs' (*al-taṣarruf fī maʾāribihim*), as repeated in the *Case of the Animals*, and contrasting the endless cycles of violence within human civilisation.[121]

Soon enough, however, matters are taken from the hands of all species, through the concluding image of a divinely sent flood, culminating the religious discourses which traverse the novel, rooted in the depiction of Jandouba as a 'blessed land' (*arḍ mubāraka*).[122] While ᶜAli first discovers the barley after al-Hajja Khadija's prayers for 'a morsel of barley bread', and the tribe celebrate its discovery as a divine boon, it is the animals who receive an 'invisible call', instructing them to take shelter on the mountain and await 'salvation'.[123] Inverting the Noah's ark story, humans are left in confusion by their unintelligible 'grunting', 'barking' and 'braying' as, like the 'merciless sun', the flood acts as a powerful leveller.[124] Finding themselves fleeing with the jerboas as though 'their fates were bound', the tribe's attention finally shifts to the animals themselves. As the barley is destroyed, some lament its loss but another asks: 'You mean the jerboas' barley?'[125] This comment, heard as though 'for the first time', provokes both hysterical laughter and weeping, as one person responds 'Hahaha. You're right, Burhan! Hahaha. It *is* the jerboas' barley!'[126]

As the water finally retreats, the novel concludes with the jerboas' 'mournful lament' (*bukāʾ ḥazīn*), providing a final, striking contrast to fable, as it is 'lost amid the people's screams, and the roaring of the flood'.[127] In the competing strands of 'human' and 'animal', 'realism' and 'fable', this unintelligible complaint has the last word, conveying struggle against the 'harshness of the environment' and 'difficulty of historical circumstance' as the final shared ground between them. Obliterating all possessions, the flood finally recalls Shaykh Abu Layla's earlier words, lamenting how 'God's country' (*bilād Allāh*) was once 'God's land' (*arḍ Allāh*), spiritually and environmentally united beyond divisions of ownership.[128] Just like the bay in which Masᶜud confronts his turtle foe in *Min Makka*, the flood creates a vision of unity through shared struggle, leaving the future of society and nation in question. As Chorin suggests, 'The underlying message, which resonates well in present-day Libya, is one of the connectivity of all things – individuals to people, people to animals and the environment – and the advantages of unity in the face of adversity.'[129]

Nazif al-Hajar: From Cain and Abel to Human and Animal

Against a backdrop of American military operations and European tourism in the 1950s, *Nazif* takes the poetics of *Min Makka* and *Fiʾran* further into the wild and mystical. Like Masᶜud, Asuf lives apart from society, but contrastingly embraces this solitude, while Cain (Qābīl), his nemesis, is violently addicted to meat, eventually hallucinating, through lack of protein or '*ṭāqa*' (energy), that Asuf has become an animal, and slaughtering him in its place. Flashbacks to the 1930s further depict Asuf's mythic relationship with the *waddān* and Cain's with the gazelle, against a backdrop of Italian incursion. Both are based on animals having saved humans' lives and calling them to recognise their indebtedness as, through the voice of a gazelle, fable articulates a creaturely ethics of self-sacrifice, and what Susan McHugh describes as 'a peculiar resignation to deprivation – rather, an embrace of emptiness – as the mindset of survival that distinguishes all of the desert's inhabitants'.[130]

Through these strands, al-Kuni ties together political critique, spiritual meditation and ecological mourning. Alongside ᶜAbd al-Raḥmān Munīf, his environmentalist poetics have been widely recognised within Arabic literature. Like al-Nayhum, he describes oil in demonic terms, as an unleashing of disease, addiction and oppression, alluding to it within his defining use of myth, and evoking what Wenzel terms 'petro-magic-realism', as he situates 'the magical and violent aspects of petro-modernity within an older fantastic tradition'.[131] In Massak Satfat, where *Nazif* is set, oil prospecting began in the 1980s, leading to severe environmental damage in an already drought-riven land.[132] While oil does not feature explicitly, the novel's title clearly alludes to it, echoing al-Kuni's description of oil extraction as the 'spilling of a mother's blood' (*nazīf damm al-umm*) as, across his writing, the repeated image of 'bleeding' (*nazīf*) brings together physical vulnerability and spiritual revelation, and emphasises the interconnections of human, animal and land.[133] The 'bleeding' of the stone thus couples with that of animals, plants and souls, within states of exception and appropriation, opening onto spiritual encounter.[134]

Specifically, al-Kuni's environmentalism is bound to his Tuareg heritage, drawing on the tribes' intimate acquaintance with the land, migrating between Niger, Libya, Algeria, and Mali, and weathering the settlement policies of postcolonial nations, resource extraction and climate change.[135] Within these contexts, al-Kuni's exaltation of voluntary exile (*ightirāb*), as spiritual freedom, is intertwined with the realities of political and ecological dispossession. Through Cain and Asuf, he juxtaposes the settled and nomadic, and Libyan and Tuareg, reflecting his assertion that the desert, rather than nation, is the 'essential origin of his literary work'.[136] While such an avowal might appear to put him at odds with other Libyan authors, his objection to centralised, authoritarian power clearly also echoes the centripetal logic of both *Min Makka* and *Fiʾran*, while his protest over dispossession extends to Libya itself. Describing Tripoli, where he spent his early adulthood, he conveys the same burden of loss as al-Nayhum, as a beloved city transforms to toxic, concrete jungle.[137]

Collective dispossession is thus mirrored in his personal exile, firstly as an environmental refugee, when drought drove his family from Tinghart in the Hamada Hamra to Wahat Adri, Ghadames and Sabha, and then as a student in Tripoli and voluntary exile in Russia and Poland.[138] As with al-Nayhum, this personal exile is bound to existential reflection on a lost wholeness and 'freedom', whose 'praises' the desert creatures 'sing' (*yusabbiḥ bi-l-ḥurriya*).[139] As Fähndrich observes, 'In al-Koni's desert everything is symbolic, impregnated by myth. Every plant and every animal, every grain of sand and every rock points beyond itself.'[140] Most often, 'signs' come in immanent form, through human–animal encounters, woven into myth, and representing the visceral 'realism' beneath magic and mysticism.

In *Nazif*, al-Kuni returns to the Cain–Abel narrative, with his protagonists' very names, Cain and Asuf, juxtaposing Abrahamic and Tuareg tradition, foundational fratricide and, in Tamasheq, the central cosmological and psychological concept of 'wilderness', 'solitude' and 'longing' (*essuf*).[141] As Ricardo Quinones remarks, Cain's murder of Abel represents a 'shattering reminder of the fragility of the human compact', dramatising 'an encounter with the lost brother, the sacrificed other, who must be gone but who can never be gone'.[142] In *Nazif*, this lost brother is figured as both the Tuareg minority and the land and its creatures. The novel's opening epigraphs further juxtapose the Old Testament story of Cain's fratricide to Qurʾanic description of animals as 'nations like you', transforming one of humanity's most famous foundational narratives into one story among many, from one species among many. Animals duly shift from the named and sacrificed of scripture to a central place within the cosmic scheme, emphasised through the playful altering of epigraphs in subsequent chapters.[143] A quote from Sophocles' *Oedipus Rex* (*c.* 429 BCE) likens Oedipus to a *waddān* rather than the bull of the original.[144] A translation of Henri Lhote's *A la découverte des fresques du Tassili* (1958; *The Search for the Tassili Frescoes*, 1959) emphasises hunters' ritual mimicking of the *waddān*, translating the original description of them 'skipping' (*sautillant*) to 'bounding on all fours' (*yataqāfaz ᶜalā arbaᶜ*).[145]

Duly, the drama of Cain and Abel shifts to that of human and animal.[146] Both Cain and his American ally, John Parker, are possessed by a voracious need to consume, personifying what Meg Weisberg calls 'the separating mind-set' of colonial and neo-colonial logic.[147] Cain's story begins when he is a baby and his family are lost in the desert. Seeing the family's plight, a gazelle sacrifices her life for his, allowing her blood to be consumed. In an inversion of Ibn Ṭufayl's *Hayy Ibn Yaqzan* (*c.*1169), Cain is weaned on gazelle blood rather than milk, and consequently is driven not towards enlightenment but to consumption.[148] As an adult, his addiction further shifts from myth to misogyny, as he compares meat-eating to bedding women, and tells Asuf, 'If you don't eat meat, then you have to live apart from other people. I see now why you've chosen to live in this empty wilderness.'[149] Eventually, Cain's addiction becomes so severe that a soothsayer predicts it will be assuaged only by human flesh, realised through entangled images of carnivorousness and cannibalism as he consumes a gazelle, described as his sister, and slaughters Asuf who transforms into a *waddān*.

John Parker's more cerebral addiction begins with his study of mysticism at university, followed by his posting to the American Wheelus Airbase. While there, he becomes fascinated with popular Sufism and the promise of gaining mystical insight through animals. In his readings, he encounters two ways of doing so. The first dictates an existence of solitude like that of Asuf, 'silencing his tongue until he lost the ability of speech, eating grass until he forgot the taste of food'.[150] The alternative is simply to consume gazelle flesh, in which, as he reads in a Sufi travel log, 'God has placed the secret (*al-sirr*)'.[151] As Parker opts for 'flesh', supplying Cain with weapons and vehicles, and assisting in the species' eradication, his fundamental misunderstanding of the animal as 'sign' and 'secret' becomes clear.

This misunderstanding is concluded through one of al-Kuni's many feverish hunt scenes, evoking what Hélène Claudot-Hawad observes as the pursuit of animals as a metaphor for the pursuit of knowledge in Tuareg tradition.[152] Such pursuit, Claudot-Hawad suggests, should be carried out with patience and respect, lest the animal bolt or injure itself in flight.[153] Disregarding this, Cain and Parker helicopter to the Hasawna Mountains, as technology allows them to eradicate the 'bonds which have preserved the balance of survival' in the desert.[154] As they scan the terrain in a long, filmic perspective, the helicopter initially shields the men from their victims' vulnerability. After descending, however, Cain catches a glimpse of the animal's gaze, longing to 'grasp' its secret, just as he longs for its meat:

> Her eyes were big and black and intelligent, speaking some unknown language, saying something to him, revealing a secret (*sirr*). A secret, yes, one he sensed but couldn't quite grasp (*lā yudrikuhu*). It's the hardest, most desolate thing in the world, to sense a secret and not grasp it (*taᶜjiz ᶜan idrākihi*).[155]

Cain's inability to read the animal's gaze goes to the heart of the spiritual and ethical centrality of animals in al-Kuni's writing. As Huggan and Tiffin comment, 'the leap required to read observed animal behaviour and imagine animal being is perhaps not as profound as we conveniently like to believe'.[156] The gazelle is simply asking to live but, unable to recognise this, Cain closes his eyes and shoots. The calf and her mother's abjection then displaces any transcendent 'secret', as Cain sees the calf 'writhing on the ground' while the mother's eyes shine with 'wretchedness' (*shaqāʾ*).[157] As she howls like a 'wolf', the uncanny image further strikingly juxtaposes an earlier chapter in which she speaks eloquently in fable, representing animals' simultaneous spiritual wisdom and stark vulnerability, as they seek to convey the 'secret' of their oneness with humanity and simple, yet urgent, desire for life.[158]

Self-sacrifice

Al-Kuni, as discussed in my introduction, cites the Kyrgyz novelist Chingiz Aitmatov and his 1970 Russian-language novel, *The White Steamship*, as a foundation for his thinking about minorities and the environment.[159] In both respects, *The White Steamship* further resonates with his own use of animal fable as a necessary means of drawing attention to human wrongs. Like *Nazif*, it depicts the mistreatment of a mother deer, the 'Horned

Deer-Mother', as mythic saviour of the Kyrgyz people, nursing the last two of its children after a massacre by an enemy tribe.[160] Despite her act of salvation, however, the children grow up to prove themselves thankless, inaugurating a custom of slaughtering her descendants, and leading her to flee into the mountains with her remaining herd, never to return. As so often with animals in al-Kuni's writing, the Horned Deer-Mother's eyes fill with 'reproach and sorrow', and she declares, 'I spoke that way [in the language of men] because otherwise you would not have understood me, and not heeded.'[161]

Echoes of this deer resonate through *Nazif*, whose own mother gazelle tries, but fails entirely, to communicate with Cain and Parker. As Saᶜīd al-Ghānamī comments, al-Kuni's writing often fluctuates between distanced, bird's eye perspectives and close-up intimacy, 'penetrating' (*yastabṭin*) the consciousness of non-human beings, and contrasting their visceral sentience to human unfeelingness.[162] In *Nazif*, this emerges through juxtaposition of the ancient wisdom of fable with the disorienting speed of car and helicopter which obliterates it.

Sheltering in the mountains, the mother tells her lonely daughter why they have remained when others have migrated south, returning to the history of their 'nation' (*waṭan*) and of 'creation' (*al-khalq*).[163] The Creator, she explains, assigned 'time', 'place' and 'body' as three frontiers to the soul.[164] All creatures must respect these bounds or risk imbalance and consequent 'perdition'. A metaphysical translation of animals' instinctual habits and habitats, the gazelle's words reflect what Oerlemans observes as the combined 'human *and* animal wisdom' of fable, rooted in a respect for otherness, and the dividing line between need and desire.[165] Continuing, the mother then describes the special covenant that ties her offspring to Cain, forged by her own mother's act of self-sacrifice for the baby and his family as they were marooned in the desert. This act, the herd leader tells her, will both forge a bond of blood between their descendants and open the 'secret' of 'creation':

> 'God (*al-khāliq*),' she said, 'honoured all creatures (*al-makhlūqāt*) and gave them life. Then, to test their endurance, He set them in the desert. He placed his secret (*sirr*) in the scarce water, and He placed a further secret in dreadful sacrifice. He who sacrifices himself to save another's life sees into that secret and wins immortality.'[166]

The gazelle's words establish creation as a test not of self-preservation but self-sacrifice (*taḍḥiyya*), which, contrary to Parker's belief in the magic power of meat, represents the true nature of 'signs' and 'secrets', as a call to respond to otherness, and recognise a shared struggle for life, binding the desert creatures.

Despite its ancient wisdom, however, fable ultimately fails, as Cain, heedless of covenants, irrevocably alters the balance of the land, annihilating its gazelles. Structured around fateful clashes between creatures, *Nazif* emphasises how civilisation renders the individual irresponsive while, like Asuf, states of hunger, thirst and isolation maintain spiritual and physical 'alertness' (*yaqẓa*), allowing creatures to engage ethically in the drama of survival. In Derridean terms, Asuf and Cain represent the opposing poles of 'carnophallogocentrism' – in which selfhood is founded on the ingestion, both symbolic and literal, of otherness – and 'eating well', as the ideal encounter with otherness, renouncing the stability of selfhood, and premised on 'absolutely limiting understanding itself, the identifying appropriation'.[167]

Blood and Flood

Like Masᶜud and his turtles, Asuf's encounters with the ever-silent *waddān* indicate the need to rebalance an upset order, unfolding in a drama of pursuit, slaughter, companionship, recognition, metamorphosis, self-sacrifice and, finally, 'bleeding' (*nazīf*) and 'flood' (*fayaḍān*). Contrary to *Min Makka*, these encounters involve reaffirming, rather than denying, the animal's mythic power while, more similarly, embracing both its unknowability and fundamental unity with the self. Within the novel's entangled narrative threads, shifting between flashback and flashforward, this is dramatised through the bonds that tie Asuf and his father to the *waddān*, eerily echoing those of Cain and the gazelle. Hovering between myth, mythic breakdown and visceral materiality, these bonds dramatise the fundamental truth of ecological and spiritual wholeness that haunts al-Kuni's writing. 'I have always been interested in the problem of the unity of creation', al-Kuni states, 'and even of the unity of creator and creation. God, man, and animal are united in a single body, named the Sahara. That is why, when we kill a *waddān* (moufflon), we harm ourselves.'[168]

After being rescued by a *waddān* from a cliff edge, Asuf's father solemnly 'swears' (*yandhur*) that neither he nor his descendants will hunt again. Signifying both 'vow' and 'votive offering', this '*nadhr*' enters them into a sacrificial relationship with the species, with the life of one becoming ransom for the other.[169] After killing a second *waddān* when drought strikes, Asuf's father thus falls to his death, mirroring the fate of a third *waddān*, which he had previously hounded to death. For years after, Asuf respects his father's vow until, one day, he finds himself compelled by an 'unknown power' to pursue the animal.[170] Unlike Cain, his pursuit is precarious as, running on all fours, he appears to transform into the animal, before being pulled along uncontrollably as the 'chase' (*muṭārada*) becomes a 'peeling away' (*saḥl*), literally opening him to otherness.[171] Blurring predator and prey, Asuf shifts the traditional paradigm of the human hunt, in which culture trumps nature, transforming prey to meat, to spiritual, creaturely journey. As the *waddān* plunges him into a pit, he faces imminent death, before being lassoed to safety by his former prey. At his most physically vulnerable, he then exchanges a gaze with the *waddān*, conveying a vision of unity on a creaturely, mythical and mystical level: 'Suddenly, in the dimness of the glow, he saw his father in the eyes of the great, patient *waddan* [. . .] The eyes that had chosen a cruel freedom without ever quite knowing why.'[172] On one level, Asuf's recognition is based in the myths surrounding father, son and *waddān*, suggesting that, following their parallel deaths, father and *waddān* have become one. On another, it reveals Asuf's perception of his kinship with the *waddān*, as patient desert creatures. Finally, as he cries out 'You're my father. I recognized you', his exclamation is described 'as if communing with his God' (*kaʾannahu yunājī rabbahu*).[173]

Through this encounter, Asuf's relationship to the desert is recalibrated, primarily through his sudden aversion to meat, even from his own goats, which, in contrast to the *waddān*, enjoy no special privilege in Tuareg myth.[174] Representing Asuf's daily survival rather than his divine rescue, and contrasting the *waddān's* prophetic 'wretchedness' (*shaqāʾ*) with their 'unruliness' (*shaqāwa*), they, too, are incorporated within the novel's ethics of 'eating well'.[175] Even when dying of starvation, Asuf refuses to slaughter them and, beyond the vows that shape his relationship with the *waddān*, this exemplifies his total openness to otherness, recalling the words of the mother gazelle that '[sacrifice] knows nothing of bargains, and doesn't look to the soul for which the sacrifice is made. Sacrifice belongs to the Almighty Creator (*al-khāliq al-ʿaẓīm*).'[176]

Following this transformation, the *waddān* further begin to mix with Asuf's goats, uniting the 'ordinary' and 'mythic' in creaturely companionship, and consoling Asuf with eyes which 'conversed in a thousand languages, spoke with a thousand tongues, without ever making a sound'.[177] As in *Min Makka*, the shared human–animal gaze, as refuge from human society, becomes an almost rhythmic refrain, through repetition, across the novels, of Mas^cud's 'silent observation', and the 'wretchedness' and 'thousand tongues' of the *waddān's* eyes. Emerging through self-sacrifice and companionship, these shared moments gravitate from the discourses imposed on animals to an interconnected vision of human, animal and divine.

Asuf's entanglement with the *waddān* is, however, continued through metamorphosis, representing the ultimate relinquishment of self and counterpoint to carnivorousness. Narrated in flashback, in a chapter entitled 'Rāqid al-Rīḥ', which, following my opening comments to this chapter, might simply be translated 'The Survivor', Asuf transforms into a *waddān* after descending into an oasis for the first time because of drought. Immediately, he is captured by Colonel Bordello, a fictional iteration of the brutal Italian military leader, Rodolfo Graziani, as he gathers troops to fight in Ethiopia. While Asuf and the other prisoners are 'packed together like sheep', Asuf transforms into a *waddān* and escapes.[178] As both Miriam Cooke and Susan McHugh suggest, this metamorphosis evokes Deleuze and Guattari's concept of '*becoming-animal*', as a state of shifting identities or 'assemblages', opposing the monolithic narratives of 'state apparatus'.[179] In a moment of exuberant liberation, and a brief escape from vulnerability, Asuf transforms into a human-*waddān*, unhurt by the shower of bullets that follows him. Transforming into legend, his metamorphosis is later interpreted by Sufi shaykhs as both '*ḥulūl*' (divine indwelling) and '*taḥawwul*' (transformation).[180] Combining human, animal and divine, it suggests, above all, how the 'becomings' of al-Kuni's writing begin, as Elmarsafy remarks, from the fundamental basis of Sufi oneness, accessed through states of extreme vulnerability, embodied by the figure of the *rāqid al-rīḥ*.[181]

Asuf's self-sacrificial death then concludes this entanglement of human, animal and divine. Repaying his father's debt, he refuses to lead Cain to the *waddān* until the crazed Cain resolves to slaughter him in the animal's stead.[182] From animal sacrifice as a rite that traditionally consolidates differences between human, animal and divine, the novel thus shifts to self-sacrifice as a rite through which they merge.[183] Crucified and with his throat cut, Asuf's death simultaneously evokes prophetic martyrdom, ritual slaughter and meaningless savagery. On an ancient fresco of a priest and *waddān*, his body 'merges' with both the rock and the image of the animal, while his severed head intones a prophetic Hadith, representing his sole refrain during the novel's last seven chapters: 'Only through dust will the son of Adam be filled' (*lā yushba*ᶜ *Ibn Ādam illā bi-l-turāb*).[184] Returning to God's condemnation of Cain in the opening epigraph from Genesis, 'thy brother's blood crieth unto me from the ground', the severed head both completes Asuf's identification with Abel and sunders him from the species of Ibn Adam.[185] In parallel, Cain's violence, the result of an addict's hallucinations, contrasts the ancient wisdom and harmony of priest and *waddān*, standing in equitable 'dignity'.

Culminating the gazelle's 'fable of sacrifice', in which all life is given for a greater whole, writing then appears on the rock, prophesying that 'when the sacred *waddan* bleeds and the blood issues from the stone [. . .] the earth will be cleansed and the deluge cover the desert'.[186] Through water and blood, the two liquids fundamental to life, the prophecy simultaneously suggests redemption, purification and annihilation, anchored in the fundamental imbalance of material, creaturely existence. Ending with the first drops of rain, the novel, like *Min Makka* and *Fiʾran*, thus seems to announce a seismic transformation to the desert, yet also leaves the future of land and nation in question, restoring *arḍ Allāh* yet also hinting at irreparable loss.

Conclusion

Discussing the imperceptibility of 'slow violence', Rob Nixon questions how we are to 'act ethically toward human and biotic communities that lie beyond our sensory ken'.[187] In the Libyan novel, the dual invisibility of the environmentally and politically excluded are interwoven in a vulnerability-of-being, demanding a broadening of the conventional parameters of attention. Beginning with al-Nayhum's 'naive Sufism', this represents a defining poetics of the Libyan novel, generated through depictions of creaturely solidarity in response to the overwhelming weight of political, social and environmental transformations. In a 1969 article, a young al-Kuni thus describes his fascination with identifying an ungraspable and momentous 'secret' (*sirr khaṭīr*) within al-Nayhum's 'rebellious Sufi philosophy'.[188] Over forty years later, in his autobiography, he elaborates this vision of al-Nayhum as a Sufi writer, embracing not only the 'oneness-of-being', but 'the oneness of all creatures within being' (*waḥdat al-kāʾināt fi hādha-l-wujūd*), and citing Ibn al-ᶜArabī's (1165–1240) famous lines to describe him:

> My heart has become capable of every form: it is a
> pasture for gazelles, and a convent for Christian monks,
> And a temple for idols and the pilgrim's Kaᶜba and
> the tables of the Tora and the book of the Koran.
> I follow the religion of Love: whatever way Love's
> camels take, that is my religion and my faith.[189]

The heterogeneous unity envisioned in Ibn al-ᶜArabī's verse resonates through all three of *Min Makka*, *Fiʾran* and *Nazif*. Shifting from symbolic to material, and prophetic to silent, animals lead humans down unexpected paths of pain and insight, away from language, security and possessions. Through fable, juxtaposing the playful wisdom of traditional narrative with harsh realism, they evoke both lost oral traditions and ties to the land, as well as the silenced subjectivities of the nation's 'others', haunted by the 'difficulty of story'. Reworking Qurʾanic narratives of Adam and Eve, Cain and Abel, Jonah, and Noah, the novels further evoke a wholeness lost to literal and figurative appropriation as, in extreme geographies, *arḍ Allāh* is reinforced beyond military and economic forces, colonial and national borders, and growing consumerism. Haunted by latent 'energy anxiety' and an aversion to excess, the novels conclude with empty-handedness as, from pre- and post-Qadhafi eras, they both dramatise the 'placelessness, homelessness or statelessness' engendered by tyrannical forms of power and embrace alternative unities through animal characters, which, unlike humans, remain at home in the world.[190]

2

The Primordial Turn

Among His signs is that He created you from clay and behold, you are human beings pervading the earth. (Qur'an 30:20)[1]

Apes, I can see now, reminded her of the passions which led to the spilling of blood. (John Berger, 'Ape Theatre')[2]

In 'The Nocturnal Visitor', the third instalment of Alessandro Spina's (né Bāsilī Shafiq Khuzām, 1927–2013) *I confini dell'ombra* (2006; *The Confines of the Shadow*, 2012), the venerable judge Sheikh Hassan is immersed in history books, whose vicissitudes he sees reflected in the ruins dotting his native Cyrenaican valley.[3] Imagining bygone kingdoms, 'richer than Iram of the Pillars', alongside the crumbling ruins they leave behind, the Sheikh envisions the valley as a dramatisation of North African historiographer Ibn Khaldūn's *Muqaddima* (1377 CE), and its exposition of the 'foundation of a city, its flowering and subsequent decay'.[4] Superfluity, Ibn Khaldūn tells him, is the cause of this decay, while the secret of Bedouin society lies in its moderation, preserving group solidarity (*ʿaṣabiyya*).[5]

Within Spina's sprawling epic of twentieth-century Libya, Ibn Khaldūn's words set national history within a pan-historic perspective, spanning Ottomans, Italians and, finally, Jamahiriyya, a culmination of 'superfluity', but also an unparalleled break with the past, as people and power are drawn irrevocably from the nomadic (*badawī*) to the settled (*ḥaḍar*). As cautionary 'signs' (*āyāt*), the valley's ruins further evoke Walter Benjamin's reading of the past as 'natural history' (*naturgeschichte*), an accumulation of melancholy traces, cast from the symbolic systems that once conferred meaning upon them, and reabsorbed into natural time.[6] This history, as Pick suggests, 'sweeps human legibility into history's catastrophic pileup', evoking 'mutability, transience and decay – the passing of the historical into ahuman nature, the passing of man into nonman, of soul into matter'.[7] Natural history, as Pick suggests, represents the sobering dissipation of human cultural meaning into the material and transient, and of human epochs into organic cycles of growth and decay, setting nation and civilisation within a wider, creaturely whole. As such, it presents an ominous warning to the Jamahiriyya, as the ruins of the past promise its inevitable demise, while the products of a new, oil-fuelled world threaten irredeemable change.

In this chapter, I pursue these interweaving discourses further, in novels which set contemporary contexts within dizzyingly distant perspectives, comprising evolutionary imaginings, interwoven with myths of creation and fall, opening from individual survival to civilisational 'flowering and decay'.[8] Immediately, such imaginings are suggestive of political allegory, with historical cycles of violence pointing inevitably to the Jamahiriyya, and al-Qadhafi identifiable in every portrait of founding fratricide and murderous primate. Beyond Libya and, indeed, nation, however, fractures are created in notions of progress more broadly, moving beyond 'founding' fathers to the animals that precede them, and seeking where humanity went wrong on its way from caves to Jamahiriyya. The Qurʾan is, once again, central to this vision, as humans' humble origins, from 'dust' (*turāb*) or 'despised fluid' (*māʾ mahīn*), are reiterated against the ambivalence of their 'stewardship' (*khilāfa*), marked by 'injustice' (*ẓulm*) and 'bloodshed' (*safk al-dimāʾ*).[9] Animals, meanwhile, feature as both the 'other' that has been sacrificed for the sake of progress and the 'self' humanity once was and still is – a reminder of its distant past, brought into uncomfortable juxtaposition with its precarious present.[10]

Typically, such reflection on 'pre-'history has tended to be isolated within the 'dense layer cake of time' explored across history, anthropology and other disciplines, maintaining a strict barrier between 'deep' and 'shallow' temporalities.[11] Despite the revolution in humanity's understanding of its origins, brought by Darwin's *On the Origin of Species* (1859), the paradigms of 'sacred history', locating a fixed origin in the Garden of Eden, have tended to migrate into secular historiography, asserting a past point from which to explore the 'ascent' of man, 'centred on the conquest of nature and the birth of political society'.[12] Against such tendencies, Daniel Lord Smail argues that modern nations must not be divorced from the 'rootless bands' of the deep past, nor should this past be consigned to 'speechlessness'.[13] While Smail does not mention the role of literature in this process, he flags the centrality of imagination, and of reconfiguring 'the level at which a story can be imagined', reconceiving 'the human condition as a hominin one'.[14] Others have explicitly incorporated the possibilities of art into this process, suggesting that 'understanding deep time lies, perhaps, in a combination of the rational and the intuitive'.[15]

In the Libyan novel, there is no reluctance to engage with humanity's deep past, dwelling on its ignominy, exploring how it arrived where it is today and questioning whether this place is to be celebrated. Combining the rational and intuitive, authors upset sacred history with animal voices and rewrite myth with deep, creaturely history at its heart. In contrast to the Arabic novel's more familiar historical turn, of recovering and rewriting bygone eras, 'saturating the novel's textual landscape with a profound longing for the past', those I explore frame the past as confusion and transgression, rooted in a trajectory of exile and loss.[16] Just as the 'subsistence survivor' of Chapter 1 contrasts the *fallāḥ* of the Egyptian novel, so does this primordial impulse, animated by monkeys and monsters, parallel its more concrete Pharaonic and Islamic *turāth*, reflecting the profound dislocation of self from other and from past under al-Qadhafi. Continuing to focus on major works by al-Nayhum, al-Faqih and al-Kuni, I explore how they shift from environmental ethics to species alienation, reflecting on creaturely origins, anxiously confronting what Santner terms humanity's 'aberrant place in the "great chain of being"', and commenting, through this, on the plight of the outcast intellectual.[17]

While most Libyan writers fell silent during the 1980s, all three of the above writers rose to a degree of prominence, responding to sporadic summons from the regime and subsequently facing accusations of passivity, if not complicity.[18] For the authors, this stand-off was a necessary means of continuing to write and, implicitly, protest, but left them in a state of constant, tenuous compromise.[19] Under threat of reprisals, they navigate between critique and obfuscation, confronting despair, isolation and powerlessness. From al-Nayhum's *al-Hayawanat* (1975, The Animals) and *al-Qurud* (1983, The Primates)[20] to al-Faqih's *Hadaʾiq al-Layl* (1991; *Gardens of the Night*, 1993) and al-Kuni's *Anubis* (2000; *Anubis*, 2002), the novels I examine represent particularly daring depictions of sovereign power and circling allegories of oppression, cast within the drama of human fall and conveying the 'difficulty of story' through returning to the imagined realms of prehistory. Unlike the authors' 'survival novels', each is stylistically and structurally distinct. The final publication of Dar al-Haqiqa, before the regime shut it down, *al-Hayawanat* was followed by five years of silence across the Libyan literary community. Depicting a totalitarian animal kingdom, it acts out the 'law of the jungle', followed, almost a decade later, by *al-Qurud*, allegorising al-Qadhafi's rise and predicting his fall through the power games of jungle baboons. Moving from the jungle, *Hada'iq* juxtaposes three worlds: modern-day Edinburgh, the fantastical city of ᶜIqd al-Murjan and Tripoli. All three are haunted by the pre-determining force of human heredity, from biological genes to mythic fallenness, dramatised through the journeys of protagonist-narrator, Khalil al-Imam. *Anubis* is similarly structured in three parts, telling of the legendary Tuareg ancestor, Anubi, whose name, signifying 'orphan' or simply 'person' in Tamasheq, makes him an allegory for all humankind. Wandering the desert in search of his father, Anubi enjoys a brief, paradisiacal stint among desert animals before founding Targ, a desert civilisation, doomed to downfall.

Despite their structural differences, all four novels present civilisational rise and fall as what might be considered counter-manifestoes to the monolithic logic of al-Qadhafi's Third Universal Theory (*al-Naẓariyya al-ᶜālamiyya al-thālitha*).[21] Claiming a 'definitive theoretical solution' to social ills and a blueprint for an ideal society, the *Green Book's* 'utopian experiment' monopolised Libyan intellectual life for decades, while the novels of al-Nayhum, al-Kuni and al-Faqih speak from the margins, through uncertain, despairing narrative voices.[22] All three are further tinged with apocalyptic anxiety over Cold War politics. In them, depiction of fantastical, nihilistic weapons indicate a global, rather than solely Libyan, vulnerability. Living between the Jamahiriyya and USSR, in the aftermath of Chernobyl (1986), al-Kuni describes the 1980s as a 'pre-adamic time' (*zaman al-fiṭḥal*), when 'stones were soft and tender', death an 'obsession' and the 'momentousness of fall' a constant threat.[23] The atomic bomb, he suggests, cast the creational order into an unprecedented uncertainty, paralleling humanity's 'expulsion from paradise'.[24] With a new awareness of vulnerability compounded by political surveillance, authors thus turned to a 'lost dimension' (*buᶜd mafqūd*) beyond the 'chains' (*qayd*) of the 'real' (*al-wāqiᶜ*) and echoing Kafka's paradigmatic turn from the panopticon of 'The Trial' (1915) to what al-Kuni interprets as the liberating transformation of 'The Metamorphosis' (1915).[25] Born of madness and confrontation with death, this lost dimension in his own work returns to dormant histories, recovering what has been forgotten and erased, as a healing and explanatory force. As Benjamin writes of Kafka: 'Everything forgotten mingles with what has been forgotten of the prehistoric world, forms countless, uncertain, changing compounds, yielding a constant flow of new, strange products.'[26]

In the novels examined here, this return appears not through eloquent fable but literary '*maskh*', an Arabic term for 'metamorphosis' defined in *Lisan al-ᶜArab* as 'the transformation of one form into an uglier form' (*taḥwīl ṣura ilā ṣūra aqbaḥ minha*) and, more generally, a 'deformed creation' (*al-mushawwah al-khalq*).[27] Appearing in the Qurᵓan to denote transformation, as divine punishment, to ape (*qirda*) and swine (*khanāzīr*), it represents in the novels I examine a painful yet revelatory move to non-human form.[28] In *Hadaᵓiq* and *Anubi*, the protagonist-narrators both recognise themselves as having gone through *maskh*, while *al-Hayawanat* and *al-Qurud* have, themselves, been read as fable-*maskh*, moving into animal kingdoms as, once again, al-Nayhum prefigures an ongoing, primordial trend within the centripetal, creaturely logic of the Libyan novel.[29]

'Animal Societies' in *al-Hayawanat* and *al-Qurud*

Within the arc of al-Nayhum's career, *al-Hayawanat* and *al-Qurud* express his profound disillusionment at the loss of home and readership following his star status in the 1960s. As cultural secretary to al-Qadhafi's short-lived Arab Socialist Union and advisor to the RCC, he initially attempted to influence the revolutionaries from within, leading to bitter fallouts with fellow authors and a persistent suspicion that he had influenced the ideas behind al-Qadhafi's *Green Book* and popular revolution.[30] After finally leaving Libya in 1973, he thereafter navigated what Taji-Farouki describes as 'a difficult path that steered between exile, home and silence'.[31] Al-Qadhafi was, allegedly, somewhat in awe of him and therefore kept him close.[32]

Undoubtedly, this proximity has troubled his legacy, with his final works on Islam and the mosque read as support of al-Qadhafi's 'direct democracy'.[33] Further research is undoubtedly needed on these connections while, here, I focus on his last novels and their latent, but staunch, critique.[34] As common insults in Arabic, *ḥayawān* and *qird* signify stupidity, recklessness and deviousness, and, in both fables, animals duly shift from the steadfast harmony of *Min Makka's* rats and turtles to brutality and submissiveness, while humans disappear altogether.

As early as 1969, the duality of 'human' versus 'animal' society (*al-mujtama*ᶜ *al-insānī wa-l-mujtama*ᶜ *al-ḥayawānī*) had become a principal means through which he addressed the new revolutionary regime, warning, with frightening foresight, of the 'cages', 'armed police' and 'gallows' that result from absolute ideologies, preventing society from 'practising its humanity'.[35] In his first encounter with al-Qadhafi at the Revolutionary Intellectuals Seminar (1970), he further opened by evoking 'cows', 'herdsman' and 'human' to symbolise the shift from autocracy to democracy.[36] In an immediate backlash, ᶜUmar al-Muḥayshī condemned his 'flowery language' and al-Qadhafi urged him to specify the identity of 'cows' and 'herdsman'.[37] Al-Kuni, also present, laments how al-Nayhum's carefully crafted language was destined to be turned against him, inaugurating a new era of semiotic tyranny.[38]

In subsequent writing, for newspapers and for his new encyclopaedic project in Geneva, al-Nayhum increasingly upholds 'humanity' as a democratic ideal, combining study of history and social Darwinism, and symbolic analysis of the Qurᵓan.[39] In *Tarikhuna* (1976, Our Past), a seven-volume history of Libya, he returns all the way to humans' cave-dwelling ancestors, identifying 'cooperation' as a lost quality, allowing their ascendance.[40] Depicting prehistory as an idyllic period in which 'God's land' (*arḍ Allāh*) was 'the people's land' (*arḍ al-nās*), he suggests that human inability to move beyond self-serving egotism has corrupted this cooperation, culminating in the creation of the atomic bomb.[41]

Both *al-Hayawanat* and *al-Qurud* dramatise this failure through the 'animality' of the 'nations' depicted. More so than the fables discussed in Chapter 1, both draw on the tradition of *Kalila wa-Dimna* as mirror-for-princes and political allegory, composed in short chapters through rhythmic, rhyming prose, repeated motifs and concluding axioms. In contrast to *Kalila wa-Dimna*, however, there is no royal court where justice is, even nominally, dispensed, nor stories-within-stories, celebrating the underdog, offering wise council and encouraging the use of wit against might. Wit and cunning, alongside violent coercion, instead become tools of political manipulation, as fable is infused with the 'difficulty of story'.

Moving from Libyan coast to jungle and from local seagulls and turtles to lions and baboons, the novels depict what Mario Ortiz-Robles calls the trope of the 'animal collective' through which authoritarian power is frequently allegorised.[42] Through the biological hierarchies of jungle animals, predicated on the dichotomy of predator and prey, human systems of exclusion and the fallacies of their 'naturalisation' are critiqued. In modern fiction, this is, of course, exemplified by George Orwell's *Animal Farm* (1945), dramatising Stalinist Russia through the revolution of barnyard animals and the premise that 'All Animals Are Equal', subverted into 'Some Animals Are More Equal than Others'. Despite al-Nayhum's denials of any connection, his fables have been explicitly recognised as the 'Libyan *Animal Farm*'.[43] 'The jungle', al-Faqih writes, 'became a symbolic version of what we saw around ourselves. Without difficulty, we could give his animals and monkeys the names of people we knew. If we were brave, we could even give them our own names.'[44] Like *Animal Farm*, *al-Hayawanat* and *al-Qurud* are structured around refrains, hinting at a moral message before collapsing into pessimism. *Al-Hayawanat* thus replaces 'All Animals Are Equal' with the vegetarian principle, 'We Don't Eat Others, and We Wish for Others Not to Eat Us'. A well-trodden theme in fable, the opposition of predator and prey, as primal subjugation of one creature by another, provides its proto-ethical core, through the uneasy juxtaposition of jungle carnivorousness and specifically human forms of predation. Responding to a question from al-Kuni concerning his use of literary animals, al-Nayhum declares:

> The human is a social animal, truly defined. [. . .] If this animal is born in human conditions, it becomes human. But if it is born in the current conditions of our closed and tyrannical Arab society, it transforms into a caged animal, plundering and stealing [. . .] I want to provoke you. I want you to tell me: we are not predators and prey. We are individuals . . . [. . .] If I push you to tell me that then I have succeeded. If I don't then I have failed.[45]

Perhaps ironically, al-Nayhum suggests that humans must overcome the 'ape within' them, while problems arise in his jungle worlds precisely through *human* traits, from the beginning of government in *al-Hayawanat* and self-consciousness in *al-Qurud*. As animals cease simply to spend their days 'following their noses' (*hāʾimīn warāʾ unūfihim*), they become exposed to dangers for which society, in al-Nayhum's view, has yet to find solutions.[46]

The overall tone of the fable is, therefore, one of fallenness, and, while a positive hope in human ascendancy underlies it, reflecting al-Nayhum's wider thought, it is marked by ambiguity, vulnerability and pessimism. Its founding principle of vegetarianism further draws it close to the Ikhwan al-Safa°'s *The Case of the Animals*, and, like *Min Makka*, 'hunger' is a driving force within it, exploring the dividing line between survival and rapaciousness, and the placing of one life above another, inherent to the dichotomy of predator and prey.

Law of the Jungle

Depicting the founding of a jungle 'government' (*ḥukūma*) by a falcon-*fgi*, wily wolf-vizier and hungry lion-king, *al-Hayawanat* moves swiftly towards a society of surveillance, with flies deployed as spies and a campaign of torture launched against all animals without official positions. Repetition is a key aesthetics, first through the appointment of animals to the government, then the hushed conversations of those not appointed, and finally their imprisonment, interrogation and torture. As al-Kuni describes, its searing portrait of the 'security forces' (*al-mu°assasāt al-amniyya*) in animal form prompted a 'powerful reaction' on all levels of Libyan society.[47] Initially published in *al-Usbu^c al-Thaqafi*, swift mediation was allegedly needed to appease the regime.[48]

Certainly, its political dimensions are unavoidable, as mockery of the naturalisation of oppression. Through syntactic parallelism, animals are described as 'created for their positions' (*khuliqa lahā*) and their positions 'created for them' (*khuliqat lahu*).[49] The hedgehog becomes head of media because he is good at 'prickling' and never looks to 'left or right' while the crocodile with his 'crocodile tears' is appointed to the Law Courts, and all animals are 'created' for consumption by the lion.[50] Through circling logic, some are appointed precisely because of their stealth, in order to explain injustices in advance. The fox and rat are thus declared essential to the government as, without them, 'nobody would know who stole the egg or silenced the rooster'.[51]

All other animals are cast into fearful silence, surrounded by flies, hiding behind newspapers with recording devices.[52] Through the rest of the fable, they represent an unsettling presence, laced with bitter humour, as when the camel spots two flies, one watching him, and the second watching the first.[53] All are then submitted to varying forms of torture, with the playful repetition of fable circling over the cowering, caged forms of pigs, donkeys and camels. The elephant, accused of 'reactionism' (*raj^ciyya*) and 'distorting the jungle spirit' (*tashwīh maṣīrat al-ghāba*), resists torture and is offered a position on the 'diplomatic path'.[54] Refusing, he is defamed and put on trial, where he continues to repeat his mantra, 'We Don't Eat Others and We Wish for Others Not to Eat Us'.[55]

The ensuing tale of persecution and crucifixion has clear overtones of Jesus' last supper and execution, leading some to criticise the novel's 'opaqueness' (*ghumūḍ*), through which its critique of government oppression is tempered by confusing religious imagery.[56] This, perhaps, was a ploy to evade censorship or cement the novel's proto-ethical critique of political carnivorousness through the exemplary martyrdom of Jesus. Whatever the case, the imagery does little to conceal critique of authoritarian tyranny as mindless brutality. Interspersing their nonsensical rhymes, the government animals sporadically declare themselves 'hungry' (*jāʾiʿ*), while the elephant, echoing the *Case of the Animals*, warns his companions, 'You will be eaten with salt, and you without it. You will be skinned alive, and you fried in oil.'[57] Serving grass at his 'Last Supper', he urges his friends to refuse, at all costs, to 'eat one another', positing vegetarianism as a fundamental ethical principle in the 'dog-eat-dog' law of the jungle.[58]

In his role as rejected prophet, the elephant may well be read as an embodiment of al-Nayhum himself, emphasised through the bleak concluding image of him, after the secret services 'cut off his tongue' and 'empty his skin', such that 'no one hears him any longer, because no one sees him any longer'.[59] Perhaps more clearly, however, it is the fable's elusive narrator who becomes a mouthpiece for the intellectual's alienation and fearful complicity. Beginning with the sing-song style of a public storyteller, declaring 'We sit together, each with his two ears', this narrator is the only potentially human presence in the novel.[60] As the animals become coerced into supporting the regime, forgetting all emotions but 'fear' and transforming into a 'museum of animal statues', the voice becomes increasingly dejected, slipping from scene to scene, but never gaining a concrete presence, fearing the regime yet seemingly immune to it.[61] Both detached and implicated, the narrator's voyeurism is described in fragmented physical terms, as watching with 'one eye' and listening with 'half an ear', and retreating from scenes of torture, 'pretending we were never there'.[62] With each repetition, the phrase alters slightly to encompass every sense and channel of communication, from 'pretending we cannot see' to 'cannot talk', 'cannot hear' and 'cannot feel'.[63] The novel's final lines conclude its complicity in proverbial style:

> Let us now part ways in health, before we meet again without it, and let the story of the jungle be a warning (*ᶜibra*) to us, for none of us says what will cause him to lose his head, and none of us hears what will cause him to lose his mind.[64]

Elusive and barely there, the narrator reflects, in physical terms, the psychological disintegration of individual and society, addressing, instead of the 'you' characteristic of al-Nayhum's earlier journalism, an ambiguous 'we', bound by fear and complicity, and embodying the literal effects of censorship on the relationship between writer and reader.[65] While concluding with a 'warning' (*ᶜibra*), the fable's only council is to remain silent as the 'age of truth' gives way to that of 'interrogation'.[66] Thus al-Nayhum predicts the years of ensuing silence, as the narrator escapes under threat of death and, from the shadows, addresses an equally ephemeral readership, threatened by censorship. Gone is what Deleuze and Guattari call the 'literature of the author or the master', as, more than ever, the Libyan novel becomes 'minor', giving voice to a threatened collective as it retreats into its 'lost dimension' (*buᶜd mafqūd*) and, in the case of al-Nayhum, to evolutionary pre-history.[67]

Evolutionary Fable

More so than any other animal, the primate reminds humanity of its animal origins and animal self.[68] Marian Scholtmeijer goes so far as to claim that 'all stories are about the struggle of a particular species of ape to invent and preserve a nonanimal identity for itself'.[69] In twentieth-century 'post-Darwinian fiction', she further indicates how various authors have begun to consciously incorporate this struggle into their writing, exemplified by Kafka's 'A Report for an Academy' (1917), and its humanised ape-narrator, Red Peter, reminding his audience that they, like him, have something 'hominid' behind them. 'Your life as apes, gentlemen', Red Peter declares, 'insofar as something of that kind lies behind you, cannot be farther removed from you than mine is from me. Yet everyone on earth feels a tickling at the heels: the small chimpanzee and the great Achilles alike.'[70]

Like 'Red Peter', *al-Qurud* evokes a 'tickling at the heels'. Its apes are, however, observed from afar rather than animated from within, monitored by an academy of 'observers' (*murāqibūn*) through whom the downfall of society is painfully diagnosed. In this, the novel instead reflects John Berger's short essay, 'Ape Theatre', in which Berger remembers boyhood visits to the zoo, when he would gaze on the caged apes as both 'intimately familiar and strikingly remote', reflecting, through their grooming, scratching and fondling, the beginnings of 'humanness'.[71] 'Their bodies, forgotten, suddenly nag, twinge, and irritate', Berger writes. 'They become impatient with their own skin.'[72] As Berger suggests, the spectacle is akin to theatre, which, more than any other art, allows for, and depends upon, the physical coexistence of two times, as the audience confronts a new world before it.[73] In *al-Qurud*, this is mimicked in the confrontation of modern 'observing' gazes with deep past as, embodying both sameness and difference, monkeys enact the shift from self-preservation to the human 'passions' of 'bloodshed'.

Set in the Budongo Forest in Uganda, a pack of baboons are monitored by a group of scientists conducting an experiment on them from a hut on a hill. Investigating whether the baboons, all of whom, like Orwell's Napoleon, are named after famous military leaders, can cooperate and employ rudimentary weapons, the observers release a cheetah among them. The novel then portrays the baboon leaders' internal struggles and inability to protect the weak as they bicker over a female, while the observers watch in growing dismay. The experiment fails as the baboons collapse into violence and the observers leave while the cheetah preys upon the vulnerable.

Unlike *al-Hayawanat*, the baboons are only gradually anthropomorphised, and initially communicate through gesture, beating their hands against their chests to indicate their positions of power.[74] As the novel progresses, however, they progressively 'ape' human society, as some start 'talking to their heads', becoming self-aware and desirous of power and status.[75] Alluding to the failed coup by RCC members in 1975, Sun-Yat-sen attempts to overthrow Hannibal. Swiftly quashed, this coup is followed by what 'looked like a trial' (*mā yushbih al-maḥkama*), despite the observers' prior conclusion that 'the baboons had absolutely no sense of justice'.[76] Through this episode, evoking the trope of the trial in both *Kalila wa-Dimna* and *Animal Farm*, al-Nayhum alludes to the publicly broadcast 'People's Court' that had become a widespread feature of

Libyan life on radio and television.[77] At its conclusion, the baboons proceed to 'mount' Sun Yat-sen, in a burlesque parody of modern, sovereign violence and the facade of justice.[78]

Beyond Libya, *al-Qurud* further alludes to the overarching instability of the 1980s. The nuclear standoff of the Cold War is symbolised by the scorpion, which Sun-Yat-sen discovers in exile and uses to regain power, inaugurating a further succession of coups as the baboons steal it from one another, seizing power for a few days before being ousted in turn. Eventually, other scorpions are found, resulting in a fruitless stalemate.[79] The leaders' names – Sinuhe, Hannibal, Hulagu and Sun-Yat-sen – further bind them into a pan-historical perspective, evocative of further, latent, allegorical equivalents, from 'Sinuhe' (Sinūḥī) as King Idris al-Sanusi to Hannibal (Hānībāl) as al-Qadhafi (who named his fifth son Hannibal in 1975).

Devoid of a triumphant underdog or voice of reason, *al-Qurud* concludes without even attempting a message. Instead, it enumerates the observers' 'conclusions' (*khawātim*) in the form of a bleak list, isolated on one page: 'The primates did not fight/nor cease fighting./They did not chase away the cheetah/nor cease chasing him around./Nothing happened/nor ceased happening'.[80] Repetition of the same negative structure emphasises the experiment's 'middling' (*bayna-bayna*) nature, concluded by a final statement followed by ellipses: *lam . . . wa-lam . . .* ('Neither did . . . Nor did . . .'). As the observers watch the primates' struggles, the fable suggests that they have not been significantly surpassed. Through repetitive syntax and structure, *al-Qurud* thus comes full circle, conveying grim stagnation.

Excluding these conclusions, the observers themselves remain silent, with their distance from the action emphasised by the adverb '*fawq*' (above), placed at the beginning of most descriptions of them. Interpretable in various ways – as politicians, intellectuals or actual ethologists – they clearly echo the detached, voyeuristic narrator of *al-Hayawanat*, no longer merely passively observing injustice but actively implicated in it as they release the cheetah. Both narrator and observers' 'gazes' are further suggestive of Masᶜud's 'silent observation' in *Min Makka*, as a thread uniting al-Nayhum's otherwise distinct novels. These later gazes are, however, stripped of the playful compassion of Masᶜud's observation, and laden with judgment, dislocation and guilt as, across a gulf, they watch powerlessly on.

Despite al-Nayhum's growing isolation, both *al-Hayawanat* and *al-Qurud* were influential works in the Jamahiriyya. Locating hidden copies in Libyan bookshops in the 2000s, Taji-Farouki suggests their continued popularity, as, while their specific allegorical dimensions fade with time, their overarching, natural historical pessimism remains.[81] At the same time, more ambivalent reactions indicate how fraught writing had become in Libya, burdened with political signification. Raḍwān Abū Shwaysha thus questions, 'what do these animals have in common with al-Ḥājj al-Zarrūq [one of al-Nayhum's most famous characters from the 1960s], and with me, as citizen?'[82] There must, he declares, be a 'goal' to these animals. Such was al-Nayhum's status that many believed he alone could challenge al-Qadhafi, leading to inevitable disappointment in his disengagement. Fāṭima Maḥmūd declares that, 'after all that has happened, the Libyan reader desperately needs a pen such as Sadiq's. But Sadiq is gone.'[83] In response, al-Nayhum declares that a return to his former writing is impossible, dislocated as he is from his fellow citizens, by geographical and emotional distance.[84] Humans duly retreat to the margins of his novels, as silent, despairing gazes, observing the 'animals' who become burdened with their worst traits.[85]

*Hada*ʾ*iq al-Layl*: A Trilogy of Worlds

Moving from al-Nayhum's jungle dystopias, al-Faqih's *Hada*ʾ*iq al-Layl* dramatises a trilogy of 'worlds', engaging tropes from across Arabic literature as it moves from the circling of fable to the journeys north of Arab students, and foreign kingdoms of *Alf Layla wa-Layla*.[86] The first volume, *Sa-ahabuka Madina Ukhra* (I Shall Give You Another City), is clearly within the tradition of Tayeb Saleh's (1929–2009) *Mawsim al-Hijra ila al-Shamal* (1966; *Season of Migration to the North*, 1969).[87] The second, *Hadhihi Tukhum Mamlakati* (The Borders of My Kingdom), then shifts to the traditional tales of *Alf Layla* while the last, *Nafaq Tudi*ʾ*uhu Imra*ʾ*a Wahida* (A Tunnel Lit by One Woman), confronts the reality of 1980s Tripoli.[88] Juxtaposing the cultural 'other' of the West and the cultural 'heritage' of *Alf Layla*, the trilogy aptly illustrates Bamia's description of the Libyan novel, torn between a rapidly transforming home, the industrialised West and a fanciful 'dreamed of' world.[89] All, however, are underpinned by the portrayal of protagonist-narrator Khalil al-Imam as a fallen Adam, prey to destructive impulses, historical traumas and political oppression. While animals do not feature prominently, political, emotional and physical vulnerability are central, and, through them, the boundaries of human and animal being are explored, as, beyond Khalil's own intentions, his inner drives increasingly dictate his actions, imagined as a 'wild being' (*kāʾin mutawaḥḥish*) or 'corrosive germ' (*jurthūm fāsid*) within him.[90] As the trilogy progresses, this 'being', or demonic double, is revealed as a primordial facet of Khalil's self, repressed and distorted by social convention, and transforming into a destructive doppelgänger, formed from subjection to creaturely states of exception, and ultimately morphing into the controlling presence of the sovereign himself. Like al-Nayhum's disillusioned 'observers', Khalil's dark stream-of-consciousness thus conveys the frustrations of an intellectual in exile, with his very name echoing al-Faqih's own as he, in turn, becomes double to the author.[91]

During the early years of the RCC, al-Faqih occupied several prestigious cultural positions, appointed, in 1972, as editor of *al-Usbuᶜ al-Thaqafi* (where *al-Hayawanat* was published) and, in 1978, as head of the Libyan Writers' Union. Completing his PhD in Edinburgh in 1982, he thereafter followed the 'diplomatic path' satirised by al-Nayhum, taking ambassadorships in Athens and Bucharest, and even penning a concluding essay to al-Qadhafi's short story collection, *al-Qarya al-Qarya*.[92] He also, however, continued to publish prolifically, and often critically. As Amlūda observes, *Hadaʾiq* is only the second novel to depict Libya under al-Qadhafi, through a suffocating vision of contemporary Tripoli, beneath noxious fumes and the gaze of security services and moral police.[93] Indicatively, it was also followed by a return to historical settings, in al-Faqih's twelve-volume colonial saga, *Kharaʾit al-Ruh* (2008; *Maps of the Soul*, 2014).

Channelled through Khalil's sombre perspective, I suggest that the trilogy's worlds are underscored by al-Kuni's 'lost dimension', confronting political violence and historical deprivation through a preoccupation with the distant and deep past. Filled with 'lament' (*nuwāḥ*), 'hunger' (*jūᶜ*) and deep-seated social conservatism, Khalil's desert childhood is described as a 'thousand-year legacy of oppression and deprivation', determining his trajectory.[94] He is, as he declares, further torn between the DNA of his paternal grandfather, a pious *faqīh*, and maternal grandfather, a merciless highway robber.[95] Finally, he is haunted by constant imaginings of humanity's fallenness, dreaming of the innocence of animal instinct and the idyll of Eden, lost to brutality and submission.

In comparison to the trilogy's east–west and reality–fantasy dichotomies, this primordial imaginary has been little examined in previous criticism. It is, however, central to its intertextual relationship to both *Mawsim*, in its depiction of latent drives, and *Alf Layla*, in its extremes of passion and innocence. It is on this latter aspect that I focus. As Ferial Ghazoul suggests, Arabic fiction has tended to adapt *Alf Layla* into political explorations of ruler and ruled.[96] Wen-chin Ouyang further understands the tales as an 'ancient empire of signs', concerning reason, desire and rulership, from which novelists adapt their own empires, commenting on modern nationhood.[97] In the trilogy, these dimensions are underpinned by Khalil's fixation on the tales as dramatisations of sex, violence and the unconscious, penetrating the 'most complex realms of the human soul'.[98] Although his PhD thesis examines the tales' influence on western literature, this primordial nexus represents his obsession, resonating through the trilogy's structure, and through contrasting imagery of virgin islands and violent desires, paradise and fall. Almost all Khalil's relationships to places and people are conveyed through metaphors and similes of aridity and fertility, desert and garden, evoking what Richard van Leeuwen calls the 'metaphoric substructure' of *Alf Layla* in the trilogy, alongside Libya's geography of baking sands and Qibli wind, symbolic of emotional and physical vulnerability.[99] Latent energy anxiety and political protest further resonate in the interstices of Khalil's monologue, through description of the land and its creatures as 'suffocated' (*makhnūq*) or 'hanging from gallows' (*mashnūq*).[100] Drawing together the disparate settings of Edinburgh, ᶜIqd al-Murjan and Tripoli, *Alf Layla* becomes an outlet for repressed, primordial emotion, and a means of coping, intellectually, spiritually and emotionally, with life within the Jamahiriyya.

Khalil's romantic entanglements further mimic the repetitive 'patterning' of the traditional tales in which words, clauses or sentences are repeated to emphasise themes or reinforce 'moralistic concerns'.[101] In the trilogy, this takes shape in Khalil's repeated movement from love to obsession, abandonment and violence, in a compulsive pattern of destruction, driven by the uncanny, demonic 'being' within him. The tales' traditional opening, of nightly entertainment and 'permitted speech', further shifts to the bleak refrain that opens and closes each volume: 'A time has gone, and the next refuses to come'. Like the rhythmic repetition of *al-Hayawanat* and *al-Qurud*, this 'third time' conveys circling stagnation, as a 'wasteland of red sand, baking beneath a motionless sun, in a sky the colour of lead'.[102] In existential, and sometimes literal terms, Khalil seeks shelter, as the nascent imbalance depicted in *Fiʾran* shifts to a world doomed, which no flood can redress.

Between Garden and Desert

In each of the trilogy's volumes, Khalil is torn between an idealised romantic relationship and an 'other woman'.[103] In Edinburgh, this is dramatised through Linda and Sandra. The first is Khalil's married landlord, compared, in exaggeratedly idyllic terms, to a 'spring of water and light' and a 'garden rose', allowing him to escape his 'heritage of instinctual fear' (*mīrāth al-khawf al-gharīzī*).[104] Above all, Linda allows Khalil to open himself to another and, seemingly, rid himself of haunting demons, 'scraping away', as he describes it, 'the accumulated muck from my cells and tissues, and exorcising the demons from the ruins of my soul'.[105] Beyond such descriptions, anchoring Linda in the innocence of Eden, she is little developed, and, after becoming pregnant, their relationship collapses. In this way, she indicates Khalil's desperate attempts to escape his past, as well as his worsening confusion of illusion and reality, as he projects the imagined innocence of Eden around him, while being driven by exemplary human, and what Santner would term creaturely, drives.

In Linda's place, Khalil moves to young undergraduate Sandra, who supposedly returns him not to a lost garden but to the wildness of instinct. Together, they embark on drug-induced orgies, regressing, as Khalil puts it, to the 'murmurs and cries of humans' first language', re-joining the 'other creatures' (*baqiyat al-makhlūqāt*).[106] On a trip to the Highlands, Khalil imagines them as Robinson Crusoe or Hayy Ibn Yaqzan and, when Sandra tells him of a tribe who spend one day each year crying to relieve repressed emotions, Khalil finds himself overcome by wails of grief, recalling not only his childhood, but a melancholy, existing within him from the 'first days of creation' (*badʾ al-khalīqa*).[107] Almost immediately, however, these tears also threaten to awaken latent violence, emphasising the precarious proximity of innocence and violence in the trilogy. Overcome by desire to strike Sandra, only the 'veneer of civilisation' holds Khalil back.[108] In another instance, when the pregnant Linda announces that she is leaving to live with her family, he imagines throwing her to the ground, driven by the dark 'creature' within him:

> That creature (*kāʾin*) had been fashioned from the mud of lean years (*min ṭīn al-sinīn al-ʿijāf*), the ashes of drought, and the shrapnel of minefields, exploding amidst women's wails, and bringing sudden death in their wake. Now, it had awoken, eating away at the human, shaped by books, legends and odes, and tickets to distant cities.[109]

In dense passages such as this, Khalil hints at the years of al-Qadhafi's 'lean' rule and the deprivation preceding it, destining him to repetition of destructive emotional states. As the trilogy progresses, this 'creature' becomes increasingly present, a schizophrenic spectre, imagined as 'animal' but formed from human trauma and states of exception, and characterised not by instinct but compulsive drives.[110]

Before leaving for Tripoli, after completing his doctorate, Khalil visits Linda and his son, suitably named Adam. Just as places and times leave their mark on Khalil, this son represents a trace of himself in Scotland, embodying the tantalising possibility of innocence. As they wave goodbye amid the Scottish fields, mother and child evoke both fresh start and happy ending within the trilogy's dark narrative threads. Both, however, are conditional on Khalil's removal of his destructive self back to the Libyan desert. Thereafter, Scotland is little mentioned, becoming another of his latent legacies, dictating his behaviour.

Returning to Tripoli, Khalil submits to the 'rites' and 'laws' of the 'tribe', ensconcing himself in society's symbolic systems and submitting to its surveillance.[111] Consenting to a loveless marriage and cloistered in an apartment building, he works as a university lecturer and, in contrast to his intense summer months in Edinburgh, three years pass uneventfully. Failing to conceive a child, it further becomes apparent that, in Tripoli, Khalil cannot inspire even the beginnings of life, as, descending into depression and psychosis, his research on *Alf Layla* shifts from sex and violence to 'metamorphosis, disfigurement, death and suicide' (*al-maskh wa-l-tashwīh wa-l-mawt wa-l-intiḥār*).[112] Signed off work, his depression becomes entangled with the wider city's malaise:

> Tripoli had embraced the modern world's tarmacked roads and high-rises, sun-scorched and windswept. But, having left the intimate shelter of their tribes, its inhabitants had not learnt to be neighbours, and cast one another the haunted stares of lifeless bodies, swaying from gallows.[113]

Like many novels from the 1970s and 1980s, al-Faqih depicts Tripoli as victim to disorienting industrialisation, while also charging it with political violence through the simile of 'lifeless bodies' (*al-insān al-mashnūq*).[114] With nowhere to flee, Khalil is immobilised beneath the watchful gaze of family, colleagues and state, and his hallucinatory journey to ᶜIqd al-Murjan becomes the only political and narrative means of shattering this stasis.

Al-Madīna al-Fāḍila

Returning to his childhood home, Khalil has a vision of his former Qur'an teacher, al-Shaykh al-Sadiq, who promises to cure his depression. Passing out amid incense fumes, he finds himself walking through a sunburnt wasteland, before reaching a palace, surrounded by gardens and fountains and populated by the viziers, merchants and cobblers of *Alf Layla*. In stark contrast to Tripoli, ᶜIqd al-Murjan abounds in fertility and riches, allowing Khalil to forget 'the hissing broadcasts' and 'drone of machinery'.[115] Echoing tales of 'shipwrecked sailors', he stumbles upon power and love, marrying the princess, Narjis al-Qulub and enacting the idealised romances of epic, binding 'erotic' and 'patrimonial' love to ensure the 'legitimacy of the kingdom'.[116]

Through this sojourn, the first volume's Edenic impulse shifts to utopic imaginings, exploring how desire and violence, run rampant in Edinburgh, might be harnessed into an ideal society. From the vizier, Shaykh Jalal al-Din, Khalil learns that the city's 'governance' (*niẓām*) is derived from observation of the 'secrets' (*asrār*) and 'wisdom' (*ḥikma*) of the natural world, to which the city must strive to be 'worthy of belonging'.[117] In this Sufi-inspired rule, citizens are not externally disciplined but recognise and maintain their own drives. Stumbling upon a ritual 'dance of the jungle', Khalil thus witnesses the participants mimicking 'the running of the jungle kingdom' in order to release the 'base emotions' of the 'unconscious'.[118] In contrast to the uncomfortable interweaving of human and animal in al-Nayhum's jungle kingdoms, human and animal traits are maintained in balance, avoiding the possibility of unintentional *maskh*.

In this and in other respects, ᶜIqd al-Murjan evokes both the fantastical cities of *Alf Layla* and the rich tradition of Islamic utopian thought, from *Hayy Ibn Yaqzan* to al-Fārābī's (d.950) 'virtuous city' (*al-madīna al-fāḍila*), in which social and cosmic harmony are similarly aligned.[119] Devoid of laws and 'state institutions' (*ajhizat al-dawla*), ᶜIqd al-Murjan further echoes certain of the Jamahiriyya's alleged fundaments as, Khalil hears, the people work only according to their 'own free will', indebted and enslaved to none.[120] Any possible nod to the *Green Book*, however, is negated by the volume's inevitable, violent end as, it transpires, the city was never more than the feverish imagining of a depressed, desperate and morally compromised inhabitant of present-day Tripoli.[121]

After Narjis becomes pregnant, Khalil gravitates to Budur, a beautiful singer. Rejecting fatherhood, once again, he inverts the motif of childless sultans, desperately seeking offspring, in numerous tales from *Alf Layla*.

The vizier, Jalal al-Din, meanwhile, becomes infected with a hubristic desire for progress, after hearing Khalil's description of the wonders of the modern world. Mistakenly interpreting them as Sufi revelation, he fashions a monstrous weapon, sinking the city into poverty through the cost of manufacturing it. Echoing the 'forbidden door' motif from *Alf Layla*, Khalil completes its destruction, unleashing a foul yellow air which returns him to Tripoli.[122] Lamenting his act, he observes:

> this was humanity's heritage (*irth*), which I carried within me – a blind, primal force, leaving prisons, torture chambers and gallows in its wake. Slumbering in the fibres of the brain, it reared its ugly head to annihilate, and to stain the beautiful with blood.[123]

Once again, the Jamahiriyya is insinuated as the inevitable outcome of fallenness, and Khalil's immersion in the world of *Alf Layla*, as therapy, instruction, transformation and illusion, comes to a brutal end. Straddling the aesthetics of spiritual revelation, fantasy and mental breakdown, the ambiguity of his sojourn evokes Mas^cud's feverish fables in *Min Makka* as, returning to Tripoli, Khalil realises that only an hour has passed and yet he is covered in blood and dust. Above all, ^cIqd al-Murjan represents a necessary psychological and literary recourse within the stifling constraints of the real, in pursuit of a 'lost dimension'.

Between Instinct and Drive

As Van Leeuwen suggests, the central theme carried over from *Alf Layla* to the trilogy's final volume is 'metamorphosis', not as magical transformation but as *maskh*, becoming synonymous with the awakening of latent, destructive drives, and the takeover of Khalil's violent doppelgänger.[124] In his disturbed consciousness, reality and illusion, and origin and *maskh*, further become disturbingly and dangerously confused. Returning to Tripoli a 'fallen Adam', he continues to immerse himself in the 'secret language' of the natural world, obsessing over the minute movements of spiders, caterpillars and ants in order to retain a fragment of his former contentment.[125] Even the consolation of Sufi spirituality soon becomes tainted, however, as, attending a *dhikr* ceremony, his initial rapture becomes swiftly nightmarish, as he hallucinates the other participants literally 'tearing at my limbs, ripping me apart' (*yumazziqūnanī wa-yatanāhabūna aṭrāfī*).[126] In young university researcher Sana^ɔ, meanwhile, he locates his next romance, the real-life copy of Budur, initially described as a woman of 'radiance' (*ishrāq*) and 'revelations' (*tajalliyāt*), before being uncovered, in all her creaturely reality, as one of 'clay' (*ṭīn*) and 'despised water' (*māʾ mahīn*).[127] Through their relationship, the compulsive circling of Khalil's life reaches its destructive climax.

This is foreshadowed as the couple drive together past Tripoli's famous statue of the Girl and Gazelle. While Khalil interprets the entwined bodies of woman and animal as a 'symbol of desire' (*ramz li-l-raghba*) and the 'intimacy of creation' (*ḥamīmiyyat al-khalq*), Sanaʾ sees only 'the alienation of a woman and her gazelle, stranded amongst the fumes'.[128] A fleeting, yet structurally central, encounter, this moment is one of many ekphrastic episodes in the Libyan novel, through which paintings and sculptures, often in the form of animals, are animated in melancholy and abandoned to ruin. In all, art, as human creation, reveals primordial truths of human creatureliness, through longing for an original wholeness and perception of its lostness. As Berger observes, such 'aesthetic moments' return the contemplator to a state of harmony, suggesting that 'we are more deeply inserted into existence than the course of a single life would lead us to believe'.[129] 'For a brief moment', Berger writes, 'one finds oneself – without the pretensions of a creator – in the position of God in the first chapter of Genesis'.[130] Images of the natural world, he continues, further represent an attempt to translate a 'message from a real bird', representing 'an organized response to what nature allows us to glimpse occasionally'.[131] Beyond the Italian imperialism that formed her, the Girl and Gazelle offers such a vision, as the naked woman curves back to embrace the gazelle behind her. Remaining in its fountain amid the cavalcades of rulers, the statue has also, however, fallen, like the city's inhabitants, into dereliction, prompting Sanaʾ's identification, and becoming a sign of both original wholeness and creaturely vulnerability.

After driving past, the couple return to Khalil's summer resort outside Tripoli where, succumbing to feverish madness, Khalil attacks Sanaʾ, imagining their sexual union as rebirth from a mythic flood, a 'form of worship, which God bestowed on the creatures of the world', and an unleashing of the 'creative power, through which the Girl and Gazelle was fashioned'.[132] 'We will become one', Khalil reflects. 'Our blood, flesh and bones. Our longing and light. The clay from which we are formed.'[133]

In reality, the rape represents the final, violent imposition of his will and, simultaneously, his loss of self-awareness and submission to the 'creature' within him. Returning to lucidity, he sees Sana°, prone and bleeding, and the true reality of his fantasies becomes clear, as a culmination of his inner struggle.[134] In visceral terms, Khalil describes his 'sinews' and 'arteries' ripped apart by his legacy of 'lack and repression'.[135] As throughout the novel, he describes himself 'trembling' (*murta*ᶜ*ish*), with 'blood pulsating beneath my eyelids'.[136] Transforming the traditional Arabic simile of the heart as caged bird, he evokes it, 'beating like a bird with blood gushing from its severed neck'.[137] As Sana° flees, he then attacks himself, declaring that 'only through the letting of blood can I free my body and soul of this monster (*maskh*)'.[138] Saved by the arrival of security guards, he reaches the climax of his destructive compulsions, paralleled in the inevitable fall of ᶜIqd al-Murjan.

From a *Bildungsroman* structure, tracking the individual's path through the world, *Hada°iq al-Layl* thus submits to the pre-determination of Khalil's demonic, creaturely double.[139] As Santner suggests, such uncanny doubles must be understood through the relationship of sovereign and creature, formed from an 'obscene paternal agency' that prohibits and commands pleasure, marking humans off as 'creatures of *drive* (rather than 'animals of *instinct*)'.[140] This, he continues, is further exacerbated in modernity, as traditional social roles collapse, leaving the individual beyond the realm of well-trodden paths. Rejecting paternity and mired in professional and political apathy, Khalil exemplifies this state, yielding to alcoholism and moving permanently to his coastal resort as summer shifts from the liminal setting of the trilogy's first volume to a symbol of permanent abandonment. Khalil's final 'other woman', Suᶜad, similarly escapes depression in drugs, sex and self-harm. Bringing the trilogy full circle, she introduces Khalil to a new phase of 'truth', beyond any redemptive 'lost dimension'. Suᶜad, Khalil decides, is the 'origin' (*al-aṣl*) and Sana° the 'copy' (*al-ṣura*), as illusions are stripped away to reveal bare neurosis.[141] Fired from the university after its English Department is closed by the authorities, he embraces a 'philosophy of idleness and play' (*falsafat al-lahw wa-l-la*ᶜ*b*), cavorting with corrupt officials and exemplifying the intellectual turned 'clown' (*muharrij al-sahra*), telling lewd stories inspired by *Alf Layla*.[142] As with al-Nayhum's fables, story is undone and Shahrazad's life-giving tales turned to payment for alcohol and drugs.[143] Writing radio serials, praising 'the beautiful deformity and dazzling ugliness of the city', Khalil becomes a mouthpiece for the regime, reconciling himself with the demonic 'other' within him, and the sovereign 'other' outside him. Embracing this 'other' as 'guide' (*murshid*) in the trilogy's concluding sentences, he finally alludes to al-Qadhafi himself, as *Murshid al-Thawra* (Guide of the Revolution), cementing the political dimensions of his demonic, creaturely double.[144]

Beyond the Sufi wisdom and natural imagery that resonate across al-Faqih's fiction, postmodern fracture prevails in the trilogy as, beneath the tropes of 'Arab student', 'ideal lover', 'prince' and 'intellectual-turned-clown', lurks only death, intoxication and a 'wild creature'. As several critics observe, links between the trilogy's volumes may appear somewhat tenuous, and this is because they are primarily formed by the repetition compulsion that sets humans apart, frustrating the communication of 'sane' story through a social and political groundhog day, underpinned by repression, amnesia and schizophrenia, as Khalil is doomed to repeat the same behaviours.[145] In this way, the trilogy moulds the patterning of *Alf Layla* into a 'third time' of 'terror' and 'fall'.[146] Throughout, Khalil seeks an 'abode', whether in the 'gardens' of romantic love or the 'shelter' of responsibility and political commitment. From the beginning, however, his destiny is exposure, exile and the circling stasis that, despite their aesthetic and structural differences, binds his trilogy to the novels of al-Nayhum and al-Kuni, and marks the primordial, creaturely dimensions of his engagement with *Alf Layla*.

Anubis: The Novel as Creaturely Myth

Of all Libyan authors, al-Kuni most vividly engages with primordial imaginings, writing and rewriting narratives of creation and fall through interweaving mythological strands. As Fähndrich remarks, 'A journey with Ibrahim al-Koni through "his" desert, the region of his childhood and youth, is a journey into the past; his personal past and that of his people.'[147] Al-Kuni's writing is, furthermore, a journey into the past of all humanity, combining the vastness of the Sahara with the dizzying distance of deep time. With 'memory' (*al-dhākira*) as a central epistemological endeavour, his writing strives both to recover Tuareg heritage, and what he describes as the 'hidden depths' (*al-jānib al-mustabṭin*) and 'absent dimension' (*al-buᶜd al-ghāʾib*) of human experience, beyond oppressive ideologies.[148] Nomadism represents an allegory of this pursuit, compounded by al-Kuni's belief in the Sahara as the birthplace of humanity before drought prompted its migration. Identifying ancient Libya as 'the oldest nation', he argues that its 'primitive language' (*lugha badʾiyya*) shaped Babylonian, Egyptian, Phoenician and Hellenic cultures, and lingers in modern Tamasheq.[149] As Elliott Colla remarks, 'The modern Twareg are, in this account, the direct descendants of the most distant Saharan past – among the very first of history's "first peoples".'[150]

Al-Kuni's fiction represents an 'interrogation' (*istinṭāq*) and 'pursuit' (*muṭārada*) of this past, seen, in *Nazif*, through the intertwined strands of Biblical, Qurʾanic and folkloric reference. Often, the very gaze of an animal is imbued with 'secrets' of creation, while the genesis of plants and animals serve as microcosms for all existence.[151] As Elmarsafy observes, 'it is precisely as a maker of fictional worlds that Al-Koni teaches, or rather narrates and recites, the entities, laws and values of the world to the reader.'[152] As 'maker', al-Kuni goes even further, placing his reader in fictional worlds which operate according to numerous accounts of creation and fall, encouraging the reader to contrast and compare, and suggesting that all accounts are valid, but none sufficient. Memory, after all, is an elusive process, and, as it struggles towards truth, repetition and reconfiguration become necessities, circling around transgression, fall and lost paradises, constituted from the mythical Tuareg oasis *Wāw*, the Biblical Eden and Platonic Atlantis.[153] Situating all within the Sahara, Luc Deheuvels notes how al-Kuni combines them 'to the point of confusion', in what Rima Sleiman interprets as a 'negation of creation', 'rewriting' Genesis and moving towards 'nothingness'.[154]

Above all, al-Kuni rejects mythic resolution, in an intertextual and aesthetic open-endedness, exemplified by his engagement with the fragile, indecipherable rock art of the Messak massif in south-west Fezzan, engraved onto rocks and boulders within its intercutting canyons. Exemplifying the creaturely, ekphrastic turn of the Libyan novel, paralleling al-Faqih's Girl and Gazelle, al-Kuni depicts this art as a record of the 'lost law' (*al-nāmūs al-mafqūd*), misplaced by the 'first ancestor', and plunging the desert into bloodshed until recovered fragments were transferred onto cave walls through the 'language of images' (*lughat al-ṣuwar*).[155] A transposition of this 'language' into fiction, paintings frequently come to life in his writing, with animals slipping from cave walls into narrative, combining flesh and stone, and blood and ink, as the 'tracks' (*āthār*) of live animals intermingle with 'remnants' (*āthār*) of the past. Long preceding Darwin's evolutionary theory, al-Kuni traces animals' centrality to human thought through these ancient images, mapping, as Berger puts it, their status as the first object of human investigation:

> To suppose that animals first entered the human imagination as meat or leather or horn is to project a nineteenth-century attitude backwards across the millennia. Animals first entered the imagination as messengers or promises [. . .] [They] interceded between man and their origin because they were both like and unlike man [. . .] The parallelism of their similar/dissimilar lives allowed [them] to provoke some of the first questions and offer answers. The first subject matter for painting was animal. Probably the first paint was animal blood. Prior to that, it is not unreasonable to suppose that the first metaphor was animal.[156]

Anchored in this primordial impulse, *Anubis* represents a fragmented, creaturely novel-myth, woven from living animal-signs, scraps of leather and ancient art, telling of the legendary Tuareg forefather, whose story precedes all others and, as al-Kuni's opening note clarifies, whose 'tribe' is the 'human tribe' in pursuit of its 'secret' (*sirrahā*).[157] A foundational figure, key to unlocking humanity's forgotten truths, Anubi is also himself haunted by uncovering the secrets of his own ancestors, demonstrating the dizzying backward spiral of al-Kuni's fiction. As McHugh notes, reading the novel is a 'profoundly disorienting experience', moving from the well-trodden paths of familiar myth into the unexpected, incomplete, and 'animal'.[158] In Tamasheq, 'Anubi' means 'orphan' or simply 'someone' and, through his exilic wanderings, al-Kuni transforms the iconic, jackal-headed god of the Egyptian pantheon into a shady, nomadic figure, shifting between 'God', 'creature' and *maskh*.[159] As al-Kuni writes in his author's note, history has 'confused' (*balbala*) Anubi's legend, entangling it in other tales as it passes from people to people.[160] Like the gardens and deserts of *Hadaʾiq*, *balbala* (confusion) further becomes a leitmotif within Anubi's own life, evoking the Tower of Babel's 'confusion of tongues', and reminding the reader of a pre-linguistic past from which confused story emerges piecemeal.[161]

The novel's concluding section, a series of aphorisms described as 'Anubis' counsel' (*waṣāyā Anūbīs*), finally brings together, in apparent clarity, the entangled dichotomies of life and death, earth and heaven, body and soul, and human and animal, from which the novel is constituted.[162] This clarity, however, remains riven with the tensions of creaturely being and the interplay of the open-endedness of 'life' (*ḥayāh*) and closure of 'myth' (*usṭūra*). As I interpret them, they put into words the wisdom of rock art, which Anubi first contemplates, then creates, translating creaturely experience into fragmented *nāmūs* in a primordial iteration of Berger's 'aesthetic moment'.

Through this 'counsel' and art, Anubi, like Khalil, embodies both fallen Adam and exiled intellectual. As al-Kuni states, his own journey to tell Anubi's story would, if he 'were able to write it', fill even more pages than the novel itself, and Anubi's story duly resonates with his own untold and untellable tale.[163] During the 1990s, when he researched and wrote it, he had finally renounced any attempt to work within the regime's cultural and diplomatic bodies and found himself under intense scrutiny.[164] Writing became a profound retreat, in which desert and deep past provide the means for figurative journeys, appeasing his longing for a homeland that no longer exists.

From Shipwrecked Sailor to Composite Creature

As with the three volumes of *Hadaʾiq*, Anubi's trajectory subverts the coming-of-age paradigm of *Bildungsroman* and heroic journey. Searching the desert for his missing father, his life unfolds through painful metamorphoses, and ultimately exile and absence, as father and leader. Through the entwining of sacred paradigms and bare, creaturely life, the novel further frustrates any possible mythic closure. Its three sections, *Akhbār zamān al-mahd* ('News from the Time of the Cradle'), *Akhbār zamān al-wajd'* ('News from the Time of Passion') and *Akhbār zamān al-laḥd'* ('News from the Time of the Tomb'), juxtapose the gravity of scripture to the materiality of birth, survival and death.[165] This is compounded by opening epigraphs from Genesis, telling of Adam's birth and expulsion from Eden.[166] As McHugh writes, 'Crisscrossing the desert, [Anubi's] confused and confusing wanderings tell the story of the birth of a nomadic people, yet they also expose a bare dependence of desert people on even simply the traces of animals.'[167] Within each section, chapters are further titled after times of day, juxtaposing the sun's movement, and the relentless continuation of earthly life, to echoes of sacred history, conveyed through ancient Tuareg terms and phrases from Genesis and the Qurʾan.

While the novel's first part describes Anubi's birth and learning of the 'names' (*asmāʾ*), I focus on the second and third parts, relaying his return to primal innocence and subsequent founding of a desert civilisation.[168] Led by the desire to locate his absent father, he departs into the desert, succumbing to dehydration and awakening within a deserted, paradisiacal valley. While paralleling the doomed structure of Khalil's trip to ᶜIqd al-Murjan, this world is not simply governed by natural wisdom, but returns to it. Awakening from unconsciousness, Anubi discovers a verdant oasis, populated by animals. Like Khalil, he appears to have undergone a princely transformation, with his face wrapped in a 'mask of soft leather (*jild*)', his chest 'clad in soft, rich hide (*jild*)' and his feet 'encased in splendid shoes of costly leather (*jild*)'.[169] Through repetition of '*jild*', al-Kuni hints, however, at the true nature of this transformation. As Anubi realises, his clothes 'adhered to my skin, like skin' (*iltiḥām al-jild bi-l-jild*), and, when crying for help, he can communicate only a 'choked rattle' (*ḥashraja makhnūqa*).[170] Inverting the paradigms of Daniel Defoe's *Robinson Crusoe* (1719), and other castaway-turned-coloniser narratives, Anubi does not proceed from wonder and fear to dominion and mastery, but returns to an ambiguous, ancient form of being. As Philip Armstrong comments, Crusoe anthropomorphises the animals of his island into his 'little family', while also putting 'layer upon layer of animal-derived cultural vestments between his body and the elements'.[171] Anubi, contrastingly, grows his own skin and painfully loses his self.

Unlike Asuf's *ḥulūl* (divine indwelling) and *taḥawwul* (transformation) in *Nazif al-Hajar*, Anubi's *maskh* is profoundly disorienting. Echoing the loss and estrangement of Kafka's 'Metamorphosis', it hints at the pressure of a tyrannical regime, forcing literature into 'lines of flight'.[172] This flight is further rooted in a terrifying encounter with the prehistoric past, embodied by a 'shadowy figure' lurking in a dark cave.[173] Described as an 'empty hide' (*jild ajwaf*) and 'stone statue', this immense 'composite creature' (*makhlūq murakkab*) is half gazelle and half *waddān*, half animate and half inanimate, filling Anubi with fear, nausea and trembling.[174] Gazing into its eyes, fear nevertheless leads to profound identification, as Anubi realises himself, too, as both a fragmented '*maskh*', 'composed from two creatures' (*mulaffaq min makhlūqayn*), and an inextricable part of a seamless whole.[175] Joining the herds, he immerses himself in their warmth and fluid union, declaring, 'I forgot even that I had forgotten'.[176] Prompted by pain, fear and vulnerability, *maskh* represents return to a lost dimension, and deeper immersion into the world of the animal than that of Asuf, as the central epistemological endeavour of memory in al-Kuni's work is, paradoxically, achieved through forgetting.

While Anubi's peaceful sojourn dramatises in novelistic form the most ancient of the Sahara's rock art, depicting therianthropic creatures, half-animal and half-human, its conclusion shifts to the dramatisation of later tableaux, of hunt and domestication.[177] As so often in al-Kuni's writing, a primal act of consumption prompts Anubi's rift from the animal world and 'fall' into civilisation. Lured by the smell of roasting flesh, he rapaciously consumes the 'charred flesh' of the prehistoric creature, set ablaze by a lightning storm.[178] Returning to *balbala*, 'composites' (*tarākīb*), of art and creature, human and animal, past and present, are blown apart, as animals shift to prey, their eyes filled not with secrets, but 'mucous', 'grains of sand', 'revulsion' and 'agony'.[179] Regaining language, Anubi then employs his reason to fashion a trap and a shelter, which, in a hubristic echo of Genesis, he enters on the seventh day and declares to be excellent.[180] Assuming 'deputyship' (*khilāfa*) for his absent father, his oasis grows, and, in further echoes of the Qur'an, he barters for 'livestock' (*anᶜām*) and 'human beings' (*anām*).[181] Animals subsequently disappear from the narrative, and from human experience, while the oasis, Targ, grows into a civilisation, destined to flourish and decay.

Targ

Paralleling ᶜIqd al-Murjan, Targ is fashioned according to natural law (*al-nāmūs*), reflecting ancient belief, from Hindu mythology to Greek philosophy, in the human body as a microcosm for society and the universe. Divided into groups, the clan of Ragh represents the 'head', that of Yet the 'torso' and that of Set the 'hands' (*maqālīd al-ḥīla*).[182] Like Khalil, Anubi is appointed ruler by dint of prophecy, and soon turns, like him, to 'entertainment' (*tasliya*) and 'play' (*luᶜba*).[183] Forging iron weaponry to attack other settlements, the tribe of Set take over and Anubi is usurped by a 'false prophet' (*zaᶜīm al-zūr*), proclaiming the law of the 'wheel' (*ᶜajala*) that dictates endless cycles of flourishing and decay.[184] Attacked in turn, Targ falls into ruin and, under the 'bitterness of subjugation and hunger', its people are viciously subdued.[185] Beginning the genealogy of the nomadic Tuareg and exiled intellectual, Anubi is sent into the wilderness where, bringing the novel full circle, his estranged son finds and kills him.[186]

Dying, he traces a 'final mark' (*wasm akhīr*) onto a 'patch of leather' (*ruqᶜat al-jild*), conveying his 'truth', not as a 'shadow' (*ẓill*) or 'illusion' (*wahm*), but as a 'human, who traversed the desert'.[187] While the mark is not described in further detail, it is perhaps in the form of a 'composite creature', as a fragment of creaturely truth among the desert's constituent memories. 'History', al-Kuni suggests, is the 'fingerprint' we leave in time, and his own novel is viscerally constructed from such prints.[188] Joining himself, as founder of the desert novel, to Anubi, as founder of the Tuareg, in a lineage of pursuit and *balbala*, al-Kuni transforms writing into quest, as well as what McHugh notes as an 'oddly anthropological process', weaving together narrative across 'geography, history, genre, and even species'.[189] From the oral narrative of shaykhs to copies of rock inscriptions on 'crumbling leather manuscripts' (*ruqa*ᶜ *jildiyya*), the novel is pieced together from the materials of Anubi's journey, echoing his own post-metamorphosis 'skin', the hollow 'skin' of his prehistoric companion, and the 'skin' on which he leaves his mark.[190]

The final word is given to his sayings, whose symmetrical brevity evokes the neatness of 'composites' (*tarākīb*), hinting at the harmonious completion to which al-Kuni's writing strives.[191] For Elmarsafy, these sayings provide the novel's *raison d'être*, following Tuareg convention in which conversations conclude with axiomatic wisdom.[192] 'It is as if', Elmarsafy writes, 'the novel only existed to enable the pronouncement of the law'.[193] For Alyn Hine, al-Kuni's aphorisms further represent a 'rejection of the novel genre', through prioritising the 'intellectual richness of empty space'.[194] As brief moments of insight, they are comparable to the gaze of an animal, or contemplation of an image on rock, and represent the necessary fragmentation of the *nāmūs* which, if completed, would spell the end of exilic pursuit, and of story. Rather than 'law', their fragmentary meditations reject political manifestoes and what al-Kuni derides as the 'culture of slogans' (*thaqāfat al-shi*ᶜ*ār*), upsetting certainties and shifting from abstraction and metaphor to creaturely physicality.[195]

Conclusion

In *The Author and His Doubles*, Moroccan author Abdelfattah Kilito observes: 'If I seem to have lost myself in the animal kingdom, it is because my subject is one of loss, deprivation, reduction, and perdition: in sum, curiously enough, metamorphosis.'[196] While Kilito's focus is the loss occasioned by bilingualism, his evocation of metamorphosis as 'reduction' also captures the lostness of Libya's primordial, censored fiction, seeking to recover home, and understand it anew through various forms of *maskh*. Describing al-Nayhum's lifelong refusal to renounce his Libyan citizenship, al-Kuni claims that his staunch loyalty inspired him, too, to creatively rediscover his nation through exilic writing.[197] In all three, nation is duly depicted at a distance, through allegories of alienation, despairing observers and outcast Adams, longing to return but grasping the impossibility of doing so. Negotiating the possibility of just Law, they similarly deny it, as, through circling, rhythmic repetition, cycles of 'flourishing' and 'decay' follow one upon another. Trapped within this 'wheel', the individual is both victim of others and of compulsive drives, revealing the thin line that divides human and *qird*, prince and rapist, and ruler and monster. Within this fruitless circle, *maskh* represents a dangerous and endangered form of being, which is, nonetheless, capable of great expression and insight. As an embodiment of al-Kuni's 'lost dimension', it evokes the ultimate failure of return to the past as Edenic idyll, as dreams of lost innocence and harmony prove illusory, in the face of the destructive impulses and drives through which human and animal become entangled.

Despite this shared focus on the primordial, the authors' writing is also strikingly distinct, as, under al-Qadhafi, their individual aesthetics became only more accentuated. In his autobiography, al-Kuni describes al-Nayhum as driven by the spectre of al-Fārābī's 'ideal city' and by an ambition for power that unsettled him.[198] In al-Nayhum's fables, this spectre remains as, through his characteristically dialogic tone, albeit newly distanced and disillusioned, his 'animal societies' diagnose the ills of society as counter-manifestoes to the Jamahiriyya. In contrast, *Hada'iq* descends into the frenzied tangle of predetermining forces, as Khalil's story progressively eludes his own narrative authority. Finally, al-Kuni returns not to the primates that humans must transcend, but to the warm pulse of the flock, beyond the simian seeds of human passions. Lifelong friends, the authors suggest both a particularly Libyan aesthetics of history and the radical changes brought by life within the Jamahiriyya.

Part II

SIGNS AND CITYSCAPES

3

God's Wide Land: War, Melancholy and the Camel

My people, here is the she-camel of God, a sign to you. Leave it to graze in the land of God and do it no harm, or else painful torment will befall you. (Qur'an 7:73)[1]

They are spiritual creatures, somehow bound up with the miracle of existence. Perhaps they are leaves which have fallen from an old tree that is no longer there, or people who have yellowed with maturity. (Muhammad Bin Lamin)[2]

Among the Libyan authors to have risen to prominence in the 2000s, ʿAbdallah al-Ghazal (b.1965) has, through his three novels and their allusive, introspective and at times horrifying aesthetics, been recognised as a pioneering new voice.[3] From *al-Tabut* (2004, The Coffin) to *al-Khawf Abqani Hayyan* (2008, Fear Kept me Breathing), his writing addresses major incidents from Libya's recent history, infused with palpable fear, hidden truths and traumas. Having lived and worked in Libya as an oil engineer for most of his adult life, the frustrated nostalgia of exile, seen in the writing of al-Nayhum, al-Faqih and al-Kuni, shifts to immediate vulnerability. Nevertheless, in many respects, his writing also remains deeply connected to that of his predecessors, and specifically al-Kuni whom he, like many Libyan authors, cites as an influence, and whose writing resonates through his own in a poetics interweaving fragile 'signs' and vulnerable creatures.[4] Through the striking parallels in their writing, I conclude my discussion of al-Kuni as a central figure within the development of Libyan fiction, elucidating aspects of his veiled yet creaturely poetics, drawn out by a reading of al-Ghazal's more explicit depictions of contemporary Libya. Together, they frame my discussion in Part II of writers from the 2000s, whose enigmatic, allegorical novels form a dense web of responses to censorship, trauma and environmental degradation, anchored in animals, art and melancholy landscapes. Toying with the censor, authors subvert what Barthes terms the 'propriety of symbolic systems', imbuing them with a shifting mix of political, psychological and spiritual import.[5] A continuation of the 'difficult stories' explored so far, 'signs' appear in more self-conscious terms, liable to exposure and simultaneously able to metamorphose and slip into the shadows. With 'fear' as the pulsing heart of his novels, al-Ghazal exemplifies this, binding present vulnerability with past traumas in a constant search for absent, healing signification. Comparing his and al-Kuni's depictions of war, I examine how both resonate beyond their immediate contexts to hint at future perils or diagnose past ills.

From the 1960s, anti-colonial struggle has featured prominently in the Libyan novel, in depictions of heroic, local resistance to the Italians. From 1969, however, this then becomes entangled with al-Qadhafi's undeclared war on his own people, as heroism shifts to stasis and disillusionment.[6] Exploring how authors weave premonitions of later dictatorship into depictions of Italian colonial aggression or, conversely, look back from contemporary Libya to the demons of Italian occupation, I draw together al-Kuni's *al-Tibr* (1989; *Gold Dust*, 2008) and al-Ghazal's *al-Tabut*, respectively depicting Italian invasion and Libya's war with Chad (1978–87). Set in the fraught yet peripheral southern Sahara, bordering Algeria, Niger and Chad, both novels shift to the margins of the political order, involving characters that fail as 'warrior' (*fāris*) and 'man of war' (*rajul ḥarb*).

Land is central to both, with its apparent emptiness belying its richness in spiritual signs, material 'treasures' (*kunūz*) that lure invaders, and 'traces' (*aṭlāl*) of historical traumas, testifying to past violence. Through the exposure of all three, the novels extend the ethics of 'animal nations' into a more visceral poetics, drawing not on fable but on the desert geography of the pre-Islamic qasida, and creating a hybrid Sufi poetics, expressive of spiritual pursuit, but also of trauma, of liberation, but also of painful, bodily dissolution, and of the elusive, creaturely 'sign', hounded by censorship and ideology. In both, the *āya* (sign) and *sirr* (secret) evoke not just Truth, but buried memory and latent protest, while the Sufi state of *fanāʾ* (passing-away, effacement [of the self]) coincides with the collapse of narrative and the literal disintegration of bodies and land.[7] *Kashf* as 'revelation' accordingly twins with *kashf* as 'exposure', entwining the unseen (*al-ghayb*) with the 'should-not-be-seen' of bare flesh and exposed land. Bound together, the 'unknown' (*al-majhūl*), 'repressed' (*al-makbūt*) and 'silenced' (*al-maskūt ᶜanhu*) are unveiled through revelation, compulsive repetition and violent appropriation, in powerful evocations of the vulnerability-of-being.

The consequent fragmentation of language and self powerfully counters what Barthes calls the fullness or richness of sign systems, as 'reality' is replaced by an 'emptiness of language' and 'retreat of signs'.[8] As Ian Almond observes, 'openness' (*futūḥ*) is emphasised in both Sufi and deconstructionist thought, signifying the limitless possibilities of semantic meaning and dramatising the 'broken ruins of one's own constructions'.[9] In al-Kuni and al-Ghazal, it is, additionally, bound to the 'openness' of vulnerability as literal and figurative woundedness, extending from characters and landscapes to the novels themselves, promising insight into spirituality and the political 'unsaid', and opening themselves to censorship in the process. The resultant symbolic universe is divorced from, and subversive of, the Jamahiriyya, leaving creaturely struggle on the land, towards an absent Truth.

Al-Ghazal has himself theorised 'Sufi narrative discourse' (*al-khiṭāb al-ṣūfī al-sardī*) as the opening up of a symbolic dimension that interacts with, and defamiliarises, realist depictions of time and space.[10] This dimension, al-Ghazal suggests, voices an 'existential Sufism' (*al-ṣūfiyya al-dhātiyya*), embodied by disillusioned outsiders, rejecting dissatisfactory reality for a deeper wholeness and suggestive of the tormented consciousnesses of Masᶜud, Khalil, Anubi and, indeed, al-Ghazal's own solitary protagonists.[11] Specifically, al-Ghazal cites al-Kuni's writing as exemplary of the twinning of 'narrative' (*sardī*) and 'Sufi' discourse, extending beyond simple use of mystical terminology to infuse the land with immanent significance, binding spirituality and physicality.[12] In al-Kuni's writing, revelation is predicated on lack of water and shelter, transforming the desert into the 'shadow' (*ẓill*) of a place, whose inhabitants are driven by Truth, rather than relationships or possessions.[13] In al-Ghazal's writing, too, the land's lacks and historical traumas fill it with signification, as spiritual awakening comes not through Sufi states of 'intoxication' (*sukr*) and 'love' (*ᶜishq*), but 'fear' (*khawf*) and visceral 'bewilderment' (*ḥayra*).[14]

According to al-Kuni, both *Nazif al-Hajar* and *al-Tibr* marked his 'rebirth' from a period of physical and mental crisis in the 1980s, prompted by the oppressiveness of the Soviet Union and Jamahiriyya, causing a complete aversion to food and retreat from social interaction.[15] The product of his retreat from the 'world of people' (*min dunyā al-anām*), the novels' central animal encounters resonate with mental and physical struggle.[16] A twin to the wild encounters of *Nazif*, *al-Tibr* depicts companion species' bonds and acts of translation, through the human protagonist, Ukhayyad, and his *mahri* (thoroughbred) camel, representing a rare example of enduring love in the Libyan novel. Taking place on the periphery of the 1920s colonial war, it alludes to a broader nexus of catastrophes in Libya and the Sahara of the 1980s. As al-Kuni writes himself within the body of the *mahri* camel, and rewrites the desert through the all-consuming bond of man and animal, the novel represents a pinnacle of his creaturely poetics.

In al-Ghazal's writing, all possibility of lasting companionship is dispelled, as he shifts from literal survival to the psychological malaise of authoritarianism, and what Santner calls the 'ceaseless and vertigo-inducing excitations and shocks' of modernity.[17] Reflecting his years as a mechanical engineer for national oil refinery, Ra'ˀs Lanuf, in the Sirte Basin, al-Ghazal locates the vulnerability of human, animal and land within the roar of mechanics and stench of oil. In my concluding section, I read his *al-Khawf Abqani Hayyan* as a creaturely portrait of modern Misrata, in which a suddenly barren palm grove becomes a battleground between government and people, melancholically mirroring its former historical significance within anti-colonial struggle. In *al-Tabut*, meanwhile, al-Ghazal depicts five months in a desert barracks during the 1980s Libya–Chad war, in which no fighting takes place, while a final, paradigm-shifting encounter comes through the death of a she-camel. In a war driven by ambition for empire and nuclear arsenal, this death appears both peripheral and cosmically portentous. Prefaced by Qurˀan 7:73, describing 'God's she-camel' (*nāqat Allāh*) as an *āya* to the people of Thamud, it also strikingly parallels *al-Tibr*, in which the verse similarly prefaces the *mahri's* captivity as the desert descends into war and famine.[18]

Through camels, the species most evocative of Libya's transformations in the twentieth century, and most intimately entangled in its changing society, this Qurˀanic intertext structures my comparison of the authors, with its nexus of human, animal and land emphasising both parallels and distinctions between them. While *al-Tibr* takes place exclusively within the hinterlands, *al-Tabut* moves from city to desert. In *al-Tibr*, the camel represents a constant companion, and even extension, of the human protagonist, with his compulsive physicality defining the novel's aesthetics and plot. In *al-Tabut*, the she-camel emerges fleetingly and inexplicably before returning, after she is killed, to haunt the soldiers. In both, however, the transgression and disintegration embodied by the Qurʾanic *nāqa* is echoed in visions of deep-seated social and environmental imbalance. As Suzanne Stetkevych comments, 'The she-camel [in the Qurʾan] functions as a symbol of fecundity and prosperity, a sign of divine blessing whose improper or forbidden sacrifice marks the disintegration, indeed, extermination, of the polity.'[19] These connotations, Stetkevych continues, are also rooted in the earlier heritage of the pre-Islamic qasida, in which the fate of camel and man are similarly bound, and in which, after their traditional desert journey (*raḥīl*), the camel's sacrifice or, contrarily, 'sacrifice-gone-wrong', may either cement tribal bonds or split them into 'mutually hostile voices'.[20]

Within modern Libyan literature, these poetic and mythic connotations are woven into new themes and aesthetics. In oral poetry, celebration of the nobility and perseverance of specific camels has shifted to lament for the entire species' lost status as 'ship of the desert' (*safīnat al-ṣaḥrāʾ*), and, as Alan Mikhail observes, one of the 'primary purveyors of usable energy until the twentieth century', when oil took their place.[21] Composed by Ibrāhīm Būṣūkāya (d.1974), the famous oral qasida 'Shāyilīnik wa-intī illī shayyāla' ('You, who once bore, are now borne') elegises this transformation through the refrain of the 'bearer' become 'borne', transported in trucks for the meat industry.[22] In fiction, too, the camel is paradigmatically vulnerable and paradigmatically creaturely, eminently subject to human whim, yet proving resistant to anthropomorphism, with its fickle temperament and idiosyncratic physicality depicted through the Arabic language's historically rich 'camel-related vocabulary'.[23] In al-Faqih's *Fiʾran bila Juhur*, Shaykh Abu Layla's camel thus starkly contrasts the eloquent jerboas, as he 'bellows' (*yurghī*), is 'agitated' (*hāʾij*) and refuses to 'sit' (*yabruk*).[24] Despite being the Shaykh's faithful companion, he is also swiftly slaughtered to ensure the tribe's survival, evoking the cohesive force of necessary sacrifice.

In contrast, the death of camels in *al-Tibr* and *al-Tabut* are markers of disintegration, while, through their spontaneous movement and incoherent bellows, they recalibrate humans' perceptions of the land as vehicles of what Mohamed-Salah Omri calls 'the Sufi journey as a reading code' in the Arabic novel.[25] This code, Omri suggests, dramatises both the development of 'individual consciousness' and a 'desire to forget and return to an original state of being', with both processes manifested in 'the gradual opening up or the unfolding of the individual self in relation to the universe'.[26] As Omri comments, the process of 'deciphering the sign' is central to the Sufi journey, inspired by the geography of the pre-Islamic qasida, in which 'reading traces' (*qiyāfat al-athr*) is a necessary art and skill.[27] Motifs from both the pre-Islamic qasida and the mystical poetry inspired by it are certainly central to *al-Tibr* and *al-Tabut*, relocating them to the desert geographies from which they originated and including central traits as listed by Michael Sells:

> *the ruins* (aṭlāl) *and traces* (rusūm) *that are effaced but somehow endure, that signify but cannot answer; the phantom of apparition* (khayāl – *a term that later came to mean 'imagination'*) *and way-stops* (maḥallāt) *along the pilgrimage; the constantly changing condition or states* (aḥwāl); *remembrance* (dhikr) *of the beloved* (al-maḥbūb); *the secret* (sirr) *entrusted from lover to beloved; the sacred or 'prohibited'* (ḥarām) *and profane or 'allowed'* (ḥalāl); *the lightning flash of an ephemeral union; the love-mad* (majnūn) *who experiences bewilderment* (ḥayra) *in the shifting emotions of the beloved and who ends in ruin* (halāk).[28]

In their depiction of departure and journey, al-Kuni and al-Ghazal's protagonists move through way-stations, driven by ruins, signs and the camel, as apparition and as *āya*, leading to bewilderment, revelation and ruin. In this, both novels are equally suggestive and disruptive of rite-of-passage, concluding not with wealth, dominion and ideal masculinity, but failure, lack and death.[29] The 'unfolding' of the Sufi journey therefore turns to vulnerability, as the self is opened to the universe through physical suffering, and land and creatures are animated through shared melancholy and fear.[30]

For Santner, melancholy permeates creaturely consciousness, distinct from mourning, as defined by Freud, in that it has neither defined cause nor resolution, representing an 'obsessive preoccupation with death, destruction, and decay'.[31] In al-Kuni and al-Ghazal's writing, it evokes political powerlessness and the appropriation of 'treasures' and fading of 'signs' behind the roar of machinery, as well as an all-encompassing cosmic melancholy, intrinsic within the being of all desert creatures. Through flashes of insight, conveyed through vulnerability, I explore how both writers shift from the motifs of the heroic qasida to *rithā*ʾ (elegy), as images of suffering animals express insurmountable, incommunicable loss as an event that 'bonds all living beings together'.[32]

Al-Tibr: The *āya* of Companion Species

Al-Tibr depicts the Sahara's imprisonment by a stream of invaders, summed up in Ukhayyad's final fate, exiled and threatened by tribes from the south and Italians from the north. 'Even God's vast wilderness (*ṣaḥrā*ʾ *Allāh al-wāsi*ᶜ*a*)', he reflects, 'could be turned into a prison – one more impenetrable than the Ottoman jail whose ruins (*aṭlāl*) he had seen in Adrar.'[33] Overtaken by plunderers, seeking the 'gold dust' of the novel's title, the desert is fleetingly restored to 'God's vast wilderness' through Ukhayyad's relationship to his *mahri*, a 'vessel' (*safina*), and *āya*, helping him read the land anew. Above all, this occurs through the dynamics of companion species, defined by Donna Haraway as any species in an 'obligatory, constitutive, historical, protean relationship with human beings'.[34] As al-Ghānamī comments, Ukhayyad and the *mahri's* companionship is central to the novel's aesthetics and plot, with each comprehensible only through the other, and the death of one necessitating that of the other and, indeed, the novel's end.[35] In this, it reflects the celebratory equation of man and mount in pre-Islamic, Tuareg and Libyan oral poetry.

Alongside the 'joy' and 'play' of companion species, however, Ukhayyad and the *mahri* also demonstrate the less idealised characteristics of 'indifference' and 'ignorance' that also feature within companion species relationships.[36] As McHugh remarks, their relationship emerges in 'decidedly unsentimental' terms, forged under 'extreme duress'.[37] Through changing power dynamics, the camel shifts between rebellion and revelation, while Ukhayyad shifts from berating him to engaging in what Erica Fudge calls the 'ongoing process of translation' of interspecies communication, as the camel integrates him into the desert's secrets.[38] Shifting from desire for his camel's 'praise' (*madīḥ*) to a co-constitutive desert *raḥīl* and, finally, perception of the desert's 'lament' (*nuwāḥ*), the novel inverts heroic paradigms. Intertwining the hardships of the early twentieth century with personal and collective crises in the 1980s, it becomes a creaturely allegory for the fate of Libya and the Greater Sahara. Channelling the demise of Tuareg tradition and Libyan national hopes through the contested, wounded body of the *mahri*, and the failure of Ukhayyad to live up to the noble expectations placed upon him, it posits all-consuming creaturely fellowship as the only possible recourse.

Qaṣīdat madīḥ and the Warrior Camel

From the first, the *mahri* is defined by Tuareg discourses, practices and hierarchies. At every juncture, characters have something to say about him or do to him, and, through him, the desert and its peoples are mapped. The son of a tribal chief, Ukhayyad receives him from the Ahaggar tribe to celebrate his 'coming-of-age' (*sinn al-rushd*).[39] A marker of nobility, central to interactions among the Tuareg upper echelons, the *mahri* delivers him to adulthood, and the expectations of his father, famous for expelling 'foreign invaders', and his 'passion for women'.[40] Ukhayyad, however, becomes overly obsessed with the camel, its pure stock and rare colouring, bragging to other young men of his 'lightness of foot' and his 'pride, fierceness, and loyalty', and singing desert epics in his honour.[41] The camel, however, fails to live up to the qualities of 'heroism' (*furūsiyya*). Longing for him to receive his own praise poem, Ukhayyad struggles to 'break him in' (*tarwīḍahu*), but is consistently frustrated as he undergoes gruesome physical changes, and becomes implicated in worsening 'scandals' (*faḍā'iḥ*).[42]

Progressively, Ukhayyad's passion for the camel leads him, too, to contravene accepted norms. As a child, he sneaks treats for the animal and, after being berated by his father for wasting food on 'livestock' (*al-dābba*) when people are going hungry, he simply states 'The piebald is not livestock. The piebald is the piebald' (*al-ablaq laysa dābba. Al-ablaq huwa al-ablaq*).[43] This statement amuses his father, but, as Ukhayyad grows to maturity, his attitude becomes less acceptable, rejecting, as his stubborn statement demonstrates, conventional hierarchies and the use of language to differentiate and define.

The novel's opening episode fully depicts his failed rite of passage through a ceremonial group camel dance, which, taking place at weddings, represents an important entertainment in Tuareg society in which young men and their camels vie for esteem.[44] To merit *madīḥ*, Ukhayyad is told that the camel must perform either in 'battle' (*maʿraka*) or 'dance' (*raqṣ*).[45] In preparation, he adorns the camel with finery from across the desert: a saddle from Ghat smiths;

an embroidered kilim rug from Touat merchants; a bridle from the Ifoghas women; and a Tamenrasset travel bag. In short, the camel is bedecked in the desert peoples' finery, as with their values of purity and nobility. It is not long, however, before he shakes off both. With the tribe organised in rings around the dancers, he erupts out of the circle in a 'frenzied motion across the dance arena', dramatising the manner in which, throughout the novel, he upsets the careful ordering of society.[46] Words specifically associated with camels describe him as 'frenzied' (*hāʾij*), and how he 'bellows' (*yurghī*) and has 'froth' (*zabad*) around his jaws.[47] Rather than the panegyric Ukhayyad had intended, both are scorned, while the camel responds to Ukhayyad's displeasure with stubborn, unswerving affection, luring him from the dictates of society.

This is demonstrated in the novel's counterpoint to the *tẹnde* as rite of passage, as the companions undergo a transformative desert journey, both echoing and inverting the pre-Islamic *raḥīl*.[48] During one of Ukhayyad's amorous adventures in a neighbouring tribe – reminiscent of Imrūʾ al-Qays' (d. *c.*565) infamous dalliances – the *mahri* contracts mange from a she-camel, suffering excruciating welts across his skin. As the infection spreads, Ukhayyad takes him to the distant Maymūn fields in search of curative silphium. The plant, however, drives the camel mad and he careers across the desert, dragging Ukhayyad behind him. Like Asuf, Ukhayyad begins to resemble the animal he is pursuing, with 'froth' appearing on his lips as he struggles to hold on. At the journey's end, he and the camel are then born anew.[49] Awakening to find himself naked, and his camel a 'solid red mass', their wounded skin joins as he climbs onto his back: 'Ukhayyad's body, now also naked, fused with the viscous flesh of the *mahri.* Flesh met flesh (*iltaḥama al-jasad bi-l-jasad*), blood mixed with blood (*ikhtalaṭa al-dam bi-l-dam*). In the past they had been merely friends. Today, they had been joined by a much stronger tie.'[50] This moment of spiritual, yet fleshly, union is described as one of 'brotherhood' (*taʾākhī*), with revelation achieved through grim suffering and 'exposure' (*kashf*), liberating Ukhayyad from his attachment to the *mahri*'s prestigious, piebald coat.[51] In contrast to the *tẹnde*, Ukhayyad relates to him beyond human systems, echoing Haraway's description of companion species: 'The task is to become coherent enough in an incoherent world to engage in a joint dance of being that breeds respect and response in the flesh.'[52]

The dance of man and camel is, however, a brief one, with the tension between it and the *tẹnde* representing a continuous tug-of-war within the novel. While opening the novel, the *tẹnde*, in fact, occurs chronologically after the journey, demonstrating Ukhayyad's continuing fluctuation between social expectations and rejection of them, creating a central uncertainty that deconstructs the novel's symbolic systems. According to traditional paradigms of passage, the desert should be restored to harmony after his adventure. Proving his maturity, he should sacrifice self and camel for his people, as his father erects a tent to celebrate his 'escape from the wilderness' (*li-istiqbāl al-zuwwār wa-l-muhanniʾīn lahu ʿalā al-salāma min al-tīh*).[53] The 'wilderness', however, continues to lure Ukhayyad, coinciding with social disintegration, intimately entangled in the bodily suffering of the *mahri*.

Marrying contrary to his father's wishes, Ukhayyad is cut off. Shortly thereafter, the desert descends into famine and war, as tribes from the south head north, fleeing drought, while the Italians attack from the north. Mirroring the Tuareg's fate throughout the twentieth century, Ukhayyad's tribe scatters, and, amid 'bloody events', he finds himself wandering among 'migrants from many tribes and nations'.[54] While preparing to battle the Italians and earn the status of *fāris*, he learns that the resistance has already been quelled and his father has died heroically in battle. After his son's birth, Ukhayyad then proves unable even to provide for his family, until, on the brink of starvation, he reluctantly agrees to pawn the *mahri* to his wife's relative, Dudu. The *mahri*, however, continues to escape his new owners, calling out to Ukhayyad until he can no longer bear their separation, and gives his wife and son to Dudu in exchange for the animal. Confirmed in his failure as father and warrior, he opts out of social expectations, and thus becomes another anti-heroic and anti-social protagonist of the Libyan novel, who can find solace only beyond the bounds of society, and through a radical rereading of the world.

'ʿAw-a-a-a-a-a-a-a'

Manifested in weather, cave paintings and dreams, *al-Tibr* is structured through a web of secrets and signs, which Ukhayyad, with the aid of Sufi shaykhs and soothsayers, attempts to comprehend. With interrogatives forming a major part of the narrative, he remains perpetually alert to the fickle desert, with every action a potential provocation to the 'unseen', whether identified with Allāh or the Tuareg goddess, Tānīt. Increasingly, these signs coalesce around the figure of the *mahri*, as Ukhayyad feverishly questions, 'Was the spark in the piebald's eyes a sign (*ishāra*)? A sign of something. One had to heed signs. [. . .] These signs were the language of God. The one who ignored them would be damned in this world.'[55] In particular, these signs become manifested in the animal's suffering, as, following Ukhayyad's immersion in the 'laxity' (*istirkhāʾ*) of oasis life, the camel returns as a 'wretched skeleton' (*haykal bāʾis*), which he interprets as a 'warning, a sign' (*tanbīh . . . indhār . . . ishāra*).[56] Throughout the novel, such descriptions of the camel as 'secret' and 'sign' form an interconnected web, culminating with evocation of the Qurʾanic *nāqat Allāh* as *āya*.[57] As the desert descends into war, the *mahri* is therefore evoked as both a warning of human overreaching and a vulnerable victim of it, with his plaintive cries echoing Haraway's comments of how, 'through our ideologically loaded narratives of their lives, animals "hail" us to account for the regimes in which they and we must live'.[58]

Despite his awareness of the camel's import, Ukhayyad spends much of the novel misinterpreting the animal's simple desires. After their desert journey, for example, he orders his castration, hoping to restore his 'purity' and, consequently, his piebald coat. The *mahri* clearly refuses the proposition: 'Agitated, the piebald reared his head. Was this his way of showing that he rejected the idea?'[59] In ignoring this refusal, described as a '*sign* of refusal' (*ʿalāmat rafḍ*), Ukhayyad fails in the translational process of their companionship, while across the novel the camel continues to 'hail' him, shifting its narrative from stable sign systems to wordless complaint, spiritual lament and creaturely emotion. While identified as the 'mirror of his rider', and a 'human being in a camel's skin', he resists anthropomorphism, simultaneously embodying 'prophet' (*rasūl*), 'friend' (*ṣadīq*), 'victim' (*dhabīḥa*) and, most importantly, 'animal' (*ḥayawān*).[60] From his heightened sense of smell to his fluctuating sexual appetite and volatile temperament, he exhibits exemplary traits of the dromedary species.[61] When Ukhayyad attempts to wipe his memory to facilitate their separation, for example, the animal sniffs him on the breeze and is compelled to seek him out, with his fidelity emerging from his olfactory powers. Even their desert journey is prompted not by a transcendent call to adventure but the camel's seasonal sexual drive, leading first to illness, then madness, injury and enlightenment.

Through his physical compulsions, the camel both lies beyond the reader's 'anthropomorphizing' grasp and, paradoxically, becomes more readable than the guarded humans of al-Kuni's writing. Whether shining with joy or dulled by illness, his expressive eyes contrast the treacherous 'glint' (*barīq*) of humans and, in the case of Dudu, the 'mask' (*qināᶜ*), 'shielding his heart'.[62] The most striking parallels between Ukhayyad and the *mahri* further result not from the camel's anthropomorphism, but Ukhayyad's compulsive physicality, as anger prompts the camel to vomit 'frothy mucus', while Ukhayyad, in parallel, spews 'yellow bile'.[63] Ukhayyad, moreover, is led to his death after smelling the camel's burning skin on the breeze, with sensory physicality driving their doomed relationship and the narrative throughout.

In this way, *al-Tibr* both confirms and contravenes what al-Kuni describes as his focus on 'symbolic' (*ramzī*) or 'veiled' (*makhfī*) speech.[64] Through 'exposure' (*kashf*) and 'disclosure' (*ifshāʾ*), Ukhayyad and camel frustrate the expectations of Tuareg nobility, demanding allusion, and Sufi spirituality, demanding 'obfuscation' (*al-tawrīya*) and 'preservation of the secret' (*ḥifẓ al-sirr*).[65] Both traditions warn against the dangers of revealing secrets under the influence of desire, and associate nobility and insight with mystification. Secrecy must, in addition, be read within the light of the Jamahiriyya, where, as al-Kuni writes in his autobiography, intentions are necessarily covered by a 'mask' (*qināᶜ*) while all 'openness' (*inbisāṭ*) is immediately exploited.[66] Duly, Ukhayyad and the *mahri's* deaths become inevitable from the moment Ukhayyad reveals the 'secret' (*sirr*) of their attachment.[67] Conveyed through a web of signs, their relationship represents a spiritual secret requiring preservation. In its 'openness', however, it also conveys a spontaneous expression of the repressed and unspoken, wordlessly protesting injustice through the affectionate connection of bodies, sharing 'the word of the secret, through limbs' (*kalimat al-sirr bi-l-aṭrāf*).[68] As al-Kuni observes in his autobiography, the veiled reticence of Tuareg nobility is no longer possible, as, within the modern world, current forms of oppression demand enraged expression rather than the allusive restraint of traditional *furūsiyya*.[69]

Approximate, muddled and often even grotesque, Ukhayyad and the *mahri*'s communication emerges through touch, taste and smell, as they are described 'licking away the tears of the other, tasting the salt and the pain'.[70] As Ukhayyad reflects, 'When the shadows of death descend, this is all creatures (*al-makhlūq*) can do.'[71] Most strikingly, the *mahri's* grunts are literally transcribed as an alternative to the veiled, appropriative human speech through which, as Ukhayyad reflects, 'all signs of heaven disappear'.[72] This 'word', '*ᶜAw-a-a-a-a-a-a*', gains significance only through Ukhayyad's interpretation of it, whether as joy, pain, protest or a plea for help.[73] From within al-Kuni's hybrid, 'minor' language, combining Tuareg and Sufi cosmologies, it represents raw, physical emotion. When Ukhayyad teases the camel about his love for a she-camel, the *mahri* thus grunts back, swaying and spraying spittle.[74] When sad or ashamed, his bottom lip and eyelids droop and he stands motionless.[75] He thus, as al-Fayturi comments, becomes the novel's true 'narrator' (*rāwī*).[76] 'The novel conceals its secrets from us', al-Fayturi writes, 'only to reveal them suddenly, through a wild flood or the anger of the camel, exposing the hidden.'[77] Echoing Haraway's comments, this is premised on the dynamics of companion species:

> *We are training each other in acts of communication we barely understand. We are, constitutively, companion species. We make each other up, in the flesh. Significantly other to each other, in specific difference, we signify in the flesh a nasty developmental infection called love. This love is an historical aberration and a naturalcultural*[78] *legacy* [italics in original].[79]

For al-Kuni, language represents 'exile' (*ightirāb*) and 'sin' (*khaṭīʾa*), driving humans from 'truth' and enveloping them in 'shame' (*ᶜār*).[80] Interspecies communication represents a return from this exile, and a shelter from the censored worlds of Jamahiriyya and Soviet Union, as Ukhayyad shifts from his initial desire for 'praise poetry' to his final perception of friendship with the *mahri* as primordial union:

> As if in a dream, he saw their friendship as it had been at the very beginning, before they were born, before they were clots in their mothers' wombs [. . .] He saw them before they were a desire that took hold of bodies, before they were even dust drifting in the endless void. He could glimpse them back when they had been merely a sound in the wind, the echo of a song, the lamentation (*nuwāḥ*) of strings played between the fingers of a beautiful woman [. . .] And now he saw it clearly: before they ever existed as anything, they had been as one being (*kāʾin wāḥid*).[81]

Despite *al-Tibr's* gruesome conclusion, in which the *mahri* is burnt to death and Ukhayyad is torn to pieces in revenge for his murder of Dudu, the unyielding affection central to *al-Tibr* represents an unassailable bond within otherwise fragmented realities.[82] Through Ukhayyad's realisation of 'oneness', and the 'lament' inherent to it, interspecies companionship further becomes an undoing of the *āya*, and what Omri describes as an 'erasure of the sign' as the ultimate goal of Sufi journey to oneness.[83] In this, the novel echoes Berger's identification of the shared impulse underlying both metaphor and interspecies solidarity, with both representing an attempt 'to re-establish – or at least a refusal to forget – a once-known unity'.[84] For al-Kuni, metaphor represents the foundation of 'creative writing', as an act of 'solemn veiling', transforming the world into symbol and 'metaphorical material expelled from its visible homeland'. 'The Metaphor', he observes, 'was given the quality of suggestion, comparable to what Muslim Sufis see in the "sign" (*āya*).'[85] In *al-Tibr*, this 'activity of solemn veiling' is undone through the 'exposure' of man and camel to one another and the universe. Thus, while al-Kuni describes literary creation as 'concealment (*tawriyya*) and effacement (*taghyīb*)', it also represents an undoing of both, exposing the vulnerability at the heart of creaturely existence, and specifically within the Jamahiriyya, Sahara and Soviet Union.[86]

While its autobiographical dimensions have been little recognised, *al-Tibr* echoes many events from al-Kuni's life, from his romantic entanglement in Russia, to the legacy of his father as a hero of anti-colonial resistance, to his own illness as a 'sign etched onto my body' (*āya marsūma fi sīmā'ī*).[87] Above all, it mirrors his self-described 'second birth' (*mīlādī al-thānī*), born of exile as he witnessed his people's dispersal from afar, and struggled to locate a different form of heroism to that of his father, predicated not on the art of war and noble, enigmatic silence, but the outpouring of concealed protest.[88] The 1980s was a catastrophic decade for the Tuareg, as they struggled against drought and the aggression and corruption of Saharan nation-states. In the early 1990s, this led to large-scale rebellion in Niger and Mali.[89] Both in the Soviet Union and Jamahiriyya, meanwhile, intellectual freedoms were drastically curtailed and economic and environmental precarity a constant concern. Witness to all, al-Kuni describes his nervous depression as a 'bleeding' (*nazīf*) of soul and body.[90] Like his *mahri*, he became a 'skeleton', exposed to overwhelming forces, and literally fading from sight.[91] Only in writing could he find a cure, in a 'policy of starvation' (*siyāsat al-tajwīʿ*), both literal and figurative, which served as a necessary protest against the bleeding of body and land, and the rapacious allure of 'gold dust' (*tibr*).[92] In parallel to '*nazīf*' (bleeding), '*al-tibr*' (gold dust) thus represents another allusion to oil, this time through the harmful impulses it awakens, rather than the ecological vulnerability suggested by the former. In the novel, it represents an opposing force to the camel as creature, pursuing his course across God's wide, but fractured, land.

Resonating through *al-Tibr*, 'starvation' and 'anxieties' (*hawājis*) thus represent central creative impulses and a lasting legacy in the Libyan novel, while the companionship of man and camel, in response, represents an unparalleled bond of love – what Pick elsewhere describes as a 'creaturely fellowship by default, self-evident and undeniable, in a world of imbalance and injustice'.[93] Reflecting upon al-Kuni's physical transformation in the 1980s, al-Fayturi writes in harrowing terms of their encounter at al-Nayhum's wake in 1993, describing al-Kuni as a metamorphosed, hybrid 'being' (*kāʾin*), combining animal alertness with deep contemplation. His words aptly convey how the author's writing had become synonymous with his self, and how he had grown to legendary status within the threatened, isolated Libyan literary community:

> Our eyes did not meet, because his looked within. A simple creature (*kāʾin basīṭ*), he seemed to fill the room with his sharp features, dark, penetrating gaze, and troubling silence. This was the son of the desert, and the child of oral heritage, but the pen had eaten his tongue so that he no longer fed on air [. . .] His angular face and body were those of the *waddān*, with which he had become one (*al-waddān alladhī yatashābah ḥadd al-immiḥāʾ*).[94]

As author, al-Kuni exemplifies the poetics of *maskh*, *āyāt* and creaturely vulnerability, demonstrated across his three novels discussed here and the many that followed, and connected both to the writing of his forebear, al-Nayhum, and to subsequent generations. Nowhere is this connection clearer than in the writing of al-Ghazal, whose characters are similarly 'readers of signs', moving between wonder and fear as they excavate the melancholy of self, nation and land.

Al-Tabut: The Poetics of Stasis

Across al-Ghazal's writing, epigraphs from the Qurʾan and Sufi writings of Ibn al-ʿArabi (d.1240) establish an overriding, visceral awareness of life and death, creation and destruction, upon which the 'disturbed depths' of 'consciousness in crisis' are enacted.[95] His short story, 'al-Bakmaʾ' (2006, 'The Mute'), is an apt example. Beginning with Qurʾan 32:7, describing humans' formation from 'clay' (*ṭīn*), its young protagonist is driven to muteness by the 'sadness' (*ḥuzn*) she perceives in human, animal and land.[96] Haunted by a sound between a 'voice' (*ṣawt*) and a 'sob' (*nuwāḥ*), she obsesses over life's yearning for its 'origin' (*aṣl*), before drowning herself in a mountain brook, and returning fertility to the land.[97] Combining myth and mental breakdown, the mute is one of many insular protagonists in al-Ghazal's writing, inhabiting landscapes scarred by metal, concrete and petrol, and embodying what Santner describes as a 'certain *skinlessness* with respect to excitations from the outside', exposed to 'the dual impact of historical violence and the structural dislocations generated by capitalist modernity'.[98] Unfolding through moments of sudden violence (*ḥawādith*) that disturb the static social fabric, from exploding landmines to colliding vehicles, his novels are, as Fāṭima Muḥammad suggests, plagued by 'signs and allusions, pointing to another, greater story'.[99] This 'other story' fluctuates between spiritual revelation, buried memory and political tyranny, while *ḥawādith* prompt not coming of age but stasis and regression, and war is dictated not by legendary *furūsiyya*, but sovereign, state power, evoking al-Ghazal's own conscription to the Libya–Chad war.

The first fictionalised account of this war, *al-Tabut* daringly challenges what is 'sayable' in Libya, broaching a particularly dark episode in the Jamahiriyya's history. Bordering Fezzan to the south, the Aouzou Strip was annexed by al-Qadhafi in 1973, under the pretext of an unratified treaty signed by Italy and France in 1935, dividing up their colonial possessions. Continuing to intervene in Chad's rapidly deteriorating political situation, he then committed 7,000 ground troops in 1980, intending to conclusively end French influence in the region, expand Libyan territory south and appropriate uranium deposits in the Tibesti Mountains.[100] According to some, a latent motivator also lay in his desire to weaken his own army and prevent possible future coups. Through sporadic clashes, the war continued in the 1980s, as widespread disorganisation and inadequate knowledge of the terrain led to flagging morale. Chad's decisive victory came with the Toyota War of 1987, and, despite a lack of official figures, Libyan losses are estimated to have exceeded 10,000. Almost universally unpopular, the war cemented the country's pariah status within the international community.[101] According to one soldier, 'We were ordered to shoot anything, even a camel caravan carrying goods across the desert [. . .] we were told to consider anything moving as an enemy.'[102]

This sense of nonsensical, indiscriminate violence echoes through *al-Tabut*, critiquing the mindset of '*jundiyya*' (soldierliness) as the governing logic of the Jamahiriyya, appropriating young lives and public funds into fruitless wars and opposing intellectual openness to military order.[103] In its opening scene, rows of soldiers are methodically vaccinated before being flown south, where they are stationed for five months. Despite lack of combat, and the delivery of regular supplies, their solitude and boredom lead to paranoia and aggression. A novel of 'pseudo-survival', and a war novel without a battle, political critique remains latent, while the novel culminates through the slaughter of a she-camel, which, as in *al-Tibr*, I explore as a concluding inversion of the heroic qasida, defamiliarising motifs of departure, journey and sacrifice.[104]

Departure

Al-Tabut opens with an epigraph from Qurʾan 6:95: 'It is God Who splits open the seed and the pits. He causes the living to issue from the dead, and the dead to issue from the living.'[105] Through this image of the biological unity of life and death, the verse introduces a central tension within the novel, between natural mortality and the unnatural biopolitics of modern war. In the opening paragraphs, the army is described in panoramic perspective, through the 'columns' (*ṭawābīr*) of soldiers, clustered on an airstrip between planes and lorries, alongside coffins (*tawābīt*) for returning their remains. Through the repeated adjectives *usṭūrī* (legendary) and *khurāfī* (fabled), the scene is cast into both a timelessly mythological and a grimly real light. Under the blazing sun, everything is animated in fragility, with airplanes becoming 'the motionless, mummified forms of fabled birds, perching amidst waves of ferocious heat', while trees are imagined as the 'scattered remnants of a defeated army'.[106] In a chaos of senses, oil and sweat mix with the exhausted 'panting' (*luhāth*) of human, animal and machine, depicting the uniform army within a wider vulnerability-of-being.

Verbs of motion intensify this physicality, forming a dense layer across the novel.[107] Conveying the powerless struggle of bodies, *talawwā* and *taqallaba* (writhe) are most prominent, describing the soldiers as they stand, 'writhing on the tarmac expanse, scorching in the summer heat'.[108] Paradoxically, *rukūd* (stasis) is also prominent as, in their 'static, illusory movement', they appear 'like a herd of sheep, panting without shade'.[109] Finally, *zaḥafa*, meaning both 'creep/crawl' and 'march', is deployed to defamiliarising effect as, despite describing an army, the former meaning is foremost, emphasised by description of the soldiers' movement as 'slow' (*baṭīʾa*) and 'snakelike' (*thuʿbāniyya*).[110] Similes and metaphors likening men and machines to suffering animals compound this, from planes described as 'half-dead lizards baking on a metal sheet' to trucks as 'small tired beetles' and soldiers as 'ants struggling beneath a dead locust'.[111] Constellated around insects, ants and flies, the narrative is alive with crawling and buzzing, as the world shifts to a fragile 'flow of life' (*dabīb al-ḥayāh*), threatened by modern war.[112]

Within this whole, the narrator is introduced only on page three, as he describes himself, 'crawling/marching along with the columns, dragging my back behind me' (*azḥaf maʿa al-ṭawābīr, wa-ajurr haqībatī*).[113] From the first, however, his consciousness infuses his surroundings with anxiety, in a continued process of pathetic fallacy, shifting to deep identification with the land, yet coupled with profound physical discomfort and dislocation from self:

> My eyes were exhausted and weeping. Distorted images gathered at their corners. Burning things. Shifting. Reaching my brain and penetrating it like needles. My head swayed. Bubbling sounds, like sluggish liquids, swam through it, twisting around the afternoon heat, spreading out and splitting clamorously open.[114]

Tortured by his body's strangeness, the narrator dwells on the sensations of skin, eyes and organs, imagining his joints as 'cold and rusty, like a steel machine' and his sweat as a 'small, slithering serpent'.[115]

Like Ukhayyad, he is no hero. In a flashback to the morning of his departure, he is terrified by his own appearance, 'like a soldier preparing for war'.[116] After a sleepless night, 'haunted by the spectre of war and departure' (*raḥīl*), he contemplates the awakening city from his balcony. Through heightened alertness, bordering on the torturous, he observes the 'human shadows' (*ẓilāl ādamiyya*) on opposite balconies, the sea 'rising and falling like the sobs of a mute Shaykh' (*nuwāḥ shaykh akhras*), and even the scratch of cats' claws on the pavement.[117] Reflecting his own fragility, the city is later described from the airstrip as 'melancholy ruins' (*aṭlāl kaʾība*), sorrowfully watching the soldiers' departure, and prefiguring description of the Aouzou army base, fading into '*aṭlāl*' as the soldiers move into the desert.[118] While suggestive of the qasida's 'way-stations', both evoke the progressive sense of disintegration brought by war.

Bidding his wife, Batul, farewell, the narrator further defamiliarises the poetic motif of the *nasīb* (departure from the beloved), as his preoccupation with physiology replaces conventional masculine desire. This is strikingly conveyed through an echo of the opening lines of Iraqi poet Badr Shakir al-Sayyab's (1926–64) famous 'Unshudat al-Matar' (1952, 'Rain Song'): 'Deep down I knew that her eyes, like palm tree forests in early light (*ka-ghābat nakhīl sāʿat al-saḥar*), were sticky globes, filled with liquids and blood vessels'.[119] Stripping the body of what Pick terms 'consolatory illusions', he is paralysed by physicality, later admitting that he was unable to consummate their marriage for three months. Like al-Faqih's Khalil, he verges on breakdown, inhabited by a 'terrified thing' (*shayʾ khāʾif*) which 'twists and turns (*yataqallab*)' and 'wails soundlessly (*yaʿwī bilā ṣawt*) like a shackled beast (*waḥsh maʾsūr*), its tongue and ears severed'.[120] Through his fragmented consciousness, speech disintegrates into soundless wailing, pulsating with smell, touch and sound. Characterised by silence and passivity, he listens and feels rather than saying or doing, as, through his desert sojourn, the novel shifts into memories, weaving the stasis of the present into that of the past. 'We only live through our past', the narrator declares, 'panting to catch up with the present moment until we hit the wall of death, breaking apart, disintegrating, dying. Death has a thousand stories, but all are woven from the same thread.'[121]

One of the narrator's first memories is prompted by the sight of stray cats pursued by a dog on the morning of his departure, reminding him of a car crash (*ḥāditha*) in which, swerving to avoid a another stray dog, he smashed into a tree. Spending a month in hospital, metal plates were inserted into his crushed thigh and, in their literal foreignness, embody the suppressed incident:

> Sometimes, I would imagine the platinum plates as dead bodies, stretched out in the interstices of my muscles, like coffins in the fleshy darkness. Repulsed, I felt them, cold as snow, as I walked. Heavy and intrusive, they were dormant machines, ready to stir into life.[122]

Combining animate and inanimate, organic and inorganic, this description exemplifies the uncanny poetics of al-Ghazal's writing, in which buried memory takes physical form, preventing comprehension and evoking radical disjuncture within a broader vulnerability-of-being.

Obsessed with locating a convincing 'relationship' (*ᶜalāqa*) between traumatic events, the narrator, like Ukhayyad, is constantly immersed in signs, attempting to fathom their potential import. In an interconnected web, flies become particularly suggestive of order and meaning, before dissolving into the unpredictability of the swarm and bleakness of mortality. On the flight to Aouzou, for example, the narrator is woken by a fly crawling across his skin. Immediately, this reminds him of his mother's death, when, visiting her in hospital, he became obsessed with a fly on the window of her room. 'I left her to writhe (*tatalawwā*)', he recalls, 'and went to the fly as it climbed up the window. With a single blow, I crushed it. Its body disintegrated into smudges of blood, smeared across the sill. When I returned to my mother's bed, I found her cold.'[123] Clinging to an abstract, absent significance in the body of the fly which, ultimately, embodies only transience and decay, the narrator reveals his inability to absorb his mother's death, and broader, immobilising preoccupation with bodily vulnerability. As Steven Connor remarks, 'The fly is more than a *memento mori*; its infuriating incapacity to see any significant difference between life and death makes it seem as though to the fly we may already have plenty of death about us.'[124]

On the plane, the fly also contrasts the unnaturalness of the soldiers' deployment into the desert. 'Like us', the narrator reflects, 'the fly had travelled south, but by its own instinct, attracted by the smell of onions, grapes and sweat, and the spots of dried blood inside the coffins. Life had led it here.'[125] Continuing, he imagines it nourishing itself on the desires and fears of the bodies around it, 'bloating its body with sticky liquids, obscene hope, and dirty, colourful secrets'.[126] Combining Santner and Pick's understandings of the creaturely, the soldiers are, together with the fly, envisioned as part of a natural whole, but also as apart from it, driven by 'obscene hopes' and 'colourful secrets', and, above all, by al-Qadhafi's expansionist ambitions and the allure of uranium. It is this drive that is dramatised through the concluding slaughter of the she-camel, as both a cosmically portentous and utterly marginal 'creaturely sign'.

The nāqa as nadhīr

As the narrator later sits guard on the mountains, overlooking his barracks, he imagines layers of uranium, 'slumbering' below him, and questions what drives humans to 'prise open the hiding places of death (*maknūnāt al-mawt*), letting the curse of annihilation (*fanāʾ*) burn through the wide land (*al-arḍ al-wāsiᶜa*)'.[127] As in al-Kuni's fiction, the hidden layers of the spiritual are thus entangled with destructive layers of the organic, while *fanāʾ* is infused with bodily vulnerability. Drawing his peripheral battalion into a global context, he then reflects on the bombings of Hiroshima and Nagasaki as defining moments of modern mortality, in which 'mute, dread energy' (*al-ṭāqa al-murᶜiba al-kharsāʾ*) reduced cities to 'isolated ruins' (*hashīm muḥtaẓar*) and 'annihilated their people' (*afnat al-bashar*).[128]

Through the rest of the novel, this entanglement of spirituality and environmental malaise continues, culminating in the slaughter of the she-camel in the penultimate chapter, 'al-Nāqa'. Introduced by Qurʾan 7:73, the chapter is steeped in the imagery of the pre-Islamic qasida as the narrator relates how three of his fellow soldiers, Zaydan, Jumᶜa and Bashir, embark on a patrol through the desert. Appearing suddenly, the camel is described as a 'phantom' (*khayāl*), whose 'slow movement' (*dabīb*) roots her within the land: 'Suddenly, there was movement. Something was moving slowly through the silent valley. Like a phantom blending into the surrounding rocks, she proceeded in large, slow paces.'[129] Described as a 'lightening bolt', the she-camel removes the 'veil from their eyes (*ghashāwat al-baṣar*)', disrupting their static lives.[130] Traversing a valley of landmines, she also, however, becomes prey to both historical traces of war and present 'bloodlust', as Jumᶜa claims the need to slaughter her, providing food for the camp and waging a 'war on death'.[131] Trigger-happy and obsessed with his 'soldierliness', his shots resonate across the novel as, through want of human victims, he guns down snakes, birds and foxes. Intolerant to all weakness or perceived deviance, he, like al-Kuni's Cain, imposes his violence on the land, declaring the 'law of the desert' (*shirᶜat al-ṣaḥrāʾ*) to dictate 'bloodshed' (*safk al-dimāʾ*).[132]

In contrast, Zaydan interprets the camel as an omen, with his repeated command to 'Leave the camel be!' (*daᶜ al-nāqa wa-shaʾnuhā*) echoing the Qurʾanic Salih. Presented as an ideal 'reader of signs', Zaydan is a farmer from the fertile region of ᶜAyn Sharshara in north-west Libya, attending to both the written *āyāt* of the Qurʾan and physical *āyāt* of the land.[133] In the camel, he perceives a sign of both wonder and warning. Attempting to wrestle the rifle from Jumᶜa, however, he is knocked aside and the camel wounded by a first bullet.[134] Running in panic, she emits a 'bellow' (*rughāʾ*) like the 'lament of a mute women' (*ka-nuwāḥ imraʾa kharsāʾ*) before her death is described in grim detail:

> She collapsed onto her front legs, with her neck a long arc on the ground. Her back legs and hump remained upright, while her tail thumped weakly against her thighs and more droppings fell to the ground. Then her body collapsed and a pain-filled bellow wrenched the air.[135]

To reach her, the soldiers must navigate the landmines, a far greater threat to their survival than lack of meat, compounding the senselessness of Jumᶜa's act.[136] As Zaydan reflects, 'Jumᶜa's claims were entirely illusory, for they had never truly been hungry'.[137] Cementing this sense of wrongful slaughter, the camel's butchered flesh turns almost immediately black, engulfing the barracks in a nauseating stench as the narrator obsessively repeats how their relationship with the desert had 'gone bad' (*fasadat*) following the 'incident of the camel's slaughter' (*mundhu ḥādithat ṣayd al-nāqa*).[138] While the camp is infested by the 'buzzing' of flies and scorpions, Jumᶜa is poisoned by a viper, with his death depicted as an act of cosmic justice:

> Jumᶜa died. He was slain by a little desert viper with a pointy tail. In the previous days, he had killed a whole array of them, as well as two foxes. Before that, his bullet had ripped apart the camel's throat and his blade had brutalised her skin and flesh.[139]

Bashir, in contrast, is overcome with grief and paranoia as the camel begins to visit his dreams.[140] Caught between the conflicting worldviews of Zaydan and Jumᶜa, he is, throughout the novel, increasingly threatened by both 'omens' (*nudhur*) and mental instability. The first of these omens is a skull which he finds in a cave, 'with tufts of silver hair still clinging to it', alongside shining cans of condensed milk.[141] Juxtaposing the artificial lustre of modern, mass-produced goods to natural death and decay, the find is one of many sites of death which litter the encampment and haunt Bashir and his fellow soldiers, from the spot where a previous soldier accidentally detonated a grenade to that of a violent ambush and mass slaughter. While Zaydan interprets these sites as omens, they also simply represent random sites of catastrophe within the melancholy of natural history. Laced with fear, the novel and its desert setting thus shift between the meaningful narratives of myth and signs, and the disintegration of mental breakdown, echoing the similar fluctuation between malaise, mysticism and grim reality that resonates across the Libyan novel, from al-Nayhum's hallucinatory Masᶜud to al-Faqih's Khalil.[142]

Insisting on burying the camel's discarded meat, Bashir begins to repeat, in an echo of al-Kuni's Asuf, that 'everything is dust and sand, everything is dust and sand' (*kull shayᵓ turāb wa-rimāl*).[143] Unable to bear both his guilt and his overwhelming perception of mortality, he then runs into the field of landmines and, in the novel's concluding image, his 'insides' (*amᶜāᵓ*) are scattered across the traumatised narrator, echoing the culminating description of Ukhayyad's torn 'limbs' (*ashlāᵓ*) in *al-Tibr*. As throughout the novel, Bashir's death appears both as the culmination of cosmic 'signs', and profound breakdown within the meaninglessness of modern war.

Finally, through Zaydan, the camel delivers a vision of oneness. Paralleling Ukhayyad's skinned and suffering *mahri*, this is conveyed first through the exposure of her flesh as Zaydan contemplates the 'layers of white criss-crossed with red veins'.[144] Later, he formulates this into a grotesque expression of wholeness:

> The camel had died, her head striking the desert floor, and here was her flesh, strung above them. What the soldiers had eaten yesterday would emerge today in their excrement, fertilised by fly eggs. Life was one huge entity. An entity which coursed, unseen, through the paths of existence, rebuilding, even in the desert, what death razed.[145]

As in *al-Tibr*, this vision of organic interconnection is followed by a more conventional experience of *fanāᵓ* centred on the camel's gaze, which Zaydan witnesses in a trance: 'The she-camel halted and turned. Her huge eyes settled into the depths of his. Their gazes joined in a halo of light as a wail of lament (*nuwāḥ wa-anīn*) flowed through him. He sensed his spirit melting into the light, and he was annihilated by it (*yufnīhi al-nūr*).'[146] Like in *al-Tibr*, the 'bellows' (*nuwāḥ*) of the wounded camel echo the 'lament' (*nuwāḥ*) of cosmic melancholy, as human language collapses, removing 'consolatory illusions' and reframing truth, in Pick's words, '[not as] a terminus of thought or resting place of concepts but the site of encounter with reality that rattles concepts and confounds thought'.[147] Such encounters, Pick quotes from philosopher Cora Diamond, can be 'turned equally toward splendour and toward horror' and, in *al-Tabut*, they sit side by side, with wondrous *āyāt* juxtaposed to painful exposure and laced with trauma, protest and melancholy.[148]

Through myth and mysticism, the camel's death dramatises the breakdown of connections between humans and earth, restored only by returning, like Zaydan, to fundamental reflection on creaturely and spiritual wholeness or like Ukhayyad to interspecies translation. Together, both *mahri* and *nāqa* draw twentieth-century Libya into the timelessness of the Qur'anic *āya*, as wider political and environmental contexts coalesce around them, concerning the destruction of *arḍ Allāh* and the unnecessary battles waged on it, from political wars to the plundering of resources. In both, these battles are depicted from the sidelines and interwoven with other webs of signification. Concluding my discussion, I track this oblique poetics further, moving to the entirely implicit 'war' of *al-Khawf*, in which the seismic slaughter of camels is dispersed into even less visible acts of suffering, conveying the slow violence of political tyranny.

Al-Khawf Abqani Hayyan: The Poetics of Horror

While *al-Tabut* is structured as a desert journey, *al-Khawf* opens with the return of its protagonist-narrator, unnamed once again, from months in a psychiatric hospital to his empty house in Misrata. For the remainder of the novel, he remains motionless in his courtyard, excavating his past in a tormented stream-of-consciousness. Haunted by what he calls the 'landmine incident' (*ḥāditbat al-lagham*), in which he lost half his foot after stepping on an old Italian mine in the palm grove behind his house, his malaise binds the personal and national, present and past, in structuring 'moments' that uncannily echo those of *al-Tabut*.[149] On one level, the narrator senses that the 'landmine incident' has served as a divine 'sign' (*ishāra*), initiating him into the 'unknown' (*al-ghayb*) and awakening within him a hidden force, which he describes as a 'slumbering beast (*waḥsh ḍārr*), curled tight around its body'.[150] Sufi poetics soon, however, shift to breakdown, seeking answers before retreating in horror, as, behind every event, lurks a web of dangerous significance. As with al-Faqih's Khalil, the 'slumbering beast' becomes increasingly threatening as, constituted through secrets, lurking within self, house and city, the novel emerges through horrifying dysphoria and, in contrast to the deserts of *al-Tibr* and *al-Tabut*, the cityscape of the 2000s is dense with hidden gazes and political precarity.

Alone in his 'desolate house' after his pregnant wife Malika leaves with their son, the narrator is characterised by trembling and bodily discomfort, imagining himself as a 'one-celled being', a 'mangy dog, crouching next to the wall', and the 'skeleton' of a car, which sits, like him, rusting in the courtyard.[151] In another echo of 'Unshudat al-Matar', his previous life troubles him like a 'sticky, decomposing corpse, floating on the waves', and, as in *al-Tabut*, he is nauseated by the stench of his own skin and obsessively visualises his heart 'pumping blood and beating weakly'.[152] Profoundly dislocated from self and past, he describes his relationships as 'rotted' (*fasadat*), fantasising about hitting his wife, whom he has reduced to 'lament' (*nuwāḥ*), and referring to his son only as 'the boy'.[153] Imagery of infection further extends even to his unborn child, as, in an ongoing obsession, he associates sperm with disease, infusing the beginnings of life with contamination as he imagines Malika's foetus transforming into a monster.[154]

This present motionlessness, it transpires, is underpinned by a web of domestic secrets, culminating in the narrator's unwitting acts of incest and fratricide, caused by his father's illicit affair. While these events are only alluded to, in the fevered depths of his monologue, imagery of collapse is centred on the family home through his father's marble tomb in the courtyard and an ancient cellar discovered during renovations.[155] Troubled by these subterranean lacunae, the narrator becomes further paranoid that the house will be appropriated, either by his friend and half-brother, Yusuf, or the government.[156] In the Jamahiriyya, home is liable to be snatched away and scandal exposed. A striking contrast to the 'protected intimacy' that Gaston Bachelard identifies with the house, integrating thoughts, memories and dreams, the Libyan house simultaneously evokes claustrophobia and exposure.[157] In *al-Tibr*, too, Ukhayyad repeatedly dreams of being trapped in a 'house of rubble' (*bayt al-anqāḍ*), tracked by an 'invisible being' (*kāʾin khafī*), while, in *al-Khawf*, the narrator's house feeds his anxieties, while being simultaneously tainted by them. Beyond its walls, the outside world is phantomic, embodied by stray dogs, the 'ghosts' (*aṭyāf*) of passers-by and 'a warm drizzle, heavy with car fumes'.[158]

As the novel progresses, this world becomes increasingly threatening. The neighbourhood children throw dirt at the narrator's car while he imagines the adults 'lurking in hidden corners, silently watching'.[159] Going further, he likens all to a 'swarm of maggots' (*jamharat al-dīdān*), battling over the spoils of oil wealth, which, when it dries up, will leave 'brothers to consume brothers'.[160] Given his own perceived monstrousness, this fallen city of ruins and ruination, zombified gazes and parasitic lifeforms, is, to a large extent, made horrific by the narrator's own troubled consciousness. At the same time, through mention of the security services intervening in disputes over land and corrupt businessmen monopolising the market with toxic, imported food, the novel alludes to a war for land and resources driven by a government that sets citizen against citizen.[161]

Paralleling this, a sense of mythic disintegration is also conveyed by the rats and oversized cockroaches which invade the neighbourhood, echoing the Biblical plagues of Egypt, and divine punishment of Thamūd.[162] While the government imports owls to kill the rats, shrieking in the skies above, the neighbourhood people spread poison indiscriminately through the streets. Mythic doom is therefore coupled with daily slow violence and neglect. In his courtyard, the narrator watches the agonising demise of a poisoned cat, fascinated by the fear 'passing through the animal's small, suffering brain', as the scene becomes a microcosm for life in the city.[163]

The Palm Grove

Together, these scenes of disintegration converge on the palm grove behind the narrator's house. Throughout Libyan fiction, palm trees are symbolic of the country's traditional ecology, and, in *al-Khawf*, become a tapestry of local history, planted by the narrator's distant ancestors in what he imagines as a simpler, more harmonious time. In following centuries, the grove then becomes home to a wandering Sufi dervish, al-Shaykh al-Marrakishi, providing a core of spiritual mysticism around which political disturbances coalesce. The most important of these comes at the beginning of Italian colonisation, with the 1912 Battle of Rumayla. One of the first cities to fall to Italian occupation, Misrata was, under the leadership of Ramaḍān al-Suwayḥilī, a centre of resistance, and the grove evokes this forgotten history, as, following their defeat, locals are hung from its trees. Whitewashing this history, the grove is then transformed to tourist attraction, complete with hot spring.[164] In later years, surrounding Bedouin shanty towns are replaced by concrete blocks, and a road constructed around it. Following its sudden barrenness, in the early 2000s, it is itself then finally condemned under the government's land development initiatives, and, in publicly resisting its removal, the narrator's friends Yusuf and Hamid are destined to disappearance and death.[165]

Through these entangled histories, the grove becomes a simultaneously nostalgic and threatening presence, embodying the disjuncture of past and present, and the profound erasure and distortion of local memory, as the narrator imagines a 'nihilistic force, crouching among its roots, and crawling to attack'.[166] Like his house, it becomes intertwined with the darkness of his mind, a 'pit of melancholy', whose roots spread through his skull like 'dark soft snakes, squeezing my blood-filled brain'.[167] Exemplifying the novel's poetics of horror, it is a 'haunted forest', combining personal and political demons, and with its concluding removal infused with presentiments of social, environmental and political change.[168] Shortly before it is felled, the solitary flight of a bird thus fills the narrator with an 'animal fear' that reality is 'on the verge of turning to violence, or perhaps to ruin (*kharāb*)'.[169] Through the din of diggers, like 'vicious insects, gnawing at the trunks', the trees leave a ruined wasteland and, half-asleep, the narrator imagines himself hearing thousands of birds crying, in an echo of Genesis, 'Cain, why have you killed your brother Abel?'[170]

Through the finality of this fallenness, the grove's story is complete, while its removal opens the land to change, embodied by the mounting unruliness of the neighbourhood children who, like the narrator, have grown forgetful of the past, but, unlike him, are thereby uninhabited, and uninhibited, by fear.[171] As the annual procession of the Sufi ᶜAysawiyya passes by his house in rhythmic, pulsing union, the children merge with the energy of the mass, feasting on sweets, while the narrator lurks in the shadows, paralysed by fear.[172] As he excavates the past, attempting to evade the demons of personal and national history, he represents an overarching, structural stasis as, once again, the Libyan novel dwells within the 'difficulty of story'.

While the national threatens to erupt into violence, the personal also reaches crisis point, as the narrator begins to confront the truth of his sibling relationships to Yusuf and Yusuf's sister Sara. These underlying events are never fully elaborated but hinted at through charged encounters and, particularly, through tortured contemplation and ekphrastic depiction of the melancholy sculptures and paintings of artist, Yusuf. While *al-Khawf* is not populated by the same, paradigm-shifting human–animal encounters as *al-Tibr* and *al-Tabut*, these paintings come vividly to life, expressive of the fear of both their creator and contemplator. In contrast to the historical ekphrasis of al-Faqih and al-Kuni, from 'Girl and Gazelle' to 'composite creature', they are based on the contemporary art of Misrata-born Muhammad Bin Lamin (Bin Lāmīn, b.1969). Through numerous references to Bin Lamin's work, which has been aptly compared to the 'haunting' quality of Libyan fiction, al-Ghazal becomes one of several Libyan authors to fictionalise fellow intellectuals and artists, transforming the novel into a refuge for creative endeavour and archive of threatened creations.[173]

Creatures and Creations

Famous for his use of unconventional materials, Bin Lamin portrays obscure human–animal forms caught in strange, static movement amid open landscapes. One series features twisted shapes fashioned from metal mesh, and another displays bullets bound with wire to form delicate, humanoid figures. Yet another applies chemical treatments to photographic paper, through which the shining outlines of human and animal are etched.[174] According to his website, 'Bin Lamin's pieces are inspired by Libya's rich cultural and artistic heritage and draw upon its history, going as far back as the ancient cave paintings in the southern mountains and the surreal identities that the country has had to endure over the centuries'.[175] Combining the primordial and natural historical, Bin Lamin envisions Libyan identity as one of *maskh*:

> His painted beings, with their deformed, disproportionate, heads and bodies, with their glowing colours of yellow, green, red, brown and blue, the colours of the Libyan landscape, reflect a torn, sometimes deformed, identity, which tries to mix the different, diverse and conflicting identities of Libya, a land of desert and sea, rural and urban, the serious and absurd. The Beings of Mohammed Bin Lamin are entombed in their colourful, deformed, submissive world.[176]

Through this world, Bin Lamin captures the essence of al-Ghazal's characters which, in a brief review of *al-Tabut*, he himself describes as nodes of 'fear', radiating out to encompass their surroundings.[177] All three of al-Ghazal's novels feature artwork from Bin Lamin on their front covers, and connections between their aesthetics are clear as artist and novelist become, equally, creatures and creators.

Al-Khawf engages with various of Bin Lamin's series, from his 'Yellow Beings' to his 'Opera of Spoons', formed from coffee stains on metal cutlery.[178] His chemical etchings are, however, foremost. Contemplating them, the narrator dwells on the violence involved in their creation:

> Their eyes bore traces of disturbance, left by the scrape of the blade across the shining paper. It was as though their cover had been removed, with the etched line marking their horrifying separation from the unknown (*al-ghayb*). With his knife, Yusuf forced them from nothingness and unknowability.[179]

This 'unveiling of forms' (*iẓhār al-rusūmāt*) presents art, like creation, as a painful, violent process of separation, as, with lowered eyelids, the creatures long for renewed oblivion.[180] While Yusuf desires them to resemble prophets, 'as light and soundless as feathers' and devoid of 'cells and enzymes', they instead resemble his tormented friends, combining the redemptive power of art with the abject and vulnerable.[181] The narrator sees himself eerily reflected in one blurred form while Bin Lamin might, indeed, see himself in Yusuf.[182] Through these ekphrastic traces, *al-Khawf* thus shifts from human–animal encounter to the 'aesthetic moment' or 'mode of attentiveness' which, for Santner, is exemplary of creaturely poetics, introducing a 'muteness' into the reading process, creating 'breaks and pauses in the movement of narrative', and suggesting that we are 'no longer inhabiting a strictly verbal universe'.[183]

Through Yusuf's 'beings' (*kāʾināt*), however, *al-Khawf* also demonstrates the vulnerability of art to the tyranny of censorship, emptying creaturely signs of their fluid meaning and refilling them with malicious intent. While attending a literary festival in Morocco, the narrator's paranoia drives him to hint publicly that Yusuf's artist's website may be an 'encoded means' (*wasīla mushaffara*) of communicating his affiliation to 'insidious organisations, threatening the land'.[184] While intending his words to be 'playful', they come out hoarse and ominous, as the 'beast' within him compels him to fatal sabotage. Several months later, Yusuf is arrested and tortured in Spain, leading to his swift degeneration and death, caused, as the narrator realises, by his own insinuations.[185] As its title suggests, fear dictates *al-Khawf* and the emotional and creative lives of its characters, caused by personal, political and historical secrets.[186] It is this poetics that distinguishes al-Ghazal's writing, prompting a rereading of the Sufi aesthetics of broader Libyan fiction through the pressures of trauma and censorship, leading to fiction structured around stasis and populated by terrifying traces.

Conclusion

Praising al-Kuni's seamless interweaving of 'narrative' and 'Sufi' discourse (*al-khiṭābān al-ṣūfī wa-l-sardī*), al-Ghazal evokes how the 'symbolic world' emerges seamlessly from the real and time becomes compacted into a 'single moment'.[187] Through this process, his novels represent a modern iteration of mystical time, expressive of the 'synchronicity of everything', in which histories and geographies are 'compressed in a moment'.[188] In both al-Kuni and al-Ghazal's writing, such mystical synchronicity is, however, also interlaced with psychological and political 'synchronicity', as a single moment echoes with wider traumas and allusive allegory. Within what Barthes calls the 'fissure of the symbolic', sign systems are imbued with shifting import, individuals struggle towards Truth through omens and *āyāt*, and, while the 'unseen' seems to hint at an underlying cosmic justice, it simultaneously collapses into unfathomable vulnerability.[189] Framing their critique of war in a vision of both symbolic fissure and organic interconnection, the authors depict land rather than nation, animated by lament and marked by ruins and ruination, as language disintegrates into physicality and camel-signs shift between wonder and warning.

In *al-Tibr*, Ottoman and Italian remnants scatter the desert, hinting at spectres of future oppression, while the synchronicity of Sufi time couples with the immediacy of 'camel time', recalibrating *arḍ Allāh*, but revealing, through immediate physical vulnerability, the precarity of creaturely existence. In *al-Tabut*, buried memories repeat themselves in the present, while the paradigmatically vulnerable, and paradigmatically mythic, *nāqa* embodies the circling 'flow of life' (*dabīb al-ḥayāh*) within the unnaturalness of modern war. In contrast to al-Kuni's fiction, *al-Tabut* turns also to the urban north which, in *al-Khawf*, becomes central to a poetics of stasis and surveillance, where signs of past, present and transcendent Truth are exposed to the powers-that-be and resonate with unspoken political violence. Through its static, trembling narrator, it exemplifies the breakdown of individual and family, community and nation, in static pursuit of an absent 'story'.

4

Absent Stories in the Urban Novel

Is there not guidance for them in how many generations we caused to perish before them, among those habitations they walk? Truly in that are signs for those who thoughtfully reflect. (Qur'an 20:128)[1]

It is almost as if one were to ask whether Benjamin's angel of history was capable of a good laugh amid all that wreckage piling up before his eyes. (Santner, *On Creaturely Life*)[2]

Cities are full of strays, of dogs and cats, of the homeless and rootless. In their darkened corners, creatures seek shelter and security. In their density, they expose the individual to the gaze, pressure and flow of the agglomeration. An exemplary site of discipline, they yet retain a pulse of their own, through the inhabitants who reinvent their histories and reconfigure their cartographies. The story of the Libyan city is one of oil and surveillance, marginality and neglect – well-trodden themes of novels from the 1960s on. Animals, when they appear, are not the eloquent beasts of desert narrative, but startled forms, traversing the human gaze, and subject, like humans, to a new, industrial world. Creeping below the radar, or flying over it, they do not, nevertheless, become the same site of shared vulnerability and paradigm-shifts as in the survival novel. Instead, humans identify with that which, like them, is static and surveyed: the statue of the Girl and Gazelle, tired, thirsty and exposed; the palm groves, savaged by diggers; and the neglected streets, choked by high rises. These are the creaturely traces that animate the urban novel, brought to life not as Sufi signs but through their exposure to sovereign power, as what Santner terms a 'dimension of *surplus value* – attaching to objects and bodies that thereby become the focal points of ceaseless economic, cultural, and political administration'.[3] Evoking the melancholy of the qasida's *aṭlāl*, these traces resonate with the mute eloquence of transience. Echoing the ominousness of Quranic *āyāt*, as 'signs' of bygone 'habitations' (*masākin*), they cast panoptic 'administration' into natural historical scope, signalling that it, too, will one day be cast from the symbolic systems which confer meaning upon it.

The rapidity of Libya's urbanisation from the 1950s has, certainly, been seismic. From a population of thirty thousand in 1911, Tripoli expanded to almost two million in the 2010s, with mass migration in the 1960s resulting in the spread of slums and unravelling of local neighbourhoods.[4] Benghazi's growth was similarly rapid. In a 1965 letter to *al-Haqiqa* editor, Rashād al-Hūnī, al-Nayhum describes his shock at returning from Helsinki to find a 'materialistic city, harsh, fickle, and uprooted', lamenting the flashy cars which choke once convivial, if deprived, urban communities.[5] Al-Faqih's Tripoli and al-Ghazal's Misrata, in turn, depict concrete jungles, subject to surveillance and engulfed by diesel, as their material memories are obliterated.

Such representations are the focus of this chapter, in Mansur Bushnaf's *al-ᶜIlka* (2008; *Chewing Gum*, 2014), Muhammad al-Asfar's *Sharmula* (2008, Sharmoula Salad) and Razzan Naᶜim al-Maghrabi's *Nisaʾ al-Rih* (2010, Women of the Wind). Like al-Ghazal, all three authors remained in Libya under al-Qadhafi, and extend the 'difficulty of story' to the concrete vulnerability of books, writers and readers. Banned in 2008, *al-ᶜIlka* has yet to be reprinted in Arabic, while al-Asfar published his first fourteen novels at his own expense, knowing their distribution would be severely limited. This material precarity echoes through their writing, in experimental narratives questioning the possibility and desirability of telling story and being heard, and continuing the visceral hesitancy of al-Nayhum's *al-Hayawanat*. Subverting tyrannical interpretation through stuttering and fragmentation, they dwell within the local, excavating forgotten margins and unofficial histories, and determinedly reclaiming the city from al-Qadhafi's infamous antipathy towards it.

Despite initial improvements to public housing, education and healthcare in the 1970s, this antipathy became swiftly apparent through what Ali Ahmida calls al-Qadhafi's cultural policy of 'bedouinisation', actively undermining urban culture and the growing middle class.[6] His principle of '*al-bayt li-sākinihi*' (the house for the inhabitant) created profound instability, as properties and individual wealth were summarily seized.[7] With individual bank accounts confiscated, Libyans became dependent upon the largess of the regime, underemployed in government positions and with no opportunities to leave or change the country.[8] As the culmination of his anti-urban stance, al-Qadhafi's short story, 'al-Madina' (1993, 'The City'), reviles the city as 'the graveyard of social interaction' and a 'biological, maggoty life, where people live and die without meaning', as 'rats', 'snails' and 'slugs'.[9]

Against this rhetoric, authors imbue the city with pathos, exposed to rulers that come and go, and painful processes of '*maskh*' (metamorphosis).[10] Returning in 2001, after decades of exile, Mattawa describes Benghazi's transformation into a 'ghost town' where 'piles of rubbish appeared with equal frequency in rich and poor neighbourhoods'.[11] Returning in 2014, Matar describes the sudden appearance of 'high brick walls', betraying a 'private disquiet' and desire to 'keep out the sun and the passing gaze'.[12] This is compounded by an eerie sense of incompleteness, haunting him since boyhood:

> Ever since I can remember, I have found the unfinished state of much of modern Libya's architecture unsettling. It expresses neglect more actively than, say, ruins or old decaying structures. When something is built, we assume it to have been built out of a sense of necessity, intent or desire. Therefore, we associate its incompleteness with deliberate negligence and carelessness, or else sudden impotence.[13]

Imbuing the landscape with an abandonment that mirrors that of its people, Matar brings Libya's modern ruination, born of 'sudden impotence' and active neglect, into unsettling confrontation with the ruins of its past and the melancholy of natural history.

In other fiction, this emerges through the visceral juxtaposition of humans and misplaced, contested and truant '*turāth*' (heritage). Discussed in my introduction, Qanāw's 'ᶜAwdat al-Qaysar' succinctly conveys many defining features of the urban novel, imbued with bitter humour as statues come alive and humans turn to stone. Returning to Tripoli from Leptis Magna, to where al-Qadhafi relegated him in the 1970s, the bronze statue of Septimius Severus is horrified by the ruins of the modern city, and convinces the dilapidated Girl and Gazelle to flee with him. Contrasting the mute 'thingness' of Benjamin's natural history, they defy their expulsion from the symbolic order, as past abandons immobile present, refusing to remain as a site of memory, instruction or warning.

In the novel, authors similarly strive to locate the story of the city's 'inner upheaval', as humans, cast from rights and agency, are juxtaposed to neglected landscapes, provoking mad laughter amid the 'catastrophic pileup' of history.[14] Depicting the 2000s, many further evoke the high-rises and boutique hotels brought by the lifting of sanctions and the country's gradual reintegration into the international fold, alongside the nominal reforms and open-door policy of Sayf al-Islam (b.1972), al-Qadhafi's second son. While the regime was courted by western politicians, Sarkozy and Blair, and by foreign oil companies keen to regain their profits, little sustained effort was placed on securing real change for the country's people. As al-Kiddi satirically evokes in his 'al-Hayah al-Qasira al-ᶜAjiba', the happy ending of a Libyan dog could be made into a biopic, so long as nothing extraneous to this 'story' would be shown. As western imports and changing skylines give only the semblance of change, authors therefore cast the familiar themes of survival, homelessness and hunger in altered landscapes and aesthetics. A sense of rapid obliteration is conveyed, alongside one of protest and revolt, reflecting the escalation of popular discontent, which culminated in the infamous 2006 Benghazi protests whose initial cause – protest against the Danish cartoons of Muhammad – led to explicit anti-Qadhafi protest and the death of at least ten men at the hands of security services. As in al-Ghazal's *al-Khawf Abqani Hayyan*, such precipitous change is hinted at in the novel, while juxtaposed to continued stasis in uncertain, improvisational narratives.

Alongside al-Ghazal, the three authors Bushnaf, al-Asfar and al-Maghrabi are prominent among the new, or returning, novelists of the 2000s. A rising star of Benghazi's theatre scene in the 1970s, Bushnaf's densely symbolic satirical writing harks back to al-Nayhum's dark humour.[15] In 1978, he was, however, one of many intellectuals to be imprisoned, until 1990, under charges of Communism. *Al-ᶜIlka* is his first novel, with its central images, of stasis and chewing gum, reflecting both his own imprisonment and the stagnation of 1980s Tripoli. Amid a litterscape, where rubbish, relics and humans exist in equal precarity, the nation chews, while the narrative is circling, stuttering and obsessed with the impossibility of its own 'story' (*qiṣṣa*).

Born and raised in Benghazi, al-Asfar has published prolifically since his first novel, *al-Mudasa* (2003, The Crushed), and short stories, *Hajar Rashid* (2003, A Guiding Stone). Vibrantly chaotic, his novels wander down unexpected paths, reflecting his vision of writing as life and life as writing. The loss of his only brother, in the massacre of Abu Salim Prison, further resonates through his novels. 'I wrote about the massacre in my first novel', he observes, 'And my second. And my third. And I was not the only one who couldn't forget.'[16] Alternating between the celebration of local heroes, the satire of government officials and traumatic loss, *Sharmula* is narrated by a fictional avatar of al-Asfar himself. Centred on the titular motif of '*sharmūla*', a simple Benghazi salad, it evokes the unofficial networks of hospitality within the city, countering the hunger and 'chewing' of the wider Libyan novel and embracing storyless-ness and fragmentation as vital, subversive impulses.

Through al-Maghrabi, finally, the compounded marginality of Libyan women's writing comes to the fore.[17] Despite growing up in Damascus, Tripoli occupies centre-stage in her 2011 IPAF-longlisted *Nisaʾ al-Rih* as, amid large-scale 'destruction' (*hadm*) and 'development' (*taṭwīr*), it stages the dramas of rich women, closeted in their apartments and fuelling themselves with coffee and cigarettes. Constructed around scandals, secrets and blackmail, their friendships represent a desperate pursuit of agency, while the narrator, an aspiring 'author' (*kātiba*), attempts to formulate them into 'story' (*ḥikāya*). Breaking from the dense symbolism and entangled narratives of Bushnaf and al-Asfar, al-Maghrabi's bare prose reflects on the tradition of 'women's writing' as coming-of-age in Libya, pondering who can tell a story and have their story told. After first drawing on the poetics of Bushnaf and al-Asfar, comparing their evocation of writing as chewing gum and *sharmūla*, and the creaturely 'signs' through which they animate their cities, I then explore how *Nisaʾ al-Rih* both marks new territory for the Libyan novel and remains rooted in the same 'difficulty of story'.

Al-ᶜIlka: The Novel as Litterscape

In the 2000s, Bushnaf began, as he describes, 'chewing' the idea for a first novel, charting Tripoli's transformation to litterscape.[18] *Al-ᶜIlka* is this novel. A repeated refrain, the verb *lāk*, *yalūk* (to chew) replaces all activities, emotions and thoughts within it, through a cast of characters on the 'margins' (*hāmish*) of life.[19] Tantalisingly hinting at personal fulfilment, 'chewing' is driven by a fundamental awareness of the need to stay still and keep quiet. The ensuing dark satire evokes the 'strange madness' that Bushnaf associates both with his own and the country's imprisonment:

> I spent twelve lean years in Libyan prisons, during which, in abject conditions, I learned patience, chewing and self-preservation. But I also learnt humour and laughter. This sense of absurdity will have a great influence on Libyan literature and art. Libyans will write with a taste of bitterness, laughing long and hard from their strange madness.[20]

Self-reflective and consciously postmodern, the third-person narrator of Bushnaf's *al-ᶜIlka* conveys this madness, totally preoccupied by the 'story' being told and, more importantly, by its impossibility, viscerally conveyed through the novel's hero who remains motionless for almost the entire narrative as the narrator attempts to enunciate his story and overcome his stasis. Paralleling this static hero is a nude, nineteenth-century statue, central to relaying the city's turbulent history from the end of Ottoman rule to the present. Carved by an Italian prisoner of the pasha, the statue frustrates 'categorisation' (*taṣnīf*) and renders mad any who 'grasp' it (*man yudrikuhu*).[21] Imagined through the heterotopic spaces of a public park and museum, both statue and hero defamiliarise the conventions of plot, characterisation and allegory as characters shift between 'stasis' (*tasammur*) and chewing, static longing and unfulfilled desire.

The resultant narration, simultaneously static and swift, reflects Bushnaf's early grounding in theatre, shifting, as critic Ṣāliḥ observes, between 'symbolism' (*al-tarmīz*) and 'alienation' (*al-taghrīb*) and grounded in an aesthetics of 'repetition' (*takrār*).[22] In Brechtian fashion, the narrator draws attention to the artifice of the story, focusing on setting and props rather than heroes, plot and grand narrative. While at one point, the narrator, in a show of certainty, declares, 'This is the story, everything else is peripheral', the peripheral, in fact, subsumes all, while human characters are decentred.[23] With two 'beginnings', entitled, 'The Beginning to Our Story' and 'But What's the Story?', its props and settings are further arranged into deceptively ordered pairs, including, 'The Statue' and 'The Statue 2', 'The Park' and 'The Park 2' and 'The Hero' and 'The Hero 2'. Regardless of the resolution suggested by this duality, however, each 'story' ultimately frustrates the narrator, who, in mock despair, declares, 'Despite all the structural and stylistic tricks (*al-ḥiyal al-inshāʾiyya al-kathīra*) we have employed to extricate ourselves from this novelistic nightmare, we remain in a state of endless chewing.'[24] As one of the narrator's 'stylistic tricks', and an exemplary 'creaturely sign', I set the statue amid the novel's broader paraphernalia of hero, gum and park. Focusing first on the hero as 'human statue', and the heroine's chewing, I examine the postmodern stasis, which provides the first layer of excavation, before moving to public park and statue, juxtaposing melancholy historical consciousness to present litterscape.

The Human Statue

The novel's impossible story is, in short, as follows: the hero and heroine, Mukhtar and Fatima, meet in a public park in Tripoli and ostensibly fall in love. Mukhtar is of a higher social class than Fatima, whose family hail from the nation's new middle-class, enriched by oil and striving after Nasser's 'Freedom, Socialism and Unity'.[25] 'Hers', the narrator remarks, 'was one of the humble families who had benefited greatly from the socialist revolution. They were able to move into flats built by Poles, Bulgarians and Egyptians and become familiar with modern luxuries like fridges, telephones and gramophones.'[26] Through Mukhtar and Fatima's nascent love story, the path is paved for the unfolding of national drama through the ins and outs of the domestic, with the narrator declaring it to follow a 'roughly Arabic template', typical of the romantic melodramas of Egyptian cinema.[27] Specifically, the narrator aligns it with the Egyptian author Ihsan ʿAbd al-Qaddus's (1919–90) short story 'al-Wisada al-Khaliya' (1957, 'The Empty Pillow') and novella *Biʾr al-Hurman* (1962, The Well of Deprivation). Both were adapted into popular films in the 1960s and 1970s and move from frustrated love story, hampered by psychological disorders and social conventions, to happy ending, in which desires are reconciled and society harmonised.

Biʾr al-Hurman provides the most consistent intertext to which the narrator's story is juxtaposed. Narrated by a celebrated Cairene psychiatrist, the novella describes the cure of young, respectable, married woman, Nahid Hatim, who, compelled by the trauma of her parents' loveless marriage, subconsciously engages in violent sexual encounters in Cairo at night, awaking the following day with no recollection. Steeped in the optimism of what *al-ᶜIlka*'s narrator terms 'bourgeois Nasserism', *Biʾr al-Hurman* is structured around the Freudian 'talking therapy', organising Nahid's confused memories into 'story', and ensuring her cure and happy ending.[28] *Al-ᶜIlka* unravels this, eschewing 'novelistic posturing' and hinting at a trauma that refuses to be formed into story within the postmodern stasis of 1980s Libya.

As the narrator states, *al-ᶜIlka* may follow an Arabic template, but it is told in the 'mode of chewing gum', a surrogate for human interaction and emotion, offering only the ephemeral promise of food, companionship and meaning. In keeping with this mode, the relationship of hero and heroine is oddly adrift from social contexts. They meet only in the public spaces of a municipal park and the Red Palace Museum, and while Fatima is at one point described 'tidying up', her domestication is limited to the area around their chosen park bench. The reasons for their separation are also unsettlingly void of recognisable motivation, and are attributed to a vague 'emptiness' (*farāgh*) and 'revulsion' (*qaraf*), contrasting their friends who meet in the park with them before moving swiftly into 'love talk' (*al-ḥadīth ᶜan al-ḥubb*).[29]

Ultimately, Fatima abandons Mukhtar because he is 'strange and unpredictable' but, above all, because he is motionless, caught first in the 'repetitive cycle of visiting park and museum' and then in stasis.[30] As she leaves him in the park, he becomes a human statue, remaining frozen for ten years and the rest of the novel, with his beard lengthening, his clothes tattered and rubbish piling around him. Consumed by the image of Fatima's retreating figure, he echoes the qasida's melancholy *nasīb*, unable to move forward and turning, himself, to *aṭlāl*. An 'abandoned lover' (*ᶜāshiq mahjūr*), his growing unkemptness further recalls the paradigmatically antisocial Majnun Layla, paralysed by impossible love and abandoned in the wilderness.[31] Rhythmically, and even ritually, the same phrases are repeated to describe his 'stasis' (*tasammur*), as 'part of a neglected park' (*juzʾ min ḥadīqa muhmala*), 'under the rain' (*taḥt al-maṭar*), for 'ten long years' (*li-ᶜashar sanawāt ṭiwāl*).[32]

Alongside his embodiment of raw longing, Mukhtar also becomes a locus for satirising contemporary ideologies, as he transforms into a city landmark, debated by intellectuals and professors of philosophy, economics and psychology, all recently returned from abroad. For the philosophy professor, immersed in Sartrean angst, he represents existential nausea, while the economics professor is concerned with the consumer trends revealed in the litter around him.[33] For each, the knowledge acquired abroad runs into the dead-end of Mukhtar, consigning them, too, to endless 'chewing'. Condemning him as a 'monument' (*timthāl*) of reactionary capitalism, the Revolutionaries soon wade in, while the security services take up undercover residence opposite him and, like the professors, succumb to a decade of motionlessness.[34]

Through their ideological agendas, intellectuals, artists and security services fail to perceive Mukhtar's fundamental suffering, 'thirst' (*ᶜaṭash*) and 'wretchedness' (*būʾs*).[35] Instead, he becomes a 'specimen' (*ᶜayyina*), transformed into 'contradictory ideas that signified everything, except himself'.[36] With his name evoking that of national hero ᶜUmar al-Mukhtar, who was similarly appropriated into the Jamahiriyya's political ideology and propaganda, he allegorises the nation's frozen, frustrated potential. In Santner's words, he, and those around him, embody a 'creaturely stuckness' prompting melancholy laughter, as the various agendas and hidden traumas of each figure compel them to empty repetition, gathered, in stylised formation, around Mukhtar.[37] At such 'points of creatureliness', Santner suggests, 'the *nonsensical* aspect' of signifying stress 'assumes an aspect of utter and nonsensical purposelessness – of repetition compulsion as a weird sort of *comedy*'.[38]

Leaving the park, Fatima, in parallel, seeks social mobility through the underground chewing gum trade. All that awaits her, however, is a life of prostitution. In contrast to Nahid in *Biʾr al-Hurman*, she is not driven by repressed memories but, as the narrator asserts, fully conscious of her actions. Unlike Nahid, her story is never resolved and her desires never harmonised to those of the nation. Fatima, in fact, becomes devoid of human desire. During their courtship, Mukhtar eagerly searches her gaze for the 'glittering shine of desire' that never transpires, relegating him to his fate as a statue.[39] Meanwhile, chewing gum appropriates all of Fatima's desire, in a world where human relationships have been subsumed by commodification for want of other alternatives: 'She altered libidinously between lemon, mint, apple and any of the new flavours that came onto the market. The act of mastication affirmed her femininity and offered her an intense sense of fulfilment.'[40] While men become obsessed with her, Fatima turns from the promise of romance, domestication and community to the insular act of chewing, delighting in the physical experience of gum, a 'pleasure' (*mut^{c}a*) which she 'senses only' (*tuḥissuhā faqaṭ*).[41]

While seemingly divorced from broader domestic contexts, in a disorienting state of stasis, Fatima and Mukhtar's frustrated romance is further gradually woven into the wider fabric of Libyan society, first through their family histories and then through the park in which their romance takes place. Mukhtar's father is a retired high-ranking officer in the Royal Police Force, fervently faithful to the former Senussi monarchy and only reluctantly engaging with the new revolutionaries. Abandoning his wife and son, he moves to a farm outside Tripoli where he drinks and brings prostitutes. One of these prostitutes is Fatima, taking the novel, as the narrator declares, further into the melodramatic Arabic template.[42] Mukhtar's mother, meanwhile, waits, motionless, for the return of her former lover, ^{c}Umar, from Istanbul, where he trades in chewing gum. In her own state of stasis, she barely notices her son's absence, and parallel motionlessness. In contrast to the lengthier description of Mukhtar's parents, the fate of Fatima's middle-class family is then sparsely narrated in a few sentences. Following her descent into prostitution, her mother and father commit suicide and her brother abandons his fight for social equality, surrendering to robotic bureaucracy – and chewing – like the rest of society.

Chewing Gum

Originally called *Sarab al-Layl* (The Night Mirage), Bushnaf changed his novel's title to *al-^{c}Ilka* following its translation into English, moving away from the poetic image of 'mirage', evocative of desert geographies, and identifying gum at the heart of the novel as litterscape. A variation on motionlessness, chewing becomes the nation's 'overriding concern' (*shughl al-nās al-shāghil*), tantalisingly hinting at personal, social or political progress behind which a true lack of agency is concealed.[43] Born of the country's economic, political and social ruin, alongside its marginality within the global order, the underground chewing gum trade replaces all economic activity, with its value elevated 'to the status of a bond' (*arṣida maḍmūna*).[44] Two decades from the discovery of oil, Libya's population is depicted as having shifted from the struggle for subsistence to the frivolous excesses of pop culture, hiding a fundamental creaturely 'stuckness'.

As the narrator declares, the nation's preoccupation with gum, alongside the other consumerist inventory of bananas, jeans and pop music, reflects its premature state of 'postmodernity' (*mā baᶜd al-ḥadātha*).[45] While other Arab nations are immersed in debates over 'modernity, the arms race, Palestine, Arab unity, social justice, UN amendments, OPEC and the price of oil, and American and British conspiracies against Libya', Libya itself shifts into post-modern, intellectual 'chewing':

> In debates, leftists and rightists argued the finer points of the issue. The former were of the opinion that teeth were a metaphor for the human race while gum represented time, whereas the pessimistic rightists, or 'nihilists' as the leftists called them, upheld the view that the gum stood for human existence, while the teeth were eternity and the act of mastication a motion that would continue ad infinitum.[46]

As with Mukhtar, the intellectuals' rhetoric becomes entangled in the stasis of gum and, as they debate the possibility of human agency – do we chew or are we chewed? – the question arises as to whether gum stands for the meaninglessness of all existence or just the meaninglessness of life in al-Qadhafi's Libya. By extension, the question arises as to whether the narrator's 'story', and story in general, is inherently impossible or impossible only in Libya. Ultimately, both lead to the question of how the novel's and the nation's postmodernism might be understood within its broader excavation of the past, leading to the stasis of the present.

Set in the 1980s, the main events of *al-ᶜIlka* coincide with the heyday of postmodernism in Europe and North America, with new forms of art, architecture, film and narrative being theorised as a 'mode', 'condition' and 'logic', notoriously controversial and difficult to define. In his landmark 1984 essay, 'Postmodernism, or, the Cultural Logic of Late Capitalism', Fredric Jameson understands it as an outcome of the commodification of culture within a newly global and technological world, identifying various defining traits that resonate with *al-ᶜIlka.* Some of these include: a merging of elite and pop culture; a shift from modern concerns with 'depth' – typified by Freud's 'repressed' – to surfaces and multiplicities; a similar move from modern emotions of anxiety and alienation to 'intensities' and affects; and a weakening of historicity.[47] All are underpinned by a fundamental breakdown in the certainty of metanarrative, and a relativising of truth claims and totalising systems.

While hugely influential, Jameson's suggestions are by no means a conclusive statement on the postmodern. They do, however, chime with Fatima's emotionless chewing and Mukhtar's extreme, immobilising longing, as well as the mockery of al-Qaddus's 'talking cure' and the narrator's eschewal of 'novelistic posturing'. Above all, however, they chime with the commodified 'chewing' that overtakes the narrative, reflected in its fragmented structure and frustrated narrator. As Bushnaf states, 'chewing' was central to his first conception of the novel, which posits itself as the inevitable outcome of Libya's postmodern mode, with its 'impossible story' reflecting the breakdown of metanarrative. From newspaper to academic articles, photos, films, poems and paintings, *al-ᶜIlka* is filled with different forms of representation, all preoccupied with how life might be captured in art and 'our hero' put into words, onto canvas or into film. All, like the narrator's story, drift into the realm of chewing gum wrappers, littering the novel's pages. Those who embark on storytelling are further destined to motionlessness and marginality, an existential commentary, but also a real reflection on the concrete difficulty of telling stories in Libya and of having them heard, through marginalisation and threat of imprisonment. *Al-ᶜIlka* thus posits a brand of postmodernism born of tyranny, which compels confrontation with the limits of language, meaning and the human.

While the narrator suggests that this condition arose somewhat prematurely in Libya, and was characterised by particularly intense 'chewing', it resonates with the wider disaffection sweeping the Arab world from the 1960s, as the optimism of nationalism and Nasserism was replaced by the rise of Islamist ideologies and the outbreak of violent political confrontations. The concomitant shift in literary discourse, from the reassurance of realism to uncertain, fragmented representation, can certainly be understood as a postmodern 'mode', albeit marked by continued political commitment, rather than what Andreas Pflitsch suggests as the 'postmodern laissez-faire' of the West.[48] Expressing an overriding skepticism in political and religious ideologies, Arabic postmodernism, as Pflitsch suggests, is precisely located in the breakdown of metanarrative as political protest. Both deeply political and deeply despairing, *al-ᶜIlka* would seem to confirm this assessment, with its narrator's 'impossible story' infused with the immediate danger of speaking and acting, while also refusing to shy from a critical vision of the present, rooted in an awareness of the catastrophic past. This awareness, too, reflects broader trends within Arabic fiction, with Pflitsch observing how authors' interweaving of literary *turāth* and narrative experimentation upsets the neat boundaries of tradition and modernity, thereby formulating what might be understood as a specifically Arabic postmodern aesthetics.[49] In *al-ᶜIlka*, material, rather than literary, *turāth* is central. Aptly, Matar describes 'excavation and memory' as one of the novel's defining poetics, yet both are bound into an overriding awareness of fracture and obliteration, conveyed through the rubble of Mukhtar's park and the turbulent fate of his beloved statue.[50]

The Park

Describing the 1920 Paul Klee monoprint, 'Angelus Novus', Benjamin formulates his best-known statement on natural history through the 'angel of history' entangled in 'debris'. Suggestive of the relationship between *al-ᶜIlka's* statue – and, indeed, of Mukhtar as statue – and the 'debris' in which they are located, the statement goes:

> This is how one pictures the angel of history. His face is turned toward the past. Where we perceive a chain of events, he sees one single catastrophe which keeps piling wreckage upon wreckage and hurls it in front of his feet. The angel would like to stay, awaken the dead, and make whole what has been smashed. But a storm is blowing from Paradise; it has got caught in his wings with such violence that the angel can no longer close them. The storm irresistibly propels him into the future to which his back is turned, while the pile of debris before him grows skyward. This storm is what we call progress.[51]

In *al-ᶜIlka*, the 'debris' that constitutes Mukhtar's park set his and Fatima's romance within a broad historical perspective, conveyed through fragmented and loosely contained stories, evocative of the phantomic traces of al-Ghazal's *al-Khawf* and its haunted palm grove. Frequented by prostitutes, drug dealers, Sufi charlatans and, of course, Mukhtar, it is a marginal, heterotopic space which nevertheless reflects the land's transformations across the centuries, from peasants' farmland to pashas' pleasure park, the battleground between Libyans and Italians, and the elegant Italian garden from which Libyans are barred. During the Senussi monarchy, it witnesses the police's violent backlash against student protesters and, under the Revolutionaries, becomes a neglected rubbish dump, following the botched nationalisation of the sanitation company. Finally, an Environmentalist, recently returned from the USA, grants it a new lease of life, leading, among other initiatives, to a 'Flower Security Squad' (*jiḥāz amn al-zuhūr*), imposing fines on any who pick its blossoms.[52] In each era, the narrator concludes, the garden is built on the 'debris' (*anqāḍ*) of previous orders and survival becomes its defining feature.[53] Destroyed by Bedouin raids and European naval assaults and submerged by the sea, it remains a 'refuge' (*malādh*) for poets, lovers and drug dealers and, 'in spite of everything, it remains a park'.[54]

The park is haunted, above all, by the ghosts of women raped, murdered or imprisoned within it, situating the fate of static Mukhtar and chewing Fatima in a genealogy of violent desire. One woman, caught by her husband with a pasha, transpires to be Mukhtar's great-grandmother, who, after the consequent murder of both husband and lover, wanders the park mad, before being found dead in the fourth year of Italian occupation. Another story concerns a singer from Fezzan, killed by another vengeful pasha, and whose songs of 'longing' (*ḥanīn*) haunt the city women, offering solace when 'places begin to suffocate them, and they long to fly away'.[55] Dramatising Libya's conflicted history, from the chaos of the nineteenth century, the women contextualise the park's current condition, in which all have retreated to their private spaces and personal chewing. Representing the collective trauma of past events, rooted in imperial, colonial and patriarchal violence, the women's stories provide the backdrop to new forms of power and surveillance.

These new, particularly modern, forms are the last to be excavated within the park as a network of gazes, directed endlessly onwards, without reciprocity. This is exemplified in one of the security services' many photos of Mukhtar, likened to a Salvador Dalí painting, and capturing all professors, intellectuals and security services, frozen in time, gazing at one another and constellated around Mukhtar:

> The first Director appears, observing the Director recently returned from Hungary, who in turn is observing our hero, followed by the Professor of Economics recently returned from America and the Professor of Philosophy

> recently returned from France. A journalist is also present, and a security agent. The security patrol considered this photograph to be the best, not knowing that they, too, were part of a larger canvas.[56]

Subsuming the aesthetics of surrealism, like that of postmodernism, within the absurdity of a surveilled state, the photo captures a nation in which human relationships have collapsed, with the shadow of dictatorship over all. Within it, all are simultaneously exposed to dominant structures of power and excluded from them, while the statue emerges as the frightening and ultimately futile potential of breaking out of these systems and opening history to alternative readings.

The Statue

As the narrator repeats, the statue channels the curse of the nineteenth century, recognised across the Arab world as the period of *nahḍa* (renaissance) and rooted in rising nationalist consciousness and processes of social, economic and political modernisation. In Libya, waning Ottoman control, exemplified by the pasha's pleasure park, was threatened by the colonial encroachment of France, Great Britain and finally Italy, with the Banco di Roma expanding its control over commerce, industry and agriculture. Meanwhile, the ascetic religious and political force of the Senussi grew in Cyrenaica. Out of this confluence of waning and growing powers, the statue is born, offering yet simultaneously denying the promise of nationhood, to be followed only by the continued operation of absolute power. A nexus for the novel's depiction of love, desire and madness, negotiating the fragile imagined community, the statue's immobilising influence on all those who encounter it disrupts straightforward notions of affiliation and identity through physical experiences of desire, longing and captivity. In other words, it exemplifies the ekphrastic, creaturely impulse of the Libyan novel, from Girl and Gazelle to prehistoric cave art to Bin Lamin's melancholy 'beings'.

The statue is housed in Libya's national Red Palace Museum, displaying artefacts from prehistory to the twentieth century. However, as the narrator declares, the statue, unlike the park, reflects none of the wider changes to Libyan society and cannot be neatly relegated to any one symbolic system. Carved by an Italian prisoner of the pasha in the dungeons of the Red

Palace, it is affiliated with no aesthetic school but simply sculpted according to its creator's 'pain' (*alam*) and 'longing' (*ḥanīn*), and expressing his subjection to stifling heat, bitter cold and longing for affection, comfort and freedom.[57] As in the myth of Pygmalion, the sculptor becomes infatuated with his creation, which, following his fluctuating moods, embodies both 'surrender' (*istislām*) and 'headiness' (*tahawwur*).[58] With head thrown back, eyes closed, and mouth formed into the longing expectation of a kiss, the statue is, as the narrator emphasises, a 'living being' (*kāʾin ḥayy*), which gains its life through 'the eyes, emotions and imagination of its audience'.[59] After the prisoner's death, the statue embarks on what the narrator calls 'its own journey through time', proving of little worth to the Italians, British, monarchists or revolutionaries.[60] In the 1970s, it is supposed to be transported to Leptis Magna with Septimius Severus, but is instead abandoned in the dungeons of the Red Palace, in 'a corridor between and outside every age' (*mamarr bayn wa-khārij kull al-ᶜuṣūr*).[61] Eventually, an archaeology professor attempts to claim it as the work of an early Libyan, but cannot verify his nationalist hypotheses, exposing him to professional ridicule. Repelling all ideological claims, the statue, like Fatima, frustrates the symbolic equating of woman, nation and heritage, expressing only history's chaotic pain, madness and longing. Combining the essence of Da Vinci's *Mona Lisa* with Michelangelo's *David*, it blurs all dichotomies: 'Our statue is an embodiment of smoothness and violence, stillness and propulsion, pleasure and pain, the angelic and the demonic, the feminine and the masculine, all dryads born in captivity, in the absence of freedom.'[62]

Through its blurring of dichotomies, the statue induces intense infatuations and mad desire in all men who encounter it, whether Italian, Sicilian, American or Libyan. Caught in the paradigmatic immobility of the *aṭlāl*, the men pleasure themselves before it, turning, like Mukhtar, to *kharāb* (ruination), as, in seeking to escape history through the statue's impossible dualities, they are simultaneously excluded from it.[63] Mukhtar himself locates the desire and surrender that Fatima withholds in it, while Fatima realises he can relate to her only as he relates to it – an impossible, static idol. For Mukhtar, the statue offers escape from stasis, not, like Fatima and her gum, in the future, but in a relic of the past that simultaneously offers escape from that past. Like Fatima's gum, however, this escape proves deceptive, as the statue, like gum, leads only to greater immobility:

> He would spread his arms as if to hug the stone woman. It was as though she were running towards him without ever reaching him, while he could never bring himself to embrace her. From that fateful moment, long before the Professor of Philosophy returned from France, his existence could be summed up as a slow succumbing to the fate of the 'existential gum' (*wujūd ᶜilka*).[64]

Offering the utopic promise of reciprocal, consummated desire, outside of all 'ages', the statue simultaneously refuses it through its eternally expectant lips. Like Fatima, its eyes are alluring but unresponsive, mirroring the insular gazes of the security service's photo, and depicting human relationships, once again, as fragmented chewing. Through complex processes of narrative mirroring, both Fatima and Mukhtar become bound to the statue, conveying the lifelessness of the present through the animation of the past, and dramatising the impossibility of any harmonious 'embrace'. Like chewing gum, the statue ultimately ends up as another layer of rubble as, freed from stasis by a psychology professor who diagnoses his condition as the product of childhood stuttering, Mukhtar uses his newfound mobility to smash it.[65] After locating Fatima in a coffee shop, changed beyond recognition through a life of prostitution and chewing, he rushes in panic to the statue, 'flinging his arms around it so violently that it fell to the floor and shattered in pieces'.[66] With this collapse, the novel concludes, suggesting, on the one hand, a potential liberation from the 'curse of the nineteenth century', and, on the other, the fate of wider Libyan *turāth*, subjected to acts of destructive annihilation that transform it from longing and desire into mute rubble. In the final paragraph, Mukhtar, the 'hero', becomes a vague 'memory' (*dhikrā*), described, once again, as 'exhausted and emaciated' (*mutᶜab wa-hazīl*), as he roams, stuttering, through the city streets.[67]

Returning to Freud, through the psychology professor's identification of Mukhtar's repressed malady, the narrator proposes stuttering (*al-taʾtaʾa*) and, by extension, shattering as 'the escape route that we propose for our text'.[68] As the wider novel suggests, however, no such escape is possible. As in Qanāw's 'ᶜAwdat al-Qaysar', the statue's departure, conveyed through the bitter humour and 'strange madness' that Bushnaf associates with Libyan fiction, poignantly emphasises the people left in its wake, in continued states of exception, as history escapes and can no longer inform the present. In the writing of both authors, who remained in Libya for most or, in the case of Bushnaf, all their lives, heritage is first reclaimed through shared experiences of vulnerability and then irrevocably lost. As Bushnaf states, his statue was inspired by a real counterpart, which he spent hours contemplating in a real park, binding his own precarity, as author, to that of the nation's *turāth*, and demonstrating how personal connections, rather than grand narratives, emerge through shared experiences of neglect, exposure and vulnerability.[69] As an alternative historical storehouse, *al-ᶜIlka* shatters the museum's solemn veneration, revealing the states of exception that lie behind the acceptable face of modern nationhood. From the park, Mukhtar moves to vagrancy while, entering the 2000s, shops fill with shampoo, bananas and magazines, and chewing gum triumphs over the stasis which, deep down, is synonymous with it.[70]

As an allegory of Libya's collapse, the novel therefore emerges through the collapse of allegory into the 'catastrophic pileup' of the past.[71] Echoing the incomprehensible cries of gazelles, jerboas and camels in the wider Libyan novel, Mukhtar's 'stuttering' concludes the search for 'story' through the visceral disintegration of human communication as, like so many Libyan 'heroes', he is left empty-handed and homeless. Tracing the fragments of Italian, Roman and prehistoric *turāth*, the novel dramatises, as recompense, the strange affiliations born of passion and vulnerability, through the disorienting coming together of humans' vital bodies and the 'thingness' of mute, historical *aṭlāl*. As the consumerist goods of a globalised world infiltrate their way into the closed state, the present, like the past, is conceived as *kharāb*, perennially excluded, and with the eroded fragments of history covered by the artificial permanence of litter. Titled *Chewing Gum* and with its English edition mimicking a Wrigley's packet, the novel eschews metanarrative in favour of commodified gum, presenting itself, like the subjects it depicts, as entangled in global capitalism and, like its statue, as a simultaneous product of exclusion.

Weaving these images into a complex genealogy of postmodern existence within totalitarianism, Bushnaf's 'litterscape' posits itself as the inevitable outcome of nineteenth-century demons, excavated through a narrator whose struggling 'story-less-ness' evokes both the precarity of speaking freely in Libya and past traumas that immobilise the present. As a rare work of Libyan fiction to have come to international attention, *al-ᶜIlka* resonates with an expectation of marginality and silence, initially confirmed by its immediate banning. Nevertheless, it asserts itself despite its 'impossible story', indicating the pressing need to recuperate narrative and reinstate agency, no matter the void to which they may be destined. Through its central images, of homelessness, hunger and stasis, it further resonates with broader trends in the 2000s, and, perhaps above all, with al-Asfar's writing, in which narrative is similarly self-conscious and haunted by creaturely signs of misplaced, neglected histories, while writing is likened not to the repetition of chewing gum, but the improvised nourishment of *sharmūla*.

Sharmula: The Novel as Nourishment

In a 2008 review of *al-ᶜIlka*, al-Asfar describes it as the first 'semiotic Libyan novel': 'Each of its narrative components – characters, settings, timeframes – is packed with signs (*dalālāt*), intersecting in a tightly-spun ball – a ball of coloured gum that's chewed, blown into a bubble and popped, so chewing might be resumed.'[72] As his words suggest, Bushnaf and al-Asfar share a similar dark humour and teasing use of word play. However, while the former's 'chewing gum' is suggestive of compulsive return to haunting preoccupations, the latter's '*sharmūla*' represents a more diffuse symbolic structure, inviting the reader to dip in and out of its various threads and evoking Miriam Cooke's definition of dissident writing as, 'not agenda-driven but improvisational', twisting and turning down unexpected paths.[73] Through food, this improvisation takes on a creaturely aspect, rooted in shared hunger and unquestioning acts of hospitality, beyond the 'stuckness' of dictatorship.

This is not, however, to neglect the darker aspects of al-Asfar's fiction concerning the horror of the regime's abuses and, particularly, its oppression of Benghazi as a 'rebel city'. Like *al-ᶜIlka*, *Sharmula* depicts a panorama of urban society, juxtaposing Benghazi's rich intellectual history and famed openness to the subdued ruins of the 2000s. Known as *rabāyat al-dhāyiḥ* (the wanderer's refuge), the city became famous in the late 1940s for opening its doors to refugees from the drought-ridden west as, while police were sent to expel them, locals left their doors unlocked. In 1955, the city then became home, alongside Tripoli, to Libya's first university, producing a flourishing literary community, exemplified by al-Nayhum and *al-Haqiqa*. Theatre flourished, too, and al-Asfar recalls seeing Bushnaf's name on posters across the city, announcing shows which he attended religiously.[74] Alongside the 'slow violence' of urban decay, Benghazi soon, however, became subject to open hostility, as al-Qadhafi perceived it to be a stronghold for support of the former monarchy, and a hub of resistance. Most of the victims of Abu Salim hailed from there, while in the 1990s, responding to the rise of Islamist opposition, al-Qadhafi besieged the city and napalmed the surrounding land. 'Benghazi residents', Chorin writes, 'recall the presence of military men with machine guns at intersections, barricades managed by Revolutionary Guard members, all of which stood in stark contrast to the calm, controlled atmosphere in Tripoli.'[75]

Evoking Benghazi as 'other' to the regime, al-Asfar formulates his poetics around the centripetal, vulnerable and resistant. 'I hate capital cities', he declares; 'I hate centrality and power. I love weakness that refuses defeat. I love trees that resist the wind, dancing and swaying to its force.'[76] Embodying this impulse, *Sharmula* is narrated by a fictionalised al-Asfar, meandering through neighbourhoods from al-Ruwaysat, where he grew up, to Maqha ᶜAyn al-Ghazala, his regular cafe and literary haunt. Constructing a progressively fuller picture of the city, he visits and revisits places, connecting them to one another and resituating them within local memory, while also alluding to the 'Popular Security Points' and other centres of institutional power – including the Centre for the Study of the Green Book – that now disrupt the landscape. Like *al-ᶜIlka*, the novel is devoid of private, domestic space, as the narrator 'scribbles' (*ukharbish*) in different locations, refusing to remain still.[77] For al-Asfar, writing and life are synonymous, and he cites Moroccan author, Muhammad Shukri (1935–2003), as exemplifying the 'regular, truthful writer, who writes like he lives'.[78] Refusing to bind his novel to the parameters of plot, structural fluidity becomes a counter-narrative to the monolithic, and a literal, literary flight from censorship and the extreme control that, al-Asfar writes, the regime exerted over individual lives: 'Even sex was regulated: many people couldn't marry until the regime organized a mass wedding or they were "gifted" a bedroom for the wedding night.'[79]

Refusing the label of intellectual (*muthaqqaf*), al-Asfar further disavows membership of the Libyan Writers' Union, revealing its corruption in uncompromising detail. Instead, he asserts himself as a '*kātib sharmūlī*' (*sharmūla* writer), 'with no connection to your newspapers, your magazines or your blogs, your "culture", your "media", or your "literary soirees".'[80] A local Benghazi salad, *sharmūla* is central to his aesthetics of writing as life. Unlike gum, it represents not commodity fetishism within political and economic stagnation, but nourishment, locality and improvisation. A mix of tomato, onion, pepper, cucumber, garlic and olive oil, it is 'simple folks' food' (*qūt al-busaṭāʾ*), and the novel opens with a lengthy description of its preparation and consumption. 'It's the food of gatherings, and the nourishment of unbounded joy and love', al-Asfar asserts, 'I have never eaten *sharmūla* alone.'[81] An exemplary form of '*rizq*' (sustenance), *sharmūla* becomes a locus of social and, indeed, ecological holism, as al-Asfar describes eating it with his wife, Amal, on the beach:

> After dousing the vegetables in the sea, we crush them in the hollow of a rock, adding olive oil, but dispensing with salt from the nearby marshes. Seawater suffices. Eating our fill from the plate of the earth, we give thanks to God. A scoop for you, a scoop for me and a scoop for our daughter, Muhja, a twinkle in our eyes. One more for the hungry who roam around us, and whom we sense but do not see. We eat, and gaze towards the horizon.[82]

Celebrating the 'decent' (*ṭayyib*), *sharmūla* evokes a community that exists beyond structures of power, while also, like chewing gum, becoming a metaphor for writing as '*tasharmīl*', eschewing 'linguistic posturing' (*al-ḥadhlaqa al-lughawiyya*), which al-Asfar describes as the 'dictatorship of the eloquent' (*diktātūriyya al-balīgh*), and instead nourishing a community of readers.[83] 'The reader is not a vessel into which we can pour our narcissistic views', he declares to Tripoli poet Rāmiz al-Nuwayṣirī (b.1972) in an excerpted interview that concludes the novel. 'We must', he continues, 'create readers with love, and invite them to write with us.'[84] Conflating 'words' with 'garlic', 'onions' and 'tomatoes', al-Asfar 'crushes' and 'mixes' his writing, 'adding whatever I like to my *sharmūla*'.[85] Within this heterogeneous mix are anecdotes of real and fictional characters, extracts from poetry and interviews conducted between al-Asfar and other authors and artists. Despite his disavowal of the 'intellectual', he exemplifies the intertextual impulse of the Libyan novel, creating literary versions of fellow authors and, beyond his fiction, writing prolific analyses of their work. In what follows, I track the narrative strands through which this polyphony emerges, from the animated figure of a carved gazelle, which al-Asfar pursues through the city, to local football matches and, finally, the literary community, caught between semiotics, censorship and 'signs'.

ᶜUmar al-Mukhtar's Gazelle

Appearing at unexpected junctures across the city and novel, al-Asfar's gazelle becomes, like al-Kuni's *waddān* and Bushnaf's statue, his literary familiar, through which he expresses buried emotions and forgotten histories. Affixed to the wall of Maqha ᶜAyn al-Ghazala, her carved figure haunts him, and he frequently imagines dialogues with her. Conveying 'calm' (*sakīna*) and 'dignity' (*waqār*), the gazelle's eyes further become a melancholy witness to Benghazi's degradation, as al-Asfar imagines her coming to life, 'shaking her short tail and her head, and bounding from the café, as I pursue her musky scent across Jamal Abdul Nasser Street'.[86] Every day, the gazelle journeys to the tomb of ᶜUmar al-Mukhtar, fifty-five kilometres south of Benghazi, in Suluq. In 1976, the hero's remains were relocated there, where he was executed, from their mausoleum in Benghazi. In the 2000s, the beloved mausoleum itself was then bulldozed overnight.[87] As with Septimius Severus, al-Mukhtar threatened al-Qadhafi's status as the nation's sole spiritual guide, and, as Mattawa sums up, the regime 'has given the old man no rest'.[88]

The gazelle's daily tour nevertheless resituates al-Mukhtar's remains at the heart of memory and map. 'Every day', al-Asfar writes, 'the gazelle journeys south to Suluq, where she arrives at the tomb of the martyr, Shaykh ᶜUmar al-Mukhtar. Grubby with dust, from the land where the hero was hung, she returns, weeping, to places rooted in pain.'[89] Through the gazelle's tears, the cartography of her tour becomes peppered with recent and historical suffering. After passing the Institute for the Disabled, she nears the Children's Hospital and weeps alongside its ghostly inhabitants who, as with reference to Suluq, resonate with hidden protest. In 1998, 453 Benghazi children were infected with HIV while at the hospital. While the regime blamed its Bulgarian and Palestinian medical staff, condemning them to imprisonment and death, the incident remains without proper investigation or international media coverage.[90] 'The case', Chorin writes, 'was highly symbolic and emotional, as it involved so many innocent children, an illness for which there is probably no greater taboo in the Middle East, and Benghazi, whose people already felt highly persecuted and underserved by the Libyan regime.'[91] As the EU and USA normalised relations with Libya, the medics' release was secured through compensatory payments, while international medical assessment deemed the incident to be most likely the result of poor hygiene procedures in the hospital. As with so many chapters of Libya's history, it remains shrouded in conjecture, with many even suspecting the regime's involvement.[92] Through the gazelle's compassionate tears, it is woven together with the Cement Factory, 'belching out poisonous dust', and the psychiatric hospital, 'shaking with screams and hysterical laughter'.[93]

Arriving at al-Mukhtar's tomb, the gazelle finds consolation. 'In Suluq', she tells al-Asfar, 'I rub off the worries that cling to my honeyed coat on the Shaykh's tomb, and keep him company awhile.'[94] To cheer the old man up, the gazelle recites the 'Qasidat al-Nakhla' ('Poem of the Date Palm') by oral poet al-Ḥājja Mabrūka ᶜAraysh, a vibrant celebration of Libyan ecology and history, 'overflowing with goodness, shade, water, transparency, health and belief'.[95] Combining praise of God with prayers for al-Mukhtar, the poem celebrates how each part of the date palm is used for food, tools and shelter, representing an antidote to the industrial, surveilled city.[96] Al-Asfar's *Sharmula* emulates this poem while, like Bushnaf's statue, the gazelle becomes a companion to the marginalised. 'I love you', al-Asfar declares, 'I love accompanying you on your outings, and slumbering next to you, an eternal carving on the wall. I'm bored of this life. I'm fed up with humans' glum faces, spent with dissimulation.'[97] Through the gazelle's 'tour', she conveys what Santner calls 'acts of testimony and transmission', operating through 'chance' and opening up the possibility of 'encounter and engagement'.[98]

ᶜAbd al-Jalil is chief among the other characters 'encountered' and 'transmitted' by the gazelle. A folk singer and local football hero, he exemplifies the 'decency' of Benghazi's 'simple folk', and his biography provides the novel's opening episodes:

> ᶜAbd al-Jalil was a human, firm, decent and blessed with wit. Lavishly generous, his door was never shut, nor would his visitors go empty-handed. [. . .] 'God gives to those who give', he would say, and ᶜAbd al-Jalil gave of everything: love; friendship; money; blood; food; and cigarettes.[99]

Through ᶜAbd al-Jalil, football, like *sharmūla*, becomes a celebration of local Benghazi, as, playing for the local team, al-Hurriya, in the 1970s, he attracts rapturous crowds:

> The playing fields of al-Muhishi will forever echo with that throng of gifted players, bringing the ball to life, and making it sing. Their feet played tunes on the fresh grass, and the ball passed between them, dancing slickly and madly. The pitch wasn't then fenced off. Spectators sat on the grass, a meter or so from the action. Sons perched on fathers' shoulders, legs dangling, heels thumping against chests, and hands clamped around necks as they yelled, 'Jalil! Jalil!'[100]

Through their movement, the players 'bring the ball to life and make it sing' (*yastanṭiqūn al-kura wa-yajᶜalūnahā tughannī*). Unlike the animated statues and mournful animals of the wider Libyan novel, it communicates immediate joy, with no thought of past or future as it flies between their feet.

In keeping with the novel's allusive symbolism, football also, however, hints at darker realities. From local community, it is incorporated within spectacles of dominance, surveillance and violence. Al-Qadhafi abhorred the collective watching of sports, particularly as they began to attract greater viewing numbers than his own televised speeches. While matches became devoid of commentary, players would be referred to by number rather than name.[101] Soon, this silent neglect escalated, as the leader's third son, al-Saᶜidi al-Qadhafi (b.1973), began playing for Tripoli's al-Ahli, and football became a proxy war between al-Qadhafi and the growing opposition. While regime-sponsored teams secured questionable victories, the opposition retaliated, with football becoming, as Mattawa puts it, 'an arena where the public could show loyalty to something other than the regime'.[102] A particularly bitter match in 2000, between Benghazi's al-Ahli and the regime-backed al-Akhdar, led to violent protests, which were allegedly a direct catalyst in the bulldozing of both al-Mukhtar's tomb and the al-Ahli stadium.[103] Al-Asfar thus weaves together a web of suppressed and unspoken incidents, through various intermediaries: through football, as a memory of collective joy; through the gazelle, as symbolic of compassion and beauty; and through *sharmūla*, as symbolic of unbounded hospitality.

ᶜAbd al-Jalil, meanwhile, dedicates his later years to coaching the Benghazi club, al-Sawaᶜid, helping the young players navigate life within the Jamahiriyya, as he gifts students money and helps soldiers secure leave. He is, nevertheless, doomed to solitude as, after catching his players shirking training, he resigns. Without family, and suffering from chronic paralysis, he sits in his wheelchair in the rain, as the gazelle runs past. Echoing *al-ᶜIlka's* Mukhtar, he becomes a static observer of a rapidly changing city, 'discarded on the pavement, like a lump of rock or rusty can'.[104] Addressing the gazelle, he similarly seeks solace in the non-human:

> I often sing to the gazelle, hoping she will turn, stop and sing for me. Oh gazelle, take me to a brook, running by a palm grove, carpeted in soft grass, and scattered with henna. Cement has overtaken us, and ashes have suffocated the green. The Cement Factory vomits dusty destruction, and brooks have become sewers, spewed out by our consumption (*istihlāk*) and our ruin (*halāk*). I sing often to the gazelle, hoping she will turn, stop and sing for me. The passers-by don't stop, hurrying past without recognition. I have, by God, become a stranger (*ṣirtu gharīban*).[105]

Bearing him imaginatively across the city, the gazelle connects ᶜAbd al-Jalil to al-Asfar, who, on her instructions, pushes him to al-Ruwaysat where both grew up.[106] Turning down forgotten streets, mingling smells are evoked in loving detail, composed of 'clover, kerosene, coal, straw and barley' and 'mixed with the chirping of birds in cages and trees'.[107]

A powerful symbol in Arabic poetry, of love, beauty and divine union, the gazelle, as creaturely sign, juxtaposes Benghazi's dust and fumes, a metamorphosing literary familiar, formed from characters' memories and imaginings. As it transpires, ᶜAbd al-Jalil's relationship with her goes back to childhood, when he would visit her in Benghazi zoo. Through his progressive stasis, he releases her from the memory of her cage, allowing her to spirit him through the city as, once again, inversions of human and animal, animate and inanimate, formulate movement, vitality and protest. Assuming a first-person perspective, ᶜAbd al-Jalil describes how he stood in the zoo, 'contemplating the gazelle for hours, and singing elegies of silence' (*mawāwīl al-ṣamt*), mourning her captivity.[108] 'And now', he continues, 'she contemplates me, when once I stood and contemplated her. Times have changed, and she contemplates me, paralysed in my chair.'[109]

The Writers' Union: Between Semiotics, Censorship and sharmūla

Alongside ᶜAbd al-Jalil, *Sharmula* sings of many unsung heroes, from nurses to cleaners to folk dancers animating wedding parties. Anchored in the daily struggles of their existence, they exemplify al-Asfar's assertion that 'stories need bodies, and bodies need stories' (*al-ḥikāya taḥtāj ilā jasad wa-l-jasad yaḥtāj ilā ḥikāya*).[110] Young struggling authors represent a particularly important layer, seeking their daily *rizq* in the world of media and publishing.[111] In exchange for a cup of coffee, aspiring writer ᶜIzz al-Din brings al-Asfar a stolen pen every day, and filches the novels of al-Nayhum, al-Kuni and, in an ironic twist, al-Asfar himself from prosperous bookshops.[112] Unwilling to bow to bureaucracy, he is reduced to vagrancy and lawlessness, as what, al-Asfar asserts, is the only means of remaining creative within the Jamahiriyya. 'There is', he concludes, 'a secret to stolen ink.'[113]

The official face of the literary scene is, in contrast, depicted in bitingly satirical terms, through the cultural and media organisations housed in al-Muntada al-Idhaᶜi (The Media Club), and the corrupt election for leadership of the Writers' Union. The first candidate, Zaᶜbur al-Saᶜi, secures votes by lavishing food and prostitutes on fellow members, while withdrawing first the 'membership card' and then the 'blood' of any who question the principles of 'freedom, socialism and unity'.[114] A fictional character, *zaᶜbūr* signifies 'cheater' and *sāᶜin* 'slanderer'. Against him is the real-life Salih Qadirbuh (b.1975), a young and talented poet, whose embrace of free verse engenders his endless 'marginalisation and mockery' (*al-tahmīsh wa-l-istihzāʾ*).[115] During his campaign speech, he reads a poem, 'Mamnūᶜ al-Ibtisāma' ('Smiling Forbidden'), in which the repeated phrase, 'Rāʾiḥat al- . . .' ('The scent of . . .') opens each line.[116] Some lines evoke political oppression, from 'The scent of jail cells, their inhabitants unknown', to 'The scent of names erased from the Civil Registry'. Others convey the melancholy of industrial ruin, from 'The scent of a kitten, crushed on rusting train tracks', to 'The scent of machines, piled in a factory'. Others concern cultural stagnation, from 'The scent of badly translated novels' to 'The scent of boredom'. A catalogue of vulnerability, the poem ordains its own fate, as, with tissues over noses, complaining of its bad 'scent', the audience leave Maqha ᶜAyn al-Ghazala en masse. Only the gazelle responds, weeping and leaving behind the dejected Salih to visit Suluq.[117]

Through each candidate, al-Asfar pits integrity against corruption, before revealing the eventual complicity of all. Salih, it transpires, is supported by the regime-backed Abu Jubur who, like all 'revolutionary men', has a guiding hand in countless businesses and initially supports Salih.[118] From the root *j-b-r*, his name, like the majority of fictional figures in the novel, is satirically loaded, connoting both 'to help up' and 'to force, compel'.[119] Moreover, al-Asfar asserts, whoever wins the elections will not enjoy power for long. 'Literature', he asserts, 'is like the revolution, it never settles down, and is always renewing itself, so as not to become stagnant.'[120] Mimicking the official rhetoric used by the regime to justify its erratic policies, he reveals the necessity of constant movement, navigating the precarity of literature and of life. Just as the leader of the Writers' Union can dissolve individual membership, so can the People's Court dissolve the Union, escalating all the way to the Minister of Culture, whose interests, belying his title, lie in 'security (*al-amnī*) rather than culture (*al-thaqāfī*)'.[121]

The transformation of reading and writing, from the 'cultural' to the 'security', traverses *Sharmula*. Representing the inverse of literary creativity, Abu Jubur is one of many who alters and erases, writing not novels but 'reports' (*taqārīr*). Slapstick journalists-turned-censors, Abu Isba[c] (Mr Finger) and al-Zarzur (The Starling) oversee these 'security readings', through the 'revolutionising' (*tathwīr*) of whatever passes their way.[122] 'Whatever newspaper or magazine you open', al-Asfar writes, 'you find The Starling. Whatever radio you switch on you find him chirping [. . .] He cheeps on literature, chirrups on Sufism and peeps on painting, politics and the culinary arts . . .'[123] Like his own *tasharmīl*, al-Asfar uses verbs from each name, *taṣabbu*[c] (to finger) and *tazarzur* (to chirp), to evoke the semiotic tyranny of the Jamahiriyya. Over several pages, he depicts both men interpreting a poem about a bird and a worm, 'fingering' it as subversive and 'chirping' of how it undermines the revolution, while neglecting its central image of bodily and existential yearning.[124] Scattered across the novel, from the description of al-Asfar's childhood encounter with a blind hoopoe to the poem itself, images of birds and traps are symbolic of the natural world more broadly, infused with a freedom for which humans yearn, yet liable to literal and semiotic traps.[125]

Juxtaposing this creaturely imagery is a cast of burlesque revolutionary men, through whom al-Asfar diagnoses the ills of literary criticism, creativity and 'signs', compounding the freighted nature of *āyāt*, *ᶜalāmāt* and *asrār* in the likes of al-Kuni and al-Ghazal. During an excerpted radio interview, famous 'semiotician' (*sīmiyāʾī*), ᶜAbd Nafsuh, describes his practice through Sufi terminology, as the 'science of signs and signals' (*ᶜilm dalālāt wa-ᶜalāmāt*), rooted in 'divination and pursuit of traces' (*al-firāsa wa-iqtifāʾ al-athr*).[126] He also, however, describes the semiotician as the 'detective of literature' (*baṣṣāṣat al-adab*), a reality dramatised by his young protégé-turned-competitor, Fathallah, who offers the security services both an 'impressionistic' and 'semiotic' description of the daily movements of a visiting Moroccan academic.[127] In a yet more evocative instance, ᶜIzz al-Din listens to a radio interview with none other than al-Kuni, concerning 'the sanctity of silence and crisis of expression' (*qadāsat al-ṣamt wa-miḥnat al-taᶜbīr*).[128] Though the interview is not described in detail, it evokes the resonant 'signs' of al-Kuni's work as a celebration of silence and a commentary on censorship. His interviewers, however, do little to unpack this. Demanding to know why al-Kuni cites the Bible rather than the Hadith, and why he does not address 'Palestine and other Arab issues', one proposes the titular stone of *Nazif al-Hajar* to signify the rocks hurled during the Intifadas, and the *waddān* to symbolise the young boy, Muḥammad al-Ḍurra, killed by Israeli gunfire in 2000.[129]

Through these portraits, part fictional and part real, al-Asfar depicts the barriers to literary creativity and, indeed, to reading in Libya. 'There are so many projects that have been aborted or miscarried when they were only beginning to stumble and crawl', he laments. 'In the clearest terms: apart from al-Nayhum and al-Kuni, Libyan literature is decidedly ordinary.'[130] In creaturely terms, he describes fiction as a child that cannot be protected, crawling uncertainly forward. His *Sharmula* counters this struggle, reanimating the literary community and portraying many characters who would be familiar only to fellow Libyans, or even Benghazians, in a defiantly local aesthetics. As he insists, he writes not for renown but survival, in the hopes of nourishing readers. While *al-ᶜIlka* represents an alternative historical storehouse of jumbled signs, al-Asfar's *Sharmula* thus represents an alternative forum for literary history, criticism and autobiography.

Occasionally, however, al-Asfar must sour his *Sharmula* by tales of 'fingers' and 'starlings', shifting from football to 'heartball, tongueball and neckball', and breaking the narrative flow with intermittent, elliptical lament:

> What is left after all this pain? What is left after ropes have strangled you, bullets riddled you, and acid melted you? What is left after the blood?
>
> . . .
>
> What?
>
> . . .
>
> I hear nothing[131]

Within the heterogeneous, joyous abundance of al-Asfar's *Sharmula*, silence and a barely articulated cry sometimes win, hinting at the interstices of vulnerability that render the novel necessary. Escalating acts of disappearance, torture and execution are mixed with food, gazelle and football, productive of the novel's improvisational dissidence as it challenges, evades and pokes fun at semiotic tyranny.

In the novel's conclusion, al-Asfar's wife, Amal, goes into labour with their first daughter, Muhja, leading to a mad yet life-affirming dash through the city, led by his gazelle and aided, in his penniless state, by friends and acquaintances. As with so many Libyan novels, paternity is presented as a precarious business. Al-Asfar must, he reflects, finish his *Sharmula* soon, to send it with friends to the Cairo Book Fair in the hopes of finding a publisher as, ironically enough, his writing denies him the very sustenance which is its theme. As he observes in an interview, his vision of himself as 'writer' is premised on the seeming marginality of the 'footnote' and a deliberate embrace of the weak yet resistant:

> I only mix with people when I need money, begging a few dinars in exchange for my novels and stories. Otherwise, I sit alone, or wander aimlessly. Even when I'm near people, I can't hear them. My hearing is weak, and I refuse the treatment that my wife and friends insist on. I like being deaf. I like everything that absents me, that relegates me to a rogue footnote, dislocated from any text (*hāmish tāʾih lā matn lahu*).[132]

In contrast to the Jamahiriyya's prying eyes and pricked ears, al-Asfar dulls his senses, allowing those around him to do and say what they like. Declaring, in *Sharmula*, that not only is his hearing weak, but his eyesight poor and his understanding slow, he states that, 'Only my walking is fast!', revealing a society where it is best to simply keep moving.[133] Describing his writing as 'narrative freaks' (*musūkh sardiyya*) and 'novelistic sneezes' (*ᶜaṭasāt riwāʾiyya*), he affirms the creativity of vulnerability: 'My understanding of beauty is rooted in disfigurement. I like burns and scars. I like cracks.'[134]

Finally, something of al-Nayhum's 'naive Sufism' resonates through al-Asfar's writing, posited, like football, gazelle and *sharmūla*, as an evasion of semiotic tyranny and celebration of locality, through the vibrant festivities of urban brotherhoods and unexpected companionships of local 'saint', ᶜAbd al-Jalil, and his gazelle. An opening epigraph from the biography of the famous Persian mystic, Ibn Khafif al-Shīrāzī (882–982), establishes this. In it, al-Shīrāzī and his fellow shaykhs prepare soup after a lengthy fast, when a bird flies into their pot and dies, leading them to discover a viper they had accidently cooked. Afterwards, all experience 'trances and states' (*aḥwāl wa-raqāʾiq*) before respectfully burying the bird. Binding the locality of Benghazi *sharmūla* to a wider historical and spiritual sphere, al-Asfar concludes the extract by observing that the term *sharmūla* originates in the *fuṣḥā* root, *tharmala*, defined, in Ibn Manẓūr's *Lisān al-ᶜArab*, as to prepare food hastily or under-cook it.[135] Alongside the extract, this commentary suggests the wonders that come from both food, not consumed but hastily improvised, and from literature, similarly spun together, and opening onto revelation. As al-Asfar remarks, the Sufi poet is a 'being who rebels against interpretation' (*kāʾin ᶜaṣī ᶜan al-tafsīr*)', who 'never offers answers' and writes instead as a salve for violence and suffering, connecting immediate, grim reality to a wider whole.[136] *Sharmula* similarly strives towards this, as al-Asfar describes himself inscribing 'Sufi *sharmūla* letters (*ḥurūf ṣūfiyya sharmūliyya*) on the skin of my gazelle, read by the sun, serenaded by the moons, and danced for by the stars.'[137]

As 'chewing gum' and *sharmūla* authors, Bushnaf and al-Asfar infuse their fiction with creaturely *maskh* as humans are entangled with statues and gazelles, negotiating intellectual survival within the Jamahiriyya through strange juxtapositions and affiliations. In *Sharmula*, deterritorialising 'lines of flight' tend to be more successful than the shattering and stuttering of *al-ᶜIlka*, yet both remain painfully attentive to the oppressive structures that delimit them, emerging within their margins and as their margins. In al-Maghrabi's *Nisaʾ al-Rih*, meanwhile, their tightly spun and chaotically diffused symbolism gives way to bleak prose, as the hesitant narrator loses control over her own narrative, excavating the double limitations of political and patriarchal oppression, blocking the 'woman author' (*al-kātiba*) and her 'story' (*ḥikāya*) from even the most tenuous 'lines of flight'.

Nisaʾ al-Rih: The Novel as Disclosure

From the earliest Libyan novels, women feature prominently, animating debates over tradition and modernity, national identity and gender relations. Such, of course, is paralleled in broader Arabic fiction, where the figure of woman as national symbol has been amply observed, laden with values concerning the ideals of citizenship, between 'authentic' past and 'modern' future.[138] In the Libyan novel, women particularly frequently feature as the long-suffering objects of male desire, malaise or mistreatment, from Masᶜud's cloistered wife, referred to as '*al-khādim*' (a woman slave) to Khalil's love interests to Ukhayyad's abandoned spouse. Fatima, in *al-ᶜIlka*, may be read as an explicit parody of these figures, caught between ideological loading, mistreatment and narrative marginalisation. Eroticised and idolised into a statue, she seeks social mobility but is ultimately abandoned and caught in solipsistic chewing. She, like the other women characters, represents the profound breakdown of emotional and social cohesion as men retreat not to domestic bliss but non-human companions, fantasies and hallucinations, abandoning wives, lovers and children as embodiments of social, political and emotional imprisonment.[139] While men transcend boundaries in their proto-ethical attentiveness to animal 'others', this rarely extends to female 'others'. By attending to women's literary presence and, above all, to their presence in writing by women, the dimensions of creatureliness and vulnerability that I have discussed so far are therefore nuanced and challenged. Is this writing, I question, expressive of the same lines of flight, and the same focus on the visceral and primordial, as that of men, and does it look to the same solidarity in vulnerability as escape from social malaise?

Since the pioneering figures of Nādira al-ᶜUwaytī (1930–2015) and Marḍiyya al-Naᶜās (b.1949) in the 1970s and 1980s, Libyan women's writing has tended to be read as sentimental and autobiographical, featuring characters' coming-of-age, rooted in the domestic and often concluding with marriage and affirmation of the social order. Despite tending towards romance, however, the double marginality of both patriarchal and political oppression remains close to the surface, resonating through psychological, bodily and emotional turmoil. The 'woman's issue' (*qaḍiyat al-marʾa*), as al-Shaylābī suggests, has preoccupied thinkers from the first days of Libyan independence, tackling deep-rooted social conservatism and the burden of honour and shame that adheres to women.[140] While al-Qadhafi styled himself as a champion of women's rights, encouraging their entry into education and work, strict patriarchy remained intact, and the position of women has continued to be an intellectual and literary concern, as well as an impediment to the flourishing of women's writing.[141] Despite this, a new generation has emerged in the 2000s, with al-Maghrabi prominent among them. Having grown up in the Libyan diaspora of Damascus, where her grandfather emigrated in 1931, she returned to Tripoli in the 1990s and her writing is situated within the aesthetics of both the urban novel and the domestic space of women's coming-of-age. Far from the hallucinations and flights of fantasy of the novels discussed so far, her writing is anchored in the bleakly real, with little, if any, compensatory, critical or transformative creaturely companionships. In novels by women and about women, I suggest, there is little possibility for desert escapes or coastal conversations with rats and seagulls. The creaturely must therefore be pursued in more abstract, fleeting terms.

In *Nisaʾ al-Rih*, Tripoli is at the heart of this poetics, serving as a melancholy stage of figurative and material vulnerability upon which the intrigues of its female characters are enacted, cloistered in their shared apartment block. Through these women, the baggage surrounding the female author and, indeed, character is dramatised through the protagonist-narrator's obsession with her status as '*kātiba*', which becomes a shield, compensating for loneliness and powerlessness, and paradoxically preventing narrative and relational openness. The only name by which she is known, the *kātiba* inspires envy and awe in her neighbours, yet fails to live up to the label as she progressively loses authority over the unfolding plot. The novel must therefore be rescued by 'papers' (*awrāq*) supplied by her neighbours and by the 'metal memory' (*al-dhākira al-maʿdaniyya*) sent in a recording device from France by her cleaner, Bahija. Together, these narrative fragments form a fragile edifice, devoid of a central narrating self or kernel of creaturely longing. Instead, story emerges through acts of transmission, compromised by the omnipresent suspicion, surveillance and scandal that necessitate dissimulation in the depiction of oneself, and prompt misinterpretation in the reading of others. Through Bahija's flight to Europe, a tension is further introduced between the stasis of Tripoli and the precarity of illegal Mediterranean crossings, debating the possibility of story between both, and framing broader dichotomies of frankness and concealment, truth and dissimulation, and origin and copy. While vulnerability, in friendship and authorship, designates a state of openness to others, *Nisa' al-Rih* maintains a web of secrets, lies and anonymity, hinting at an underlying wound and at invisible structures of power. Both of these restrict the possibilities of relationship and story as the narrative voice disintegrates through self-doubt and oppression, and the author ultimately abandons literary aspirations for motherhood.

In this disintegration, *Nisa' al-Rih* arguably goes further towards the 'difficulty of story' than other Libyan novels, in which narrative voice, while uncertain, remains clearly identified with a central self. In *al-ᶜIlka*, the narrator, though frustrated, constantly restates his story while, in *Sharmula*, there is no doubt that the *sharmūla* is al-Asfar's. Contrastingly, a fragmented polyphony underlies *Nisa' al-Rih*, expressive not of joyful plurality but of uncertainty and duplicity. In contrast to *al-ᶜIlka*, its absent 'story' (*ḥikāya*) concerns not Libya's 'impossible allegory', but who is permitted to tell a story and have their story told, as well as the anxiety of having one's story forcibly unveiled. While the author longs to align herself with the city's 'great male authors', her neighbours wish to be 'heroines' (*baṭalāt*), escaping reality through ephemeral 'illusions' (*awhām*). The author's *ḥikāya* becomes, however, synonymous with scandal and 'disclosure' (*al-bawḥ*), debunking the romantic vision of the female author with a 'room of her own', expressing women's experience against male tradition. Creaturely consciousness, of hunger and thirst, survival and the primordial, therefore appears far from the picture of strong coffee, beauty treatments and text messages. However, as the novel gives way to lies and blackmail, four short chapters, dispersed through the main plot, and shifting from first to third person, strikingly escape the mesh of dissimulating voices. Forming the basis for my concluding analysis, after first discussion of the author and her 'characters', I explore how, in them, Tripoli is animated in melancholic longing, as a surface upon which the manias of modernity and political oppression are enacted.

Women of the Building

Through its titular 'women of the wind', *Nisa' al-Rih* suggests, and simultaneously frustrates, the transgressive female counter-communities that have featured across Arab women's writing, challenging monolithic religious, social and ethnic identities through alternative, counter-cultural friendships.[142] Neighbours in the same building, the women are described as 'silly' (*tāfihāt*), constructing their lives around material pleasures, scandals and affairs, while their 'fragile relationships' (*ᶜalāqāt hashsha*) are predicated on lies and blackmail and restricted to 'sessions in closed rooms' (*jalasāt al-ghuraf al-mughlaqa*).[143] Fuelled by coffee and smuggled alcohol, their friendships, as the author observes, are like 'bad fabric that tears at the first touch'.[144] Whether secret second wives or mistresses, their lives unfold through 'continuous, enervating ringtones and illicit whispers'.[145] In contrast to the breakdown of language in *al-ᶜIlka* and *Sharmula*, collapsing into stutters and sneezes under the weight of political sloganeering, the women use language to manipulate and conceal as the only means of assuming agency. Huda is a second wife, whose husband, ᶜAdil, encourages her to befriend his unwitting first wife, Safa', using the women's friendship as a pretext for bringing his families together. Despite ᶜAdil's clothes strewn over Huda's flat, Safa' remains willfully ignorant, but their friendship progressively deteriorates until, when ᶜAdil is suddenly hospitalised, Huda realises her own fundamental inability 'to be angry, happy or sad when I want'.[146] Huda's marriage further confines her to friendships based on 'emotional blackmail' (*al-ibtizāz al-ᶜāṭifī*). While disliking Yusra, a profligate adulteress, Yusra's knowledge of her 'secret' forces their friendship, and all within the building exist within a similar network of secrets whose disclosure would 'cause numerous houses to collapse'.[147] Described as a 'stage', the women play their parts, as their talk fills with 'blame and censure, laughter and release, dance and joy, and tears and futility'.[148]

Yusra exemplifies this turn to intrigue and role-play. On one pivotal night – the 'night of the women of the wind' – she becomes trapped in her lover Kamal's flat, after a former lover, Munir, threatens to expose her. After scheming her way home, she rings the author in the early morning to describe her ordeal, beginning her obsession with sublimating her life into story, whatever the dangers involved in doing so. Using the author's premarital relationship with rich businessman ᶜAbd al-Majid as leverage, she invites herself for coffee not, as the author comments, as a 'request' but as an 'obligation and order' (*farḍan wa-amran*).[149] 'She wanted', as the author comments, 'to see her love story (*qiṣṣat ḥubbihā*), which resembled no other, in the pages of a novel.'[150] On several occasions, the author likens her to a 'modern-day Shahrazad' as, at dawn, she finishes not 'what she had been allowed to say' (*al-kalām al-mubāḥ*), but her 'disclosure' (*al-bawḥ*).[151] Embodying the frustrated aspirations of Tripoli women, alternating between 'seductress, good wife, tender mother, and crazed lover', Yusra's stories cause the author to vomit in disgust and ultimately abandon any attempt to convey her 'love story, which resembled no other'.[152] In this way, between the two, the notions of confession, testimony and understanding are deeply unsettled, as they become entwined with latent power dynamics and desperate forms of emotional blackmail.

Within the novel's broader plot, moreover, the value of Yusra's unparalleled love story is further radically questioned, as story, at least within the confines of Tripoli, emerges not as a reflection of hidden truths and creaturely companionships, but as lie and illusion, compensating for stasis and powerlessness. Rather than Yusra's love story, the novel is therefore propelled by the clearer trajectory of Bahija's journey to Europe. Ridding herself of the intrigues of the city, she speaks to the recording device, imagining herself 'born anew, without past, without nation, and without friends'.[153] On the boat, fear casts aside 'masks' to reveal 'faces, exhausted and wretched from waiting', and brought together from across 'God's wide country (*min bilād Allāh al-wāsiᶜa*)'.[154] In the vein of the 'survival novel', this exemplary state of exception becomes a form of creaturely heterotopia, prompting frankness and solidarity across borders. Associating her journey with rebirth, Bahija longs to be reborn into life, law and narrative, imagining herself as a 'child, fallen from the womb, inspected by the smuggler – a doctor, who would judge her suitability for the life to come'.[155] Resonating with openness, born of immediate precarity, Bahija's journey further allows the Tripoli women's stories to be partially unfolded as, whispering into the recording device, she reports the author and her friends' stories back to them, revealing their secrets and trying to understand their motivations, as though spiriting them away from Libya.[156]

Despite this flight, however, the novel remains circular and self-enclosed, as, nine months later, the stories are returned to the author from Paris, concealed in baby's clothes and delivered by her husband.[157] During this period, she has turned from literary aspirations to imminent motherhood, declaring 'It makes me smile to remember when I thought I could write a novel, after no more than some prose pieces and poems, which everyone thought was prose anyway.'[158] Bahija's journey, and frank confessions, are thus subsumed into the continued stasis and dissimulation of life in Tripoli.

Paralleling Bahija's flight, the women's building is further condemned to demolition, as revealed in the penultimate chapter, 'Mukhaṭṭaṭ al-Hadm min ajl al-Taṭwīr' ('Demolition for the Sake of Development'). Echoing the fragile cityscapes of *al-ᶜIlka* and *Sharmula*, personal fragility is mirrored in the urban fabric, destined for oblivion, unless precariously preserved in story. It is, furthermore, revealed that, from the novel's beginning, the author has been aware of this fate and of the consequent temporariness of her friendships and stories. 'It was as though', she writes, 'these places which had been torn down were earmarked for the events of this novel alone, before returning to oblivion.'[159] Through this ending, precarity and concealment are reinforced. Lying to the women about her new address, the author concludes by announcing her husband's decision to take her on his travels and by confirming her pregnancy. Alongside the building's destruction and Bahija's flight, both promise an ephemeral move beyond stasis. However, while the 'wind' of the novel's title suggests flight and freedom, the novel depicts, above all, 'women of the building', whose demolition confines them to only transitory homelessness, as story crumbles into rubble. Like the novels of al-Asfar and Bushnaf, story-less-ness is at its heart, as even the potential liberation of creaturely flights must concede to continued stasis.

Al-Kātiba

Like her friends, the author inhabits a solitary universe, with her modern flat, both claustrophobic and exposed, representing another iteration of simultaneous homelessness and imprisonment. The second wife of a businessman, constantly travelling abroad and whom she admits to treating with coldness and silence, her wider family is barely mentioned while, like the other women, her every move is policed.[160] Friendships further render her vulnerable to blackmail and condemnation by association. Being an author thus becomes a form of sublimation for fear, anger and frustration. From the first, however, her authorial voice is unstable, as she admits that, having become pregnant, she has given her materials to another, identically named *kātiba*, who, unlike her, has already published a novel and can therefore better 'fill the gaps'.[161] Having made this confession, it becomes unclear, through the rest of her first-person narrative and the papers and recordings that supplement it, to what extent this second author has tampered with the first author's original materials. In a second confession, she further admits to a fundamental lack of inspiration. Trawling her memory for 'story', she finds nothing and thus resorts to extracts from Bahija's recording device in which she herself features as a character, interspersed with papers from friends.[162] As the novel progresses, authorial agency thus becomes dispersed, while the *kātiba* shifts from literary aspirations to 'gossip' (*tharthara*), and from observer to 'participant' (*ṭaraf*) in unfolding scandals. In contrast to both *al-ᶜIlka* and *Sharmula*, in which writing represents pursuit of truth or chaotic nourishment, the author's desire to write becomes a surrogate for truth and companionship, compromising any form of creaturely testimony or solidarity. Having discovered Bahija's intentions to travel to Europe, one of her first responses is to beg her to record her journey and, in case of the boat sinking, to preserve the recording device in a plastic bag.[163] As Bahija reflects, 'it was not people who interested her so much as filling paper with ink and printing it [. . .] She was a mad woman. A woman who did not care for the lives of others, except insofar as they aided her novel.'[164] Concerning the building's other women, the author admits that they are 'not friends' but 'silly women', whom she prompts to 'disclose their secrets' (*al-bawḥ bi-asrārihinna*), manipulating their desire to be part of 'story'.[165]

While the author encourages others' disclosure, she reveals little of herself, except, that is, for her premarital relationship with ᶜAbd al-Majid, first discovered by Bahija and Yusra. Like her husband, ᶜAbd al-Majid is never fully depicted, remaining a spectral presence, dictating women's lives from afar, and tainting their pursuit of friendship and story.[166] In a telling contrast to the ekphrastic impulse of al-Kuni, al-Ghazal and Bushnaf's writing, mention of a painting, gifted to the author by ᶜAbd al-Majid, becomes a source not of creaturely reflection, but scandal and exposure. The painting is, in fact, never described, remaining a blank question mark, significant only in Bahija's recognition of it from the businessman's house and consequent realisation of the author's indiscretions.[167]

Beyond such intrigue and the spectral presence of businessmen, the author longs to be courted by a 'great writer' (*kātib kabīr*), yearning for an alternative form of community and communication.[168] In Libya, however, any such community is compromised, with no escape to be found even in the novels of others. While working for a publishing house, eventually shut down by the regime, she discovers a 'whole archive of abandoned manuscripts by well-known and young authors alike. Strewn neglectfully on shelves and in cardboard boxes, water seeped into them from the rusted windows.'[169] Alongside the books' concrete vulnerability, their subject matter is similarly consigned to historical margins:

> Almost none mentioned Tripoli, my poor city, oppressed even by its authors, whether by neglect or design, I couldn't tell. All I knew was that I wanted to read Libyan authors who spoke about me, the people in the streets where I walked, the fish restaurant on the coast, and the cafés where they themselves sat, talking culture over coffee, and debating one another's writing. They travelled on spoken memories, without a single signature or seal to point to their lost domain. And so their words and theories drifted into the void, as they arose and moved on.[170]

Just as she longs for a literary voice, the author longs to be represented in literature, identifying her own marginality with that of the city as a whole. Lamenting its neglected architecture, from the Girl and Gazelle to the Arch of Marcus Aurelius, she testifies to 'ruination' (*kharāb*) and the 'scattered stones' (*ḥijāra mutanāthira*) of 'bygone civilisations' (*ḥaḍārāt bādat*), as well as to censored novels and phantomic authors.[171] In doing so, she strikingly echoes tropes from the bleak urban landscapes of al-Faqih, al-Ghazal, Bushnaf and al-Asfar (perhaps some of the 'great authors' of whom she dreams), and this melancholy backdrop becomes the stage for the intrigues and frivolities of her neighbours who, unlike those great authors, represent her only lasting companionship.[172]

Through the voice of the *kātiba*, al-Maghrabi thus presents a bleak portrait of creative and creaturely decline, poisoned by patriarchy and politics. 'Money and a room of one's own', it transpires, are not the primary blocks to female creativity, but a city-wide malaise in which all find themselves excluded from law, as from literature.[173] Within this bleak perspective, the recurrence, at key junctures, of short chapters, shifting from first to third person, and from private intrigue to creaturely wholeness, represents the centre of the novel's subversive ethics and vulnerable compassion. Serving almost as an anonymous creaturely diagnosis, they place women's lies and dissimulation into a broader perspective of disorientation, loss and fear. Significantly, their author – whether the first *kātiba* or the second – remains unclear, or, rather, anonymous, as, resonating with vulnerability and rage, the chapters approach the precarious heart of political injustice and leave themselves open to accusation and persecution.

Tripoli, the Pseudonymous

The very first chapter of *Nisaʾ al-Rih,* 'Ṭarābulus: Mizāj Mutajaddid' ('Tripoli: The Ever-Changing'), concerns the city's economic opening and the proliferation of consumer goods in the 2000s, presenting a surface facade of material pleasures beneath which an absent core is progressively revealed. 'Tripoli', the opening sentence declares, 'is a fickle, whimsical city, infatuated with frivolities and luxuries' (*tahwī al-lahw wa-l-taraf*).[174] 'Cafés generate cafés' (*maqhā yastansikh maqhā ākhar*), always liable to close or transform overnight in a constant process of 'replication' (*istinsākh*), frustrating 'permanent, inviolable memory' (*dhākira dāʾima mamnūᶜa min al-intihāk*).[175] Caught within rootless change as replication replaces origin, Tripoli is, as in *al-ᶜIlka,* a place of postmodern 'chewing', predicated on copying, dissimulation and repetition, through want of, or fear of, authenticity and openness. Echoing the 'accelerated rhythms of capitalist temporality' that compound Benjamin's understanding of natural history, melancholy transience is compounded by the rapid accumulation of the 'detritus' and 'junk' of 'enslaved and enslaving objects'.[176] Through this acceleration, the city is caught in a heedless mania, exposed to unspecified external forces, as, with the 2000s, neglect and stasis are compounded by the sudden interests of rich businessmen: 'Always shifting, places cannot remain still. All that slumbers and sleeps is unexpectedly seized by sudden twists and turns (*ḍalāl mufājiʾ*), as, each morning, the old is erased to make way for the modern and new.'[177]

Exemplary of what Santner describes as the 'paradoxical mixture of deadness and excitation, stuckness and agitation' of the modern city, Tripoli is further caught within social and political surveillance, as 'copying' becomes a means of avoiding recognition as author or agent.[178] As the second of the city-focused chapters, 'Ṭarābulus: Madīnat al-Asrār' ('Tripoli: City of Secrets'), reveals, each inhabitant is caught in a web of secrets, from personal illusions to pursuit of others' scandals to flight from buried anxiety:

> Some cities seem productive only of sorrow and worry, but there are always pockets of life and speech within them. Warm places where intimacy can be found. The people of Tripoli long to unravel her secret codes, and to find answers to their relentless anxiety (*qalaqihim al-lajūj*) [. . .] Each creates a personal history (*tārīkhan yakhuṣṣuhu waḥdahu*), imagining themselves as television heroes, while recognizing, deep down, the simple fact of their marginality (*annahum mujarrad unās muhammashīn*).[179]

Echoing the rich language of 'secrets' throughout the Libyan novel, the short chapter shifts between hidden yearning, concealed scandal and fear of exposure. Contrasting these fleeting intrigues, the city itself is then animated as a geography of stillness and slumber, struggling under the weight of its inhabitants: 'Every night, Tripoli closes the door on her secrets, resting her head on a pillow of sand and drifting into sleep. But then her people awake, pouring their woes into her sea after drinking her sweet water, while raising their voices in renewed rancour.'[180] This animation continues in the third chapter, 'Ghawāyat al-Mudun al-Qadīma' ('The Seduction of Ancient Cities'), in which the old city is described as choked by high-rises, emptied of its former inhabitants and 'worn away by longing' (*muhtariʾa bi-l-ḥanīn*), asking after its 'children' among the temporary lodgers that crowd its alleys.[181] Only the poets hear its 'sighs' (*anīnahā*), however, as al-Maghrabi depicts a city torn between shadowy businessmen on the one hand and artists and writers on the other, absent from the novel's main action and perceptible only as phantoms of former times.

In the last of the Tripoli-centred chapters, 'Ṭarābulus: Madīna Mustaᶜāra' ('Tripoli, the Pseudonymous/Metaphoric'), the language of 'secrets' is then compounded into a city-wide schizophrenia, between outer appearances of virtue and an underside of scandal, as well as between the grimness of reality and desperation of illusions, as all live in fear of those who 'spy on the city's defeats and disappointments' (*yatalaṣṣaṣ ᶜalā khaybātihā wa-hazāʾimihā*).[182] In Tripoli, living story and telling story are equally precarious, with 'prying eyes' (*ᶜuyūn mutalaṣṣiṣa*) reaching every corner, and necessitating constant 'metaphor' or 'pseudonym': 'Tripoli is a pseudonymous city, just like our names, which we never reveal when divulging our turbulent pain' (*al-bawḥ bi-mā yakhtalij fī al-ṣadr min alam*).[183] Like the cityscapes of *al-ᶜIlka*, *Sharmula* and, indeed, *Hadaʾiq al-Layl* and *al-Khawf*, Tripoli's inhabitants endeavour to carve out creaturely cartographies, as they 'dwell in truth (*yaskun al-ḥaqīqa*) while fashioning their story from illusion, desiring freedom but achieving it only by abandoning reality and travelling to their second Tripoli'.[184] Through this 'second Tripoli', al-Maghrabi hints at flights of longing fantasy, transporting narrative to animated coastlines and dreamed-of cities. There is, however, no extended elaboration of this 'second city' which remains consigned to darkness and anxiety while the narrative moves through frustration, blackmail and lies, between those who 'dig Libya's earth for money and deals' and the phantoms of 'good people who die of love for her soil and sea' (*al-ṭayyibūn al-mawtā ᶜishqan li-turābihā wa-baḥrihā*).[185] Combining al-Asfar's evocation of the 'simple' (*al-basīṭ*) and 'good' (*al-ṭayyib*) with Bushnaf's nod to Majnun Layla, 'dying from love', al-Maghrabi evokes, in fleeting terms, the shadows of creaturely solidarity within claustrophobic spaces of fear and intrigue. The novel thus emerges through the wistful yet dissimulating tales of its cloistered women, held together by brief chapters which open out onto the panorama of Tripoli's melancholy history and shifting geography, in creaturely solidarity with the women and the lies they must tell.

Conclusion

In an article in 2011, following the beginnings of the February uprising, al-Asfar wrote for the *New York Times*: 'Libyans have been patient for a long time, but our patience was not cowardice. We waited for the moment of true inspiration, and now that it has come and the time is right, we have achieved our goal, with a courage and motivation that has astonished the world.'[186] The urban novel of the 2000s captures this painful, patient waiting. Evoking the vulnerability of story and book, 'signs' resonate with instability, exposure and occasional glimpses of truth, while authors and intellectuals chew, or wander the margins. As heroes shift to stasis, story is defamiliarised through 'whispers', 'stutters' and 'disclosures', *rizq* shifts to gum, coffee and cigarettes and the city is animated in melancholy vulnerability, traversed by sighs, longing statues and darting gazelles. All are haunted by the rhythmic repetition of motifs and turns of phrase, from 'chewing' to 'ten long years' to gazelle tears, evoking the similarly ritual circling of al-Nayhum, al-Faqih and al-Kuni.

Through Mukhtar's stasis and Fatima's chewing, *al-ᶜIlka* stages the breakdown of romance as, from national allegory of fragmentation, it progresses to the fragmentation of allegory, into melancholy, postmodern protest. *Sharmula* and *Nisaᵓ al-Rih*, meanwhile, conclude with pregnancy and childbirth, tantalisingly evocative of change, yet similarly haunted by circling and stasis, between painful past and ominous future. In Part III, 'Children of the Land', I explore this further, in novels which return to the 1960s as a decade of possibilities evoked through the bewildered vulnerability of childhood and haunted by the spectre of the Jamahiriyya.

Part III

CHILDREN OF THE LAND

5

Too-Long-a-Tale

When the earth quakes – a shattering quake!
And the earth casts up its loads!
And man says: 'What ails it?'
That day it shall tell its tales,
For your Lord will have inspired it!

(Qur'an, 99:1–5)[1]

To listen to and tell a rush of stories is a method. And why not make the strong claim and call it a science, an addition to knowledge? Its research object is contaminated diversity; its unity of analysis is the indeterminate encounter. (Anna Tsing)[2]

In 'The Animal That Therefore I Am', Derrida writes: 'And in these moments of nakedness, under the gaze of the animal, everything can happen to me, I am like a child ready for the apocalypse, *I am (following) the apocalypse itself*, that is to say the ultimate and first event of the end, the unveiling and the verdict.'[3] In his encounter with otherness, under the gaze of the animal, Derrida evokes a child's bewilderment, in which all is open to change, from apocalypse to sudden revelation. Upturning the stable bounds of selfhood and ethics, the animal returns him to the immediacy of childhood perception, restoring the world from convention to wonder and precarity. Such moments of encounter inform my final chapters, exploring how coming-of-age or *Bildungsroman* (novel of formation) is predicated upon the individual's opening onto a creaturely whole, in which, as across children's stories and imaginaries, the land is animated in holistic union, and animals and plants treated as partners in an often overwhelming world. Returning to the 1960s and 1970s, such encounters and comings-of-age are framed by seismic transformations, as cities are rocked by earthquakes, drought and mass migration, and delimited by the ominous spectre of the Jamahiriyya. As throughout my analyses, sudden rupture with the past is a defining framework, as the transitional period of childhood, in all its openness to apocalypse and sudden revelation, coincides with what Pierre Nora describes as the 'increasingly rapid slippage of the present into a historical past that is gone for good', in a period when 'anything and everything may disappear'.[4] In addition to childhood memory, I therefore explore the memories and tales passed on by older relatives, as the 'difficulty of story' emerges through both the unsettling of *Bildungsroman*, opened onto creaturely being through moments of 'encounter', and the backward-looking impulse of 'too-long-tales', threatened by forgetfulness.

For Franco Moretti, the *Bildungsroman* represents the exemplary literary form of modernity, in which the dynamism and instability of youthful protagonists convey the heady possibilities and sudden, irrevocable dislocations of industrial, urban society.[5] As they cast off the 'useless dead-weight' of tradition, and reconcile themselves to new social structures, their emerging consciousnesses take on a collective aspect, enacting the possibilities of the 'imagined nation'.[6] In nineteenth-century Europe, Moretti comments, the *Bildungsroman* 'contained the unpredictability of social change, representing it through the fiction of youth: a turbulent segment of life, no doubt, but with a clear beginning, and an unmistakable ending.'[7] In the twentieth century, meanwhile, the upheavals of war and growth of impersonal state institutions began to shake such certainties, producing a 'veritable tradition of counter-*Bildungsroman*', in which adult maturity is increasingly seen as an unattainable and undesirable outcome.[8]

In modern Arabic *Bildungsroman* and autobiography, narratives of childhood feature particularly prominently, as Tetz Rooke suggests.[9] Sometimes, childhood serves as an exploration of social mobility in the form of a '"success story", where the unimportant child hero overcomes a handicap – physical, emotional, or social – and surmounts a series of difficulties before the "breakthrough" which is adulthood'.[10] Often, too, childhood is romanticised as a haven from troubling adult experience and recuperation of an ideal, freer self. In other cases, childhood marks premature initiation into trials and traumas that haunt adult life. In each case, childhood is, as Rooke suggests, 'not just the beginning of the story of life, it is also the end of the discourse of the self', suggestive of buried truths and stifled memories, sought through writing.[11]

In the Libyan novel, successful transitions from childhood to adulthood are rare. Paralleling the poetics of survival, primordiality and stasis, youthful vulnerability stands at the heart of a flurry of memoirs, some autobiographical, some fictional, from the late 1990s and 2000s.[12] Narrated by nine-year-old Slooma, Hisham Matar's *In the Country of Men* (2006) is a prominent example, and I examine it in my final chapter through the shared dimensions of 'encounter' and 'too-long-tales'. First, however, I explore its predecessors in the Arabic Libyan novel, in Ahmad Yusuf ᶜAqila's *al-Jirab: Hikayat Najᶜ* (2006, A Sack of Village Tales), Ahmad al-Fayturi's *Sarib* (2000, A Long Story) and Najwa Bin Shatwan's *Wabr al-Ahsina* (2006, The Horse's Hair). Through the perspective of young children, all three hint at 1969 as a year beyond which adulthood becomes a precarious domain to navigate, while, between colonisation, war and dictatorship, the 1960s offer the fragile possibilities of nationhood and adulthood-to-come. Caught in the forcefield of environmental, social and political change, the child embodies bewilderment and the spectre of future loss, and the *Bildungsroman* concludes with bleak outlooks on the future, and even the disappearance or death of the child. Far from 'origin stories' tracking monumental shifts in consciousness, of child becoming adult and land becoming nation and Jamahiriyya, they articulate the precarity of creaturely being.[13]

Exploring this, I focus, in one strand of my analyses, on the encounter with animal others. As critic Muḥammad al-ᶜAmāmī comments, the child's witnessing of animal slaughter, particularly at Eid, represents a significant theme in early Libyan fiction, exemplified by al-Nayhum's short story, 'al-Rajaʾ min al-Hajj al-Zarruq' (1967, 'A Request from Hajj Zarruq'), in which a young boy desperately shelters his sheep from the tyrannous butcher, Hajj Zarruq, and Khalīfa al-Fākhirī's (1942–2001) *Mawsim al-Hikayat* (1974, Season of Stories), in which another boy is similarly left distraught by the 'bloody festival' (*al-ᶜīd al-damawī*).[14] Prompting children to question the adult world into which they must grow, scenes of slaughter are laden with symbolic significance as, through their sheep companions, children become receptive readers of 'creaturely signs'. Dramatising what Santner terms, 'one's "thrownness" into a dense matrix of natural historical signification', the child must literally 'stomach' what the animal's death conveys within society, as well as its allegorical significance within the narrative, bound to wider social, political and historical contexts.[15]

Prompting profound change in the lives of the children, such encounters are paralleled by broader, historical shifts which, in a second strand of analysis, I explore through memories of the early twentieth century, and traditional folklore, conveying natural historical pessimism in the future of the land and its inhabitants. Contrasting the rejection of 'dead-weight' tradition that Moretti recognises in the European *Bildungsroman*, children's voices merge with the stories and memories of older, particularly female, relatives. Dialect terms, *kharārīf* (folk tales) and *sarīb* (a long, rambling tale), designate such narrative. With the first connoting *kharīf* (autumn) and the second *sarab* (the flow of a river), *sirb* (a flock of birds) and *sirāb* (a mirage), they suggest the meandering of natural history, embedded in the land and countering official versions of history which, as Nora suggests, arise to compensate for the loss of lived tradition as, through the 'acceleration of history', there is a need to construct pasts and fashion roots.[16]

In Libya, memory and history represent a particularly troubled terrain. Al-Qadhafi actively erased all history prior to 1969, restricting the school curriculum to Green Book ideology and evoking early periods of Italian rule and British and American influence only to bolster his own rhetoric. Italian colonisation has also been clouded in both deliberate Italian amnesia, perpetrating images of Italian settlers as *brava gente* (decent people), and general scholarly neglect, sidelining Libya's early twentieth-century history behind the all-consuming figure of al-Qadhafi.[17] It was not until the 1990s that the Libyan Studies Centre in Tripoli began to record oral memories from Italian concentration camps and to transcribe poetry and song composed in them.[18] The colonial period has thus been caught between what Paul Ricoeur describes as an 'excess of forgetfulness' on the one hand and, occasionally, an 'excess of memory', through al-Qadhafi's virulent rhetoric, channelled into escalating acts of aggression and oppression against his own people, under the pretence of defence against foreign interference.[19]

In the interstices of this fraught history, individual memories of migration and imprisonment, haunting the present or threatening to fade into oblivion, are interwoven in the *Bildungsroman* as an essential facet of children's relationship to the world around them. As Ahmida describes, 'For the generations of the colonial period, the first half of the twentieth century was indeed a long tragedy. Hard times shaped the personal and collective memory of generations. This collective memory was conveyed to children of my generation through stories, songs, proverbs, and oral poetry.'[20] Resonating with these traces, the *Bildungsroman* is rooted in a heritage of struggle and deprivation. As Sālim al-ᶜAbbār observes, popular tales flourished in Libya in years of drought to distract children from their hunger.[21] Colonisation, too, produced its own cast of ghouls, with literal horrors filtering into the folkloric imaginary.[22]

Foregoing organising structure as a distortion of the free flow of memory, the Libyan *Bildungsroman* pursues this heritage as what Benjamin calls the 'counsel' of traditional narrative, rooted in lived connections to land and past.[23] At the same time, it confronts the vulnerability of this memory, to the horrors of colonisation that resist 'telling', the dawn of old age and the dislocations of modernity. Shifting from the 'liberating magic' that Benjamin associates with fairy tale, enframed stories move to the 'nightmare' of myth and grim determinism, initiating children into histories of suffering, denying happy ending and home, and weaving together present and past vulnerability as the voices of elderly relatives falter and fall silent.[24]

Mimicking oral narrative, ᶜAqila's *al-Jirab* is a mosaic of anecdotes of the semi-nomadic society of 1960s Jabal Akhdar, interspersed with relatives' memories of war, recorded 'without order' (*dūn tartīb*), in over one hundred anecdotes of varying length, from memories of hunting for truffles or herding goats to stories of war and penury.[25] Weaving together historically defining moments with the minute interconnections of human, animal and land, *al-Jirab* exemplifies the novel as creaturely memory, as the boy's emerging selfhood is bound to community and land.

Labelled both 'autobiography' (*sīra dhātiyya*) and 'novel' (*riwāya*), al-Fayturi's *Sarib* then shifts from the patterns of oral folklore to feverish stream-of-consciousness, setting the paradigm for the troubled juxtaposition of youthful coming-of-age and precarious memory. Its young protagonist lives alone with his Berber grandmother in 1960s Benghazi, immersed in her stories and venturing through the rapidly changing city. Occupying a significant portion of the novel, the grandmother tells, in parallel, of her journey through the Libyan desert, from Gharyan to Benghazi, during the Second World War. Among the framed tales that intersperse these memories, I focus on her final tale, narrating the beginning of human domination of animals and enshrining its counsel as the primordial dichotomy of predator and prey.

Lastly, Bin Shatwan's *Wabr al-Ahsina* exemplifies the *Bildungsroman* as failed formation, underpinned by primordial pessimism. Primarily narrated by an unborn foetus, it is subtitled 'Nuṣūṣ fī al-Takwīn wa-l-Nashʾa' ('Texts Concerning Creation and Growth') and framed by a satirical take on the Adam and Eve narrative. In ensuing chapters, it traces the foetus's genealogy from them, moving into the body and, from there, the experiences of the mother. Through this defamiliarising perspective, Bin Shatwan marks a new departure for Libyan women's writing, anchored in the symbolic, visceral and primordial, while also exemplifying broader trends in childhood memory, from ʿAqila's *ḥikāyat al-najʿ* to al-Fayturi's *sarīb* to the French and English *Bildungsroman* of Kamal Ben Hameda and Matar, which I turn to in my final chapter.

Among these *Bildungsroman*, only *al-Jirab* and *Sarib* establish what Phillipe Lejeune calls the 'autobiographical pact' with the reader, in which author, protagonist and narrator are understood to be one and the same.[26] There are, however, clear autobiographical dimensions to the others, too. Recognising the fluid boundary between autobiography and fiction, I do not dwell at length on this dimension of the narratives, but analyse them together through their conscious interweaving of memory and imagination, as well as the narrative strategies through which present is woven into past and the self opened onto a creaturely whole, as coming-of-age falters and lessons of the past are tested by new realities. Beginning with ʿAqila's *al-Jirab*, I frame my discussion by briefly exploring the harmony of story and land, human and animal, old and young to which his writing gives voice. I then move to a more extensive discussion of *Sarib* and *Wabr al-Ahsina*, in which the alignment of child and community is fractured and individual and collective memory underpinned by imagined tales of primordial fall.

Al-Jirab: To Listen Closely

Best known as a short story writer, ʿAqila published his first collections in the 1990s, exemplifying the folkloric and ecological poetics of Libyan fiction through simple, evocative vignettes of human, animal and land, reminiscent of parable or meditation. Echoing al-Kuni's description of al-Nayhum, critic al-Ṭayyib Jamāzī describes how ᶜAqila imagines 'the oneness of being as the oneness of living being' (*waḥdat al-wujūd hiya waḥdat al-kāʾin al-ḥayy*), listening with the 'ear of Solomon' and awakening 'symbolic layers' within creaturely being as his language 'creeps with the insects and flies with the birds'.[27] Muḥammad Falḥi similarly describes his writing as 'brimming with majesty and melancholy, and weaving together humans and other living beings in a tumultuous world'.[28]

After serving for eight years in the army, ᶜAqila has lived his whole life in the verdant region of Jabal Akhdar, which provides the beating heart of his writing, situated in the east of Libya and in striking contrast to the desert landscape that lies beyond. In the 1920s, it was also a centre of anti-colonial resistance and of the mass internment of local people. With his writing inextricably linked to the contours and histories of this region, ᶜAqila interweaves its momentous but marginalised history into closely-observed images of the cohabitation of flora and fauna, juxtaposing natural exposure and political states of exception.[29] Through intimate attention to the terrain, his writing exemplifies creaturely memory as, in Kari Weil's definition, a method of 'reading and sensing those memories that are stored in the bodies of other animals, as in our own'.[30]

ᶜAqila's only novel, *al-Jirab* is an autobiography of his childhood, moving seasonally between the lower slopes and upper caves of Jabal Akhdar, facing hunger and flooding and witnessing the coming and going of British military bases, and of the Senusi monarchy. Like his stories, the novel represents 'attentive listening' (*inṣāt*), weaving boyhood impressions into the memories and tales of relatives.[31] In the foreword, he describes it as both the 'tale of a child' (*ḥikāyat ṭifl*) and the 'tale of a hamlet' (*sīrat al-najᶜ*), in which he serves not as hero but as 'eyewitness' to events 'as they happened'.[32] As this suggests, his creativity is anchored in the village's oral traditions. 'I want this text to be read in a single breath', he declares, 'just like the oral Libyan tale, in all its abandon and unstructured flow.'[33] The narrating I is, as this suggests, decentred both within the community and the natural world, alternating between wonder, exposure and loss. This is immediately apparent as the novel opens by describing a childhood 'without roof or walls', embarking not on a description of ᶜAqila's boyhood self, but a list of spring plants that cover the mountain's southern regions in spring, conveying sensory overload through the evocative economy of his botanical enumeration:

> The valleys and ravines were scattered with retem [juniper] and sidr trees, while the planes and lowlands were covered in saxaul shrubs, saltbushes, aloe vera, anabasis, spiky milk vetch and dryas, redolent with the scents of sage-brush, zaatar, thymelea, mallow and chrysanthemums.[34]

Listing more than thirty plants, ᶜAqila challenges the limits of translatability in his intimate knowledge of the local terrain, with his act of naming representing not appropriation but the literal rooting of narrative in the land.

Subsequent sections describing his early childhood further establish him within a natural, rather than social, framework, while culture is depicted as emerging from encounters with nature, from the songs that accompany truffle hunting to digging for jerboas and chasing rats.[35] Echoing environmentalist Paul Shepard, language, emotion and selfhood are formed from encounters with the land and its creatures in a 'kind of miniature presentiment – that the human species emerged enacting, dreaming, and thinking animals and cannot be fully itself without them'.[36] Steeped in Qurᵓanic and folkloric spirituality of 'wonder' (*ᶜajab*) and 'signs', nature is infused with the 'liberating power' of fairy tale, dramatising Benjamin's description of its 'complicity with liberated man'.[37] Echoing a prophetic Hadith, the boy associates spiderwebs with Muhammad's flight to Medina, and the lark with his footprints, in which they are said to have built their nests, becoming a repository of 'secrets' (*asrār*).[38] Folk tales are similarly rooted not in the 'heroism and chivalry' of the Bani Hilal, but the playful interconnections of Umm Bsisi, to which, he declares, 'we listened with every fibre of our being' (*fi layālī Umm Bsīsī nunṣit bi-kull jawāriḥinā*).[39]

Gradually, however, vulnerability begins to taint this boyhood wonder, through dramas of life and death witnessed during his years as a goatherd. In a series of anecdotes, ᶜAqila evokes scenes open only to those who work in proximity to nature, and the different emotions they prompt. Describing his dog's sudden pursuit of a rabbit, the boy is astonished as the rabbit is snatched instead from the air by an eagle, prompting him first to resent the injustice done to his dog and then to rejoice that, 'before it died, the rabbit soared'.[40] A flood, meanwhile, brings his first experience of mortality, sweeping sheep and goats through the valley: 'The ravines overflowed and I will forever remember that terrifying vision: sheep and goats swirling and summersaulting amidst the current, desperately clinging to life. That was my first encounter with death.'[41] Situating pivotal moments of 'formation' within the natural world, the boy becomes attuned to the spectacle of creatures' 'clinging to life' (*al-tashabbuth bi-l-ḥayāh*).[42]

Scenes of slaughter are particularly paradigm-shifting, beginning with the loss of the boy's childhood goat, which he had carefully nurtured, only for his father to select it as the first to be killed. As in broader Eid memories, the sight of its blood prompts visceral identification, a lifelong aversion to meat and an association of slaughter with betrayal and sin:

> My stomach turned, I couldn't breathe and felt the ground surge beneath me. Fleeing the scene, sobs welled, and I cursed them all, feeling as though I had myself been slaughtered, and refusing to watch as they consumed the meat. Ever since, I have regarded meat with discomfort, and associated slaughter with betrayal.[43]

In later anecdotes, the goat's slaughter becomes a haunting refrain, resurfacing at moments of vulnerability with which it is identified, from a mourning mother dog, circling the well into which her pups have been thrown, to the boy's whipping at school, to the chopping down of a beloved tree.[44] Through each encounter, resonating across the numbered vignettes, the idyll of childhood is juxtaposed to adult pragmatism, social discipline and modern land management. The pine tree, particularly, combines the momentousness of encounter and sudden eradication of memory. 'I imagined that I could see the tree's blood on the digger's teeth', he recalls; 'I wondered how it had resisted, how it had struggled before it fell [. . .] I sensed a deep emptiness within me. Something in my being, in my memory, had been irrevocably swept away.'[45] Through memory and imagination, ᶜAqila focuses not on dissecting social or political malaises, but on the physical and emotional dimensions of the suffering exposed, exemplified by the mourning mother dog:

> For days, she circled the well, her teats swelling with milk as she growled, pressing her belly against the ground so the milk would leak out, and stretching her head into the dark mouth to listen to the howling of her pups which grew progressively fainter in the deep. That was the second time I cursed my father.[46]

In other instances, childhood idyll is further juxtaposed to demons of the past. In an eloquently pastoral scene, the boy describes his sister, Maryam, taking her cow to pasture, dwelling on the stillness of the view as the morning fog sluggishly lifts, a dog 'sniffs the breeze, in search of a particular scent', and 'snails wend their way up boulders, tree trunks and tombstones, leaving shining trails behind them'.[47] Suddenly, from this stillness, an explosion blows the valley apart, as a leftover landmine from the Second World War is detonated. Amid the ensuing chaos, Maryam survives while her cow is killed: 'Maryam sat next to the black crater left by the explosion, gazing at the remains of her cow, at the severed head, and at the cloth, spattered with blood and dung, that hung from her horns'.[48] While Maryam's safety prompts joy, the scene then shifts to the bull, mourning his companion: 'He began to bellow, sharply, frighteningly and continuously, his tongue dangling, saliva dripping in long threads from the corners of his mouth, padding the ground with his right hoof and gazing, bewildered, upon his female.'[49] All the cows and bulls gather and are described as 'holding a wake' (*manāḥa*), suggestive both of human ritual and the shared, creaturely suffering underlining it.[50] Maryam, meanwhile, cannot move beyond the sight of her dead cow, continuing to gaze at it while the valley empties, with the short scene concluding with repetition: 'Maryam turned to her cow's severed head, contemplating her wide, glassy eyes, and the cloth, spattered with blood and dung, that hung between her horns'.[51]

Rather than embarking on an elaborate description of emotion, ᶜAqila leaves such scenes to resonate with wider significance, entwining human psychology in land and creatures, as he moves from central scenes of human activity to the imperceptible and closely observed lives of species on its margins. In an interview, he describes his attempts to 'spiritualise' (*rawḥana*) the non-human and inanimate, widening the 'horizons of place, movement, shape and relationships' and thereby countering not just the 'objectification' (*tashayyuʾ*) of the non-human, but also of the human.[52] For ᶜAqila, experiences of loss and objectification should draw humans closer to their non-human others and, in this, he aptly evokes Benjamin's comments on Kafka's 'attentiveness' as a 'natural prayer of the soul', including 'all living creatures' and emerging through prose that, to the extent possible, inhabits the emotions and physicality of these creatures.[53]

Perception of shared vulnerability also frames more explicit description of life under the Italians, as ᶜAqila remarks that, despite the horrors of their youth, his relatives' spirits 'remained intact' (*lam tatashawwah arwāḥuhum baᶜd*), and they would still 'mourn even the death of their dogs'.[54] He would, he describes, often request his mother to tell him about the Maqrun Camp, where she was imprisoned at fifteen. 'She would close her eyes and shake her head', he writes, 'then tell me it was too long a story' (*sarīb ṭawīl*).[55] Suggestive of a tale that cannot easily be told to a child, breaking with the optimism of fairy tale, the mother's voice echoes through subsequent sections, testifying to life in the camps and dwelling on the daily search for food as the land becomes striated with 'tents lined up in ranks, as far as the eye could see' and 'bodies swaying in the distance'.[56] Summing up, her list of the camp's distinguishing features contrasts with the opening enumeration of natural flora in the Jabal Akhdar: 'Troops, loudspeakers, trucks, whips, gallows, and barbed wire – that was the Maqrun Camp, and all its gates led only to death, in the cemetery beyond.'[57] Meaningful connections between land and people, and between the people themselves, are sundered. Voicing the growing hopelessness of Libyan folklore, confronting war and starvation, the mother imagines asking the birds to deliver her news to the Mountain, before remembering that all her relatives have been expelled from it. The internees, meanwhile, find themselves caught between collaboration and 'Italianisation', or death.

While the first sections of *al-Jirab* combine melancholy memory with encounters in nature, the second focuses on the boy's years at boarding school, initiated into a world of discipline and momentous political transformations. Perhaps primarily, this stage marks the further loss, both individual and collective, of spontaneous intimacy with the natural environment, suddenly seen in terms of efficiency and productivity:

> In geography, we learned that our nation enjoys the longest Mediterranean coast of any nation, and that our sea is alive with fish, practically jumping onto the beaches. So why were we eating roots and weeds? Why did we turn our backs on the sea, chasing a flock of sheep, panting behind a distant cloud, looking no further than the horns of our goats?[58]

From a world viewed through the horns of a goat, the boy is initiated into order and urbanisation as, along with the region's other families, his mother and father settle in a nearby town.[59] Here, the novel concludes, though, in its open-ended structure of short, numbered anecdotes, it leaves room for more stories and meditations on creaturely life.[60] With no dramatic ending it is, as its title suggests, an open *jirāb* or *sarīb ṭawīl*, in which childhood represents not a 'stage' but, as ᶜAqila declares, a 'state of astonishment' (*ḥālat al-dahsha*).[61] This state re-establishes the vital connection between story, nature and life, opening from individual memory to recover what ᶜAqila calls the region's 'fractured self' (*dhātinā al-mutashaẓẓiyya*) from 'marginalisation' (*tahmīsh*) and 'effacement' (*taghyīb*).[62] Observing how the term '*kharārīf*' connotes the season when fruits 'are collected' (*tukhraf*), while the 'narrator' (*rāwī*) provides 'irrigation' (*rayy*), ᶜAqila's 'sack' roots narrative in nourishment and growth, allowing for moments of melancholy and suffering within the structuring framework of *inṣāt*.[63] In the novels that I explore next, the nourishing capacity of story remains, albeit further tainted by melancholy, inflecting and infecting memory, and disrupting states of astonishment and fairy-tale endings.

Sarib: Underdogs and Unhappy Endings

In *Sarib*, al-Fayturi exemplifies the Libyan *Bildungsroman* as counter-*Bildungsroman*, caught between haunting past and precarious future as 'too-long-tales' overwhelm *kharārīf* and, at the novel's end, the narrating boy disappears. While ᶜAqila insists on not 'weighting' (*ithqāl*) his memories but leaving them open to land and creatures, al-Fayturi infuses his narrative with myth, hallucination and reminiscing voices.[64] 'This fevered narrative', Mattawa writes, 'alternates between a young protagonist and his grandmother and moves in and out of reality, history, and myth, from the character Nuss Enssaiss [*sic*] (whose name means "halfy half") of the local folk-tale to Berenice, daughter of Magas of Cyrene, after whom Benghazi was once named.'[65]

Born in Benghazi, al-Fayturi is of the generation of Bushnaf and al-Asfar, and has described his coming-of-age amid the first 'stern and serious' graduates of the new Libyan University.[66] Launching himself, at only sixteen, as a journalist, working for *al-Fajr al-Jadid*, he represented the heady possibilities of Libya's literary golden age. Like Bushnaf he was, however, imprisoned from 1978 to 1988 and, in returning to his childhood in *Sarib*, weaves this curtailed youth into the voice of his grandmother, with their experiences of exposure and loss reflecting upon one another.[67] A Berber from the region of Gharyan, the grandmother's memories concern her journey of more than one thousand kilometres to Benghazi during the Second World War, fleeing German, Italian and British fighting. Through her voice, al-Fayturi both evokes the embattled land as proxy battleground for the Allies and Axis Powers and alludes to the plight of Libya's oldest minority, banned, under al-Qadhafi, from speaking Amazigh and even from using Amazigh names. Her tales, increasingly under threat from forgetfulness and rejection, may be read as a dramatisation of this threatened heritage.

The first pages of the novel nevertheless depict the boy listening rapturously to his grandmother's stories and watching as she feeds the birds that flock to her courtyard. In the isolated idyll of their home, in the raised ground of al-ᶜUlwa, their harmonious existence is central, as he describes them huddled around the stove or on their shared mattress, which, to him, seems 'limitless' and to exist 'at the beginning of time' (*fī bidāyat al-zaman*).[68] Together, his 'play' (*luᶜba*) and her 'stories' (*ḥakī*) form a barrier to the wider world.[69] She is further depicted as a magical, metamorphosing creature. Said to love 'all things small' (*kull shayᵓ ṣaghīr*), she is particularly fond of ants, prompted by their mention in the Qurᵓan and their industriousness, matching her own as what her grandson calls *al-marᵓa al-namla* (the ant lady).[70] Through work, she comments, 'the ants fortify their bodies and preserve themselves and their offspring, never harming anyone who does not harm them.'[71] So close is her connection to them in fact that, finding her absent one day, her grandson even believes her to have metamorphosed into one and to have become their 'guest' (*ḍayfa*).[72] With a high-pitched voice 'like the cheep of a bird' (*mithl zaqzaqat ᶜuṣfūr*) and an 'inhuman face' (*wajh ghayr ādamī*), she is described 'twittering' (*tunāghī*) to lambs passing with their shepherd and, when lost in thought, reverts to Amazigh which, unable to understand, her grandson calls the 'speech of birds' (*manṭiq al-ṭayr*).[73] This connection to the non-human powerfully inflects his own vision of the world as he, in turn, contemplates the ants' 'comings and goings', moving from 'astonishment to astonishment' (*min dahsha li-dahsha*) in the creatures which 'she loved as she loved me'.[74]

The non-human and the not-completely-human are also the heroes of her first fairy tales, where the underdog emerges victorious through use of wit and the help of animal companions. Her first tale, 'Nus Ansis' ('Halfy

Half'), is a well-known folk tale, telling of a boy, born of minute stature, who is persecuted by his six 'full' brothers. Together with his ram companion, the halfling boy embarks on adventures, outwitting his older brothers and a flesh-eating ghoul. A running motif through the rest of the novel, Nus Ansis dramatises the power of the 'small', aligned with the natural world.[75] Within fairy tale tradition, his tale is characterised by a quest for home, in which, as Jack Zipes suggests, 'the underdog, the small person, uses his or her wits not only to survive but also to live a better life'.[76] Benjamin describes fairy tales in similar fashion, as the 'first tutor' of both children and humankind, demonstrating how 'cunning' might be used to shake off the 'nightmare' of myth:

> In the figure of the wiseacre [fairy tale] shows us that the questions posed by the myth are simple-minded, like the riddle of the Sphinx; in the shape of the animals which come to the aid of the child it shows that nature not only is subservient to the myth, but much prefers to be aligned with man.[77]

Such is the message of the grandmother's first tales. The same cannot, however, be said of her final tale, in which animal companion shifts to fearful prey, and the hopeful purpose of fairy tale gives way to a bleak myth of fall, in which humanity's 'cunning' is turned to destruction, prompting flight as a condition of survival and condemning happy endings.

The Wiles of Ibn Adam

Echoing the Ikhwan al-Safa°'s *Case of the Animals against Man*, the grandmother's 'Tale of Ibn Adam' recasts human subjugation of animals as etiological fable, describing how animals got their lairs but doing little to sugar-coat it. Returning to 'the land of human and jinn', when 'Ibn Adam's' 'wiliness' (*ḥīla*) ensures that he 'conquers all things in the world' (*ghalaba kull shay° fī al-dunyā*), the story describes his failure to become a noble master:

> Ibn Adam, dagger in hand, shot after Bull, taking hold of him in a flash, and throwing him to the ground. But, as he was readying himself to slit Bull's throat, the animal bellowed into his face: 'You have forgotten all the goodness I have given you! And now you plan to be my executioner, devouring my meat, and gobbling my hide and hooves'.[78]

Shocked by the monstrosity of Ibn Adam, the wild animals send Porcupine to investigate. After much searching, Porcupine locates the culprit. Ibn Adam first serves him milk from Goat, only to then slaughter Goat's son, Kid, in his honour. Appalled, Porcupine flees to the other beasts where he refuses to tell his tale until they dig him a deep burrow in which to hide. Having done so, the animals listen to his tale before themselves scattering in fear, searching for 'refuge' (*maljaʾ*) in mountain caves or burrows.

With the story's harsh realism contrasting the usual flights of fantasy of the 'just-so story', Ibn Adam becomes the only flesh-eating ghoul in what might be termed the first 'postcolonial fable', inaugurating, as Pick elsewhere suggests, 'the vexed relations between man and nonman'.[79] Concluding her tale, the grandmother then continues seamlessly into her own memories, identifying with the non-human's flight and using the same word 'refuge' (*maljaʾ*) to describe both animal habitats and the bombed building where she shelters after the Second World War:

> Since then, all wild beasts have fled (*harabat al-wuḥūsh*), each choosing a hiding place and refuge (*maljaʾ*). Some retreated to mountain caves, some dug into the ground and some escaped to deserted terrains. They scattered across the land just as we did, settling in Benghazi where hunger had rooted itself, and war had razed everything to the ground. We sought refuge (*maljaʾ*) in a dilapidated building, its walls crumbling.[80]

Shortly after arriving in Benghazi, the grandmother continues, she begins to hear the word 'Libyan' for the first time on the radio and to see people campaigning for independence in the war-torn streets. She rejoices, but without understanding why, simply trying to survive the man-made and natural obstacles that continue to threaten her existence as the city is shaken by flooding and the Palestinian *nakba* threatens to return her sons to another war zone.[81] Meanwhile, her story of Ibn Adam, with dagger in hand, serves as a haunting reminder of humanity's history, based on the scattering of fellow creatures.

Moving seamlessly from tales to memories and back again, the grandmother dramatises the vulnerability of storytelling counsel as she slips increasingly between sleep and meandering *sarīb*. As the boy remembers, she sporadically fetches a mysterious 'chest' (*ṣundūq*) from under her bed, prompting her to sing, cry and launch into her 'strange tales' (*ḥikāyāt gharība*), often in Amazigh.[82] These tales concern her journey across the Libyan desert, fleeing war and starvation with her six children. While her grandson imagines her as a proud figure, followed by a flock of children, heroism is firmly dispelled by her all-consuming preoccupation with survival as, shifting into the voice of her younger self, she questions:

> If my children and I truly come from you, Lord, why must we consume other beasts to survive (*lima aḥtāj hādhihi al-dawābb*)? Why must I consume other life to live, obeying the call of the wastelands as my belly hounds me and I hound anything with a belly of its own (*tuṭāridunī baṭnī wa-uṭarīd kull dhī baṭn*)?[83]

Repeating the Qurʾanic word '*dābba*' (beast/animal), she describes how the 'Christians in their tanks attacked every beast' and the Italians planted landmines 'not wanting a single beast to live'.[84] As creature, she herself oscillates between predator and prey and, hounded by hunger, embodies both at once. The aftermath of war, meanwhile, is personified as the flesh-eating *ghūla* of her folk tales, 'not wanting other mothers to have children of their own' (*lā tuḥibb an yakūn li-ghayrihā ṣighār*).[85] All unfolds in chaos, without rhyme or reason. 'We didn't know why those Christians were fighting', she reflects. 'We had no time to know. Knowledge was for the full-bellied.'[86]

Continuing, she weaves these memories further into tales of internment under the Italians: 'They told me that that Italian, Graziani, governor of Cyrenaica, had packed the tribes in there, row on row, from Tobruk to Abyar. Them, their camels and goats, with no water, food or protection from the burning sun and bitter night wind.'[87] Reference to the tribes and their herds, 'row on row', poignantly envisions the shared vulnerability of human and animal, emphasised by the sudden disciplining of a traditionally nomadic society. Her memories then slip into fragmented and nightmarish visions: 'Howling all around. A headless man seeking a sip of water. A naked woman, her hands protecting her young, her lower half gone. Cackling and whispered speech. An Italian, his belly open, running mad and naked.'[88] In these images of bodily incompletion, the 'halfling' nature of Nas Ansis gains a grotesque, horrifying dimension as, from the idyllic world of childhood where 'security' (*amān*) reigns, the grandmother's courtyard shifts to melancholy memory, flight, and a story whose sole counsel concerns Ibn Adam in whom trust cannot be found (*lā amān fīhi*).[89]

Coming-of-Age in Creaturely Memoir

As the grandmother becomes increasingly disoriented, the boy's parents remove him from her care, announcing his transition to the world of men, employed in his father's shop and marauding with his young uncle. While at first resenting this change, he soon discovers the written word of comic books and novels, displacing his grandmother's *sarīb* which, after all, signifies not just a 'long story' but an overly long one, fragmented, repetitive, without clear beginning or ending, and failing to form the past into a meaningful narrative:

> At that moment, I felt bored of her repetitive stories, realizing that she did not know all the things that I knew. We suddenly stood on opposite sides of a divide, as I began to unpick the riddles of letters and then words, while, to her, they remained as stubborn, indecipherable 'squiggles'. Her memory was made of sand, scattered by the Qibli wind, while mine stood to attention before me, in neat lines and printed shapes. Filled with pride, I pitied the forgetful old woman, shaken by every passing breeze and telling her tales again and again.[90]

Following his grandmother's 'Tale of Ibn Adam', the boy demands, 'Who are you talking to grandma?', as she responds 'I'm talking to myself' (*naḥkī li-rūḥī*).[91] This sudden dislocation is rendered all the more poignant by the fact that the tale's counsel was intended as consolation for the boy's failed trip to the zoo, as a violent sandstorm covers the city in red dust, as though 'spattered with blood'.[92] Life, the grandmother suggests, is always open to such transformations, prompting flight and upsetting the best-laid plans.

Despite their growing separation, it is this ever-changing state of Benghazi that remains as their common ground. Just as ᶜAqila roots his *Jirab* in the silent and open spaces of Jabal Akhdar, Benghazi is the structuring backdrop of *Sarib*, animated in mythic imaginings and chaotic transformations. For the grandmother, it is a sanctuary from the vagaries of nature and war, described as 'the dwelling place of human, jinn and everything in between' (*maskan al-jinn wa-l-ins wa-mā baynahumā*).[93] Playing on the root *f-t-ḥ*, as both 'conquering' and 'opening', Benghazi, for her, 'has never been conquered, for it is a place of eternal openness' (*lam tuftaḥ marra fa-hiya al-tafattuḥ al-abadī*).[94] At the same time, Benghazi is itself vulnerable, an 'old woman' (*ᶜajūz*) whose sufferings are bound to her own, as it is bombed and scattered with landmines, then overtaken by night clubs and casinos.[95]

The boy, meanwhile, opens the city onto a wider cast of Greek gods, discovered at school. Animating the city in divine form, he imagines her visiting him at night:

> Her wrinkled face shone as the rising sun hit the salt flats. The sea was in her eyes and she was shrouded in blue. [. . .] Benghazi cradled me in her lap, soothing me as I fell in love. 'You were born from water, just as I was', she murmured, 'You have lived on the salt of my bread. Before your father Adam married Eve, Zeus, King of the gods, fell in love with Tanit, goddess of Libya. They were married and I their offspring, created from the merging of the far horizon, the ocean's depths and the earth's clay.'[96]

While exulting in Benghazi's origins, combining Libyan and Greek mythology, the boy soon experiences his own encroaching sense of 'emptiness' (*farāgh*), in a city where flight and fracture, both internal and external, are constant threats and *Bildungsroman* becomes increasingly troubled and turbulent. After a bout of illness, he desires only 'destruction' (*al-hadm*) and 'forgetting' (*al-nisyān*). Trampling ants and laying his grandmother's yard with bird traps, he is declared 'man of the house' by his uncle and, echoing Qurᵓan 6:38, declares: 'There was not a beast that crawled on the ground which did not become my prey' (*mā min dābba tadibb ᶜalā al-arḍ illā wa-ṣārat ṭarīdatī*).[97] Evoking earlier Qurᵓanic imagery, of ants as astonishing *āyāt*, the change within him is evident.

This adolescent angst is then aggravated by a litany of traumatic experiences, beginning, as in ᶜAqila's *al-Jirab*, with the paradigm-shifting slaughter of a beloved gazelle, given to the boy as a gift and which he had spent days caring for. To an even greater extent than in *al-Jirab*, this moment has a visceral effect on him and, seemingly, the city around him. Tricked into eating its meat, he 'vomits its flesh out of the sheer horror of what I had discovered' (*min hawl mā ᶜaraftu*) and imagines himself to have eaten his 'own flesh'.[98]

Sinking into what he terms 'gazelle-blood fever' (*ḥummā dam al-ghazāl*), the narrative then embarks on nightmarish visions in which he makes a mad flight through Benghazi as it 'bares its fangs', haunted by packs of stray dogs, thieves and kidnappers on its outer margins.[99] 'The gazelle raced through my veins', he recalls, 'and I began baaing and bleating (*akhadhanī thughāʾ thumma ba^{c}ba^{c}a*) and barking at the dogs of the salt flats, before fleeing to deserts in which land and sky had grown dry alike.'[100]

From these feverish hallucinations, the narrative escalates into traumas both personal and historical. As the boy recovers from his fever, the country is struck by cholera and, shortly after, his little brother is hit by a car before his eyes. This is conveyed in brief, fractured terms: 'I had been playing with him when the car careered into the shop, crushing my brother, and spattering his brains across my sleeves. I heard my dad yelling across the shop, and, in the sheer terror of what had happened (*min hawl mā ḥadatha*), I told him that everything was fine.'[102] Relayed in only a few sentences, amid the novel's fevered pace and juxtaposing voices, the brother's death represents one of many fragmented, yet structurally central, memories of precarity and loss. The same phrase, '*min hawl mā ḥadatha*' and '*min hawl mā ^{c}arafatu*', bind together these swiftly ensuing experiences of terror, concluded by both his frustrated trip to the zoo, as Benghazi is engulfed by biting sand, and his grandmother's 'Tale of Ibn Adam', offering rejected counsel and consolation.

Like his grandmother, the boy also perceives the city's wider vulnerability to flooding, storms and drought, alongside mass demolition. He is particularly disturbed by the removal of the salt flats, Benghazi's 'white robe'. Picturing himself as Nus Ansis, he confronts the construction workers in their forklifts, imagining them as the attacking army of the Qurʾanic Surat al-Fil (The Elephant), bringing war elephants, but turned to ashes by birds, punishing their '*kayd*' (guile).[102] Surat al-Zilzal (The Earthquake) then echoes through the description of the catastrophic year of 1963, in which an earthquake in the city of Marj, some eighty kilometers east of Benghazi, left over three hundred people dead, and mass student demonstrations led to brutal police backlash.[103] Describing how the streets become 'a dough of clay and human flesh' (*^{c}ajīn min al-ṭīn wa-l-laḥm al-basharī*), the boy's memories, like his grandmother's, move from the enchanted and folkloric to the fear-filled, infused with human vulnerability, and echoing back to his brother's death and his growing estrangement from both his grandmother and himself:

> This isn't Benghazi, Grandma. That's the hidden truth I admitted, but she no longer heard me, and I no longer heard her. I was yelling from a valley and she was calling from above. That's what I said to myself, though my self no longer heard either. Then a timber truck hit my blond-haired brother, my little Issa, and then our home turned into a parking lot for lorries, where they belched out burning oil. That's what I said, as Benghazi turned her back.[104]

This sense of loss culminates in the boy's own disappearance at the novel's end, during a patriotic march in which schoolchildren parade through the city, chanting the name of King Idris and imagining themselves as 'men of the next generation'.[105] The boy, however, drifts away and is lost, as the narrative voice switches, for the first time, from first to third person: 'Darkness descended, he did not return, and his grandmother wept.'[106] A terrible storm arises and the novel ends as birds return to their nests, dogs and cats huddle on piles of rubbish and there is no sign of the boy: 'Police cars trawled the streets, and no one came, and there was no news of the missing boy (*al-ghāʾib*).'[107] Once again, as animals find shelter in the turbulent city, the human is irrevocably lost. Ending with the disappearance of the narrating I, just as manhood and nationhood are negotiated, the boy becomes 'Nas Ansis', the novel's ambivalent underdog, attempting to find his way home, but destined to flight and, like his grandmother, 'absence' (*ghiyāb*). Within the complex entanglement of mythologies, memories and histories that the novel brings together, the tale of Ibn Adam therefore provides its most consistent counsel, that some are consigned to eternal flight and others to pursuit. Despite the disappearance of nomadic tradition, dramatised through the grandmother's growing forgetfulness, al-Fayturi's novel thus announces that it, too, is *sarīb*, and that the coming-of-age of *Bildungsroman* is, in fact, recovery of this *sarīb* after its initial rejection. In this way, the novel provides an exemplar of the *Bildungsroman* as 'creaturely coming-of-age', looking not to the future but the histories of the past, underpinned by primordial pessimism.

Wabr al-Ahsina: First People and Unborn People

Shifting from child to unborn foetus, Bin Shatwan's *Wabr al-Ahsina* goes even further in this direction. From conception to gestation, the novel both dwells in the space of the body and opens from cells and DNA onto imagined encounters with interlocutors from Libyan and world history, echoing Pick's description of 'a particular approach to literature whose orientation is exterior rather than interior: writing that does not express the humanistic self-awareness of the autobiographical subject, lacks self-transparency, and partakes of the creaturely opacity of language'.[108] This defamiliarising, opaque perspective is characteristic of all Bin Shatwan's early fiction. *Madmun Burtuqali* (2008, Orange Content) is narrated by a river as it observes the people on its banks, their lives spilling into its waters. *Al-Malika* (2008, The Queen) is divided into 'partial pictures' (*ṣuwar maqṭaᶜiyya*), presenting a compellingly disjointed vision of Libya. Often taking the form of fable, these riddle-like 'pictures' hint at a fuller story that cannot be told, shifting to the forgotten and imperceptible, whether a new-born fly, a microbe under a microscope or, in 'ᶜId Khatiᵓ' ('A Flawed Festival'), a sheep slaughtered at Eid.[109]

Describing the social and political restrictions imposed on women authors in Libya, Bin Shatwan observes how such allusive, visceral narrative became a necessity, shaped, from childhood, by suspicion and surveillance, as teachers were unwilling to believe that she had written her homework herself while, in adulthood, the regime hounded her, enticing her first to become its mouthpiece and then levelling threats against her.[110] Summing up, Bin Shatwan describes how she 'turned to symbolism as the essence and background of my tales when dealing with Libya'.[111] *Wabr al-Ahsina* certainly tests the bounds of the *Bildungsroman*, in both its dense symbolism and structural fragmentation. Bookended by two poems, its six 'texts' depict the lineage of a single family, stretching from a 'Libyanised' Adam and Eve to an unborn child in the 1960s, and moving from a panorama of humanity to a microscopic examination of the body's genetic make-up. The first poem is Philip Larkin's 'This Be the Verse' (1971), introducing the motif of human 'genealogy' (*nasl*) at the novel's heart, focused on the unshakeable influence of biological and historical 'heritage' (*irth*):

> They fuck you up, your mum and dad.
> They may not mean to, but they do.
> They fill you with the faults they had
> And add some extra, just for you.[112]

Following this, the first three texts are narrated from a third-person perspective and the last three by the foetus. Through both, Libya's harsh social conditions, and particularly those of its women, are explored, alongside primordial reflection on the boundary between human, pre-human and non-human.

Identifying misery (*būʾs*) at the heart of human lineage, the first 'text' is a satirical rewriting of Adam and Eve through the contexts of modern Libya, entitled 'Mustakhraj Rasmī min Sijil Wāqiᶜa Wilādat Rabb al-ᶜĀʾila' ('Official Extract from the Record of the Patriarch's Birth'). Concerning the marriage of the first humans, the text opens with satirical questions: 'What kind of car brought the couple? Who received the good news about the bride's virginity and, indeed, the groom's, since Adam knew no woman before or after Eve?'[113] Following the wedding, Adam is then spared the costs of the '*zūra*', the first visit a bride makes to her family, typically necessitating great expenditure. Eve, however, regrets having no one to prepare traditional remedies for her after giving birth, as the novel shifts between Libyan localities and fundamental, existential isolation.[114] 'Adam could not manage to stifle the icy feeling that crouched over him', the narrator relays, 'and began to complain constantly about the misery of life. Eve attributed this to his solitude.'[115]

To overcome his 'solitude' (*waḥda*), Eve submits to endless pregnancies and the family rapidly extends, with discord erupting when one son kills his brother in jealousy over who is to marry their sister. While doing so, he is observed by a 'lame, dusty raven' (*ghurāb aghbar aᶜwar*), echoing the Qur'anic bird that teaches Cain to bury Abel.[116] Despite the primal nature of the act and the mythic imagery which frames it, the language describing the strife that causes it and results from it is anchored in political rhetoric, referred to as 'factionalism' (*taḥazzub*) and 'partisanship' (*tashayyuᶜ*).[117] Stemming from it, Adam and Eve's offspring descend into violence, with men killed and women enslaved. In a particularly despairing comment on humanity, Eve sorely regrets not taking the contraceptive pill, while medical imagery is woven into social satire as she suffers an 'anaemia of understanding' (*faqr al-fahm*) and Adam dies from a 'social clot' (*jalṭa ijtimāᶜiyya*).[118] The passage concludes by relating what has gone before to both Libya and humanity:

> Since then, fraternal enmity (*ḥādithat ᶜirāk al-ikhwa*) has been relayed in over a hundred ways, in every tongue. As Libyans, we have our own particular

> form of conflict-management (*idārat khilāfātinā*), famous the world over: we declare our hero to be right in all cases, without so much as a raised eyebrow, and regardless of whether he is victim or perpetrator.[119]

Following this pessimistic vision of history's 'conflict-management', the third 'text', 'Ḥāᵓ min Nasl Ḥamad' ('Ḥā' from the Line of Ḥamad'), depicts the pre-Islamic practice of *waᵓd* (female infanticide through burial alive), through returning to the Qurᵓanic raven which circles over men as they bury their daughters. 'The ground', the narrator states, 'was sated with the decomposed bodies of buried girls' (*al-mawᵓūdāt al-mutaḥallala*).[120] Before the invention of axes, men dig graves with their bare hands, distancing 'shame' (*ᶜār*), and sparing only a few girls 'for mating and pleasure'.[121] Tying Libya's oil reserves into a deep historic vision of women's abuse, the girls' burial is further linked to the formation of 'the largest land oil deposit on the face of the earth'.[122] Through these combined threads, the text provides a complex addition to what Hanadi al-Samman has identified as the 'waᵓd archetype' in modern Arabic literature.[123] Tracing how the term has been used to condemn authoritarian regimes, 'burying' dissent, the motif, she suggests, has become 'the epitome of personal and political erasure', as women are imagined as 'heirs of an archaic, albeit extinct, practice intended to eradicate traces of the female buried body and silence their recently resurrected bodies'.[124] It is this archaic practice that provides the backdrop to the foetus's narrative, as one girl, Haᵓ, escapes to become the distant ancestor of Hamad, protagonist of the third text, 'Sīn min Nasl Ḥamad' ('Sīn from the Line of Ḥamad'). Taking place after the 'fourth flood' (*al-ṭūfān al-rābiᶜ*) and against the context of Ottoman rule and Bedouin rebellion, it relates the marriage of Hamad to Ahwaywa, and the adventures of their son, Husayn, as nomadic peoples struggle against conscription, elevated taxes, imprisonment and forced labour. Husayn, meanwhile, who longs only for 'sun, sky and land', represents the distant ancestor of the unborn child, shifting to Libya of the 1960s and to the human body in the final three texts.[125]

The Pre-human

In the first of these texts, 'al-Maᶜbar' ('The Crossing'), the harshness of life in the new nation means that the child's conception is delayed by the exhaustion of her father, foreman of a team of labourers building a highway from Fezzan to Ajdabiya in order to join 'the nation to the people and the people to the nation'.[126] Characteristic of *Bildungsroman*, individual and collective formation are joined but, still in heaven, the child worries that, through the harshness of life, her mothers' eggs will have 'gone bad' (*madhirat*), anchoring struggle within life's very beginnings.[127] Forming queues, she and the other unborn children are divided into those destined for a life of luxury and those destined for labour, 'marginalised' (*muhammash*) and 'luckless' (*rāqid al-rīḥ*).[128] Discussing their futures, the children learn that, in Libya, their youth will be short or non-existent, in a nation where 'times are hard', as it 'still struggles to steer the ship of life' (*lā tadrī kayf taqūd safīnat al-ḥayāt*), while its children must 'grow up before we are ready' (*yajib an nakbur qabl al-awān*).[129] The children, in other words, prepare for the type of childhoods depicted in *al-Jirab* and *Sarib*, but stripped altogether of fairy-tale power, astonishment and complicity with nature. Their collective wait is, furthermore, paralleled to that of the country, praying for changed circumstances and brighter horizons.[130]

In 'Faḍā᾽ al-Salsūl' ('The Space of the Spine'), the child finally takes form in the body of her father, perceiving her ancestors in the 'jelly of millions of humans' on the walls of a dark tunnel: 'Inside this tunnel were secrets and events, frozen in place since the depths of time [. . .] Here, I was able to see the plasma of millions of humans, from a time unknown to all but the King of Time, the One who decides the course of events.'[131] As she looks further into these 'cells' and 'nuclei', the girl perceives that they have already determined her own future, 'planting the seeds of my being, formed in the flesh and blood, the body and spirit, the mind and emotion'.[132]

In both her father's and her mother's bodies, the girl further watches the drama of these ancestors' lives unspool through vignettes of Libyan history, as she passes through 'chambers', analysing her fitness to be born. Notable among the vignettes is a list of 'speakers' (*qā᾽ilūn*), one of whom is oral poet al-Minifi, reciting his opening lines, 'I have no illness but this place of Egaila [ᶜAqila]/the imprisonment of my tribe/and separation from my kin's abode.'[133] Later, she even comes to al-Sadiq al-Nayhum and his 'bitter humour'.[134] At one point, too, she engages in dialogue with the spectre of King Idris, whose surveillance extends even 'into the womb'.[135] Together, these voices convey history as 'catastrophic pileup', a tumultuous accumulation of people and events pointing every now and then to the unspoken outcome of the Jamahiriyya. In this way, Bin Shatwan opens out the levels of what has been forgotten such that, as Benjamin notes of Kafka, and as I earlier cited in reference to al-Kuni's deep historic perspective, 'Everything forgotten mingles with what has been forgotten of the prehistoric world, forms countless, uncertain, changing compounds, yielding a constant flow of new, strange products [. . .] "Here the very fullness of the world is considered as the only reality [. . .]".'[136]

Finally, in the last text, 'Wabr al-Aḥṣina', following her 'animalisation' (*laḥẓat ḥaywanatī*), the girl arrives in her mother, ᶜAwaysha's, body.[137] While there, she learns of the mother's life as a young girl and her marriage at thirteen, perceiving her difficult existence and the hardship of pregnancy. 'My carrier is tired, and I am too', the foetus observes. 'All day she has worked like a mule, with no one relieving her.'[138] On the walls of the womb, the girl further discovers advice left by those that went before her, urging those that follow to take pity on their 'carrier' and not reject her meagre food. In an extended passage, the foetus reads one of these babies' 'diaries' (*yawmiyyāt*), from her time in the womb to the miscarriage of her twin brother to her own premature death as a teenager.[139] Even from before birth, the baby is thus introduced to vulnerability as the first, shared state, rooted, as Pick puts it, 'in bodies exposed to time and [. . .] at the mercy of gravity'.[140] As in al-Maghrabi's *Nisa' al-Rih*, Bin Shatwan structures her *Bildungsroman* through the reproductive capacities of the woman's body, as well as its status as a site of shame and honour. In *Wabr al-Ahsina*, however, this bodily proximity becomes a means for closer knowledge of the shared suffering of mother and daughter, and of assessing the viability or desirability of life.

Eventually, the baby is pulled from her mother's belly, screaming not to be brought into the world: 'I wanted to return to where it was better, where I would not be transformed into what I did not want to be, where everything was fresh like clay (*ṭāzij ka-l-ṣalṣāl*) and it was possible to change forms, wipe them away or recreate them (*iᶜādat khalqihi*)'.[141] As in so much Libyan fiction, the baby expresses a deep ambivalence towards the process of creation and the suffering to which it leads, while, delivered into the world, her wish is realised as complications lead to the death of both her and her mother:

> My mother took me or I took her. For the first and last time, she saw that her husband cared, that he was clinging to her survival, gathering her children together and praying for her to live. But she did not respond, for she had gone with me to the world from which I had come to her.[142]

Through both the 'first humans', Adam and Eve, and the 'pre-human' narrator, Bin Shatwan infects Eden and the womb, pre-eminent symbols of human innocence, with alienation and hardship, observed on social, biological and mythical levels. The formation of humanity, nation and child are interwoven, shifting between historical panorama and visceral flesh. Following the final text, a poem, 'Farāgh al-Imtilāʾ' ('The Emptiness of Filling'), duly returns from the child's voice to a broad vision of human violence and dispersal:

> Ever since Cain killed Abel
> and the raven got involved,
> the comedy has developed
> with knives and axes,
> poison and rifles,
> bombs, gases
> and chemicals . . .
> The Earth kept turning,
> and life did not cease,
> preserving those who gave life to us.
> They poured forth as it emptied
> and it became full.[143]

Seen in a profoundly negative light, the scriptural act of human 'dispersal' is, as in Larkin's 'This Be the Verse', imagined as the transmission of violence in ever more sophisticated forms. In each 'text' of *Wabr al-Ahsina*, this generational process is envisioned in different manners, with its inevitability conveyed through myth, genetics and social custom, from Libya's pre-Islamic past to its Ottoman rule to its Independence. These contexts and narratives emerge as a tangle of circumstances which lead the unborn child to read, in the diaries of her older sister, that the existence of the *rāqid al-baṭn* (the sleeper in the belly) is far preferable to that of the *rāqid al-rīḥ* (the sleeper on the wind) who 'beds down in the wilderness, and possesses nothing'.[144] In this, we may understand the poetics of childhood – and pre-childhood at that – as another iteration of Libya's early fictional poetics of survival, discussed in Chapter 1, in similar relation to the *rāqid al-rīḥ*.[145]

Conclusion

The childhood novels of ᶜAqila, al-Fayturi and Bin Shatwan may be divided into the dichotomies of past and present and old and young, as well as those of male and female and, indeed, human and non-human. Yet all are entangled. The boys' voices merge with their older selves and with the voices of their female storytellers, while Bin Shatwan's foetus resonates with the tales of her ancestors, from the literary voices of al-Minifi and al-Nayhum to the 'diaries' of earlier foetuses, inscribed in her parents' bodies. Places, too, are entwined. Childhood home and village, and the human body itself, are presented as innocent havens or hybrid places of shelter, where histories, myths and beings come together at the mercy of war and the vicissitudes of nature. Libya as nation is therefore overwhelmed by Libya as stage for creaturely struggle, while the *Bildungsroman*, as 'novel of formation', concludes in perpetual childhood, disappearance or premature adulthood. Just as 'coming home' is frustrated in tales-within-tales, so it is in the authors' texts, which instead return to melancholy memory and primordial fall, whether through Adam and Eve's marital woes or 'Ibn Adam' who 'conquered all things'. The creaturely, however, represents not just a reminder of inevitable flight, but an expression of solidarity, resurrecting shared origins and locating vitality in orality and plurality. The revival of both childhood and memory further represents not regression but survival. Establishing alternative notions of home and recuperating past ways of being, it counters the headiness of forward movement, unbuilding the nation and returning to the lost power of storytelling as collective wisdom, countering the characteristic individualism and future orientation of the modern *Bildungsroman*.[146]

6

'Une histoire de mouche': The Libyan Novel in Other Voices

Until, when they arrived at the Valley of Ants, an ant said: 'O ants, enter your dwellings lest Solomon and his troops should crush you unawares'. (Qurʾan, 27:18)[1]

Precarity is that here and now in which pasts may not lead to futures. (Anna Tsing)[2]

Discussing the growing prominence of diasporic Arab literature in languages other than Arabic, Hilary Kilpatrick refers to 'those scattered works which cannot even be organised into a minority tradition because there are so few of them'.[3] Such applies, in the Libyan tradition, to the writing of both Hisham Matar (b.1970) in English and Kamal Ben Hameda (b.1954) in French. In the past decade, both authors, and particularly Matar, have risen to prominence, recognised for their literary depictions of Libya, and becoming two of the country's most recognised voices. In view of Libya's large diaspora, their numbers will undoubtedly also grow in coming years, raising the question, as Kilpatrick frames it, as to what writings they can be meaningfully related and, specifically, what Nouri Gana calls their '"hidden affinities" with Arabic literary traditions'.[4]

Both Ben Hameda's *La compagnie des Tripolitaines* (2011; *Under the Tripoli Sky*, 2013) and Matar's *In the Country of Men* (2006) take childhood as their starting-point, setting them, on the one hand, within the ranks of canonical, diasporic and postcolonial *Bildungsroman* such as Azouz Begag's *Le Gone du Chaâba* (1986; *Shantytown Kid*, 2007), Arundhati Roy's *The God of Small Things* (1997) and Khaled Husseini's *The Kite Runner* (2003). On the other hand, their local aesthetics are manifestly clear. Conveying the palpable heat and dazzling sunlight of boyhood summers, their novels are anchored in childhood bewilderment, steeped in folklore and Qurʾanic spirituality, and constructed around curtailed comings-of-age. Interwoven with the intimate memories of older relatives, they are framed by wider, creaturely perspectives on the land and its inhabitants. While Ben Hameda prefaces *La compagnie des Tripolitaines* with an excerpt from a fictional chronicle, '*Le livre des mouches*' (The Book of Flies), framing his protagonist-narrator, Hadachinou's, coming-of-age with the history of a 'fly nation', *In the Country of Men* opens with reference to Tripoli's 'every person, animal and ant', conveying an imaginative, creaturely collective, harking back to the Qurʾanic 'nations like you'. As what Deleuze and Guattari term 'minor writers', writing within French and English from the perspective of minority, migrant experience, their novels are thus marked by deterritorialising 'lines of flight', giving voice to a marginal collective within 'major' languages.[5] In both, however, the 'collective' to which they give voice is Libya itself, as they return, in literary imaginings, from geographic and linguistic exile to the land and its creatures. Pursuing the same theoretical perspectives that informed Chapter 5, I therefore track the interaction of *Bildungsroman*, creaturely encounter and memory in both, while taking into account the different circumstances of the novels' writing, publishing and reception. Within English and French markets, I suggest that they are marked not so much by silence and the 'difficulty of story' as by the weight of responsibility of telling story.

By dint of their idiosyncratic trajectories, both Ben Hameda and Matar further represent distinct outliers within diasporic, Francophone and Anglophone, fiction. In French, the likes of the Moroccan Tahar Ben Jelloun (b.1944) and Algerian Assia Djébar (1936–2015) have established a prominent tradition of Maghribi literature, addressing anti-colonial struggle, national independence and immigrant experience.[6] Ben Hameda does not fit clearly within this tradition, however, with his French unmarked by the same imperial legacy, and neither France nor its immigrant communities featuring in his Libya-centred prose. In a review of *La compagnie des Tripolitaines*, Matar writes that 'his book bears the particular tone of an author severed from the source' and this, in fact, is a defining feature of both authors' writing.[7]

Moving to England for boarding school as a lone sixteen-year-old, Matar remained in the UK for several decades, but admits to feeling torn between identities, relocating to New York in the 2010s, and frequently returning to Egypt and Uganda where he spent much of his early adolescence. While recognised as Arab British or Anglo Arab (or hyphenated versions of each), he represents what Layla El Maleh calls a 'wanderer'.[8] Like Ben Hameda, he does not address the more familiar concerns of Arab British fiction, from the responsibility of 'cultural translation' to the negotiation of hybrid identities.[9] In fact, Britain often fades from the picture in his fiction, with *In the Country of Men* set between Libya and Egypt, and the West featuring only through the 'yellow hair' of the young narrator's American Aunt Cathy.[10] In his second novel, *Anatomy of a Disappearance* (2011), Europe makes an appearance, but primarily as what Christopher Micklethwait terms 'ambiguous, jumbled chronotopes' of boarding school and holiday resort.[11]

In contrast, both Ben Hameda and Matar attend to Libya as an urgent concern, conveying personal loss and collective anger and suffering. In doing so, they set themselves within the ranks of broader Libyan authors. Due to their wider readership, they also, however, bear the 'representational burden' of serving as spokespeople for a country in which they have not lived for decades.[12] Amid the surge of interest in the Arab world following 9/11, Libya and its maverick leader proved particularly fascinating, emerging, as they were, from decades of political isolation. Despite this, few Libyan authors were translated into English. Anglophone writers such as Matar and poet Khaled Mattawa therefore provided rare literary perspectives on the country.[13] Slated as the 'Libyan *Kite Runner*', Samir el-Youssef cynically suggests that *In the Country of Men* was 'snapped up' as a 'convenient window' on Libya and deliberately 'shoehorns in Libyan politics under Gaddafi'.[14] 'Who would publish a book about the troubles of a Libyan child', el-Youssef questions, 'when, in the eyes of the western media, the whole country is reduced to the delusions of Gaddafi?'[15]

Given the intimate entanglement of politics and the personal in the Libyan novel, el-Youssef's criticism is unfair. While in censored Arabic novels the Jamahiriyya lurks as an ominous spectre behind the child of the 1960s, Matar's novel shifts to the 1970s, where it insidiously infects daily life. Coinciding with Libya's rehabilitation into the 'world community', *In the Country of Men* depicts, for Chorin, 'an unquantifiable darkness that lurked behind the otherwise benign-looking façade'.[16] With its evident cynicism, El-Youssef's critique thus suggests the loaded reception of Libyan and, more broadly, Arab novels in English and French. Matar himself critically assesses how *La compagnie des Tripolitaines* was interpreted by its French reviewers as a 'critique of Arab patriarchal society', reducing its complex depiction of a 'richly cosmopolitan society of Arabs, Catholics, Jews and second- and third-generation Italians conscious of the past and looking towards an uncertain future. It's a society turned in on itself, breathless from colonialism and bewildered by modernity.'[17] As an Anglophone novel of 'world literature', Margaret Scanlan further suggests that *In the Country of Men* provided an important, nuanced glimpse of Libya's 'domestic space' for western audiences consumed by the simplistic dichotomies of the 'war on terror'.[18] While true, *In the Country of Men* is decidedly also for Libyans, speaking to the broader poetics of silenced, creaturely traces in the country's fiction. Almost immediately, it was translated into Arabic and smuggled into the country, while Matar describes hearing how his Uncle Mahmoud, in a prison cell in Abu Salim, heard an interview with him on BBC Arabic, filtering its way into the remotest corners of the closed state.[19]

Underpinning the fraught domain of cross-cultural interpretation, I therefore emphasise the centrality of creaturely vulnerability in both authors, haunted by the same 'difficulty of story' as their compatriots, though informed not so much by censorship as linguistic exile, and not so much by 'readerless-ness' as the burden of representation.[20] While Matar describes linguistic exile as 'the deepest and most peculiar dimension of exile that I have experienced', Ben Hameda evokes a double alienation from the Tripoli dialect of his youth, first through the 'parrot-tongue' (*lughat al-babghāʾ*) of his schoolboy *fuṣḥā*, and then through French.[21] The response of both is to open language to what Ben Hameda calls the 'questioning' (*tasāʾul*) of the child, vividly recalling the sensations of boyhood and thereby overcoming the linguistic barrier that separates it from adulthood and authorship.[22]

This opening emerges in both authors through a strongly imagistic vein, infusing the natural world with wonder and bewilderment. While Matar's narrator, Slooma, reads censored fear in curtailed birdsong and describes his loneliness as a 'sick dog', Hadachinou shifts between an inquisitive 'field mouse' and dejected 'Sloughi'. From within French and English, this imagery opens onto a wider, creaturely collective, moving from linguistic exile into palpable expressions of vulnerability and solidarity, between children and the world around themselves. Above all, it evokes the overwhelming 'time of childhood' as what Ben Hameda calls the 'here and now' (*l'ici et le maintenant*), eroded through exile and initiation into 'the codified voice' (*la parole codifiée*) of education and memorisation of Qurʾan and *Green Book*.[23] Countering this codification, Ben Hameda strives towards the 'child's voice' (*la parole de l'enfance*), associated with his mother's Tripoli dialect, as well as with the 'language of birds' (*le langage des oiseaux*) and 'dialect of water and wind' (*le dialecte de l'eau et du vent*), encountered on boyhood wanderings.[24]

Both authors further weave personal loss into the collective memories of historical suffering that were central to my discussion in Chapter 5. In the preface to his French translation of al-Minifi's foundational oral qasida, 'Ma Bi Marad', Ben Hameda describes it as, 'a poem escaped from the abysses of hell, a forgotten voice (*parole oubliée*) that traces all the tortures inflicted on the poet's tribe, as though a foreword to those that blighted Europe'.[25] Al-Minifi, he continues, can only 'inhabit his wound', imagining the 'meadows of his childhood' as he is 'exiled within his native land'.[26] Identifying his own exile with that of al-Minifi, Ben Hameda specifically emphasises *childhood* lost, as the penultimate stanza's 'loss of my land' (*faqdit bilādī*) becomes, in French translation, the 'loss of my *childhood* land' (*la perte des contrées de mon enfance*).[27] His first novel, *La compagnie des Tripolitaines*, meanwhile, ties together the *parole oubliée* of historical suffering with the *parole de l'enfance* of Hadachinou, inflecting 1960s Tripoli with imaginings both fanciful and painful, and framed by the tales and memories of the titular 'Tripolitaines' – the Arab, Berber, African and Italian women among whom Hadachinou grows up.

In his memoir, *The Return* (2017), Matar similarly evokes al-Minifi's enduring influence since studying his poem at school in Libya, describing his younger self as 'haunted' by the twenty-third stanza and its 'image of the aged child', which he translates as follows:

> How many a child have they taken and whipped?
> The poor young flowers return confused,
> made old without having lived (*ṣāf min dūn jaylihi*).[28]

Evoking the child's premature aging through the verb '*ṣāf*', signifying, in dialect, the dying of flowers with the arrival of 'summer' (*ṣayf*), al-Minifi contrasts the natural passage of time with the unnatural brutality of the Italian whip, through which children, alternatively translated, 'grow older than their years'.[29] In Matar's rendition, *ṣāf* becomes 'made old', removing all traces of nature's redemptive, renewing beauty and indicating a decisive poetics within his fiction, whereby the vulnerability of growing up within a dictatorship taints land, sun and sea with fear and disorientation. Specifically, the aged child is suggestive of *In the Country of Men*'s Slooma, caught, in the summer of 1979, between the insidious Revolutionary Committees, the hysterical fervour of public execution and the breakdown of family relations. Opening and closing with Slooma's departure for Egypt, which parallels Matar's own, it is set over one summer, tantalisingly evocative of al-Minifi's *ṣāf*.[30] During this summer, Slooma is caught between his mother's compulsive 'telling', exemplifying the breakdown of the storyteller's counsel, and the very impossibility of speech in a state of surveillance, where every utterance is precarious. Together, both his and Hadachinou's narratives reflect the curtailed childhoods of the Arabic Libyan *Bildungsroman* and, to an even greater extent, the struggle to relay memory as literal silence or compulsive repetition dramatise the fraying of communicable experience.[31] Beginning with *La compagnie des Tripolitaines*, I focus on the melancholy exile read onto Hadachinou by an older self, and framed by the subversive myths of origin and '*histoires de mouches*' relayed by women.[32] Through *In the Country of Men*, I then explore how the fragile balance of the 1960s shifts to the outright horror of the 1970s. In both, I read the shared, creaturely vulnerability of memory and of making sense of a bewildering world.

La compagnie des Tripolitaines: Women's Histories and Flies' Histories

In Ben Hameda's first, autobiographical prose work, *La mémoire de l'absent* (2001, Memory of the Absent), he recounts his Tripoli childhood and departure for France in the early 1970s, following his internment in a psychiatric institution. Both a precursor to *La compagnie des Tripolitaines* and its unspoken conclusion, it is narrated by a reflective adult, but introduces the poetics of loss that resonates through his later novel as a haunting subtext:

> Those who never left, whether by choice or lack thereof, languish in prison or madness, in silence or oblivion. Time having wrought its pacifying work, I no longer yearn, but Libya remains a source of pain. Melancholy, powerless and alone, the Mediterranean is its sole companion. Between the time of memory and forgetting, I choose memory, anchoring me in the joyful company of others. Between the time of childhood and of exile, I choose childhood, anchoring me in life.[33]

Structured as a vivid tour of Tripoli's winding alleys, *La mémoire* both dramatises the 'joyful company of others' and confronts its loss on interweaving levels: through the geography of youth, transformed by urbanisation; the people, forgotten in death, imprisonment or madness; and the ideologies of patriarchy, colonisation and dictatorship, poisoning relationships. On the smallest scale, this is located within Ben Hameda's family and his father and mother's determined silence. Closeted in office and mosque, his father speaks not to express himself, but to repeat Qur'anic verses, or 'to order and inform'.[34] This 'codified voice', Ben Hameda writes, leaves 'nothing to spontaneity, laughter or improvisation', and is accompanied by his mother's refusal to indulge in memories or even bedtime tales.[35] Responding to intimate questions with proverbs, or the resignation of the word *maktūb* (written/destined), she denies her son's desire for story, and Ben Hameda describes his childhood sense of 'powerlessness, abandonment and exile', prefiguring his later geographical exile.[36]

His mother and father's limited speech further prefigures literal censuring under al-Qadhafi. In a series of anecdotes, Ben Hameda describes the disappearance of his favourite bookshops and libraries, and the literary figures who haunted them.[37] On the front page of a 1973 newspaper, he recalls an image of the celebrated poet, al-Jilānī Ṭuraybshān, 'with head shaven and gaze disoriented, under the cynical, provocative title: "Look at your Revolutionary Poets Now!"'[38] Recalling his own sectioning, after attempting to acquire the works of Marx, he describes his fellow internees 'endlessly circling, like a herd of cattle in an enclosure', motionless with 'stupor'.[39] The traumas that render story difficult, embodied by Ben Hameda's mother, are thus joined to the immediate precarity of telling or reading, resulting in the paradigmatically wordless condition of 'cattle' (*bétail*) and 'stupor' (*hébétement*).

Tripoli's physical transformation conveys further loss, with the repetition of the relative clause '*qui n'existe plus*' (which no longer exists) emphasising the city's literal and figurative transformation into 'an anxious, deformed and enslaved city'.[40] This is compounded by an awareness of its historical subjugation to what Ben Hameda elsewhere calls 'banners of the absurd' (*les étendards de l'absurde*), denying otherness and operating on the logic of original precedence , whereby land is claimed as the sole property of its 'first' and 'legitimate' inhabitants.[41] Countering these 'banners', Ben Hameda returns to hybrid histories and palpable, lived connections to the land, both in *La mémoire de l'absent* and, above all, in *La compagnie des Tripolitaines*.[42]

Like *La mémoire de l'absent, La compagnie des Tripolitaines* is structured through Hadachinou's wanderings, struggling from silence to story and between the codified and spontaneous. While set in the 1960s, it is further dedicated to the wives and mothers of the Abu Salim victims, framing its depiction of pre-Qadhafi Libya with the regime's worst crime and thereby binding past, present and future.[43] The opening epigraph compounds this, with an excerpt from a fictional *Livre des mouches* (Book of Flies), relaying Libya's history from the first Phoenician invasion (*c.*1200 BCE) and penned by an anonymous fly historian from the *Peuple libre des mouches* (Free Nation of Flies).[44] Combining mythic, colonial and pseudo-scientific discourses, the fly describes Libya's 'true natives' (*vrais indigènes*) as 'savage, hairy, toothless barbarians', 'cannibals', 'Cyclops' and 'hermaphrodites', blurring male and female, human and animal, and real and fantastic, in a hybrid vision that upsets any notion of homogenous, authentic origins.[45] So too does the overall use of a fictional epigraph which, on the one hand, echoes Herodotus's canonical *Histories* (440 BCE) and its description of Libya's 'dog-faced' and 'headless' creatures but, on the other, thoroughly defamiliarises the 'Father of History' through its fly narrator.[46] Among all the peoples that settled in Libya, the extract suggests, flies alone have remained constant, undermining the fleeting ideologies of empire. The land's 'true natives', meanwhile, survive amidst 'steep cliffs and mountains', roamed by fearsome beasts, and overlooked by a merciless sun, further anchoring the nation's origins in aridity, hunger and fear.[47]

While suggestive of national allegory, parodying al-Qadhafi's *Green Book* and Jamahiriyya, the *Livre des mouches* and *Nation libre des mouches* are rooted in the creaturely, with the chronicler's chief concern being to feast on human flesh. As allegory, they may therefore best be understood through Benjamin's concept of the term in which, as Bernard Cowan remarks, the abstract idea is infused with the messiness of transient reality, and 'the signs perceived strike notes at the depths of one's being, regardless of whether they point to heaven, to an irretrievable past, or to the grave'.[48] Outlasting all foreign settlers, the fly, as 'creaturely sign', is a reminder that the root and destiny of all is brute matter, collapsing symbolic systems into decomposing elements and highlighting the underbelly of waste and decay that society elevates through legends and ideology.

In its final lines, the extract concludes by describing Libya's subjugation to foreign invaders as punishment for primordial male betrayal. Echoing myths of the North African Amazons, the fly reports that women were originally the warriors while men raised their children.[49] These men were, however, tempted by the arrival of the Phoenicians, offering silphium, alcohol and gold. Renouncing their prophetess, Maboula, they therefore submitted to the foreigners, relegating women to 'bellies into which they emptied their desires' (*des ventres où se vider*).[50] This betrayal, the fly reports, marks the beginning of Libya's colonial history as the dying Maboula condemns the men's descendants to enslavement.

In this messy tale of origins and fall, Ben Hameda inaugurates the fault lines that traverse the novel, and the histories of women within it, exemplified by Hadachinou's Great Aunt Nafissa as she laments the succession of Greek, Roman, Vandal, Arab, Turkish and Italian invaders:

> Apart from their bellies and their pricks, the only thing men are interested in is destroying with one hand what they've just created with the other. I remember the war, the famine and the way women were raped when the Italian soldiers entered Tripoli: they spread shame and loathing through the city. After the Greeks, the Romans, the Vandals, the Arab tribes and the Turks, it was their turn to try out their virility on our bodies. And they're still at it now, they're just wearing different clothes. Sewer rats, the lot of them.[51]

This, then, is the melancholy history and folkloric memory that haunt Hadachinou in his coming-of-age. While the '*Livre des mouches*' may appear an incongruous epigraph to the novel as *Bildungsroman*, it clearly echoes through it, as a pan-historic preface to Hadachinou's bewilderment. Furthermore, it announces his later literary allegiance to the tales of his youth. In a later section of the novel, it is, for example, echoed in another '*histoire de mouche*', in the form of a framed tale told by Hadachinou's Great Aunt Nafissa. It may therefore be read as a stylised take on this tale, infusing it with parody of nation and ideology, and emphasising the creaturely, rather than the words of a famous literary idol, as the frame for Hadachinou's solitary coming-of-age.

'Deep in the House, no one'

Perennially alone, Hadachinou avoids both the boisterous company of other children and the stern silence of his father. Yearning for the company of his mother and her friends, he is often excluded from their intimate gatherings, and wanders the city, with his dreamy curiosity serving, as Matar interprets it, as an allegory for the young Libya:

> The figure of Hadachinou – which in Libyan-Arabic dialect means 'What is this' – seems to be the question mark that hangs over the fate of the nation. His curiosity, dreaminess, timid inquisitiveness and resistance are an allegory for the young country's desire and potential.[52]

Through his protagonist's very name, Ben Hameda inflects French with both Tripoli dialect and childhood perplexity, while Hadachinou's solitary detachment hints at both the nation's traumatic past and uncertain future. In fragmented terms, the novel's opening pages depict him awakening in a seemingly empty house beneath a brilliant, indifferent sun:

> Light spilt over the house and the walls and the corridor and the kitchen . . . which is where I went in the hope of finding something to bury the sense of exile that was beginning to overwhelm me. I gobbled a piece of fruitcake, then hurtled down the stairs like a punctured balloon. The magic of waking had given way to a feeling of powerlessness. Nothing.[53]

Combining the 'here and now' of child's time, steeped in the magic of fairy tale, with loss, read onto childhood by an older self, or perhaps present within it all along, this description conveys the competing forces within the novel, exemplified by the image of the punctured balloon, as fantasy shifts to dejection. Light, too, represents a source of both dreaminess and anxiety, intimacy and exposure, reflected in the English translator's rendition of the novel's title not as the literal 'In the Company of Tripolitanian Women', but 'Under the Tripoli Sky'. With the sun described as 'static and jealous' and the horizon as 'disinterested', this is emphasised as Hadachinou describes himself through a litany of animal images, alternating between an 'alley cat beneath a freshly lit sky' and a 'lost sloughi', trailing around 'under a shameless, merciless sun'.[54] Pursuing his mother and her friends, he becomes a 'hunting lion' (*le fauve à l'affût*), 'playful dog' and excited 'little field mouse', then, rejected by them, a 'cockerel plucked of his tail feathers'.[55]

From the first, these animal similes, drawing together boyish imagination and bewilderment, are further framed by the structuring juxtaposition of Hadachinou's circumcision and the slaughter of a sheep at Eid, which begins the novel. Echoing the broader tradition of Eid memories in Libyan fiction,

Hadachinou observes the butcher, casually whistling pop songs, before being captivated by the scene of mortality before him:

> I witnessed the ceremony with a mixture of amazement, curiosity and quasi-morbid delight. The sheep's silence, its eyes changing colour, its furious bleating as it faced the deafening void (*en face du néant assourdissant*), the children standing round in a circle holding their breath, and the springing fountain of blood. [. . .] Rivulets of slow-flowing blood, smaller streams coagulating.[56]

Juxtaposing 'silence' to 'furious bleating', a dream-like quality is introduced into the scene, linking the present moment to the 'millennial ancestral ritual' of slaughter.[57] As Hadachinou himself submits to the knife, held down by a group of men, he further identifies with the 'deafening void' in the animal's eyes: 'I gaze up at the ceiling and picture the glassy look in the sheep's eyes on the day of sacrifice, a look full of renunciation.'[58] Through the sheep's paradigmatic powerlessness, Hadachinou describes a moment of profound distress in which, for the first time, he is propelled from the 'here and now' of childhood:

> I lower my eyelids to protect myself and, for the first time, delve deep inside myself to find the place where I can safely watch episodes of my life [. . .] Lost in this indefinable chasm (*cette indicible béance*), I suddenly became aware of an explosion of women's laughter from the kitchen, a burst of cheerful voices lilting with the sheer joy of life and jostling together like a mass of balloons released to mark a feast day.[59]

The 'indefinable chasm' into which Hadachinou retreats recalls the 'deafening void' he perceives in the sheep's eyes, with both dramatising his passage into knowledge of both social discipline and inescapable mortality, through the stern, silent figures of men. In contrast, women's joy returns him from his chasm, like a 'mass of balloons', continuing the novel's swift movement between childhood wonder and fear and loss. Women, above all, emphasise this movement, representing both embodiments of joy, adoration and fantasy for Hadachinou, and his principal initiators into melancholy, collective memory.

Flytopia

Hampered by past traumas, Hadachinou's grandmother is unable to tell stories altogether. 'I only know stories about war and suffering', she declares. 'You'll learn them soon enough from books . . . or by yourself.'[60] Hadachinou's mother is similarly story-less, and, whenever alone with her son, begins what he describes as 'lamentations again and again'.[61] Most strikingly, however, this sense of the 'difficulty of story' emerges through the *Histoire de la petite mouche des mouches* ('Story of the Little Fly of Flies'), told by Hadachinou's Great Aunt Nafissa, and immediately recalling the novel's opening epigraph from the *Livre des mouches*. Shifting from its panoramic view of eras, conveyed through the official discourse of a 'fly nation', to the microscopic view of nostrils and eyeballs, conveyed through the homely voice of a little fly, the story reiterates the species' delight in cycles of war and drought.[62] Rather than banishing the possibility of 'home', as in al-Fayturi's 'Tale of Ibn Adam', Aunt Nafissa shifts to 'fly home', located in the 'putrefying bodies' of humans.[63] Filled with orifices, excrement and decay, the little fly presents a 'flytopia' where human importance is radically undermined, represented as an organic whole and literally seen from the inside out: 'My father liked nostrils best. He would sneak inside them with my older brothers and sisters, and spend ages in there. Sometimes they would have their siesta inside, and they even defecated there [. . .] Those were feast days (*C'étaient jours de fête*).'[64] As darkly disturbing as it is unsettlingly entertaining, the story is said to be Hadachinou's favourite, and told in order to distract Siddéna, his family's young black maidservant, from the loss of her family. At the same time, Aunt Nafissa impresses its seriousness upon them. As she tells them, her stories 'carry in them memories of our countries, particularly the country of women' (*la mémoire de nos contrées, surtout celle des femmes*).[65]

At first, it is unclear why the fly's memories should be related to the 'country of women'. When considered in the light of Hadachinou's grandmother, however, the tale simply points to the difficulty of telling *human* stories about Libya, and particularly the experience of its women. Provoked by Siddéna's suffering, and emerging from the suffering of women before her, the story both acknowledges it and moulds it into a form that can be told to a child, provoking both laughter in the flies' feast and melancholy in its human substance, and the chronic fracture of civilisation that underpins it. Conveying the grotesque, folkloric spirit of Bakhtin's carnivalesque, the 'feast of fools' shifts to that of 'flies', representing not a joyous reversal of social hierarchies, but a grim awareness of mortality, born of the war and deprivation underpinning popular Libyan folklore.[66] Concluding as the little fly remembers his grandmother telling him 'about the world' as he lay happily replete at night, the universal image of one generation imparting wisdom to another stands in poignant contrast to Hadachinou's own story-less grandmother.[67] If the *Nation libre des mouches* represents the 'other' to Libya, in a land where mortality cannot be masked, the *petite mouche* represents the 'other' to Hadachinou in a land where childhood is ephemeral.

'Made from clay and filth'

Much of the latter half of *La compagnie des Tripolitaines* is devoted to the voices of Hadachinou's other aunts and women friends, interwoven with his own memories. Through each of their voices, conveying Jewish, Berber and African lore, the novel evokes the lingering plurality of the 1960s, before the remaining Jewish communities, continuously inhabiting the land since the third century BCE, were expelled in 1967 and, following 1969, al-Qadhafi ousted the Italians, and began his oppression of Berber and African minorities. Together, the women recognise themselves as 'Tripolitaines', an identity both more local and more expansive than that of 'Libyan', and thereby countering the officialness of 'banners of the absurd', claiming precedence in the land. In a series of origin and exile myths, shortly preceding the little fly's tale, moreover, the women further distance themselves from the 'species' of man and the Abrahamic genealogy of Adam and Eve, tracing their lineage instead from the natural world.

Fella, a Jewish friend of Hadachinou's mother, claims to be 'not so much a fallen angel as one who's been let down (*pas déchu, déçu*)'.[68] Immersed in a state of mystical love for the Divine, she describes how the Divine rejected her, revealing Himself instead to men, 'made of clay and filth'.[69] Finally, she declares all women to be angels, 'who don't know it', after having deserted God when they realised 'he was a male god and all he was interested in was his prick and his belly, like all men, his faithful creatures (*ses fidèles créatures*)'.[70] Tibra, a Berber, then claims descent from the once powerful Amazons: 'I'm from a different species, a wilder, more ancient creature (*une autre faune plus ancienne*). Like all women (even if some have forgotten it), I'm directly descended from the Amazons, the warrior goddesses promised to the wind and wedded to the Infinite.'[71] Siddéna, too, claims descent from the trees, while her people, as she tells Hadachinou, were banished and condemned to enslavement for trying to find the 'source of the light'.[72] Finally, Hadja Kimya, the local soothsayer, also of African origin, imagines herself 'born before time, born of a sugary flower the colour of silk' and portrays herself as a force of both creation and apocalypse, directed against men as, from her breath, 'whole worlds are born and wonders, dreams and wind'.[73]

Shortly preceding the 'Story of the Little Fly of Flies', the disparity between it and these origin myths initially appears striking, as Aunt Nafissa laughs at Hadja Kimya's fanciful words, while her 'fly stories' make Hadja Kimya 'shake with laughter'.[74] Contrasting flytopia to paradise lost and the materiality of human vulnerability to light, wind and a 'sugary flower', the stories are, however, only superficially at odds, with all revealing a need to imagine history through defamiliarising perspectives while accepting the suffering inherent to it.

After questioning his Qurʾan teacher about his own identity, meanwhile, Hadachinou is told only that he is 'an Arab and a Muslim'. Resenting the 'frozen, mummified language' of classical Arabic, he begins to fear that, in rejecting it, he will have no identity, becoming a 'faceless body'.[75] As ever, Aunt Nafissa comes to the rescue, reassuring him that no one truly knows their origins, which must therefore be sought only in the gaze of other creatures:

> You come in through my eyes, you're in my blood (*tu peuples mon sang*), adding to my mind, travelling through my kingdom, my gardens, my labyrinths, then you come through my mouth, you emerge, soft kisses . . . Another person's eyes are your origins and your kingdom. But these other people can't see *you* if they're blinded by their search for an illusion, for the Invisible One.[76]

Through the inner spaces of mouth and eyes, Aunt Nafissa's words shift from the grimness of fly invasion to spiritual connection, suggesting that answers must be sought on a small scale, within the microcosm of each human, recognising both alterity and deep interconnectedness. As Matar suggests, *La compagnie des Tripolitaines* is 'imbued with questions of lineage and authenticity', but also moves beyond them, into what Nafissa describes as a 'state of pure wonder and recognition', resonating with Sufi overtones.[77] Emerging through the folkloric and creaturely, as well as the *parole de l'enfance* and *contrée des femmes*, this state counters monolithic myths of origin and appropriation, which, through the opening epigraph, are cast into a broad historical perspective stretching back to the Phoenicians. Once again, the novel therefore represents not coming-of-age but recuperation of past ways of knowing and imagined origins, ending not, as in al-Fayturi's *Sarib*, with Hadachinou's disappearance, but his reabsorption into his Aunt Fatima's circling rhyme, which also begins the novel, '*Seven girls inside a flute. The ghoul twirls and twirls and eats one of the girls. Six girls inside a flute. The ghoul twirls and twirls and eats one of the girls. Five girls inside a flute . . .*'[78] Through this echoing refrain, Ben Hameda gives the final word to childhood play behind which lurks Tripoli's transformation into the 'anxious, deformed and enslaved city' that he addresses in *La mémoire de l'absent*, and that similarly resonates through Matar's *In the Country of Men*, responding, in the darkest terms, to the questions posed by Hadachinou's 'timid inquisitiveness'.

In the Country of Men: The Problems of 'Telling'

While the title of *La compagnie des Tripolitaines* announces its depiction of a secluded female community, the title of *In the Country of Men* announces its unsparing depiction of power relations through the bewildered consciousness of a child. As Matar reveals, the novel was first conceived as a poem, 'about a boy in the garden, in the mythical garden, as it were, picking ripened fruit'.[79] As with so much Libyan fiction, innocence lost is at its heart, as Slooma desperately attempts to construct his bewildering surroundings into meaningful narrative, while the 'here and now' of childhood comes increasingly under attack. As Matar observes, 'There is something quite unique about children, the present seems eternal and there isn't really any experience of time passing.'[80] Through this 'eternal present', Slooma becomes unable to piece together past, present and future, increasingly resorting to fanciful but fragile narrative strategies and imaginings. Framed by the adult 'Suleiman', forty days after his father's death, the novel marks, on one level, the end of mourning when the bereaved can discard their black clothes and move beyond loss. Most of the novel, however, slips back to nine-year-old Slooma, in the summer of 1979, leading to his departure, as he is confronted by immobilising horrors. As Matar expresses: 'He (Suleiman) is trying to mend the fracture, the point at which his personal narrative had been amputated. This is why the prose shifts between the contemplative, reflective poise of an adult and the bewilderment of a child.'[81]

'Fracture' further marks the stories that Slooma's mother, Najwa, compulsively tells him about her forced marriage at fifteen.[82] As Noor Hashem observes, the novel's characters are defined by their relationship to narrative, which is further intimately entwined in their agency or lack thereof.[83] While some characters successfully mould narrative into action, others retreat to silence or repetition and, as Micklethwait comments, the novel thus provides 'a discourse on, and in some ways against, the redemptive qualities of narrative in the face of state terror and oppression'.[84] Within this forcefield, Slooma seeks to preserve his 'child's voice', imagining himself beyond the parameters of the 'country of men', while Najwa struggles to move beyond the point when, forced into marriage as a child herself, her own narrative was severed. As the older Suleiman reflects, her fate was sealed by 'men's words', whose binding force stripped her own ability to imagine, speak and do, echoing through her own relationship with her son.[85]

Contrary to the conventional bedtime tale, Najwa begins her 'telling' only as Slooma is drifting off: 'Just when sleep was curling itself around me, she started her telling. Her mouth beside my ear, the smell of her medicine alive in the room.'[86] Prompted by alcohol, which Slooma believes to be 'medicine', she laments the loss of her books, destroying her appetite for reading and her faith in Shahrazad, a former idol, who, she realises, bowed to tyranny, asking not for a 'room of her own', but simply 'To live'.[87] Without beginning or ending, Najwa's elliptical and repetitive telling contrasts the vital impulse of Shahrazad's tales, as she forgets what she has 'told', and begs Slooma the next day 'not to tell, not to tell'.[88] While critiquing Shahrazad's simple demand for life, she, too, is resigned to bare survival. Opposing her husband's anti-government activities, she declares, 'Here it's either silence or exile, walk by the wall or leave.'[89] Following on from the '*sarīb ṭawīl*' of ᶜAqila's *al-Jirab* and al-Fayturi's *Sarib*, as indeed from the 'story-less-ness' of Hadachinou's grandmother, she embodies the all-encompassing difficulty of relaying experience, between the momentous social and political transformations of the 1960s and 1970s.

After her 'telling', Slooma physically struggles to contain his mother's words, holding his mouth shut and unable to eat or laugh.[90] When confronted with traumatic experiences of his own, however, he also begins to crave them, attempting to piece them into a narrative 'straight and clear and simple'.[91] Through the 'liberating magic' of fairy tale, he further inserts himself into them, as a hero, arriving on a 'white horse' and bringing stacks of books. Reframing the traditional rescue of the princess in terms of 'rescuing the girl she once was', he even rethinks his own origin story, imagining his mother marrying her childhood friend and him as their joyful offspring.[92] While these creative interjections offer hope of moving Najwa's 'telling' forward, Slooma's own relationship to words is, however, soon compromised. Living opposite a senior official from the security services, the family must display outward loyalty to al-Qadhafi and, as Slooma hears his mother praising the regime, he begins to grasp the use of words to dissemble. As books are burned and phones tapped, all avenues of communication are compromised.

TV and radio convey only propaganda and scenes of interrogation, in which 'telling' takes on a dangerous aspect, the product not of Najwa's traumatic compulsion but immediate, physical coercion.

In keeping, Slooma also begins to use words to blame and humiliate. After his best friend Kareem's father is arrested, he betrays his secrets to their other friends, before being enticed by Sharief, a member of the Revolutionary Committees, to reveal his father's headquarters in Martyrs' Square. As Barbara Harlow comments, the theme of story thus shifts into 'acts of tale-telling, even tattling', as 'Suleiman tells his father's story, giving away its characters and their setting, and thereby compromising, and so indeed changing, the entire plot.'[93] Unsettlingly, Sharief is repeatedly described as having an 'old woman's voice', furthering the inversion of storytelling, as the paradigmatic conveyor of collective wisdom turns into a pernicious manipulator of words.[94]

Alongside what Harlow terms his 'tattling', Slooma also retreats from language altogether, pelting the neighbourhood beggar, Bahloul, with stones and growling wordlessly, while the old man responds with a 'horse-like scream'.[95] Confused by his own actions, Slooma sinks into self-loathing and, retrospectively, the adult Suleiman reflects that, 'In a time of blood and tears, in a Libya full of bruise-checkered and urine-stained men, urgent with want and longing for relief, I was the ridiculous child craving concern.'[96] In the 'country of men', story shifts to 'telling', 'informing' and a 'horse-like scream', obliterating childhood wonder, while Slooma struggles to reanimate the land through imagination and myth. In what follows, I explore this first through his imaginative engagement with natural imagery, and then through the historical 'traces' of Leptis Magna and Septimius Severus, reflecting both the non-human and ekphrastic underpinning of the Libyan novel's creaturely poetics.

'Every person, animal and ant'

In *The Return*, Matar evokes the 'appetite for an authentic acquaintance with nature' that marked his childhood, dissipating over years of suffering, loss and initiation into adult complications.[97] *In the Country of Men* painfully dramatises this loss, as Slooma's surroundings are gradually tainted by violence and fear. In the novel's first sentences, his playful evocation of the coexistence of humans, animals and ants is thus juxtaposed to the perspective of the older Suleiman, recalling his last summer before leaving for exile in Egypt:

> I am recalling now that last summer before I was sent away. It was 1979, and the sun was everywhere. Tripoli lay brilliant and still beneath it. Every person, animal and ant went in desperate search for shade, those occasional grey patches of mercy carved into the white of everything.[98]

Through reference to 'every person, animal and ant', Slooma playfully transforms Tripoli from 'country of men' into a hideout for creatures big and small, caught in equal stasis. An omnipresent force in the novel, the sun evokes physical exposure, while also hinting at omnipresent political surveillance from which all must shelter. Setting the tone for the ensuing narrative, the scene establishes memory as a creaturely endeavour, rooted in shared exposure and search for shelter.

As in *La compagnie des Tripolitaines*, this is continued through animal simile, conveying Slooma's impetuous movements and alternative perception of time, space, shape and colour. Going to the beach, he describes how 'I walked like an insect, my elbows raised up to my ears, my back arched, my feet curling against the heat.'[99] Glimpsing his blind Qur°an teacher's eye behind his thick lenses, he refers to it as 'open and searching for light like a snail waking up in the rain'.[100] Upset by his mother's stories, he is reluctantly lured from his silence like 'a cat teased out from beneath a bed', while his mother is described as 'a small nervous fish alone in the deep' and 'her eyes like a bird's, dark and full of grief'.[101] Despite their brevity, these similes produce a sustained poetics across the novel, transforming the 'country of men' into one of insects, moths and butterflies, and revealing both Slooma's desire to imagine the world otherwise and the undercurrent of melancholy that marks his imaginings.

Often, similes differ significantly from reality, further demonstrating his increasing disorientation. The secret service car that comes for his neighbour, Ustath Rashid, is described 'billowing dust as if it were the only creature in the world', and then as a 'giant dead moth in the sun'.[102] After witnessing his father working undercover for the resistance, Slooma becomes distracted by his sunglasses, likened to 'the humpbacks of turtles over his eyes'.[103] Elaborating, he evokes their unnatural shade, unsettling his harmonious vision of nature, 'painted by God':

> The sky, the sun and the sea were painted by God in colours we could all point at and say the sea is turquoise, the sun banana, the sky blue. Sunglasses are terrible, I thought, because they change all of this and keep those who wear them at a distance.[104]

In the novel's first pages, the ambiguous, artificial shade of the sunglasses conveys the first breakdown of a child's describable world, prompted by Slooma's realisation of the secrets that distance people, transforming 'turquoise', 'banana' and 'blue' into opaque, indefinable emotions.

As the world becomes less describable, Slooma resorts to lengthier, interconnected and more visceral similes. Upset by his mother, he describes himself as a 'sick dog gnawing at its own limbs' while, after his father returns from detention, he exudes 'the stink of a dog the boys and I had found one day on our way back from school dead with a swarm of flies buzzing around its bloated belly'.[105] In the novel's final pages, both 'dogs' coalesce in a vision of Suleiman, awaiting his mother's arrival in Alexandria, 'like a faithful dog still waiting, confident that his owner will come to reclaim him'.[106] Through each 'dog', the tenuous bonds connecting Slooma, his mother and father are conveyed through smell and touch, with all pointing to Suleiman's designation as 'Stray Dog' by the regime, following his exile to Egypt.[107] Through the novel's broader web of animal similes, this exclusionary political label is thus reinscribed with the creaturely vulnerability of sickness, longing and bewilderment.

In stark contrast, one of the most poignant moments of domestic harmony and childhood wonder comes through the family's joint care of a herd of cows, which Slooma's businessman father imports from Scotland, opening onto a brief, yet significant, proto-ethical encounter. Unable to leave the cows alone, Slooma spends his evening, 'turning around the truck, looking up at their pink titties, climbing to stare into their peculiar eyes'.[108] Slooma's mother and father join him in tending to the cows and, briefly, the traumatic events of the wider novel are transcended, with his father 'making sure each cow got its share' and his mother singing to them, 'like a little girl unaware of herself'.[109] Restoring the child's 'eternal present', Slooma later incorporates the cows into his fairy tale of rescue, imagining him and his mother running away to Scotland, 'surrounded by cows with big, beautiful, glassy eyes'.[110]

This moment of childish care is, nevertheless, soon subsumed within the wider troubles that press upon Slooma. Like the animals and ants which introduce the novel, the cows are discomfited by the oppressive heat, mooing in distress all night, and leading the family's neighbours to complain ominously. With sun and surveillance aligned once more, the sheer difficulty of existing within the nation is evoked on environmental and political levels, while

Slooma's psychological unease continues to taint the world around him, as well as his fantasies and dreams. Hearing a bird fall silent in his garden at mid-morning, he reads 'embarrassment' onto it.[111] Following his father's detention, he dreams of him transforming into a fish 'lost in the deep' and, like the other creatures of his imaginary, desperately seeking shelter.[112]

A Myth of Mulberries

Entangling images of paradise, fall, sun and surveillance, the novel's central garden scene encapsulates Slooma's 'spoilt' relationship with nature. Playing beneath the blazing heat, he feasts on ripe mulberries before succumbing to sunstroke and awakening to find the Revolutionary Committees invading his home. Together, these images set what Matar elsewhere describes as the country's 'private disquiet' and 'determination to keep out the sun and the passing gaze' within a framework of primordial fear.[113] Initially, as Slooma plays, the intense sun reminds him of his Qur'an teacher's warnings concerning the 'bridge' to 'Hell Eternal'.[114] Countering this frightening spectre, he constructs his own mythology concerning the neighbourhood's last mulberry tree, which he inserts into the Qur'anic story of Adam and Eve:

> I decided that mulberries were the best fruit God had created and I began to imagine young lively angels conspiring to plant a crop in the earth's soil after they heard that Adam, peace and blessings be upon him, and Eve, peace and blessings be upon her, were being sent down here to earth as punishment. God knew of course, He's the Allknowing, but he liked the idea and so let the angels carry out their plan.[115]

In contrast to the Sheikh's Hell Fire, Slooma imagines a benevolent fall, in which angels 'make life easier'.[116] As Hashem suggests, his story represents a 'creative reappropriation' of religious discourse, allowing him 'to imagine and make it possible to enact agency'.[117] In other words, he inserts the liberating power of fairy tale into the grim determination of myth, imagining nature as complicit with fallen humanity, providing it with a fruit that can flourish in the 'country of men' and watched over by a benevolent God rather than an omnipresent leader. Thereafter, mulberries provide an antidote to fear. When faced with the sight of his severely beaten father returned from detention, Slooma literally 'alters' his eyes 'to look only for small dark creatures', shifting his field of perception to the ecology of mulberries and the ants that feed on them.[118]

Inevitably, however, mulberries become entangled in shame and sickness as Slooma compulsively gorges himself on them, before realising that Bahloul has been watching him throughout.[119] Panicked by this observing gaze, he tries to 'look', 'seem' and 'feel' innocent, uncomfortably aware of his 'red' hands as he returns inside. Thereafter, the fruit are marked by shame as, wetting himself, he smells their 'rotten' scent, then describes his mother's incomprehensible words as 'ripened mulberries in the dirt, good only for ants'.[120] After telling his 'myth' to family friend, Moosa, the latter, distracted, replies only that 'They're a small, soft, stoneless fruit like any other', while his father spits them out, ignoring Slooma and recounting his experiences of torture.[121]

Alongside Slooma's fall from innocence, mulberries also convey a sense of national disintegration and unease, with reference to the 'armies of ants' that consume them alluding, as Hashem comments, to the government's appropriation of national resources.[122] Forming a web of references across the novel, this imagery of ants conveys a range of allegorical significance, forming a nexus of creaturely signs of symbolic, historical and spiritual purport. This begins, of course, with the opening image of 'every person, animal and ant', and extends to the visceral discomfort of Slooma biting into an ant-infested date, or watching as ants consume his mulberries. For Hashem, these 'unproductive and sinister' encounters directly contrast the 'parable of mindfulness and responsibility to cohabitant creatures' represented by King Solomon in the Qur'an's Surat al-Naml. Hearing the frightened beings in the 'Valley of Ants', Solomon thanks God for His gift of attentiveness to all living creatures.[123] In contrast, *In the Country of Men* dramatises a profound breakdown of the fanciful connections that Slooma struggles to establish.

In an echo of Aunt Nafissa's *Histoire de mouche*, Slooma also references his Uncle Khaled's epic verse play, *The Feast of Ants*, which he describes as telling 'the history of our country'.[124] While the play's contents are not described, the titular ants invite various allegorical readings. Perhaps they are tyrannous rulers feasting on the country's resources, or the country's citizens claiming what is theirs or, like Aunt Nafissa's flies, they may simply represent the literal presence of ants themselves, as the only 'nation' to have benefited from Libya's war and wastage.[125] A final interpretation, echoing Slooma's ant-infested date, might even read the ants as the substance, rather than consumers, of the feast, further suggested by the fact that it is 'The Feast of Ants', rather than 'The Feast of *the* Ants'. Presumably, the original Arabic title would have been *walīmat al-naml*, an *iḍāfa*, in which the ants' passivity or agency is suitably ambiguous.

Whatever its contents, the play is fated never to tell the country's story nor, like Slooma's 'myth of mulberries', to envision a happy ending. Put in the shed by Slooma's grandmother after Uncle Khaled leaves for America, it is itself consumed by chickens. Although the result of a comic mishap, its loss inevitably evokes the banning and burning of books under al-Qadhafi. Between ants and chickens, the allegorical and material, it dramatises the precarity of narrative within the 'country of men', in which every word and symbol is loaded with dangerous potential and destined, like Slooma's mulberries, for ruin. Through Slooma's own telling of the poem's fate, it becomes a creaturely allegory within a creaturely allegory, entwining layers of symbolic and literal imagery.

Leptis Magna

Alongside these images of mulberries, ants and cows, *In the Country of Men* is further scattered with ekphrastic imagery, centred on Slooma's determination to become an Art History Professor like the family's neighbour, Ustath Rashid. Demonstrating this interest, he recalls, at pivotal junctures, the professor's impromptu lessons on art and archaeology as a frame of reference for understanding the present. He also, however, begins to read the vulnerability of the present onto relics from the past, echoing the strange affiliations and inversions of human and stone across the Libyan novel.[126] A chronological reference point for ensuing events, his visit to Leptis Magna with the professor and his students represents the axis of this imaginary, beginning as a paradigmatic childhood outing and fleeting vision of what Slooma's final summer in Tripoli might have been before it was tainted by later events. In the painted image of a Maenad (a female follower of Dionysus), Slooma experiences the first stirs of desire:

> I came close to her, traced my finger round the dark swirl of her bellybutton. I turned my finger round the pink centre of her nipple. Then my eyes fell on her dark lips. I kissed them, hearing my own breath against the cool dry stone. Something like guilt or fear made me withdraw. I felt a swirl of excitement in my belly. Her eyes seemed to be looking at me. I quickly kissed her again and ran to catch up with the others.[127]

Paralleling the 'swirl' of the paint with the 'swirl' of his own desire, Slooma's physical reaction to the stone momentarily consumes him, reminiscent of his absorption in the cows imported by his father. Gazing into the Maenad's eyes, the wider contexts of the present and past fade away as she is animated through his childish wonder.

Excitement, however, soon shifts to the solitary vulnerability that Slooma reads in the other ruins. Paralleling his animal similes, he animates the ancient city's solitary arches through the disorientation of old men 'trying to remember where they were going'.[128] As with the broader *turāth* of the Libyan novel, these disoriented old men poignantly evoke the living inhabitants of 1970s Tripoli, 'urgent with want and longing for relief', as present trauma is entangled with the melancholy of natural history. This is, above all, conveyed through Ustath Rashid's spontaneous recitation of the North African scholar and poet, Sīdī Maḥraz's (d.1022), lament for Carthage:

> Why this emptiness after joy?
> Why this ending after glory?
> Why this nothingness where once was a city!
> Who will answer? Only the wind
> Which steals the chantings of priests
> And scatters the souls once gathered.[129]

Through the structured, often repetitive, questioning of traditional elegy, marking the fall of cities and 'bearing witness to the devastating effect of violence on the human psyche', classical poets such as Sīdī Maḥraz give form to collective grief, allowing for ritual healing and drawing together a renewed community from the rubble of a collapsed order.[130] In contrast, Slooma's narrative strategies, as well as the elegy of his older self, Suleiman, to father, country and childhood, fail to construct such meaning, as the harmonious connections between present and past, as between human and nature, are progressively threatened.

Two days after the trip, Ustath Rashid is taken by the security services, representing, as Micklethwait suggests, the novel's 'spacio-temporal nexus', beyond which childhood is sundered and the professor's voice, bridging past and present, silenced.[131] The chronology of events surrounding it also becomes confused as, it turns out, the opening scene, in which Slooma first sees his father working undercover in Martyrs' Square, in fact takes place following both events. Septimius Severus, whose statue stands in the Square, and whose arch stands in Leptis, represents a nexus for this chronological confusion and Slooma's underlying bewilderment. As Sakr comments, there is a sense of 'mystery and conspiracy' in the 'sculpture's ambivalent relations to the symbols of the revolution', echoing the other misplaced and contested *turāth* of the Libyan novel, and compounded by the bewilderment of a child, unable to piece them together.[132] As Slooma observes his father in Martyrs' Square, the statue reminds him of al-Qadhafi, 'waving his arm as the tanks passed in front of him on Revolution Day'.[133] In Leptis, preceding the scene chronologically, Ustath Rashid contrastingly refers to Septimius as 'our Grim African, both a source of pride and shame', and describes his statue as 'Urging Libya to look towards Rome'.[134] Through these nuanced references, he conveys the figure's entanglement in both former, Roman imperialism and present resistance, anchored in an understanding of Septimius as an indigenous, historical Libyan leader, and figurative alternative to al-Qadhafi.[135] Overwhelmed by this complexity, Slooma simply flees to his bedroom upon returning home from the square, retreating into his 'picture book on Leptis Magna'.[136]

The spectacle of Ustath Rashid's televised execution, which Slooma witnesses with his mother, is further juxtaposed to the lessons the Professor gives Slooma on how to read art. Observing his mother's 'beautiful' but 'lifeless' appearance, Slooma compares her to the Fayum portraits that decorate Egyptian mummies and, as the Professor moves to the gallows, recalls his 'peculiar statement': 'And because no one likes to remember the dead dead, the painters did their best to make the person look alive. [. . .] If you look closely you can see the shadow of death in the picture.'[137] In stark contrast to this nuanced perception of the 'shadow of death', mortality is central to the spectacle of the Professor's execution. In a tone of detached incomprehension, Slooma describes the TV camera's clumsy movements, the crowd's chanting and the flowers that sporadically fill the screen before, suddenly, shifting to the execution in gruesome detail, from the 'yellow' froth around Ustath Rashid's mouth to the 'punching' and 'cheering' spectators.[138] In the Jamahiriyya, death is not compassionately mourned but rendered public, as a reminder of the state of exception at the nation's heart, nullifying lessons from the past. In processing the scene, Slooma therefore returns to his own incongruous similes, describing the professor moving 'the way a shy woman would resist her friends' invitation to dance', while the crowd, grabbing his legs, are likened to 'children happy with a swing they had just made'.[139] Despite these efforts to transform mortality, the scene continues to haunt him, returning to the paradigmatic mortality of the slaughtered sheep: 'Shut or open, my eyes continued to see the slim figure of Ustath Rashid swinging in mid-air, the dark stain of urine expanding around his groin, his ankles shuddering one last time the way sheep kick after slaughter.'[140]

Through Ustath Rashid's death, Slooma's relationship to art history is severed, with the grown Suleiman admitting that he never accomplished his dreams of becoming a professor. Bookending its presence in the novel, Leptis is mentioned for the last time by Slooma's mother, enticing him to leave by telling him that Egypt's pyramids are 'much bigger' than Leptis.[141] As the grown Suleiman describes the following years of exile, in which life is filled with friends and academic success, this suggestion of the pyramids' superiority conveys his sense of loss and guilt, hinting at why, despite his success, he cannot accomplish his childhood ambitions. While the pyramids are imagined as the proud heritage of a nation in which a child might grow up happy, Leptis evokes that of 'disoriented' and 'bruise-checkered' men, in which a child's longing has no place and which nevertheless remains central to Slooma's self and drive to understand the world. His early relationship to Leptis, Septimius and the Fayum portraits leaves him with knowledge that cannot be transferred into academic discourse and so he escapes through the clinical whiteness of a Cairo pharmacy, finding the solution to his mother's 'illness' not through story but repetitive, clinical control: 'I stand in a white coat most of my days, behind a counter in an air-conditioned pharmacy in Cairo. It's a bit of a joke. After all the hopes of becoming an art historian like Ustath Rashid, a high-flying businessman like my father [. . .].'[142] Within his bleached pharmacy, the ominous sun of Suleiman's childhood finds its antidote in sterile air-conditioning, while the whiteness of his coat replaces his mulberry-red hands and the indeterminacy of his father's sunglasses, whitewashing his emotional, intellectual and sensorial disorientation.

Yet, as John Kearney notes, Suleiman's future is by no means certain, nor his past resolved, as his narrative concludes.[143] It is unclear whether he will return to Tripoli or recuperate the narrative agency lost through his 'myth of mulberries'. As Hashem remarks, the novel itself does not represent a 'clear' and 'simple' narrative, but mirrors Najwa's circular, elliptical 'telling'.[144] It concludes, furthermore, with a return to the simplest and most literal iteration of the 'child's voice' as, glimpsing his mother arriving in Alexandria, Suleiman repeats the same, primal syllable: '"Mama," I say and say it again and again until she sees me. "Mama! Mama!"'[145] As with the circling rhyme that concludes *La compagnie des Tripolitaines*, *In the Country of Men* concludes with the child's 'eternal present', lost in his mother's arms amid the weight of history.

In his next novels, too, Matar continues returning to this 'eternal present', as to traces of personal, familial and national history. Through them, he seeks to piece together a fragile story, circling around the disappearance of his father, Jāballāh Maṭar, in 1990, snatched by Egyptian police and rendered to Libya. From Slooma's imaginings, traces of story shift to more concrete form. In Matar's second novel, *Anatomy of a Disappearance* (2011), they are located in poems, newspapers and history books, which protagonist-narrator Nuri investigates after his father's disappearance, questioning what Harlow terms the 'indexicality of Libya and its history'.[146] In his memoir, *The Return* (2016), Matar then details his own campaign to find his father, alongside stories of other imprisoned relatives.[147] Filled with chance encounters and haunting clues, some real, some imagined, *The Return* emerges through what Santner terms 'acts of testimony and transmission', countering the defining vulnerability of creatureliness through the solidarity of shared narrative, surmounting the bewildered imaginings and tacit whispers of *In the Country of Men*.[148]

Most prominently, Matar includes a translation of a short story, from 1957, by his own father, 'In the Stillness of the Night: A Libyan Tale'. Tying the beginnings of modern Libyan literature to its diasporic iterations in his own writing, Matar contextualises the story by observing that 'Oil was yet to be discovered', Libya was 'trying to drag itself into modernity', and authors 'clearly saw the art of fiction as part of the national effort to drive up literacy and education'.[149] Conveying this nationalist impulse, Jāballāh Maṭar sets his story during Italian occupation, depicting the heroic struggle of nomadic herders:

> Despite the spectre of the enemy, who threatened everyone on this land, Ahmed and his uncle had ventured out to these plains to tend to their livestock. Nothing mattered to them more than the well-being of their flock. Fear was kept at bay because they had sufficient weapons and ammunition, which, on a previous confrontation, they had captured from the enemy.[150]

Like the novels of Chapter 1, the story frames the conflict of nomads and invading Italians through the poetics of survival, outlining the past from which Libya struggles. Through the herders' paramount concern for their flocks, it further echoes al-Minifi's 'Ma bi Marad', lamenting lost ways of life and weaving together individual, collective and creaturely memory.

Through these traces of story, Matar becomes an archivist, translator and close analyst.[151] In all, he is compelled by fragility, stating that, 'I start with very little: the more fragile, the better. The thread has to feel like it is about to snap.'[152] Whether a rediscovered story or the image of a child in the garden, such beginnings establish the vital connection between story and survival, mirroring the terms in which Matar, in *The Return*, describes his Uncle Mahmoud's memories: 'His stories were an attempt to bridge the vast distance that separated the austere cruelty of Abu Salim and the world outside. Perhaps, like all stories, what Uncle Mahmoud's recollections were saying was: "I exist".'[153]

Conclusion

In an autobiographical article for *The Guardian*, Matar describes a 'ritual of becoming a man', in which he witnesses the slaughter of a herd of deer while on a hunting expedition with his uncles in the Libyan desert.[154] Concluding with description of the dead deer, 'their colour only slightly darker than the desert floor', the moment captures the 'here and now' of both *La compagnie des Tripolitaines* and *In the Country of Men* as, through moments of vulnerability, the boys' consciousnesses are transformed and the nation's past and future complexly entangled in creaturely signs. As in the Arabic Libyan *Bildungsroman*, the curtailed childhoods of both novels evoke not the crystallisation of national consciousness but precarity and loss. Between catastrophic past and silenced future, *La compagnie des Tripolitaines* emerges through punctured balloons, immobilising sunlight and indefinable emptiness, while *In the Country of Men* dwells in what Matar elsewhere calls the 'private moment', exploring how, within totalitarianism and its disregard for the private, people 'love differently' and 'listen to music differently'.[155]

Such 'private moments' have underpinned all my analyses of the Libyan novel, through shadowy encounters of human, animal and land on secluded coastlines or in neglected parks. While writing in French and English, it is,

I suggest, this shared imaginary, of encounter and transformation, which makes of Ben Hameda and Matar 'minor authors', inflecting their novels with 'lines of flight' that parallel the Libyan novel in Arabic. Discussing his decision to write in English, Matar suggests it as a strategy to avoid the silencing of dictatorship:

> One of the objectives of dictatorship is to retard you, is to make you either silent or imprisoned or underground. Or so angry and loud that even the people who agree with you have no patience to listen to you. So that's part of this project. How do you do the opposite? How do you be restrained? And somehow, writing in another language, and a language that I do have a love affair with, has given me this ability to be a little bit distant. In some ways it has abstracted the reader for me.[156]

Matar's comments on the need for patience, distance and restraint speak eloquently to the narrative strategies of the broader Libyan novel, as 'minor literature', in Arabic, French or English, deterritorialising political ideology, and confronting reader-less-ness or misinterpretation. As per Matar's statement, the Libyan novel resonates with restrained rage, shying from grand narrative and anchored in bewilderment, survival and the primordial, aware of the precarity of story and the need for it to proceed tentatively, alongside its absolute necessity for survival.

Afterword: Breaking Fevers and Strange Metamorphoses

Then Libya became a desert, the heat drying up her moisture. Then the nymphs with dishevelled hair wept bitterly for their lakes and fountains. (Ovid, *Metamorphoses*)[1]

Between his arms, she transformed into wildernesses, valleys and ravines, thundering with creatures whose movement he could hear but not see. Dancing, he was swept away in this wild festival. (Bushnaf, *al-Kalb al-Dhahabi*)[2]

In *Thuwwar Libya al-Sabirun* (2011, Libya's Patient Revolutionaries), published at the dawn of the Libyan uprising, Muhammad al-Asfar evokes, in exuberant terms, how 'The Libyan people are now brothers of mankind. We can speak freely to those in the Arab world and elsewhere whom we have longed to meet, and can embrace them without fear.'[3] A precipitous, joyful response to escalating popular protest, al-Asfar's words convey many of the themes, of stasis, patience, estrangement and longing, that distinguish the Libyan novel's creaturely poetics, in its attentiveness to shared vulnerability and expression of fragile affiliations. For al-Asfar, becoming 'brothers of mankind' represents a newfound ability to tell stories and to embrace, long confined to the margins, but tantalisingly proffered by sudden, feverish transformations.

Protests first erupted in Benghazi amid the wider events of the Arab Spring in February 2011. Catalysed by the 17th February 'Day of Rage' (*yawm al-ghaḍab*), commemorating the killing of protesters by security services in 2006, they spread rapidly across the country and soon turned to clashes and outright combat.[4] Within a week, rebel forces had claimed much of the east of the country and begun making incursions into the west.[5] A new dawn of rights and solidarity suddenly seemed possible.

The government, however, reacted with predictable brutality.[6] Indiscriminately, loyalist forces fired on congregated groups, armed or unarmed, while, in March, the government geared up to retake Benghazi from the new National Transitional Council (*al-Majlis al-Waṭanī al-Intiqālī*), prompting the beginning of NATO airstrikes on 19th March. Months of fighting ensued, as bastions of the regime crumbled, culminating, on 19th October, with the capture and killing of al-Qadhafi in Sirte. As prisons were opened, relatives reunited, and 'stray dogs' welcomed home, Libya's liberation seemed complete. Through the uncovering of mass graves and registering of the many missing, however, the extent of the regime's abuses also began to unfold, alongside the toll of months of fighting.

Since then, the telling of story has become no easier in Libya, with little time to take stock of past horrors amid a rapidly disintegrating present. Internal tensions within the NTC, compounded by a lack of administrative framework, eroded centralised governance, while armed militias took over major cities and commercial assets, alongside the insurgent Islamist forces of Ansar al-Sharia and branches of Islamic State. Commenting on the state of the country in 2015, Bushnaf grimly observes:

> Today, Libyans have begun chewing on one another's flesh. Gratuitous killing has become our favourite gum. Before, the regime had a monopoly on violence. Now, it has become a collective activity, in which we are participants, rather than merely spectators.[7]

Since Bushnaf wrote those words, the country has become further divided between the Libyan National Army (*al-Jaysh al-Waṭanī al-Lībī*) under general Khalīfa Ḥaftar (b.1943) in the east, and the UN-backed Government of National Accord (*Ḥukūmat al-Wifāq al-Waṭanī*) in the west. Over years of chaos, large numbers of the population have fled abroad and oil revenues have fallen dramatically. Further atrocities have unfolded through revenge killings, targeting those perceived to have regime connections. With over 40,000 inhabitants driven from their homes in 2011, Tawergha, in the north-west, became a ghost town as the country's black population were indiscriminately labelled as mercenaries of the regime and submitted to acts of ethnic cleansing. Rising numbers of sub-Saharan migrants, seeking passage to Europe, have further resulted in horrifying incidents of slavery and people-trafficking.

Amid the rise of social conservatism and religious radicalism, the rights of women have disintegrated, alongside freedom of speech and protest.

Faced with a dark present and uncertain future, alongside the continued pressures of censorship, fiction has retreated, once again, to the margins. In the immediate aftermath of the regime's collapse, there was a first, marked turn to stark prose, stripped of symbol and fantasy, and facing past horrors in unflinching detail. Both Ṣāliḥ al-Sanūsī's *Yawmiyyat Zaman al-Hashr* (2012, Diaries of the Final Congregation) and Fāṭima al-Hājī's *Surakh al-Tabiq al-Sufli* (2016, Screams from the Bottom Rung) detail the mass imprisonment and torture of students and intellectuals in the 1970s. ᶜUmar al-Kiklī's *Sijjiniyyat* (2012, Prison Sketches) depicts prison life in similarly vivid terms, while al-Qadhafi himself features as a demonic character in al-Kiddī's *Hurub Marish wa-Thawratuha al-Thalath* and Nouri Zarrugh's English-language *The Leader* (2017). Turning from her more familiar, fragmented allegory, Najwa Bin Shatwan's 2017 IPAF-shortlisted *Zaraʾib al-ᶜAbid* (2017, Slave Pens), addresses the country's slave communities in the early twentieth century.

In a landmark anthology, *Shams ᶜala Nawafidh Mughlaqa* (2017, Sun on Closed Windows), a new generation of authors, all under the age of thirty, has also come to light. Through short stories, poems and one novel excerpt, the anthology presents both strikingly new themes and aesthetics, and connections to the past. Its offerings range from Aḥmad al-Bukhārī's (b.1985) *Kashan* (2012), written in dialect, and telling of four young men from opposite poles of life, plotting to destroy and recreate Tripoli, to the prose poetry of Ḥusām al-Thanī (b.1984) evoking the precarity of war in stark declarations:

> I am my anxious beloved, refusing to be reassured that I am well.
> I am my brother, who speaks not to me of the stench of corpses.
> I am the last of the food, stolen as the electricity is cut.[8]

In his introduction to the anthology, al-Fayturi, whose novel *Sarib* I discuss in Chapter 5, binds these new voices to those of past decades. Drawing parallels between the present and past conditions of precarity in which the country's authors must write, he describes the 'gasping flow' and feverish pace of the anthology's poetry and prose, evoking their sudden outpouring of protest and emotion, yet also echoing the stirrings of turmoil that mark his own *Sarib*.[9]

Following the anthology's publication, however, the implications of renewed censorship also became swiftly apparent, as authors and editors faced a torrent of online abuse and death threats, with several forced into hiding with their families.[10] The government's Ministry of Culture condemned it, too, claiming it had not gone through the appropriate vetting processes and confiscating all available copies. Specifically, a sex scene from *Kashan* sparked outrage, indicating a heightened, socially conservative turn to censorship, between 2012, when the novel was first published, and 2017, when the anthology appeared. In contrast to the Jamahiriyya's centralised 'gaze', the incident reveals how, amid the various powers vying for control of the country, oppression has become unpredictable and multifaceted, and the rules of censorship and self-censorship ill-defined.

Amid these turbulent circumstances, I dedicate my final comments to poetics that have remained constant. While unfolding in changed circumstances, they remain rooted in the fragile connections that authors establish between one another's writing, and between writing and land, material heritage and living creatures, as furtive glances within the panopticon. From al-Nayhum's *Min Makka*, I have traced this lineage through authors forced apart by exile, imprisonment and surveillance, but coming together through strange lines of flight, and the affiliations of humans and the imagined lives of other creatures and creations, made from flesh and stone. Specifically, the statue of the Girl and Gazelle has proved a lasting topos, poignantly evocative of rising violence. In 2014, the statue, still standing in its central Tripoli roundabout, was covered with a veil, hit in the stomach with bullets, and finally removed to an unknown fate by an unidentified militia group. In the country at large, its disappearance has coincided with the wider destruction of Sufi mosques and Greek and Roman heritage by Islamist groups. Turning to this last chapter in the statue's history, young author, Muhammad al-Naᶜas (al-Naᶜās, b.1991), imagines its final days in his short story, 'Majnun Ghazala' (2014, 'Ghazala's Madman'), which went on to win the new Khalīfa al-Fākhirī prize in 2015. The story's narrator, a policeman, recently relocated from his village to the capital, becomes obsessed with the statue, and particularly with the Girl, resenting the gazes of passers-by and their polarised condemnation and lust.[11] Imagining the statue's cracked bronze as a sign that the girl is struggling to break free of her metal prison, and looking to the gazelle in a 'cry for help', he dreams of rescuing her from her exposed plinth at the centre of history's long, 'catastrophic pileup':

> They all passed her by: Italians; Italianised Libyans; Arabised Libyans; Africanised Libyans and Libyanised Libyans. Four-wheel drives sped by, and men with clubs, Kalashnikovs and heavy artillery. People wrote for her and against her, and jokes and anecdotes were spun around her. A Shaykh in a mosque called for her to be covered with a niqab. Another called for her to be destroyed. An intellectual wrote a poem about her, and another wrote a story. And so the Arabs continued to quarrel over their women.[12]

Once again, the statue is placed at the centre of both historical neglect and ideological weighting, bringing her to life in a surplus of surveillance, administration and contestation. An eminently 'creaturely sign', the Girl and Gazelle in al-Na^{c}as's story allegorises the plight of women, as of art, forced into signifying schemes, delimiting what they are permitted to mean. As 'sign', however, the statue also disassembles these schemes as, gazing upon it, Majnun, like his namesake, Majnun Layla, turns his back on society, as 'all stories scattered, all humans, and all words' (*tāhat kull al-qiṣaṣ, kull al-bashar, kull al-kalimāt*).[13] Succumbing to sunstroke under the interminable Tripoli sky, beside the statue, he sinks into a hallucinatory fever, imagining the girl coming to life and ordering him to help her escape. In a permanent state of disorientation, he abandons his job and home, and embraces homelessness and madness, beside the roundabout. As so often in the Libyan novel, imagined flight and surreal affiliations are thus born of exposure to the force of nature and of surveillance. On 4th November 2014, however, Majnun and the statue's narrative then concludes as the statue is removed in a van by gun-wielding men, coinciding with the actual date of its disappearance. In the process, the 'story' (*qiṣṣa*)which inhabits and animates it, formed from Majnun's repressed longings and memories, is depicted as fleeing into the wilderness, leaving only 'emptiness' (*farāgh*) behind.[14] Majnun commits suicide and 'absence' provides the story's final word: 'The men did not notice him. No one noticed him, for the mad are never noticed. The truck bore the statue away and disappeared into the distance. Majnun laughed. He remembered something. And then he was gone (*thumma ghāba*).'[15] As across Libyan fiction, a fragile creature/creation is momentarily filled with the longing 'stories' of the human who gazes upon it, before fading, like its human companion, into oblivion.

Elegised at the hands of one author, the disappeared Girl and Gazelle is, nonetheless, soon re-captured in the pages of another, demonstrating the ongoing power of fiction to confront an increasingly unstable present in Libya. Concluding my discussion of the Libyan novel, bridging pre- and post-2011 periods, I therefore turn to its next appearance in Mansur Bushnaf's *al-Kalb al-Dhahabi* (2019, The Golden Dog), in which he turns explicitly to the Tripoli statue.[16] Through its rich exploration of humans and other creatures and creations, the novel places transformation, hybridity and lines of flight at the heart of an alternative Libyan lineage of world literature, resonant with the themes and aesthetics addressed throughout my chapters. Through brief discussion of it, as what might almost be termed a 'creaturely manifesto' for the Libyan novel's humans, animals, statues and land, I explore some of its most significant themes, and how they reflect the wider poetics discussed throughout my analyses, and explicitly celebrate them as defining characteristics of Libya's literary brilliance.

Written after a long search for new story, since the publication of *al-'Ilka* in 2008, *al-Kalb al-Dhahabi* is set in the 1960s and tells of a dog, metamorphosed into a man after travelling from hinterland to coast, and being adopted and seduced by an Italian woman in whose bed he transforms. Caught in permanent confusion, the protagonist, as both the dog Libeccio (the Italian term for the Qibli wind) and the man Sa^cid, sees his plight mirrored in that of the Girl and Gazelle, caught in an ever-metamorphosing city, which 'turns all creatures to human monsters' (*tamsakh kull shay' ilā maskh ādamī*).[17] Like *al-^cIlka's* 'chewing' (*lawk*), *maskh*, connoting both 'metamorphosis' and 'monstrousness', is the novel's feverish leitmotif, commenting on social transformation, vulnerability, and the power and possibility of story. As in *al-^cIlka*, the narrative voice is markedly self-conscious, though, this time, fully identified with Bushnaf, as he describes himself, a man of sixty, sitting in a Tripoli cafe, and chewing on his words. This time, too, Bushnaf, like his peer, al-Asfar, definitively embraces the 'difficulty of story', describing himself as a writer who 'likes his words to come out imperfectly' (*nāqiṣa*), and whose stories unfold through 'digression' (*istiṭrād*).[18] Inhabiting plot, character and imagery, *istiṭrād* becomes a literary manifestation of *maskh*, an unstable and fluctuating state, posited not just as a necessary response to censorship and strange, feverish transformations, but the foundation of Libya's literary brilliance.

Binding his novel to a lineage of literary and artistic metamorphoses, Bushnaf's references range from the prehistoric cave art of the Tadrart Akakus, depicting hybrid 'dog-men', to the transformations of Ovid, Apuleius, Kafka and, of course, the imagined metamorphosis of Girl and Gazelle[19]. Those acquainted with Libyan fiction may also note broader parallels to the creaturely poetics of ᶜUmar al-Kiddi's dog Ramadan, Miftāḥ Qanāw's Septimius Severus and al-Kuni's human–*waddān* composites, while Bushnaf himself cites al-Nayhum's *al-Hayawanat* and *al-Qurud* as exemplary Libyan literary '*maskh*'.[20] The legends of his own tribe, the Warfalla, are another intertext, referred to as 'the stories of the ancients, and my mum' (*asāṭīr al-awwalīn wa-ummī*).[21] *Al-Kalb al-Dhahabi* is, as he states, inspired by 'Libyan tales, full of jinn, ghouls and angels, donkeys, gazelles, wolves, dogs and hyenas', in which animals talk while 'humans stand in silent astonishment'.[22] In this lineage, both global and local, Bushnaf highlights metamorphosis as a foundational artform within 'human legacy' (*al-mīrāth al-insānī*).[23] As it transpires, however, he also posits it as a particularly *Libyan* legacy, taking a particularly monstrous form in the country's modern literature.

As the novel's title suggests, Lucius Apuleius' second-century *The Golden Ass* (Asinus Aureus) is its most important intertext and, from the first, Bushnaf highlights the Numidian-Gaetulian Apuleius as a 'man from our North Africa (*rajul min shamālinā al-ifrīqī*). Referencing his *Apologia* (158/9), which was delivered in Sabratha, he even suggests that *The Golden Ass* may well have been written in Tripoli (then Oea).[24] Roman Tripolitania would, he proposes, have provided fertile ground for such satirical literary metamorphosis, just like the city where he now sits, whose people, caught in precipitous change, have always loved 'mockery of the human being' (*al-sukhriya min al-kāʾin al-ādamī*).[25] For Bushnaf, Apuleius is a fellow writer of the margins, redefining story as he is 'absorbed by the vagaries of Tripoli life, venturing on romantic adventures, and suffering the same *maskh* as his golden donkey and his hero, Lucius.'[26] Recent scholarship would tend to agree. Exploring Apuleius's Romano-African identity, Ellen Finkelpearl suggests that his provincial yet 'Romanised' status is integral to his experimentation with literary animality, in a novel filled with 'problematic identity, hazardous migrations, and experimentation with alternate modes of being'.[27] In drawing on this central intertext, Bushnaf focuses his own novel on the similar deconstruction of borders and boundaries, drawing human stories into the 'oven of metamorphosis' that is Tripoli, and depicting shared vulnerability as a condition that prompts this metamorphosis.

As Bushnaf boldly declares, however, his story also goes against the grain of traditional literary metamorphosis, representing an 'exemplary Libyan *maskh*'

(*maskh lībī bi-imtiyāz*), in which literary motifs are turned on their head.[28] His novel is, indeed, not about a man turned dog, but a dog turned man. Playing on the Qurʾanic notion of *maskh*, as transformation into a lower form of being, he echoes the characteristic inversions of Libyan fiction, in 'praise' (*madīḥ*) of animals and 'mockery' (*hijāʾ*) of humans, challenging political hierarchies through upending traditional anthropocentrism, and dwelling on the particular plight of the '*kāʾin ādamī*'.[29] In Saᶜid's visceral disorientation, he dramatises the melancholy of specifically *human* creaturely being, alienated from seemingly simpler, more vital forms of life. In the wider Libyan novel, such forms of vitality are encountered, or imagined, only fleetingly, through the shared gaze or fragile companionships of human and animal. In *al-Kalb al-Dhahabi*, however, they represent a constant source of loss and yearning.

Bushnaf also asserts that, though his novel represents an '*umthūla*' (example/proverb), it is not intended to assert a reassuring moral, instead representing a 'fluid' (*sāʾil*) or 'unrestrained' (*munfalit*) 'allegorical game' (*laᶜb alījūrī*), irresistibly evocative of broader 'creaturely signs'.[30,] Resisting interpretation, it unfolds not through educational journeys but feverish exposure to nature and war. 'From Ovid to Kafka', Pick comments, 'narratives of the transformations of species have served as a vehicle for discussing human identity, its failings and flaws.'[31] In *al-Kalb al-Dhahabi*, however, Libeccio/Saᶜid's complex species identity eludes the stable identification of failings, flaws or identities, indicating flight, fear and flux as the only constant truths. In contrast to Lucius' transformation in *The Golden Ass*, widely understood as a warning against bodily appetites and meddlesomeness, Saᶜid's transformation is, above all, a dramatisation of vulnerability. While Lucius-turned-donkey resents the loss of his upright stature, Libeccio-turned-man is made nauseous by his new posture, and frequently described 'curling up' (*yankamish ᶜalā nafsihi*) in physical and psychological discomfort.[32]

This is coupled by Saᶜid's consistent confusion and passivity to external events, as he is tamed by his new Signora. Saᶜid, Bushnaf states, 'wanted to be as she wanted him to be', refraining from urinating at will and only occasionally baring his teeth in a canine snarl.[33] Despite his efforts, however, he experiences continuing spells of feverish disorientation, returning him to a dog-like state. These spells specifically coincide with the turbulent events of the 1960s, as both rural migrants and stray dogs are driven by drought and hunger to city slums, and Libeccio-Saᶜid must attempt to find his 'home' among them. Swept along in their current, he exemplifies the pulse of natural history, in which, as Pick puts it, 'the agent – the one who, as we say "makes history"' is replaced by 'the creature overtaken by or lost in history'.[34] Unable to understand if he should rejoice or rage in the unfolding events of September 1969, he resorts to incomprehensible 'howls' (*ᶜuwāʾ*) which, in an ironic twist, become a mouthpiece for the new Revolutionary regime.[35] His secret canine origins also, however, become a constant liability. Hearing the Signora describe Libyans as '*kilāb*', and the monarchy and then RCC's designation of political dissenters in identical terms, Libeccio-Saᶜid struggles with the otherness within himself. Through the novel's unrestrained 'allegorical game', packs of stray dogs represent both literal embodiments of the precarity of rapid urbanisation and environmental change, bringing humans and animals into unfamiliar forms of proximity, and literal and symbolic embodiments of the biopolitical exclusions of the modern nation. 'The war on dogs had', Bushnaf observes, 'turned into a nationalist project to reform the country', coinciding with the exiling of dissidents and 'settling' (*tawṭīn*) of migrants.[36] Caught between species, as between the carcases of dogs piled on rubbish dumps and the humans pursued as 'stray dogs', Saᶜid's exposure is complete: 'He would flee to his kennel at night, curling into a ball (*yankamish fīhi ᶜalā nafsihi*), like a dog afraid of humans, and a human afraid of dogs.'[37] Inverting the literary motif of what Ortiz-Robles calls humanity's metaphoric 'fall' into the 'animalisation' of modern biopower, Libeccio falls into human being while, as both human and dog, he must navigate the 'piles of rubbish' and the surveillance that haunt the Libyan novel in an anxious refrain.[38]

In another, closely related, refrain, *al-Kalb al-Dhahabi* further expresses a persistent yearning for lost fertility, echoing back to al-Kuni's 'lost domain' (*buᶜd mafqūd*) of myth and deep history, rooted in imaginings of formerly green geographies. Saᶜid thus fantasises that, through his howls, he might return Tripoli to lush valleys and flowing ravines:

> His howls filled the wilderness and populated the emptiness, blowing the thunder of life into the silence of millennia, while packs of gazelles ran with wolves, hyenas and foxes, and eagles, hawks and falcons flew overhead, chasing one another as they had done before the drought and metamorphosis (*qabl al-jafāf wa-l-taḥawwul*).[39]

Within this extended primordial imaginary, Bushnaf alludes frequently to the 'Akakus dog-men' (*rijāl al-Akākūs al-kilāb*) as embodiments of former fertility, and the 'wailing of Ovid's nymphs' (*nuwāḥ ḥūriyāt Ūfīd*) as lamentations for it.[40] As throughout the Libyan novel, the sun and Qibli wind stand in juxtaposition, as literal and allegorical forces of aridity, exposure and surveillance, submitting the land to motionlessness as well as to sudden, irrevocable transformation. Through both, *maskh* is emphasised, once again, not as moral instruction but exposure, prompting feverish states through deprivation of water, shelter, rights and agency. In the heat of the perennial desert sun, the allegorical framework of story, moral argument and meditation collapses into vulnerable, creaturely being.

All is further framed by Libya's defining, and ideologically-loaded, division between coast and desert, settled and nomadic, Mediterranean and African, of which the statue of the Girl and Gazelle becomes the novel's ultimate 'allegorical game'.[41] Animated in longing, the statue's 'sighs' (*anīn*) drift through the city, mourning the transformation of creaturely lives into signifying systems, as, in typically 'fluid' fashion, Bushnaf shifts between reading it as an allegory of nation, ecology and artistic creation. Imagining the statue to have started life in the form of two desert gazelles, fleeing hunters, he describes how they are then caught in an Italian artist's 'suffocating cage of clay' (*qafaṣ al-ṣalṣāl al-khāniq*), falling victim to his imperial desire to bring together desert and coast, and turned into human and stone.[42] The initial freedom, and subsequent vulnerability, of the desert gazelles thus echoes the plight of the dog, Libeccio, whose very name indicates his own 'Italianisation', as all three enter the turbulent space of Tripoli. More broadly, the stifled, metamorphosed state of each creature becomes a poignant commentary on the 'long petrification' (*taḥajjur ṭawīl*) of the country at large, cemented under al-Qadhafi, and through which story and art shift between processes of appropriation and liberation, with the latter necessarily predicated on digression and *maskh*.[43]

Refusing the 'petrification' of stable allegorical meaning, Bushnaf finally also suggests that his whole novel might, in fact, be simply a means of communicating his own, unspeakable love story, as Tripoli lies beneath the 'dust of black plague' (*ᶜujājat al-ṭāᶜūn al-aswad*), sweeping away Girl and Gazelle and forcing authors into 'loose, allegorical darkness' (*al-ghabash al-umthūlī al-faḍfāḍ*).[44] He would, he suggests, like to fill his story of the statue with 'emotions', 'sensations' and 'curves' but is content simply to mention it before it fades into oblivion.[45] He similarly alludes to his own youthful love affair only through brief mention of the momentarily 'bared breasts' (*al-nahdayn al-munfalitayn*) of a mountain girl amid the ruins of Leptis Magna. Repeatedly, however, he also suggests that the erotic tale to which they allude may, in fact, represent the novel's utmost 'secret' (*sirr*), paralleled in Apuleius's scandalous affair with the widow Pudentilla, which, Bushnaf suggests, was similarly translated into the form of human-animal transformation.[46] Describing both the physicality of bared breasts and the unruliness of allegory, the adjective '*munfalit*' (free/unrestrained) evokes the possibilities of unhampered emotion to which his own story strives. The breadth of history, from rock art to Jamahiriyya, is thus juxtaposed to intense points of passion, as the novel emerges in flight from stasis and censorship, fragmenting plot and narrative, and confronting the borders of individual, national and species identity, as well as symbolic meaning. In the fever of metamorphosis, Libya's current transformations, under a 'black plague', are imagined within both the broad scope of transformations past and the private moments of creatures, navigating the desert sun and the passions which cannot be expressed.

Notes

Introduction: A Nation of Others

1. Trans. Tarif Khalidi.
2. Al-Kiddi, 'al-Hayah', p. 223 (trans. p. 57).
3. Ibid.
4. Al-Kuni, *Watani Sahra' Kubra*, p. 74.
5. Diana, 'Libyan Narrative', p. 26; Vandewalle, *A History of Modern Libya*, p. 33.
6. Vandewalle, *A History of Modern Libya*, p. 42.
7. Anderson, *The State and Social Transformation*, p. 255.
8. Vandewalle, *A History of Modern Libya*, p. 74.
9. Alongside his own 'animal rhetoric', al-Qadhafi was himself branded the 'mad dog' of the Middle East by Ronald Reagan in 1986.
10. Ṣāliḥ, *Ufuq Akhar*, p. 17.
11. Ibid., pp. 18–19.
12. This prominence of animals in Libyan fiction was first noted by Lynx-Qualey ('The Animals in Libyan Fiction').
13. Gross, 'Introduction', p. 2.
14. Huggan and Tiffin, *Postcolonial Ecocriticism*, p. 3.
15. Notable exceptions are studies of Saudi-Jordanian ʿAbd al-Rahman Munif's *Mudun al-Milh* (Ghosh, 'Petrofiction', pp. 431–40, and Nixon, *Slow Violence*, pp. 68–102), as well as Sinno's 'The Greening of Modern Arabic Literature', pp. 125–43. For introductions to environmental history and the MENA region, see also Alan Mikhail (ed.), *Water on Sand: Environmental Histories of the Middle East and North Africa* (Oxford: Oxford University Press, 2012); and Diana K. Davis and Edmund Burke III (eds.), *Environmental Imaginaries of the Middle East and North Africa* (Athens, OH: Ohio University Press, 2011).
16. Weil, *Thinking Animals*, p. 5; Scholtmeijer, *Animal Victims in Modern Fiction*, p. 300.

17. Ahmida, 'Libya', p. 311. For an account of earlier prose writing in Libya, see al-Faqih, 'The Libyan Short Story', pp. 67–95.
18. Chorin, *Exit Gaddafi*, p. 39.
19. Metz, *Libya*, p. 40.
20. Quoted in Harlow, 'From Flying Carpets', p. 443.
21. Taji-Farouki, 'Sadiq Nayhum', pp. 261–4; Davis, *Libyan Politics*, p. 73.
22. Al-Kuni, *ᶜUdus al-Sura 1*, p. 224.
23. Taji-Farouki, 'Sadiq Nayhum', p. 273.
24. Saleh, 'Libya's Intellectuals Under the Gaddafi Dictatorship'; al-Qadhafi, *Al-Qarya al-Qarya, al-Ard al-Ard wa-Intihar Raᵓid al-Fadaᵓ*. See also the three volumes of essays commissioned on al-Qadhafi's writing: *Dirasat wa-Abhath fi Adab al-Qadhafi* (Benghazi: al-Lajna al-Shaᶜbiyya al-ᶜAmma li-l-Thaqafa wa-l-Iᶜlam, 2009).
25. Amnesty International, 'Long Struggle for Truth', p. 2.
26. Al-Asfar, 'Libya's Patient Revolutionaries'.
27. Sakr, *'Anticipating' the 2011 Arab Uprisings*, p. 50.
28. Mattawa, 'Libya', p. 227.
29. Chorin, *Exit Gaddafi*, p. 46.
30. Taji-Farouki, 'Sadiq Nayhum', p. 266.
31. al-Būᶜīssī, *Naᶜthal*, back cover.
32. Sakr, *'Anticipating'*, p. 65; Foucault, *Discipline and Punish*, p. 214.
33. Ishtaywī, *Thaman al-Hurriya*, p. 18.
34. For a comprehensive list of Libyan novels published from the 1960s to 2000, see Abū Dīb, *Muᶜjam al-Muᵓallafat al-Libiyya*, pp. 145–70.
35. Sakr, *'Anticipating'*, p. 65.
36. Al-Maqhūr, 'Hawl al-Qissa al-Libiyya', p. 135. For further studies of the Libyan short story see, in Arabic, al-Hāshimī (ed.), *Khalfiyyat al-Qissa al-Libiyya al-Qasira*; and, in English, al-Faqih, 'The Libyan Short Story'; and Diana, '"Literary Springs" in Libyan Literature', p. 441.
37. Al-Maqhūr, 'Hawl al-Qissa al-Libiyya', p. 139.
38. Rooke, 'Mahattat', pp. 117–18.
39. Hassan, 'Towards a Theory of the Arabic Novel', p. 28.
40. Al-Fayṣal, *Dirasat fi al-Riwaya al-Libiyya* and *Nuhud al-Riwaya al-ᶜArabiyya al-Libiyya*. Other introductions include: Burhāna, 'Al-Riwaya al-Libiyya: al-Nashᵓa wa-l-Tatawwur', pp. 349–76; Bin Jumᶜa, *Al-Riwaya al-Libiyya al-Muᶜasara*; al-Mismārī, *Dhakirat al-Kitaba: Qiraᵓat fi al-Qissa wa-l-Riwaya al-Libiyya*; and Ṣāliḥ, *Fi al-Thaqafa al-Libiyya al-Muᶜasira*.
41. Al-Hājī, 'al-Zaman fi al-Riwaya al-Libiyya'; Amlūda, *Tamthilat al-Muthaqqaf fi al-Sard al-ᶜArabi al-Hadith*; al-Mālikī, *Jamaliyyat al-Riwaya al-Libiyya*; and al-Shaylābī, *al-Qadaya al-Ijtimaᶜiyya fi al-Riwaya al-Libiyya*.

42. Diana, *La letteratura della Libia*.
43. Allen, 'A Different Voice', p. 151.
44. Sakr, *'Anticipating'*, p. 65.
45. Abū Dīb, *Muʿjam al-Muʾallafat al-Libiyya*, p. 147.
46. Examples include: Muḥammad ʿAlī ʿUmar's *Aqwa min al-Harb* (1962) and *Hisar al-Kuf* (1964); Khalīfa ʿAbd al-Majīd al-Muntaṣir's *Mabruka Batala min Libiya* (1970); and Muḥammad Ṣāliḥ al-Qammūdī's *Ramadan al-Suwayhili: Riwaya Tarikhiyya* (1971).
47. Kashlāf, *Kitabat Libiyya*, p. 176. Muḥammad Farīd Siyāla's *Iʿtirafat Insan* (1961) is the first extant Libyan novel, followed by the likes of al-Qammūdī's *Thalathun Yawman fi al-Qahira* (1971), Aḥmad Naṣr's (b.1941) *Wamid fi Jidar al-Layl* (1974) and Rajab Miftāḥ Abū Dabbūs' *Fi al-Manfa* (1975).
48. Bamia, 'The African Novel: Northern Africa', p. 25.
49. For further analysis, see Ṣāliḥ, *Fi al-Thaqafa al-Libiyya al-Muʿasira*, pp. 66–85.
50. al-Quwayrī, *Min Mufakkira*, p. 11.
51. Ibid., p. 39.
52. Taji-Farouki, 'Modern Intellectuals', p. 298; Hābīl, 'Waqiʿ al-Riwaya al-Libiyya', p. 36.
53. Al-Faqih, 'Sahib al-Nufudh', p. 46.
54. Taji-Farouki, 'Modern Intellectuals', p. 325.
55. Shalqam (ed.), *Hiwar*, p. 18.
56. Al-Kubtī (ed.), *Turuq Mughattah bi-l-Thalj*, p. 320.
57. Al-Burhāna, 'al-Riwaya al-Libiyya', p. 351; see also Ṣāliḥ's discussion of the forgotten and frustrated 'seventies generation' in *Ufuq Akhar*, pp. 59–63.
58. Ahmida, *Forgotten Voices*, p. 56.
59. Ṣāliḥ, *Ufuq Akhar*, pp. 20–2.
60. Al-Kuni, *ʿUdus 1*, pp. 177–8.
61. Al-Shaylābī, *al-Qadaya al-Ijtimaʿiyya*, p. 160.
62. Allen, 'Rewriting Literary History', p. 254.
63. Al-Kuni, *ʿUdus 1*, pp. 368, 392; *ʿUdus 2*, p. 401.
64. Allen, 'Rewriting Literary History', p. 254. Al-Kuni has rarely also been compared with other Tuareg authors, such as his contemporary, the Tuareg-Nigerian poet, Mahmoudan Hawad (b.1950).
65. See, for example, al-Fayturi, 'Marthiyat al-Zawal', pp. 40–8, and Salam, 'Zahira Adabiyya Libiyya', pp. 149–51.
66. Bamia, 'The African Novel', p. 25.
67. Hābīl, 'Waqiʿ al-Riwaya al-Libiyya', p. 38.
68. Chorin, *Translating Libya*, p. 4.

69. Deleuze and Guattari, 'What Is a Minor Literature?', p. 16.
70. Ibid.
71. Vermeulen and Richter, 'Creaturely Constellations', p. 3.
72. See Qur'an 11:6.
73. Benjamin, *The Origin of German Tragic Drama*, p. 85.
74. Vermeulen and Richter, 'Creaturely Constellations', p. 4.
75. Benjamin, *Illuminations*, p. 118. Beatrice Hanssen describes Benjamin's reading of Kafka as a way to 'reinscribe the theological into a seemingly abject realm of animality' (Hanssen, *Walter Benjamin's Other History*, p. 152).
76. Santner, *On Creaturely Life*, pp. 27, xix.
77. For Foucault's discussion of biopower, see *The History of Sexuality, vol. 1, The Will to Knowledge* (1976). Agamben's thinking on humanity and animality is most clearly presented in *Homo Sacer: Sovereign Power and Bare Life* (1995) and *The Open: Man and Animal* (2002).
78. Pick, *Creaturely Poetics*, p. 26.
79. Ibid., p. 193.
80. Derrida, 'The Animal that Therefore I Am', p. 373. For an elucidation of Derrida's arguments on animals and the 'proto-ethical', see Calarco, *Zoographies*, pp. 103–49.
81. Pick, *Creaturely Poetics*, p. 5.
82. Ibid., p. 186.
83. Al-Asfar, *Sharmula*, p. 218.
84. Anderson, *Imagined Communities*, pp. 7, 25.
85. Ohrem, 'Animating Creaturely Life', p. 8.
86. Al-Faqih, *Fi Hija' al-Bashar*, p. 7.
87. Ibid., p. 84.
88. Qanāw, 'ᶜAwdat al-Qaysar' in *ᶜAwdat al-Qaysar*, pp. 17–24. For further discussion of the real-life plight of the statue of Septimius, see Higgins, 'How Gaddafi Toppled a Roman Emperor'.
89. Santner, *On Creaturely Life*, pp. 197, 206–7.
90. Pick, *Creaturely Poetics*, p. 184.
91. Mattawa, 'Introduction'.
92. Ohrem, 'Animating Creaturely Life', p. 6.
93. Al-ᶜAwkalī, 'Hiwar maᶜa al-Qass Ahmad Yusuf ᶜAqila', p. 176.
94. Atkinson, 'Encountering Bare Life', p. 155.
95. Ahmida, *Forgotten Voices*, p. 44.
96. Matar, *The Return*, p. 153.
97. See al-ᶜAbbār, *Maqalat fi al-Turath al-Shaᶜbi*, pp. 83–93, in which he discusses the legacy of Italian colonisation on popular Libyan folklore.

98. Al-Minifi, 'Ma bi Marad', p. 21 (trans. Mattawa). For an analysis of the language of this difficult poem, see Zaydān, 'al-Qasida al-Shaᶜbiyya', pp. 54–71.
99. See ᶜAbd al-Rasūl al-ᶜUraybī's *Abwab al-Mawt al-Sabᶜa* (1994), in which al-Minifi's verses are 'wailed aloud'.
100. Yaeger, 'Literature in the Ages of Wood', p. 442. For coinage of the term 'petrofiction', see Ghosh, 'Petrofiction', p. 29.
101. Al-Kuni, *ᶜUdus 3*, pp. 108–9.
102. Nixon, *Slow Violence*, p. 72. Al-Kuni literally describes oil as the 'letting of a mother's blood' (*nazīf damm al-umm*) (*ᶜUdus 3*, pp. 101–11).
103. Nixon, *Slow Violence*, p. 15. Little has been documented of the full-scale of Libya's environmental damage, due to its current political instability. For a brief overview, see 'Oil- and Gas-related pollution in Libya', *The Telegraph* (via *Wikileaks*), 31 January 2011, https://www.telegraph.co.uk/news/wikileaks-files/libya-wikileaks/8294826/OIL-AND-GAS-RELATED-POLLUTION-IN-LIBYA.html (last accessed 1 July 2019).
104. Gifford, 'Pastoral', pp. 45–6.
105. Al-Qadhafi, *al-Qarya al-Qarya*, p. 5.
106. Woodward, *The Animal Gaze*, pp. 69, 130; Woodward and McHugh (eds), *Indigenous Creatures, Native Knowledges*, pp. 2–3.
107. Tlili, *Animals in the Qurᵓan*, p. 146.
108. Tlili, 'The Meaning of the Qur'anic Word "dābba"', p. 146. See Qurᵓan 6:38, 4:97, 29:56 and 39:10.
109. Qurᵓan 4:97.
110. Woodward, *The Animal Gaze*, p. 3.
111. Elmarsafy, *Sufism in the Contemporary Arabic Novel*, p. 2; Phillips, *Religion in the Egyptian Novel*, p. 201.
112. Al-Kuni, *Nazif al-Hajar*, p. 130 (trans. p. 106).
113. On the status of animals in classical Sufi thought, and particularly in Ibn al-ᶜArabi's writing, see Chittick, 'The Wisdom of Animals'; and Khan, 'Nothing but Animals'.
114. Pick, *Creaturely Poetics*, pp. 185–6; Elmarsafy, *Sufism*, pp. 1–2.
115. For an alternative reading of animals through the concepts of '*tawaḥḥush*' (becoming wild/beastly) and '*tagharrub*' (estrangement/alienation), see el-Ariss, 'Return of the Beast', p. 62
116. For further discussion of the *raḥīl*, see Stetkevych, *The Mute Immortals Speak*, pp. 3–54.
117. Ibid., p. 138.
118. Al-Ghadeer, *Desert Voices*, p. 79.
119. Ibn Qutayba, *Kitab al-Shiᶜr wa-l-Shuᶜaraᵓ: al-Juzᵓ al-Awwal*, pp. 563, 565.

120. Margoliouth, 'Abu'l-ʿAlā al-Maʿarri's Correspondence', pp. 297, 318.
121. For an overview of traditional Arabic allegory, see Heath, 'Allegory in Islamic Literatures', p. 85.
122. Irwin, 'The Arabic Beast Fable,' p. 40. See also Christine van Ruymbeke's discussion of the terminology of 'fable' to describe the collection in *Kashefi's Anvar-e Sohayli: Rewriting Kalila and Dimna in Timurid Herat* (Leiden: Brill, 2016), pp. 68–71.
123. Irwin, 'The Arabic Beast Fable', p. 40. For an introduction to the *Risala's* broader contexts, see Goodman, 'Introduction', pp. 1–56. See also Kassam, '*The Case of the Animals versus Man*', pp. 160–9
124. Montgomery, *Al-Jāḥiẓ: In Praise of Books*, p. 55.
125. Ibid.
126. Marzolph and van Leeuwen, *The Arabian Nights Encyclopaedia*, p. 478. See also al-Ghazoul, who comments on overlaps between the *Risala* of the Ikhwan al-Safaʾ and animal fable in *Alf Layla wa-layla*, 'Qisas al-Hayawan', pp. 134–52.
127. Fudge, 'Underworlds and Otherworlds', p. 257.
128. Aḥmad Shawqī's *Shawqiyyat* (1888) contain numerous animal verse fables, commenting on the British occupation of Egypt. Jubrān Khalīl Jubrān's *ʿAraʾis al-Muruj* (1906) is a good example of romantic imagery, while Munīf's environmentally-oriented *al-Nihayat* (1977) contains an inserted passage from *Kitab al-Hayawan*.
129. Examples include: Ghāda al-Sammān's *Bayrut 75* (1975) and *Kawabis Bayrut* (1976); Hudā Barakāt's *Harith al-Miyah* (1998); Zakariyā Tāmir's *al-Numur fi al-Yawm al-ʿAshir* (1980); and ʿAbd al-Hādī Saʿdūn's *Mudhakkarat Kalb ʿIraqi* (2012).
130. See the three Moroccan novels longlisted for the 2014 IPAF: Yūsuf Fāḍil, *Taʾir Azraq Nadir Yuhalliq Maʿi* (2013); Ismāʿīl Ghazālī, *Mawsim Sayd al-Zanjur* (2013); and ʿAbd al-Raḥīm Laḥbībī, *Taghribat al-ʿAbdi* (2013).
131. For discussions on the influence of folklore see: al-Dalnasī, 'Adab al-Qissa fi Libya', p. 177; and al-Miṣrātī, *Al-Mujtamaʿ al-Libi*, p. 35.
132. Al-ʿAbbār, *Maqalat fi al-Turath al-Shaʿbi*, pp. 93–9.
133. Ibid., pp. 97, 99.
134. For an introduction to Libya's prehistoric rock art, see Jitka Soukopova, *Round Heads: The Earliest Rock Paintings in the Sahara* (Newcastle upon Tyne: Cambridge Scholars Publishing, 2012).
135. Herodotus, *The Histories*, p. 372.
136. Khushaym, *Tahawwulat al-Jahsh al-Dhahabi*, p. 9.
137. Al-Fayturi, 'al-Hibi wa-l-ʿAqid'; al-Kuni, *ʿAdus 1*, p. 374.

138. Shalqam (ed.), *Hiwar*, p. 32.
139. The absence of modern and oral poetry from my analyses is another worthy criticism. Having toyed with incorporating it in different ways, I found the constraints of time and space to be too great to do it justice. I hope this will be a project for the future. Those interested in the history of modern Libyan poetry and analysis of its major trends may refer to Ṣāliḥ, *Ufuq Akhar*, pp. 31–50, and *Fi al-Thaqafa al-Libiyya al-Mu*ᶜ*asira*, pp. 11–17.

Chapter 1: Animal Fable in Novels of Survival

1. Trans. Tarif Khalidi.
2. Kafka, *The Complete Stories*, p. 351.
3. '*Rāqid al-rīḥ yalqā al-*ᶜ*aẓm fī al-karsh*'. 'Stomach' refers to tripe, the edible lining of cattle and sheep stomachs, which, of course, ought to be free of bones.
4. Selim, *The Novel and the Rural Imaginary*, p. 24.
5. Higgins, *Economic and Social Development of Libya*, p. 37.
6. Huggan and Tiffin, *Postcolonial Ecocriticism*, p. 27.
7. All translations of al-Nayhum are my own. To date, *Min Makka* has been translated only into Italian (*Da la Mecca a qui*, trans. Diana and Galiero (Torino: Le Nuove Muse, 2007)).
8. See: Ramsay, 'Breaking the Silence', pp. 149–72; Fouad and Alwakeel, 'Representations of the Desert', pp. 36–62; and Elmusa, 'The Ecological Bedouin', pp. 9–35.
9. Other examples of Libyan survival novels include: Mubārak al-Duraybī's *Tuyur al-Masa*ᵓ (1984); ᶜAbdallāh Minwar al-Difārī's *al-Hattab* (1984); Sālim al-Hindāwī's *al-Tahuna* (1985); ᶜAbd al-Rasūl ᶜUraybī's *Tilka al-Layla* (1994); and Muḥammad al-ᶜArīshiyya's *al-Ayyam al-Akhira fi* ᶜ*Allaj* (2006).
10. Elmarsafy, 'Ibrahim al-Koni's Hybrid Aesthetic', p. 190.
11. Wright, 'Wilderness', p. 15.
12. *Nazif*, p. 5; *Fi Hija*ᵓ *al-Bashar*, p. 7.
13. Tlili, *Animals in the Qur*ᵓ*an*, p. 148.
14. Derrida, 'The Law of Genre', p. 63; see also Huggan and Tiffin, *Postcolonial Ecocriticism*, p. 153.
15. DeLoughrey and Handley, 'Towards an Aesthetics of the Earth', p. 8.
16. Ibid.
17. Patterson, *Fables of Power*, pp. 15–16.
18. See Harel, 'The Animal Voice', p. 10, in which she discusses this scepticism.
19. Le Guin, *Buffalo Gals*, p. 10.
20. Harel, 'The Animal Voice', p. 13.
21. Oerlemans, 'The Animal in Allegory', p. 5.

22. Ibid., p. 6.
23. Baker, *Picturing the Beast*, p. 124.
24. Ibid.
25. Ibid., p. 159.
26. Chorin, 'Homeless Rats'; Taji-Farouki, 'Sadiq Nayhum', p. 255; and Elmusa, 'The Ecological Bedouin', pp. 32–3.
27. Qurʾan 27:18–22.
28. Goodman, 'Introduction', p. 40.
29. Ikhwan al-Safa', *Epistles of the Brethren of Purity*, pp. 38–9.
30. Pick, *Creaturely Poetics*, pp. 189–90.
31. Ibid., p. 190.
32. Shalqam (ed.), *Hiwar*, p. 39.
33. al-Fayturi, 'al-Hibi wa-l-'Aqid'.
34. Al-Kubti (ed.), *Nawaris*, p. 93.
35. Taji-Farouki, 'Sadiq Nayhum', p. 263.
36. Wenzel, 'Petro-magic-realism', p. 452; al-Nayhum, *Kalimat*, p. 264.
37. Al-Nayhum, *Min Qisas al-Atfal*, pp. 11–20.
38. Chorin, *Exit Gaddafi*, p. 2; Elvira, *La letteratura della Libia*, p. 72. Taji-Farouki, 'Sadiq Nayhum', p. 256.
39. Al-Nayhum, *Min Qisas al-Atfal*, pp. 21–30.
40. Al-Nayhum, *Kalimat*, p. 29.
41. Al-Fayturi, 'Najm al-Nujum'.
42. For further discussion of al-Nayhum's Islamic thought, see Taji-Farouki, 'Modern Intellectuals', pp. 317, 297–99.
43. Fromm, *The Sane Society*, pp. 23, 65.
44. Ibid., p. 23.
45. Al-Huni, 'al-Tariq ila Inkar al-Dhat', p. 48.
46. Al-Nayhum, *al-^{c}Awda al-Muhzina*, pp. 92, 115.
47. Ibid., pp. 159, 173.
48. Ibid., pp. 56, 131.
49. Ibid., pp. 85, 82.
50. Nixon, *Slow Violence*, p. 4.
51. Al-Nayhum, *al-^{c}Awda al-Muhzina*, p. 174.
52. Al-Faqih, 'Sahib al-Nufudh', p. 47.
53. Phillips, *Religion in the Egyptian Novel*, p. 195.
54. Shalqam (ed.), *Hiwar*, pp. 28–9. For discussion of Hemingway's influence on al-Nayhum, see ^{c}Ayyāsh, 'Athr Irnist Himinjway', pp. 58–90.
55. Al-Fayturi, 'al-Hibi wa-l-^{c}Aqid'.

56. See al-Nayhum's discussion of al-Hallaj in *Alladhi Yaʾti wa-la Yaʾti*, pp. 67–72.
57. Al-Kubtī (ed.), *Turuq*, p. 322.
58. *Min Makka*, pp. 5–6. In wider Libyan fiction, black protagonists also feature in Muḥammad al-^{c}Amāmī's *Kawami Ayaya* (2003), al-Ghazal's *al-Qawqa^{c}a* (2006) and Bin Shatwan's *Zaraʾib al-^{c}Abid* (2016).
59. See ^{c}Aṭiyya, *Fi al-Adab al-Libi*, p. 47, who comments on the connotations of the name, Mas^{c}ud al-Tabbal (Mas^{c}ūd al-Ṭabbāl), with slavery and African stereotyping.
60. Altaleb, 'The Social and Economic History of Slavery in Libya (1800–1950)', p. 16.
61. Ibid., p. 168.
62. Wright, *The Trans-Saharan Slave Trade*, p. 165. For discussion of Black Africans in Libya, see Chris Dunton, 'Black Africans in Libya and Libyan Images of Black Africa', in *The Green and the Black: Qadhafi's Policies in Africa*, ed. René Lemarchand (Bloomington, IN: Indiana University Press, 1988), pp. 150–66.
63. *Min Makka*, p. 30.
64. Ibid., pp. 112.
65. Ibid., p. 100. On the different species of turtle along the Libyan coast see Hamza, 'Libya: Sea Turtles in the Mediterranean', pp. 157–69.
66. *Min Makka*, p. 131.
67. Ibid., p. 53.
68. Ibid.
69. Ibid., p. 55.
70. Ibid., p. 82.
71. Ibid.
72. ^{c}Aṭiyya, *Fi al-Adab al-Libi*, p. 90.
73. *Min Makka*, p. 41.
74. Ibid., pp. 88, 97, 100.
75. Ibid., p. 99.
76. Fromm, *The Sane Society*, p. 34.
77. ^{c}Ayyāsh, 'Athr Irnist Himinjway', p. 85; Burhāna, 'al-Sukhriyya', p. 13.
78. *Min Makka*, pp. 65–6.
79. Ibid., p. 65.
80. Ibid.
81. Ibid.
82. Ibid., pp. 79, 98.
83. Ibid., p. 83.
84. Ibid., p. 84.
85. Ibid., p. 126.

86. Ibid., pp. 79, 84.
87. Ibid., pp. 76–7.
88. Ibid., p. 109.
89. Al-Nayhum, *Mihnat Thaqafa Muzawwara*, p. 32.
90. Tlili, *Animals in the Qur'an*, p. 243.
91. For discussion of spirituality in *Min Makka*, see: al-Hindawi, 'al-ᶜĀ'id ila Binghazi', p. 40; al-Huni, 'al-Tariq ila Inkar al-Dhat', p. 48; and Bushnaf, 'Bi-l-Yusra: Min Huna ila Makka'.
92. On the concept of '*murāqaba*' (observation) in Sufi thought, see al-Qushayri, *al-Qushayri's Epistle on Sufism*, pp. 202–5.
93. *Min Makka*, pp. 105 and 125–6.
94. Ibid., pp. 128–9.
95. Ibid., pp. 116–17 and 128–9. See Burhāna, 'al-Sukhriyya', p. 12, where the irony of the section is discussed.
96. Qur'an 37:139–48.
97. *Min Makka*, p. 136.
98. Ibid., pp. 146–7.
99. Al-Faqih, *Fi'ran,* p. 5. Translated passages from *Fi'ran* are taken from the published English translation, which I have further referenced, in addition to the original Arabic, throughout most of my analyses, for ease of reference.
100. Ibid.
101. Sakr, *'Anticipating'*, p. 52.
102. Al-Qadhafi, *al-Qarya al-Qarya*, p. 23.
103. Al-Faqih, *Thalath Majmuᶜat*, pp. 43–53.
104. Al-Faqih, 'Foreword', p. viii.
105. Al-Faqih, *Khams Khanafis*, pp. 11–19.
106. *Fi'ran*, p. 52 (trans. pp. 40–2).
107. ᶜAqila, *Khararif Libiyya*, pp. 107–15.
108. *Fi'ran*, p. 53 (trans. p. 43).
109. Ibid., p. 9 (trans. p. 6).
110. Qur'an, 27:17–19.
111. Ibid., pp. 20–1.
112. Ibid., pp. 91, 215 (trans., pp. 73, 177).
113. Ibid., p. 174 (trans. p. 143).
114. Ibid., p. 161 (trans. p. 132).
115. Ibid., p. 162 (trans. p. 133).
116. Ibid.
117. Ibid., p. 164 (trans. p. 134).
118. Ibid., pp. 196, 203 (trans. pp. 161, 166).

119. Ibid., p. 202 (trans., p. 165).
120. Ibid., p. 206 (trans. p. 169).
121. Ikhwan al-Safa°, *Epistles of the Brethren of Purity*, p. 39.
122. *Fi°ran*, p. 37 (trans. p. 28).
123. Ibid., pp. 57, 232 (trans. pp. 45, 190–1).
124. Ibid., p. 239 (trans. p. 197).
125. Ibid. p. 247 (trans. p. 203).
126. Ibid.
127. Ibid (trans. p. 204).
128. Ibid., p. 38 (trans. p. 28).
129. Chorin, 'Homeless Rats'.
130. McHugh, 'Hybrid Species and Literatures', p. 292.
131. Wenzel, 'Petro-Magic-Realism', p. 487.
132. Anag et al., 'Environment, Archaeology, and Oil', p. 67.
133. Al-Kuni, *ᶜUdus 1*, p. xviii.
134. Al-Kuni describes his novels' titles as their 'secret code' and 'the conscience of the work' (*ᶜUdus 1*, p. 390).
135. Research suggests the Sahara has expanded 10 per cent since the 1920s (Thomas and Nigam, 'Twentieth-Century Climate Change over Africa', pp. 3349–70). In his autobiography, al-Kuni also evokes the French nuclear tests, Gerboise bleue, conducted in the Algerian Sahara in the 1960s and leading to enduring toxicity (*ᶜUdus 1*, p. 73).
136. Fähndrich, 'The Desert as Homeland', p. 331.
137. Al-Kuni, *ᶜUdus 2*, pp. 37, 222.
138. Al-Kuni, *ᶜUdus 1*, p. 8.
139. Sperl, '"The Lunar Eclipse"', p. 247.
140. Fähndrich, 'The Desert as Homeland', p. 331.
141. Rasmussen, 'The People of Solitude', p. 609.
142. Quinones, *The Changes of Cain*, p. 3.
143. See Rossetti, 'Darkness', p. 51, for discussion of al-Kuni's use of epigraphs.
144. Al-Kuni, *Nazif*, p. 83 (trans. p. 65). Translated passages from *Nazif* are taken from the published English translation, which I have further referenced, in addition to the original Arabic, throughout most of my analyses, for ease of reference.
145. *Nazif*, p. 33; Lhote, *A la découverte*, p. 134. The published Arabic translation has '*qāfizīn*' (Ḥasan (trans.), *Lawhat Tasili*, p. 154).
146. Elmarsafy, *Sufism*, p. 128.
147. Weisberg, 'Spiritual Symbolism', p. 55.
148. See Deheuvels' comparison of *Hayy Ibn Yaqzan* and *Nazif*, 'Le lieu de l'utopie', pp. 37–8.

149. *Nazif*, p. 23 (trans. p. 14).
150. Ibid., p. 131 (trans. p. 106).
151. Ibid., p. 130 (trans. p. 106).
152. Claudot-Hawad, *Éperonner le Monde*, p. 104.
153. Ibid.
154. Van Leeuwen, 'Cars in the Desert', pp. 63–4.
155. *Nazif*, p. 143 (trans. p. 116).
156. Huggan and Tiffin, *Postcolonial Ecocriticism*, p. 154.
157. *Nazif*, p. 146 (trans. p. 117).
158. Al-Kuni, *ᶜUdus 2*, p. 213.
159. Al-Kuni, *ᶜUdus 1*, p. 374.
160. Weisberg also notes parallels to the Buddhist Jataka tale, 'The Banyan Deer' ('Spiritual Symbolism', pp. 59–61).
161. Aitmatov, *The White Steamship*, pp. 64–5.
162. Al-Ghānamī, *Malhamat al-Hudud*, p. 109.
163. *Nazif*, pp. 123–4 (trans. p. 100).
164. Ibid.
165. Oerlemans, 'The Animal in Allegory', p. 6.
166. *Nazif*, p. 126 (trans. p. 102)
167. Derrida, '"Eating Well"', p. 283.
168. Al-Kuni, 'Le discours du désert', p. 298.
169. *Nazif*, pp. 55–6 (trans. p. 35).
170. Ibid., p. 64 (trans. p. 46).
171. Ibid., p. 68 (trans. p. 49).
172. Ibid., pp. 79–80 (trans. p. 61).
173. Ibid., p. 80 (trans. p. 61).
174. Casajus, *La tente*, p. 104.
175. *Nazif*, p. 92 (trans. p. 71).
176. Ibid., p. 126 (trans. p. 102).
177. Ibid., pp. 99–100 (trans. pp. 78–9).
178. Ibid., p. 93 (trans. p. 73).
179. Deleuze and Guattari, *A Thousand Plateaus*, pp. 34–7; McHugh, 'Hybrid Species', p. 299; Cooke, 'Magical Realism in Libya', p. 13.
180. *Nazif*, p. 94.
181. Elmarsafy, *Sufism*, p. 125. See also al-Ghazoul, 'al-Riwaya al-Sufiyya', p. 35.
182. *Nazif*, p. 94 (trans. p. 74).
183. Rasmussen, 'Animal Sacrifice', p. 157.
184. *Nazif*, p. 165 (trans. p. 135). Asuf's repeated phrase is from *Sahih al-Bukhari*, Chapter 84, 'Kitāb al-Riqāq', no. 6072: '*wa-lā yamlaᵓ jawf Ibn Ādam illā al-turāb*'.

185. *Nazif*, p. 5 (trans. p. 1).
186. Ibid., pp. 165–6 (trans. p. 135).
187. Nixon, *Slow Violence*, p. 15.
188. Al-Kuni, 'Wa-l-Shi^c^r Aydan', pp. 71–2.
189. Al-Kuni, *^c^Udus 1*, p. 58; Ibn al-^c^Arabi, *Tarjuman al-Ashwaq*, p. 67.
190. Ouyang, *Poetics of Love*, p. 66.

Chapter 2: The Primordial Turn

1. Trans. Tarif Khalidi.
2. Berger, *Why Look at Animals?*, p. 39.
3. From a Syrian Maronite family, Spina grew up in Benghazi, before fleeing al-Qadhafi in 1979. While writing in Italian, he draws throughout his writing on Arabic tradition and Libyan localities.
4. Spina, *The Confines*, p. 344.
5. Ibid., p. 342.
6. Benjamin, *The Origin of German Tragic Drama*, p. 166.
7. Pick, *Creaturely Poetics*, pp. 73–4.
8. Ibn Khaldūn also suggests humanity's emergence from the 'world of monkeys' in a 'gradual process of creation' (*The Muqaddima*, p. 75).
9. See Qur'an 15:33, 32:8, 2:30.
10. Tlili, *Animals in the Qur'an*, pp. 240–2.
11. Shryock and Smail, 'Introduction', pp. 8, 5.
12. Ibid., p. 9.
13. Smail, *On Deep History*, pp. 4, 44.
14. Shryock and Smail, 'Introduction', p. 15.
15. Talasek, *Imagining Deep Time*, p. 2.
16. Ouyang, *Politics of Nostalgia*, p. vi.
17. Santner, *On Creaturely Life*, p. 105.
18. Al-Faqih and al-Kuni were recipients of the *al-Gaddafi International Prize for Human Rights*, 2002.
19. See al-Kuni, *^c^Udus 3*, pp. 563–4.
20. Taji-Farouki and al-Kubtī suggest that *al-Qurud* was published in 1975 by *Dar al-Haqiqa*, with *al-Hayawanat* following in 1984 (Taji-Farouki, 'Sadiq', pp. 257–8; al-Kubtī (ed.), *Turuq*, p. 347). However, in the 1978 discussion, *Hiwar*, *al-Hayawanat* is discussed and *al-Qurud* is not (Shalqam (ed.), *Hiwar*, p. 31).
21. Al-Qadhafi, *The Green Book*, p. 4 (original text). On the pervasiveness of the *Green Book* in education and the media see Ishtaywī, *Thaman al-Hurriya*, pp. 43–6.
22. Anderson, *The State and Social Transformation*, p. 267.

23. Al-Kuni, ʿUdus 1, p. 405.
24. Ibid., p. 409.
25. Ibid., p. 406; ʿUdus 2, p. 401.
26. Benjamin, Illuminations, p. 131.
27. Ibn Manẓūr, Lisan al-ʿArab: al-Juzʾ al-Rabiʿ, p. 23.
28. Qurʾan 5:60.
29. Bushnaf, al-Kalb al-Dhahabi, p. 39.
30. Al-Kuni, ʿUdus 2, p. 46.
31. Taji-Farouki, 'Sadiq', p. 265.
32. Al-Fayturi, 'al-Hibi wa-l-ʿAqid'.
33. These include: Sawt al-Nas (1987), al-Islam fi al-Asr (1991) and Islam did al-Islam (1994), discussed in Taji-Farouki, 'Modern Intellectuals', pp. 297–332.
34. Taji-Farouki, 'Sadiq', p. 262. Compounding his political disillusionment, al-Nayhum divorced his Finnish wife in the early 1970s and revoked his children's Libyan passports, a sharp contrast to the preface of Min Qisas al-Atfal: 'Seven Libyan Tales, Dedicated to the Citizen K. N. [al-Nayhum's son]', p. 9.
35. Al-Nayhum, Kalimat, pp. 237, 244.
36. Ansell and al-Arif (eds), The Libyan Revolution, p. 254.
37. Ibid.
38. Al-Kuni, Watani Sahraʾ Kubra, p. 69.
39. Al-Nayhum, Fursan, pp. 32–3; Kalimat, pp. 275–80.
40. Al-Nayhum, Tarikhuna 1, p. 50.
41. Shalqam (ed.), Hiwar, p. 5.
42. Ortiz Robles, Literature and Animal Studies, pp. 145, 176.
43. Shalqam (ed.), Hiwar, p. 31.
44. Al-Faqih, 'Sura Qalamiyya li-Sadiq al-Nayhum'.
45. Shalqam (ed.), Hiwar, pp. 32–3.
46. Al-Nayhum, al-Hayawanat, p. 19.
47. Al-Kuni, ʿUdus 2, p. 244.
48. Ibid.
49. Al-Hayawanat, p. 14.
50. Ibid., pp. 6, 14–15.
51. Ibid., p. 124.
52. Ibid., p. 19.
53. Ibid., p. 54.
54. Ibid., pp. 52, 48.
55. Ibid., p. 65.
56. Shalqam (ed.), Hiwar, p. 36.

57. *Al-Hayawanat*, pp. 32–3. See Goodman and McGregor (trans.), *The Case of the Animals*, p. 123.
58. *Al-Hayawanat*, p. 66.
59. Ibid., p. 119.
60. Ibid.
61. Ibid., pp. 78, 81.
62. Ibid., p. 81.
63. Ibid., pp. 37–43.
64. Ibid., p. 135.
65. Ibid.
66. Ibid., p. 35.
67. Deleuze and Guattari, 'What Is a Minor Literature?', p. 17.
68. For discussion of other monkeys in Libyan fiction, see Olszok, 'Creaturely Encounters', pp. 238–70.
69. Scholtmeijer, 'What is "Human"?', p. 139.
70. Kafka, *The Complete Stories*, pp. 269–70.
71. Berger, *Why Look at Animals?*, p. 45.
72. Ibid., p. 44.
73. Ibid., p. 50.
74. Al-Nayhum, *al-Qurud*, pp. 15, 56.
75. Ibid., pp. 83–4.
76. Ibid., p. 21.
77. Chorin, *Exit Gaddafi*, p. 46.
78. *Al-Qurud*, p. 22.
79. It is perhaps significant that al-Nayhum wrote *al-Qurud* after having worked on the *Mawsuᶜa al-Silah al-Musawwara* (1979), published by Dar al-Mukhtar.
80. *Al-Hayawanat*, p. 109.
81. Taji-Farouki, 'Sadiq Nayhum', p. 257.
82. Shalqam (ed.), *Hiwar*, p. 33.
83. Ibid., p. 52.
84. Ibid.
85. Three decades after *al-Hayawanat*, al-Būᶜīssī's *Naᶜthal* (2006) represents its successor, also recognised as a 'Libyan Animal Farm', and depicting events from the past decades in explicit form through a herd of goats.
86. All translations from *Hadaᵓiq* are my own, though I have, in some cases, included page references to the published translation.
87. Ahmida, *Forgotten Voices*, p. 56.
88. El-Enany, *Arab Representations*, p. 144.
89. Bamia, 'The African Novel', p. 25.

90. Al-Faqih, *Nafaq*, p. 252.
91. For connotations of the name Khalil al-Imam (Khalīl al-Imām), see Ahmida, *Forgotten Voices*, p. 58.
92. Al-Faqih, 'Hawl Qissatay al-Mawt wa-l-Farar ila Jahannam', in al-Qadhafi, *al-Qarya al-Qarya*, pp. 133–43.
93. Amlūda, *Tamthilat al-Muthaqqaf*, p. 15 (Fawziyya Shallābi's *Rajul li-Riwaya Wahida* (1985) preceded it).
94. *Nafaq*, p. 248.
95. Al-Faqih, *Sa-ahabuka*, p. 50.
96. Ghazoul, *Nocturnal Poetics*, p. 135.
97. Ouyang, *Poetics of Love*, p. 139.
98. *Sa-ahabuka*, p. 11 (trans. p. 6). See Beaumont, *Slave of Desire*, for an analysis of the tales in similar, psychoanalytic terms, through a Lacanian focus on the 'traumatic kernel' that defines the subject in his relation to the Law' (p. 32).
99. Van Leeuwen, *The Thousand and One Nights*, p. 77. See also al-Shaylābī who discusses contrasting imagery of light and dark in the trilogy (*al-Qadaya al-Ijtima*ᶜ*iyya*, p. 260).
100. *Nafaq*, p. 236.
101. Pinault, *Story-Telling Techniques*, pp. 18, 21.
102. *Sa-ahabuka*, p. 7.
103. See Amlūda's analytical diagram of these relationships, *Tamthilat*, pp. 189–90. Amlūda understands them as revolving around the three themes of 'discovery' (*iktishāf*), 'betrayal' (*khiyāna*) and 'violence' (ᶜ*unf*), tallying with my understanding of the trilogy's primordial imagery (p. 190).
104. *Sa-ahabuka*, p. 42.
105. Ibid.
106. Ibid., p. 164 (trans. p. 114).
107. Ibid., p. 174 (trans. p. 121).
108. Ibid.
109. Ibid., p. 131 (trans. p. 89).
110. Santner, *On Creaturely Life*, p. 195.
111. Al-Faqih, *Hadhihi*, p. 4.
112. Ibid., p. 14 (trans. p. 179).
113. *Nafaq*, p. 236 (trans. p. 472).
114. Ibid.
115. *Hadhihi*, p. 38.
116. Ouyang, *Poetics of Love*, pp. 34, 138.
117. *Hadhihi*, p. 29.
118. Ibid., p. 71.

119. Al-Fārābī, *On the Perfect State*, p. 231.
120. *Hadhihi*, p. 34
121. Ibid., p. 235.
122. Van Leeuwen, 'The Forbidden Door', p. 76.
123. *Hadhihi*, p. 155–6 (trans. p. 288).
124. Van Leeuwen, *The Thousand and One Nights*, p. 88.
125. *Nafaq*, pp. 7–8, 12–13.
126. Ibid., p. 137 (trans. p. 398).
127. Ibid., p. 75.
128. Ibid., p. 239 (trans. pp. 474–5).
129. Berger, *Why Look at Animals?*, p. 59.
130. Ibid., p. 58.
131. Ibid., p. 60.
132. *Nafaq*, pp. 245–9.
133. Ibid., p. 246 (trans. p. 478–9).
134. Ibid., p. 251.
135. Ibid., p. 248 (trans. p. 481).
136. Ibid., p. 245.
137. Ibid., p. 246.
138. Ibid., p. 250 (trans. p. 482).
139. Ibid., p. 253.
140. Santner, *On Creaturely Life*, pp. 194–5.
141. *Nafaq*, p. 256.
142. Ibid., pp. 254–5 (trans. p. 487). This alludes to the banning of foreign-language teaching in 1986, following Tripoli's bombing by US planes (Orafi, 'Libya: Intentions and Realities', p. 314).
143. *Nafaq*, p. 257 (trans. p. 486).
144. Ibid., p. 255. For further analysis of the depiction of the alienated intellectual in *Hada'iq*, see Amlūda, *Tamthilat*, pp. 235–7. Amlūda also draws a comparison to other alienated figures in the Libyan novel. Earlier mention of 'Harun al-Rashid in modern clothes' may also allude to al-Qadhafi (*Nafaq*, p. 180, trans. p. 430).
145. Van Leeuwen, *The Thousand and One Nights*, p. 77.
146. *Nafaq*, p. 258 (trans. p. 488).
147. Fähndrich, 'The Desert', p. 339.
148. Al-Kuni, *ᶜUdus 2*, p. 342.
149. Al-Kuni, *Bayan: Lughz al-Tawariq 1*, p. 16.
150. Colla, 'Ibrahim al-Koni's Atlas of the Sahara', p. 188.
151. See, for example, 'Mawlid al-Tirfas' in *al-Qafas*, pp. 9–18.

152. Elmarsafy, *Sufism*, p. 108.
153. For discussion of al-Kuni's 'paradise', see Deheuvels, 'Le lieu de l'utopie', pp. 26–42.
154. Deheuvels, 'Le lieu de l'utopie', p. 26; Sleiman, 'Ville, oasis, desert', p. 44.
155. Al-Kuni, *Diwan al-Nathr al-Barri*, p. 81.
156. Berger, *Why Look at Animals?*, pp. 15–16.
157. Al-Kuni, *Anubis*, p. 7 (trans. p. xvii). Translated passages from *Anubis* are taken from the published English translation, which I have further referenced, in addition to the original Arabic, in most of my analyses, for ease of reference.
158. McHugh, 'Hybrid Species', p. 291.
159. El-Zein, 'Mythological Tuareg Gods', p. 207.
160. *Anubis*, p. 6 (trans. p. xvi).
161. Ibid., p. 21 (trans. p. 8).
162. Ibid., p. 209.
163. Ibid., p. 6.
164. Al-Kuni, *ᶜUdus 2*, p. 59.
165. *Anubis*, pp. 13, 69, 125 (trans. pp. 1, 49, 97).
166. Ibid., pp. 13, 69.
167. McHugh, 'Hybrid Species', p. 292.
168. *Anubis*, p. 20.
169. Ibid., p. 71 (trans. p. 51).
170. Ibid., p. 77 (trans. p. 56).
171. Armstrong, *What Animals Mean*, p. 14.
172. Al-Kuni, *ᶜUdus 1*, pp. 378, 401; Deleuze and Guattari, 'What Is a Minor Literature?', p. 21.
173. *Anubis*, p. 76 (trans. p. 55).
174. Ibid., p. 77 (trans. p. 56).
175. Ibid., p. 78 (trans. p. 56).
176. Ibid., pp. 79 (trans. p. 58).
177. Blundell, 'African Rock Art of the Northern Zone'.
178. *Anubis*, p. 82 (trans. p. 60).
179. Ibid., p. 81 (trans. p. 61).
180. Ibid., pp. 93, 119–20 (trans. pp. 70, 94).
181. Ibid., p. 100 (trans. p. 128); see Qurᵓan 5:1 and 40:79.
182. Ibid., p. 153 (trans. p. 121).
183. Ibid., p. 156 (trans. p. 123).
184. Ibid., p. 183 (trans. p. 146).
185. Al-Kuni increasingly depicts villainous leaders in the 2000s. Sakr, for example, describes *al-Waram* (2008) as 'one of the most scathing parodies of a dictator's figure in the history of Arab literature' ('*Anticipating*', pp. 55–8).

186. *Anubis*, p. 198 (trans. p. 158).
187. Ibid., p. 207 (trans. p. 168).
188. Al-Kuni, *ᶜUdus 4*, p. 30.
189. McHugh, 'Hybrid Species and Literatures', p. 291.
190. *Anubis*, p. 6 (trans. p. xvi).
191. Ibid., p. 76 (trans. p. 55).
192. Elmarsafy, *Sufism*, p. 197.
193. Ibid., p. 115.
194. Hine, 'Empty Spaces', p. 36.
195. Al-Kuni, *ᶜUdus 2*, p. 254.
196. Kilito, *The Author and His Doubles*, p. 101.
197. Al-Kuni, *ᶜUdus 2*, p. 46.
198. Ibid., p. 43.

Chapter 3: God's Wide Land: War, Melancholy and the Camel

1. Trans. Tarif Khalidi.
2. Chorin, *Translating Libya*, p. 18
3. See al-Mālikī, 'Muqaddima', p. 4, and al-Asfar, 'Riwaᵓi Yanhit ᶜAwalimahu min Sakhr al-Mutakhayyal'.
4. Al-Ghazal, 'al-Sufiyya fi al-Nass a-Riwaᵓi al-ᶜArabi'.
5. Barthes, *The Empire of Signs*, pp. 3–4.
6. Depictions of other wars include: ᶜAlī Fahmī Khushaym's *Inaru* (1998) depicting North African tribes from the fifth century BCE battling Persian forces; al-Sanūsī's *Mata Yafid al-Wadi* (1981) depicting the 1973 October War; and al-Buᶜīssī's *Fursan al-Suᶜal* (2008) depicting the Soviet–Afghan War of 1979–89.
7. See Fazlur Rahman, 'Bakāᵓ wa-Fanāᵓ', EI2, vol. 1, p. 951.
8. Barthes, *The Empire of Signs*, p. 4.
9. Almond, *Sufism and Deconstruction*, pp. 7, 17, 43. On Sufism as the 'opening up' of literary creation in the Arabic novel, see also Elmarsafy, *Sufism*, pp. 1–12.
10. Al-Ghazal, 'al-Sufiyya fi al-Nass al-Riwaᵓi al-ᶜArabi'.
11. Ibid.
12. Ibid.
13. Al-Kuni, *ᶜUdus 1*, p. 129; *ᶜUdus 4*, p. 29.
14. For discussion of these different '*aḥwāl*' (spiritual states), see al-Qushayri, *al-Qushayri's Epistle on Sufism*, pp. 93–4, 142–48, 325–35.
15. Al-Kuni, *ᶜUdus 1*, p. 368.
16. Ibid.
17. Santner, *On Creaturely Life*, p. 80.
18. Al-Kuni cites the almost identical 11:64.

19. Stetkevych, *The Mute Immortals*, pp. 28–9.
20. Sells, 'The Muᶜallaqa of Ṭarafa', p. 23. The pre-Islamic War of Basūs (494–534 CE), between the Taghlib and Bakr tribes, was also prompted by a camel's wrongful slaughter, giving rise to the popular expression, 'Lā nāqa lī fīhā wa-lā jamal' ('I have no camel in this affair') (Abū al-Faḍl al-Maydānī, *Majmaᶜ al-Amthal* (Beirut: Dar al-Maᶜrifa), vol. 2, p. 220).
21. Mikhail, 'The Fallow between Two Fields', p. 14.
22. Fanūsh, *al-Ibl fi al-Shiᶜr al-Shaᶜbi*, pp. 203–8. Fanūsh indicates how Būṣūkāya's basic refrain was adopted and elaborated upon by others, most prominently Ibrāhīm Būjalāwī (1914–91). He further notes how, in other poems, the theme of bereft mother camels features prominently in critique of the meat industry (p. 206).
23. Irwin, *Camel*, p. 79.
24. Al-Faqih, *Fiᵓran*, p. 10.
25. Omri, *Nationalism, Islam and World Literature*, p. 141.
26. Ibid., p. 140.
27. Ibid., p. 133.
28. Sells, *Early Islamic Mysticism*, pp. 70–1.
29. El-Ariss, 'Return of the Beast', p. 73.
30. Omri, *Nationalism, Islam and World Literature*, p. 141.
31. Santner, *On Creaturely Life*, p. 43.
32. Al-Ghadeer, *Desert Voices*, pp. 78, 73.
33. Al-Kuni, *al-Tibr*, p. 139 (trans. p. 151). All extended translations from *al-Tibr* are from the published English translation, which I have further referenced, alongside the original Arabic, in most instances, for ease of reference.
34. Haraway, *Companion Species Manifesto*, pp. 11–12.
35. Al-Ghānamī, *Malhamat al-Hudud al-Quswa*, p. 73. See also al-Fayturi, who discusses parallels between Ukhayyad and his camel and Ṭarafa's *Muᶜallaqa* ('Marthiyat al-Zawal', p. 42).
36. Haraway, *Companion Species Manifesto*, p. 12.
37. McHugh, 'Hybrid Species', p. 285.
38. Fudge, *Pets*, p. 68.
39. *Al-Tibr*, p. 14 (trans. p. 15).
40. Casajus, *La tente*, p. 105.
41. *Al-Tibr*, p. 7 (trans. p. 5).
42. Ibid., p. 8 (trans. p. 7).
43. Ibid., p. 20 (trans. p. 18).
44. Casajus, *La tente*, p. 98.
45. *Al-Tibr*, p. 8 (trans. p. 6).

46. *Al-Tibr*, p. 11 (trans. p. 10).
47. Ibid.
48. Stetkevych, *The Mute Immortals*, p. 29.
49. *Al-Tibr*, p. 38 (trans. p. 39).
50. Ibid., pp. 42, 45 (trans. pp. 44, 47).
51. Ibid., p. 45 (trans. p. 47).
52. Haraway, *Companion Species Manifesto*, p. 62.
53. *Al-Tibr*, p. 52 (trans. p. 55).
54. Ibid., p. 68 (trans. p. 74).
55. Ibid., p. 32 (trans. p. 34).
56. Ibid., pp. 109–10 (trans. p. 118).
57. Ibid., p. 83 (trans. p. 91).
58. Haraway, *The Companion Species Manifesto*, p. 17.
59. Ibid., p. 53 (trans. p. 57).
60. Ibid., pp. 11, 25, 144, 105.
61. Irwin, *Camel*, pp. 9–10.
62. *Al-Tibr*, p. 103 (trans. p. 114).
63. Ibid., pp. 92, 81 (trans. pp. 100, 89).
64. Al-Kuni, *ᶜUdus 3*, p. 161.
65. Mohammad Ali Amir-Moezzi, 'Sirr', EI2 (accessed online).
66. Al-Kuni, *ᶜUdus 2*, p. 354.
67. *Al-Tibr*, p. 70 (trans. p. 76).
68. Ibid., p. 47 (trans. p. 50).
69. Al-Kuni, *ᶜUdus 3*, p. 163.
70. *Al-Tibr*, p. 25 (trans. p. 26).
71. Ibid.
72. Ibid., p. 126 (trans. p. 135).
73. See al-Ghānamī, *Malhamat al-Hudud*, pp. 72–3.
74. *Al-Tibr*, p. 12 (trans. p. 13).
75. Ibid., p. 19 (trans. p. 17).
76. Al-Fayturi, 'Marthiyat al-Zawal', p. 44.
77. Ibid.
78. 'Natureculture' and 'naturalcultural' are terms frequently used by Haraway to counter the binaries of 'nature' and 'culture' imbedded within modern, western intellectual traditions, and to emphasise the place of humans and their social constructs within a broader whole, formed from entangled ecological, biological and cultural dimensions.
79. Haraway, *Companion Species Manifesto*, pp. 2–3.
80. Al-Kuni, *ᶜUdus 1*, pp. 71–2.

81. *Al-Tibr*, p. 105 (trans. p. 113).
82. Ibid., p. 150.
83. Omri, *Nationalism, Islam and World Literature*, p. 135.
84. Berger, *Why Look at Animals?*, p. 52.
85. Fähndrich, 'The Desert', p. 335.
86. Al-Kuni, *ᶜUdus 3*, pp. 110, 350.
87. Ibid., p. 485. See also p. 126, where al-Kuni makes the autobiographical dimension of *al-Tibr* explicit.
88. Al-Kuni, *ᶜUdus 1*, p. 368.
89. Within this context, al-Kuni's *mahri* may be paralleled to the *Stammering Camel* of Nigerian-Tuareg poet, Hawad (b. 950), an Amazigh-language political journal, first published in 1990. The journal's manifesto, written by Hawad, declares, 'The *Stammering Camel* was born in 1990, seizing his voice from silence. He stammers because his tongue is like that of the Tuareg, mutilated by domination, gagged by exile. He has chewed on his steel muzzle, he has swallowed his tongue and spits out a stream of uninterrupted words, like bubbles of bile and blood. He speaks of your silence, and invites the mute to stand up, groan and stammer with him' ('Le journal touareg en tifinagh', *Hawad*, https://www.editions-amara.info/le-journal-touareg-en-tifinagh/ (last accessed 8 July 2019)).
90. Al-Kuni, *ᶜUdus 3*, p. 468.
91. Ibid., pp. 397, 371, 356.
92. See al-Fayturi ('Marthiyat al-Zawal', pp. 40–8) who also identifies 'lament' as central to the camel's depiction.
93. Pick, *Creaturely Poetics*, p. 184; al-Kuni, *ᶜUdus 3*, pp. 404, 349.
94. Al-Fayturi, *Sirat Bani Ghazi*, p. 140.
95. Al-Mālikī, 'Muqaddima', p. 5.
96. Al-Ghazal, *al-Sawʾa*, p. 79.
97. Ibid.
98. Santner, *On Creaturely Life*, p. 51.
99. Muḥammad, 'al-Khawf Abqani Hayyan'. See also the semantic link that el-Ariss draws between 'modernity' (*ḥadātha*) and the 'event' (*ḥadath*), positing Arab modernity not as linear progress or 'catching-up', but as unfolding through 'accidents and trials', 'centred on the body' (*Trials*, p. 3).
100. Wright, *Libya, Chad and the Central Sahara*, p. 132.
101. Hilsum, *Sandstorm*, p. 142,
102. Ibid.
103. For discussion of the army and conscription under al-Qadhafi, see Ishtaywī, *Thaman al-Hurriya*, pp. 46–56.

104. Al-Ghazal, *al-Tabut,* p. 169. All translations of al-Ghazal's novels are my own.
105. Trans. Tarif Khalidi.
106. *Al-Tabut,* p. 11.
107. For an in-depth discussion of these verbs of motion, see Muḥammad al-Rajūbī, 'al-Ab[c]ad al-Dalaliyya fi Af[c]al al-Haraka bi-Riwayat al-Tabut li-[c]Abdallah al-Ghazal', PhD Thesis, Yarmouk University, 2011.
108. *Al-Tabut,* p. 11.
109. Ibid., p. 12.
110. Ibid., p. 31.
111. Ibid., pp. 44, 105, 31, 50.
112. Ibid., p. 14.
113. Ibid.
114. Ibid., pp. 14–15; for further discussion of pathetic fallacy in the novel, see al-Mālikī, *Jamaliyyat,* p. 99.
115. *Al-Tabut,* pp. 59, 18, 17.
116. Ibid., p. 25.
117. Ibid., p. 22.
118. Ibid., pp. 12, 69.
119. Ibid., p. 182.
120. Ibid., p. 234.
121. Ibid., p. 169.
122. Ibid., p. 20.
123. Ibid., p. 54.
124. Ibid., p. 27.
125. Ibid., p. 55.
126. Ibid.
127. Ibid., pp. 160–1.
128. Ibid.
129. Ibid., p. 241. See al-Mālikī's discussion of the camel as a mythical element of the novel, *Jamaliyyat,* p. 100.
130. *Al-Tabut,* p. 241.
131. Ibid., p. 242.
132. Ibid., p. 247.
133. Ibid., p. 142.
134. Ibid., p. 241.
135. Ibid., p. 248.
136. Ibid., p. 250.
137. Ibid., p. 260.

138. Ibid., pp. 268, 288.
139. Ibid., p. 295.
140. Ibid., p. 283.
141. Ibid., p. 226.
142. Ibid., p. 243.
143. Ibid., p. 299.
144. Ibid., p. 251.
145. Ibid., pp. 258–9.
146. Ibid., p. 297.
147. Pick, *Creaturely Poetics*, p. 186.
148. Ibid. See also Diamond, 'The Difficulty of Reality', p. 61.
149. Al-Ghazal, *al-Khawf*, p. 28.
150. Ibid., p. 27.
151. Ibid., pp. 12, 15, 16.
152. Ibid., pp. 10, 13.
153. Ibid., pp. 25, 29, 144.
154. Ibid., p.
155. Ibid., p. 9.
156. Ibid., p. 108.
157. Bachelard, *The Poetics of Space*, pp. 3, 6
158. *Al-Khawf*, pp. 9, 126, 135, 151, 89.
159. Ibid., pp. 118, 258.
160. Ibid., pp. 141, 128.
161. Ibid.
162. The Dam of Maʾrib is said to have been weakened by an infestation of rats, following the polity's neglect of its maintenance, and leading to the scattering of the South Arabian kingdom of Sabaʾ (Stetkevych, *The Mute Immortals*, p. 24).
163. *Al-Khawf*, p. 138.
164. Anderson, *The State and Social Transformation*, p. 212.
165. *Al-Khawf*, pp. 34, 72–5, 131, 233.
166. Ibid., pp. 13, 178.
167. Ibid., pp. 9–10.
168. Ibid., p. 226.
169. Ibid., p. 220.
170. Ibid., pp. 226, 254.
171. Ibid., p. 223.
172. Ibid., p. 259–60.
173. Chorin, *Translating Libya*, p. 18

174. Bin Lamin's artwork can be viewed on his Blogspot, http://binlamin.blogspot.com/ (last accessed 8 July 2019), and via 'MBL Binlamin Art', *fineartamerica*, https://fineartamerica.com/profiles/mohammad-binlamin.html (last accessed 8 July 2019).
175. Bin Lamin, 'Blogspot'.
176. Ibid.
177. See al-Asfar, 'Riwaʾi Yanhit ᶜAwalimahu Min Sakhr al-Mutakhayyal', who quotes Bin Lamin's comments on the centrality of fear to al-Ghazal's novels.
178. *Al-Khawf*, pp. 221–2.
179. Ibid., p. 58.
180. Ibid., p. 58.
181. Ibid.
182. Ibid., p. 97.
183. Ibid., p. 152; Santner, *On Creaturely Life*, p. 148.
184. *Al-Khawf*, p. 179.
185. Ibid., p. 269. Bin Lamin was himself imprisoned in Abu Salim Prison during the first months of the February 2011 Uprising.
186. *Al-Khawf*, p. 282.
187. Al-Ghazal, 'al-Sufiyya fi al-Nass al-Riwaʾi al-ᶜArabi'.
188. Phillips, *Religion in the Egyptian Novel*, p. 20.
189. Barthes, *Empire of Signs*, p. 4.

Chapter 4: Absent Stories in the Urban Novel

1. Trans. Tarif Khalidi.
2. Santner, *On Creaturely Life*, p. 146.
3. Ibid., pp. 81–2.
4. Baldinetti, *The Origins of the Libyan Nation*, p. 3; Ahmida, 'Libya, Social Origins of Dictatorship', p. 74.
5. Al-Kubtī (ed.), *Nawaris al-Shawq*, p. 96.
6. Ahmida, 'Libya, Social Origins of Dictatorship', p. 74
7. Vandewalle, *A History of Modern Libya*, p. 106.
8. Anderson, *The State and Social Transformation*, pp. 265–8.
9. Al-Qadhafi, *al-Qarya al-Qarya*, p. 6.
10. See my broader discussion of this term, p. 68.
11. Mattawa, 'Dispatches', pp. 264–70.
12. Matar, *The Return*, p. 51.
13. Ibid., p. 148.
14. Pick, *Creaturely Poetics*, p. 73.

15. See his discussion of al-Nayhum, 'Bi-l-Yusra: Min Huna Ila Makka'.
16. Al-Asfar, 'Libya's Patient Revolutionaries'.
17. Since 2011, al-Maghrabi has faced regular death threats for her outspoken views on gender and religion.
18. Al-Asfar, 'Mansur Bushnaf: Bin Walid wa-Misrata Shakkalata Wijdani'. Originally titled *Sarab al-Layl* (The Night Mirage), Bushnaf changed the novel's title to *al-^{c}Ilka* following its translation into English as *Chewing Gum*. Darf Publishers are preparing a second Arabic edition, titled *al-^{c}Ilka*, and I reference their unpublished pdf for the Arabic, as well as using, and referencing, the English translation when citing from extended passages. In some instances, I have referenced only the Arabic, where the English has not conveyed a phrase or translated it loosely. An earlier version of my discussion of *al-^{c}Ilka* was published as Olszok, 'The Litterscape and the Nude', pp. 1–19.
19. Bushnaf, *al-^{c}Ilka*, p. 43.
20. Al-Asfar, 'Mansur Bushnaf: ^{c}Ashriyya al-^{c}Ilka al-Libiyya'.
21. *Al-^{c}Ilka*, p. 18.
22. Ṣāliḥ, *Ufuq Akhar*, pp. 115–16. Bushnaf's first play, *Tadakhul al-Hikayat ^{c}Inda Ghiyab al-Rawi* (The Entanglement of Narratorless Stories), was staged in Benghazi. *^{c}Indama Tahkum al-Jirdhan* (When Rats Rule) was scheduled to be staged but banned by the security services before its opening. See Al-Asfar, 'Mansur Bushnaf', who describes the first. See also Ṣāliḥ's broader discussion of a later play, *al-Su^{c}adaʾ*, in *Ufuq Akhar*, pp. 112–17.
23. *Al-^{c}Ilka*, p. 67 (trans. p. 73).
24. Ibid., p. 112 (trans. p. 121).
25. Ibid., p. 67.
26. Ibid., p. 36 (trans. p. 41).
27. Ibid.
28. Ibid.
29. Ibid., p. 12.
30. Ibid., p. 31 (trans. pp. 34–5).
31. Ibid., p. 8.
32. Ibid., p. 42.
33. Ibid., p. 8 (trans. p. 5).
34. Ibid., p. 44 (trans. p. 50).
35. Ibid., p. 50.
36. Ibid., pp. 50–1.
37. Santner, *On Creaturely Life*, p. 148.
38. Ibid., p. 146.
39. *Al-^{c}Ilka*, p. 12.

40. Ibid., p. 9 (trans. p. 6).
41. Ibid., p. 39.
42. Ibid., pp. 32–3 (trans. pp. 36-37).
43. Ibid., p. 7 (trans. p. 4).
44. Ibid.
45. Ibid., p. 54 (trans. p. 59).
46. Ibid., p. 7 (trans. p. 4).
47. Jameson, *Postmodernism*, pp. 1–54.
48. Pflitsch, 'The End of Illusions', p. 29.
49. Ibid., p. 33.
50. Matar, 'A Tree that Scarcely Fruits'.
51. Benjamin, *Illuminations*, p. 257.
52. *Al-ᶜIlka*, p. 84 (trans. p. 83).
53. Ibid., p. 25.
54. Ibid.
55. Ibid., p. 86 (trans. p. 88).
56. Ibid., p. 50 (trans. pp. 55–6).
57. Ibid., p. 16 (trans. p. 15).
58. Ibid., p. 72.
59. Ibid., p. 71.
60. Ibid., p. 18 (trans. p. 18).
61. Ibid., p. 17.
62. Ibid., pp. 72 (trans. pp. 79–80).
63. Ibid., p. 63.
64. Ibid., p. 18 (trans. pp. 18–19).
65. Ibid., p. 111.
66. Ibid., p. 116 (trans. p. 125).
67. Ibid., p. 116.
68. Ibid., pp. 113–14 (trans. p. 121).
69. Al-Asfar, 'Mansur Bushnaf: ᶜAshriyya al-ᶜIlka al-Libiyya'.
70. *Al-ᶜIlka*, p. 116.
71. Pick, *Creaturely Poetics*, p. 73.
72. Al-Asfar, 'ᶜIlkat Bushnaf'.
73. Cooke, *Dissident Syria*, p. 85.
74. Al-Riyāḥī, 'Al-Riwaᵓi al-Libi'.
75. Chorin, *Exit Gaddafi*, p. 55.
76. Al-Asfar, *Sharmula*, p. 55. All translations of *Sharmula* are my own.
77. Ibid., p. 99.
78. Ibid., p. 100.

79. Al-Asfar, 'Libya's Patient Revolutionaries'.
80. *Sharmula*, p. 93.
81. Ibid., p. 9.
82. Ibid., p. 64. See my earlier discussion of *rizq*, pp. 18, 36–8.
83. Ibid., pp. 279, 97.
84. Ibid., p. 287.
85. Ibid., p. 93.
86. Ibid., p. 29.
87. Al-Zughaybī, 'Darih ᶜUmar al-Mukhtar'.
88. Mattawa, 'Dispatches from Benghazi', p. 266.
89. *Sharmula*, p. 35.
90. Chorin, *Exit Gaddafi*, pp. 131–3.
91. Ibid., p. 132.
92. Ibid., p. 134.
93. *Sharmula*, pp. 31–2.
94. Ibid., p. 39.
95. Ibid., p. 40.
96. Ibid.
97. Ibid.
98. Santner, *On Creaturely Life*, p. 140.
99. *Sharmula*, p. 15.
100. Ibid., p. 16
101. Ishtaywī, *Thaman al-Hurriya*, pp. 125–9.
102. Mattawa, 'Dispatches', p. 267; Chorin, *Exit Gaddafi*, p. 54.
103. Al-Zughaybi, 'Darih ᶜUmar al-Mukhtar'.
104. *Sharmula*, p. 35.
105. Ibid., p. 36.
106. Ibid., p. 37.
107. Ibid., p. 178–9.
108. Ibid., p. 34.
109. Ibid., p. 35.
110. Ibid., p. 116.
111. Ibid., p. 149.
112. Ibid., p. 131.
113. Ibid.
114. Ibid., p. 86.
115. Ibid.
116. Ibid., pp. 70, 74.
117. Ibid., p. 79.

118. Ibid., p. 82.
119. Hans Wehr, *Arabic–English Dictionary* (4th edn), p. 132.
120. *Sharmula*, p. 92.
121. Ibid., p. 91.
122. Ibid., p. 225.
123. Ibid., p. 235.
124. Ibid., pp. 217–18.
125. Ibid., pp. 113–18, trans. 'The Hoopoe', pp. 137–43. See also Olszok, 'Creaturely Encounters', pp. 108–12.
126. Ibid., p. 206.
127. Ibid., pp. 194–5.
128. Ibid., p. 137.
129. Ibid., pp. 141–3.
130. Ibid., p. 285
131. Ibid., pp. 28, 285.
132. Al-Riyāḥī, 'Al-Riwaʾi al-Libi'.
133. *Sharmula*, p. 276
134. Ibn Manẓūr, *Lisan al-ᶜArab: al-Mujallad al-Hadi ᶜAshar*, pp. 82-3.
135. Al-Riyāḥī, 'Al-Riwaʾi al-Libi'.
136. *Sharmula*, pp. 107–8.
137. Ibid., p. 100.
138. Elsadda, *Gender, Nation, and the Arabic Novel*, p. 4.
139. Ibid., p. xxi.
140. Al-Shaylābī, *al-Qadaya al-Ijtimaᶜiyya*, p. 311.
141. Obeidi, *Political Culture in Libya*, pp. 168–97. For an account of the young woman author, Fawziyya Shallābī's, relationship with al-Qadhafi, see Shalqam, *Ashkhas hawl al-Qadhafi*, pp. 91–108.
142. al-Nowaihi, 'Reenvisioning National Community', p. 22.
143. Al-Maghrabi, *Nisaʾ al-Rih*, pp. 20, 84. All translations from *Nisaʾ al-Rih* are my own.
144. Ibid., p. 84.
145. Ibid., pp. 17, 52, 55.
146. Ibid., p. 103.
147. Ibid.
148. Ibid., pp. 172, 175.
149. Ibid., p. 107
150. Ibid., p. 56.
151. Ibid., p. 137.
152. Ibid., p. 66.

153. Ibid., p. 35.
154. Ibid.
155. Ibid., pp. 36, 171.
156. Ibid., pp. 190–1.
157. Ibid., p. 191.
158. Ibid., p. 9.
159. Ibid., p. 181.
160. Ibid., pp. 22, 59, 48, 100.
161. Ibid., pp. 9–10.
162. Ibid., p. 9.
163. Ibid., p. 41.
164. Ibid., p. 41.
165. Ibid., p. 20.
166. Ibid., p. 33.
167. Ibid., p. 125.
168. Ibid., p. 86.
169. Ibid.
170. Ibid., pp. 86–7.
171. Ibid., p. 87.
172. Ibid., pp. 87–8.
173. Woolf, *A Room of One's Own*, p. 4.
174. *Nisa' al-Rih*, p. 7.
175. Ibid.
176. Santner, *On Creaturely Life*, p. 60; Benjamin, 'Surrealism', p. 210.
177. *Nisa' al-Rih*, pp. 7–8.
178. Santner, *On Creaturely Life*, p. 81.
179. *Nisa' al-Rih*, p. 42.
180. Ibid.
181. Ibid., p. 80.
182. Ibid., p. 122.
183. Ibid.
184. Ibid.
185. Ibid., p. 123.
186. Al-Asfar, 'Libya's Patient Revolutionaries'.

Chapter 5: Too-Long-a-Tale

1. Trans. Tarif Khalidi.
2. Tsing, *The Mushroom at the End of the World*, p. 37
3. Derrida, 'The Animal', p. 381.

4. Nora, 'Between Memory and History', p. 7.
5. Moretti, *The Way of the World*, p. 8.
6. Ibid.
7. Ibid., p. 230.
8. Ibid., p. 232.
9. Rooke, *In My Childhood*, p. 10.
10. Ibid., p. 104.
11. Ibid., p. 101.
12. Earlier, more traditional, examples of Libyan autobiography and *Bildungsroman* include ʿAbdallāh al-Quwayrī's *al-Waqadat* (1984) and Kāmil Ḥasan al-Maqhūr's *Mahattat: Sira Shibh-Dhatiyya* (1995).
13. Anderson, *Imagined Communities*, p. 204.
14. Al-ʿAmāmī, *Qutʿan al-Kalimat al-Mudiʿa*, pp. 48–51; Al-Nayhum, *Tahiyya Tayyiba wa-Baʿd*, pp. 97–104; al-Fākhirī, *Mawsim al-Hikayat*, p. 30; see also Olszok, 'Creaturely Encounters', pp. 61–98.
15. Santner, *On Creaturely Life*, p. 33.
16. Nora, 'Between Memory and History', p. 15.
17. Ben-Ghiat and Fuller, 'Introduction', p. 2; Ahmida, *Forgotten Voices*, p. 45.
18. Ahmida, *Making of Modern Libya*, p. 194.
19. Ricoeur, 'Memory, History, Forgetting', p. 13.
20. Ahmida, *The Making of Modern Libya*, p. 2.
21. Al-ʿAbbār, *Maqalat*, pp. 99–100.
22. Ibid., p. 97.
23. Benjamin, *Illuminations*, p. 86.
24. Ibid., p. 102.
25. ʿAqila, *al-Jirab*, p. 5. All translations of *al-Jirab* are my own.
26. Lejeune, *On Autobiography*, pp. 3–30.
27. Jamāzī, 'Qiraʾa fi Majmuʿa Darb al-Halazin', citing also from critic, Fāṭima al-Zayyānī. See my earlier discussion of al-Kuni, al-Nayhum and Sufi oneness, pp. 62–3.
28. Falḥi, 'Darb al-Halazin: Bayn al-Bashar wa-l-Tabiʿa'.
29. Al-Barʿaṣī, 'Ahmad Yusuf ʿAqila'; ʿAqila's collections include: *al-Khuyul al-Baydaʾ* (1999); *Ghinaʾ al-Sarasir* (2003); *Darb al-Halazin* (2010); and *Ghurab al-Sabah* (2010).
30. Weil, 'Matters of Memory', p. 401; al-Barʿaṣī, 'Ahmad Yusuf ʿAqila'.
31. ʿAqila, *Khararif Libiyya*, p. 13.
32. *Al-Jirab*, p. 9.
33. Ibid.
34. Ibid., p. 13.

35. Ibid., p. 16.
36. Shepard, *The Others*, p. 4.
37. Benjamin, *Illuminations*, p. 102.
38. *al-Jirab*, pp. 62–3.
39. Ibid., pp. 53–4.
40. Ibid., p. 23.
41. Ibid., p. 15.
42. Ibid.
43. Ibid., p. 21.
44. Ibid., pp. 22, 107, 124–5.
45. Ibid., p. 125.
46. Ibid.
47. Ibid., pp. 50–1.
48. Ibid.
49. Ibid., p. 52.
50. Ibid.
51. Ibid.
52. Al-Awkalī, 'Hiwar', p. 176.
53. Ibid.; Benjamin, *Illuminations*, p. 132.
54. *Al-Jirab*, p. 23.
55. Ibid., p. 40.
56. Ibid., p. 43
57. Ibid., p. 41.
58. Ibid., p. 136.
59. Ibid., p. 136.
60. The 2012 edition of *al-Jirab*, which I use, is, in fact, supplemented by extracts concerning the events of September 1969, added after al-Qadhafi's fall from power in 2011.
61. *Al-Jirab*, p. 82.
62. ᶜAqila, *Khararif Libiyya*, p. 9.
63. Ibid.
64. *Al-Jirab*, p. 9.
65. Mattawa, 'Dispatches', p. 265.
66. Al-Fayturi, 'Kitab Hayati'.
67. Ibid.
68. Al-Fayturi, *Sarib*, p. 9. All translations of *Sarib* are my own.
69. Ibid.
70. Ibid., pp. 31, 33.
71. Ibid. p. 33.

72. Ibid.
73. Ibid., pp. 31, 34.
74. Ibid., p. 33.
75. Ibid., pp. 44–52.
76. Zipes, *Fairy Tales*, p. 174.
77. Benjamin, *Illuminations*, p. 102.
78. *Sarib*, p. 87.
79. Pick, *Creaturely Poetics*, p. 54.
80. *Sarib*, p. 90.
81. Ibid., p. 67.
82. Ibid., p. 40.
83. Ibid., pp. 35.
84. Ibid., pp. 40–1.
85. Ibid., p. 38.
86. Ibid., P. 35.
87. Ibid., pp. 41–2.
88. Ibid., p. 42.
89. Ibid., pp. 31, 87.
90. Ibid., p. 81.
91. Ibid., p. 91.
92. Ibid.
93. Ibid., p. 64.
94. Ibid.
95. Ibid.
96. Ibid., pp. 72–3.
97. Ibid., pp. 60–1.
98. Ibid., p. 82.
99. Ibid.
100. Ibid.
101. Ibid., p. 60.
102. Ibid., p. 96.
103. Ibid., p. 120.
104. Ibid., pp. 119, 122.
105. Ibid., pp. 122–4.
106. Ibid., p. 125.
107. Ibid., pp. 126–7.
108. Pick, *Creaturely Poetics,* p. 80.
109. Bin Shatwan, *al-Malika*, p. 155.
110. Al-Ageli, 'Shubbak interview'.

111. Ibid.
112. Larkin, 'This Be the Verse', p. 88.
113. Bin Shatwan, *Wabr al-Ahsina*, p. 8. All translations of *Wabr al-Ahsina* are my own.
114. Ibid., p. 9.
115. Ibid., p. 11.
116. Ibid., p. 14. See Qur᾿an 5:31.
117. *Wabr al-Ahsina*, p. 13.
118. Ibid., pp. 15–16.
119. Ibid., p. 16.
120. Ibid., p. 20.
121. Ibid., p. 19.
122. Ibid., p. 20.
123. Al-Samman, *Anxiety of Erasure*, p. 53.
124. Ibid.
125. *Wabr al-Ahsina*, p. 17.
126. Ibid., p. 35.
127. Ibid., p. 41.
128. Ibid., p. 37–8.
129. Ibid., p. 48.
130. Ibid., p. 37.
131. Ibid., p. 54.
132. Ibid.
133. Ibid., p. 61; al-Minifi, 'No Illness But This Place' (trans. Khaled Mattawa).
134. *Wabr al-Ahsina*, p. 96.
135. Ibid., p. 112.
136. Pick, *Creaturely Poetics*, p. 73; Benjamin, *Illuminations*, p. 131. See my earlier discussion of al-Kuni, p. 68.
137. *Wabr al-Ahsina*, p. 67.
138. Ibid., p. 101.
139. This passage extends from page 99 to 178, though is not clearly demarcated from the voice of the first foetus.
140. Pick, *Creaturely Poetics*, p. 188.
141. *Wabr al-Ahsina*, p. 184.
142. Ibid., p. 185.
143. Ibid., p. 185.
144. Ibid., p. 152.
145. See my earlier discussion of the term '*rāqid al-rīḥ*', p. 35.
146. Benjamin, *Illuminations*, p. 88.

Chapter 6: '*Une histoire de mouche*': The Libyan Novel in Other Voices

1. Trans. Tarif Khalidi.
2. Tsing, *The Mushroom*, p. 61.
3. Kilpatrick, 'Arab Fiction in English', p. 46.
4. Gana, 'Introduction', p. 11.
5. Deleuze and Guattari, 'What Is a Minor Literature?', p. 16.
6. Reeck, 'France', p. 613.
7. Matar, 'A Tree that Scarcely Fruits', accessed online.
8. Al Maleh, 'Anglophone Arab Literature: An Overview', p. 19.
9. Hassan, *Immigrant Narratives*, p. 33.
10. Matar, *In the Country*, p. 145.
11. Micklethwait, 'Zenga Zenga and Bunga Bunga', p. 184.
12. Hassan, *Immigrant Narratives*, p. 6. Following the February 2011 uprisings, Ben Hameda and Matar wrote for *Le Monde* and *The Guardian* about the evolving situation in Libya.
13. Hassan, *Immigrant Narratives*, p. 3. See also Gana, 'Introduction', p. 27.
14. El-Youssef, 'The Curse of Topicality'.
15. Ibid.
16. Chorin, *Exit Gaddafi*, p. 4.
17. Matar, 'A Tree that Scarcely Fruits'.
18. Scanlan, 'Migrating from Terror', p. 267.
19. Matar, *The Return*, p. 60; for Arabic translations of Matar's work, see: *Fi Bilad al-Rijal*, trans. Ibrāhīm Sukayna (Stockholm: Dar al-Muna, 2007) and *Ikhtifa*ʾ, trans. Muḥammad ᶜAbd al-Nabī (Cairo: Dar al-Shuruq, 2012).
20. Matar and Ben Hameda have both translated Libyan poetry and prose into English and French (al-Asfar, 'Wet Sleeves', trans. Matar; and al-Minifi, 'Poème d'Aguila', trans. Ben Hameda, in Ben Hameda (ed.), *Le livre du camp d'Aguila*).
21. Ṣāliḥ, 'al-Riwaʾi Kamal Bin Hamida'.
22. Ibid.
23. Ben Hameda, *La mémoire de l'absent*, pp. 21–2.
24. Ibid., pp. 24–5.
25. Ben Hameda (ed. and trans.), *Le livre du camp d'Aguila*, p. 12. The translation is accompanied by oral testimonies from other internees of the camps.
26. Ibid.
27. Ibid., pp. 48–9. Italics are mine.
28. Matar, *The Return*, p. 156; the Arabic is taken from al-Minifi, 'Ma bi Marad', in *Le live du camp d'Aguila* (ed. Ben Hameda), p. 43.

29. In analysing this stanza, written, like the rest of the poem, in Cyrenaican dialect, I have relied upon Sulaymān Zaydān's commentary, 'al-Qasida al-Sha^{c}biyya', p. 57.
30. Matar left in 1979, when he, too, was nine years old.
31. Benjamin, *Illuminations*, p. 84.
32. See Olszok, 'Creaturely Memory', for comparison of *La compagnies des Tripolitaines* and *Sarib.*
33. Ben Hameda, *La mémoire*, p. 9. All translations from *La mémoire* are my own. For Ben Hameda's first poetry collections, see: *Fragments de Lumière* (Paris: L'Harmattan, 1999) and *Le saint je: Poème monosyllabique* (Paris: L'Harmattan, 2003).
34. *La mémoire*, p. 19.
35. Ibid., pp. 24, 64.
36. Ibid., pp. 62–3.
37. Ibid., p. 44.
38. Ibid.
39. Ibid., p. 47.
40. Ibid., p. 57.
41. Ben Hameda, 'Dans les sables', p. 48.
42. *La mémoire*, pp. 25, 12.
43. Ben Hameda, *La compagnie*, p. 7. All translations are from the published *Under the Tripoli Sky*, and I have referenced both the French and English, except in instances where the translation has omitted a particular phrase.
44. Ibid., p. 11.
45. Ibid., p. 9 (trans. p. 9).
46. Herodotus, *The Histories*, p. 372.
47. *La compagnie*, p. 9 (trans. p. 9).
48. Cowan, 'Benjamin's Theory of Allegory', p. 110.
49. Ibid., p. 9; Herodotus, *The Histories*, pp. 343–5.
50. *La compagnie*, p. 12 (trans. p. 11).
51. Ibid., p. 38 (trans. p. 35).
52. Matar, 'A Tree that Scarcely Fruits'.
53. *La compagnie*, p. 16 (trans. p. 15).
54. Ibid., pp. 15, 67 (trans. pp. 15, 62).
55. Ibid., pp. 54, 66, 51, 59 (trans. pp. 50, 60, 47–8, 54).
56. Ibid., p. 17 (trans. p. 16). See my earlier discussion of Eid memories, pp. 173–4 and 179.
57. Ibid., p. 17.

58. Ibid., p. 21 (trans. p. 20).
59. Ibid., p. 21 (trans. p. 21).
60. Ibid., pp. 100–1 (trans. pp. 95–6).
61. Ibid., p. 45 (trans. p. 41).
62. Ibid., p. 97 (trans. p. 93).
63. Ibid., p. 97 (trans. p. 92).
64. Ibid., p. 98 (trans. p. 93).
65. Ibid., p. 97 (trans. p. 92).
66. Bakhtin, *Rabelais and His World*, p. 10.
67. *La compagnie*, p. 98 (trans. p. 92).
68. Ibid., p. 83 (trans. p. 78).
69. Ibid., p. 84 (trans. p. 78).
70. Ibid., p. 85 (trans. p. 80).
71. Ibid., p. 90 (trans. p. 85).
72. Ibid., p. 76 (trans. p. 71).
73. Ibid., p. 94 (trans. p. 89).
74. Ibid., p. 97.
75. Ibid., p. 102 (trans. p. 97).
76. Ibid., p. 104 (trans. pp. 98–9).
77. Matar, 'A Tree that Scarcely Fruits'; *La compagnie*, pp. 103–4 (trans. p. 98).
78. *La compagnie*, p. 109 (trans. p. 104).
79. Gana, 'An Interview with Hisham Matar'.
80. Tarbush, 'That Last Summer in Tripoli'.
81. Gana, 'An Interview with Hisham Matar'.
82. Kearney, 'Traumatised Narrators', p. 124.
83. Hashem, '"The Feast of the Ants"', p. 40.
84. Micklethwait, 'Zenga Zenga', p. 172.
85. Ibid., p. 173.
86. *In the Country*, p. 11.
87. Ibid., pp. 16, 171.
88. Ibid., p. 1.
89. Ibid., p. 53.
90. Ibid., p. 124.
91. Ibid., p. 11.
92. Ibid., p. 167.
93. Harlow, 'From Flying Carpets', pp. 442–3.
94. *In the Country*, pp. 62–3.
95. Ibid., pp. 118, 217.

96. Ibid., p. 166.
97. Matar, *The Return*, pp. 125–6.
98. *In the Country*, p. 1.
99. Ibid., p. 216.
100. Ibid., p. 47.
101. Ibid., pp. 20, 79.
102. Ibid., p. 5.
103. Ibid., p. 35.
104. Ibid., p. 5.
105. Ibid., pp. 153, 199.
106. Ibid., p. 244.
107. Ibid., p. 230.
108. Ibid., p. 30.
109. Ibid., p. 30.
110. Ibid., p. 148.
111. Ibid., p. 174.
112. Ibid., p. 84.
113. Matar, *The Return*, p. 51.
114. *In the Country*, pp. 45–6.
115. Ibid., pp. 47–8.
116. Ibid., p. 211.
117. Hashem, '"The Feast of the Ants"', p. 47.
118. *In the Country*, p. 211.
119. Ibid., p. 49.
120. Ibid., pp. 64, 73.
121. Ibid., 59, 212.
122. Ibid., 47.
123. Hashem, '"The Feast of the Ants"', p. 39. Qur'an 27:18–19.
124. *In the Country*, p. 146.
125. Hashem, '"The Feast of the Ants"', p. 54.
126. See my earlier discussion of ekhprasis, pp. 21, 83, 86–7, 122 and 140–1.
127. *In the Country*, p. 28.
128. Ibid., p. 26.
129. Ibid.
130. Sperl, '"O City Set Up Thy Lament"', pp. 2, 30.
131. Micklethwait, 'Zenga Zenga', p. 174.
132. Sakr, '*Anticipating*', p. 63.
133. *In the Country*, p. 4.
134. Ibid., pp. 26, 4.

135. Ibid., pp. 26, 4. See my earlier discussion of Septimius Severus, p. 21.
136. Ibid., p. 8.
137. Ibid., pp. 183–4.
138. Ibid., p. 187.
139. Ibid., pp. 186–7.
140. Ibid., p. 189.
141. Ibid., p. 222.
142. Ibid., p. 231.
143. Kearney, 'Traumatised Narrators', p. 135.
144. Hashem, '"The Feast of the Ants"', p. 52.
145. *In the Country*, p. 245.
146. Harlow, 'From Flying Carpets', p. 444.
147. Matar, *The Return*, p. 133.
148. Santner, *On Creaturely Life*, pp. 140-141.
149. Matar, *The Return*, p. 133.
150 Ibid., p. 135.
151. Hassan, *Immigrant Narratives*, p. 160.
152. Matar, 'Author Spotlight'.
153. Matar, *The Return*, p. 52.
154. Matar, 'Once Upon a Life'.
155. Kunzru, 'Hisham Matar'.
156. Ibid.

Afterword: Breaking Fevers and Strange Metamorphoses

1. Bushnaf, *al-Kalb al-Dhahabi*, p. 72.
2. Ovid, *Metamorphoses*, Book II: 237–9, trans. A. S. Kline (accessed online April 6, 2020: https://ovid.lib.virginia.edu/trans/Ovhome.htm).
3. Al-Asfar, 'Libya's Patient Revolutionaries'.
4. Chorin, *Exit Gaddafi*, pp. 187–8.
5. Ibid., p. 191.
6. Ibid., p. 194.
7. Al-Asfar, 'Mansur Bushnaf: ᶜAshriyya al-ᶜIlka al-Libiyya'.
8. Al-Fayturi, 'Shams', pp. 55, 57.
9. Ibid., pp. 33, 58.
10. PEN International, 'Libya: Fears for Safety of Writers and Editors over New Literary Collection'.
11. Al-Naᶜas, 'Majnun', pp. 465, 476.
12. Ibid., pp. 476–7; Pick, *Creaturely Poetics*, p. 73.
13. Al-Naᶜas, 'Majnun', p. 468.

14. Ibid., p. 484.
15. Ibid.
16. At the time of going to press, *al-Kalb al-Dhahabi* is still in unpublished manuscript form, once again illustrating the real difficulties of telling Libya's stories. Darf Publishers intend to publish it in 2020/21.
17. Bushnaf, *al-Kalb*, p. 24.
18. Ibid., pp. 64, 47.
19. Ibid., pp. 4–5, 39, 43.
20. Ibid., p. 39.
21. Ibid., p. 4.
22. Ibid., p. 3.
23. Ibid., p. 2.
24. Ibid., p. 51.
25. Ibid., p. 2.
26. Finkelpearl, 'Marsyas the Satyr', p. 31
27. *Al-Kalb*, p. 3.
28. Ibid.
29. Ibid., pp. 84, 96.
30. Ibid., pp. 96, 8.
31. Pick, *Creaturely Poetics*, p. 79.
32. *Al-Kalb*, pp. 18, 21, 32, 103, 104.
33. Ibid., p. 11.
34. Pick, *Creaturely Poetics*, pp. 73–4.
35. *Al-Kalb*, p. 88.
36. Ibid., p. 42.
37. Ibid., p. 32.
38. Ortiz-Robles, *Literature and Animal Studies*, p. 81.
39. *Al-Kalb*, p. 57.
40. Ibid., pp. 39, 51.
41. Ibid., p. 95.
42. Ibid., p. 28.
43. Ibid., p. 4.
44. Ibid., p. 53.
45. Ibid., p. 29.
46. Ibid., pp. 53, 72.

Bibliography

Note: In cases where multiple editions of novels exist, I have given the first publication date and, in brackets, the date of the edition I have used.

Primary Sources

Abū Dabbūs, Rajab Miftāḥ, *Fi al-Manfa* (Benghazi: Manshurat Maktabat Qurina li-l-Nashr wa-l-Tawzi^c, 1975).

Abū Harrūs, ^cAbd al-Qādir, *Nufus Ha^ɔira* (Tripoli: Madad li-l-Tiba^ca wa-l-Nashr wa-l-Tawzi^c wa-l-Intaj al-Fanni, 2010); first published: Tripoli: Maktabat al-Farjani, 1957.

^cAqīla, Aḥmad Yūsuf, *al-Jirab: Hikayat Naj^c* (Benghazi: Wizarat al-Thaqafa wa-l-Mujtama^c al-Madani, 2012); first published: Tripoli: Dar al-Bayan li-l-Nashr wa-l-Tawzi^c wa-l-I^clan, 2003.

al-Aṣfar, Muḥammad, *Sharmula* (Latakia: Dar al-Hiwar li-l-Nashr wa-l-Tawzi^c, 2008), partially trans. Ali Azeriah, 'The Hoopoe', *Banipal*, 40 (2011), pp. 137–43; and Hisham Matar, 'Wet Sleeves', *Words Without Borders*, July 2006, https://www.wordswithoutborders.org/article/wet-sleeves (last accessed 27 June 2019).

Ben Hameda, Kamal, *La mémoire de l'absent* (Paris: L'Harmattan, 2001).

Ben Hameda, Kamal, *La compagnie des Tripolitaines* (Tunis: Éditions Elyzad, 2011), trans. Adriana Hunter, *Under the Tripoli Sky* (London: Peirene Press, 2014).

Bin Shatwān, Najwā, *Madmun Burtuqali* (Cairo: Dar Sharqiyyat li-l-Nashr wa-l-Tawzi^c, 2007).

Bin Shatwān, Najwā, *Wabr al-Ahsina* (Cairo: Markaz al-Hadara al-^cArabiyya, 2007).

Bin Shatwān, Najwā, *al-Malika* (Sirte: Majlis al-Thaqafa al-^cAmm, 2008).

al-Bu^cīssī, Wafā^ɔ, *Na^cthal* (Dar al-Ruwad, 2012).

Būshnāf, Manṣūr, *al-^cIlka* (unpublished manuscript); first published: *Sarab al-Layl* (Cairo: Libya li-l-Nashr, 2008), trans. Mona Zaki, *Chewing Gum* (London: Darf Publishers, 2014).

Būshnāf, Manṣūr, *al-Kalb al-Dhahabi* (unpublished manuscript, due to be published by Darf in 2020/21.

al-Faqīh, Aḥmad Ibrāhīm, *Thalath Majmu^c^at Qisasiyya* (Tripoli: Qita^c^ al-Kitab wa-l-Tawzi^c^ wa-l-I^c^lan, 1981).

al-Fākhirī, Khalīfa, *Mawsim al-Hikayat* (Benghazi: Al-Dār al-Jamāhiriyya li-l-Nashr wa-l-Tawzīʿ wa-l-Iʿlān, 1994).

al-Faqīh, Aḥmad Ibrāhīm, *Hada^ʾ^iq al-Layl: Sa-ahabuka Madina Ukhra; Hadhihi Tukhum Mamlakati;* and *Nafaq Tudi^ʾ^uhu Imra^ʾ^a Wahida* (London: Riad El-Rayyes, 1991), trans. Russell Harris, Amin al-Ayouti and Suraya Allam, *Gardens of the Night: A Trilogy* (London: Quartet Book, 1995).

al-Faqīh, Aḥmad Ibrāhīm, *Khams Khanafis Tuhakim al-Shajara* (Cairo: Dar al-Shuruq, 1997).

al-Faqīh, Aḥmad Ibrāhīm, *Huqul al-Ramad* (Cairo: Dar al-Shuruq, 1999).

al-Faqīh, Aḥmad Ibrāhīm, *Fi^ʾ^ran Bila Juhur* (Cairo: Dar al-Hilal, 2000), trans. *Homeless Rats* (London: Quartet Books, 2011).

al-Faqīh, Aḥmad Ibrāhīm, *Fi Hija^ʾ^ al-Bashar wa-Madih al-Baha^ʾ^im wa-l-Hasharat* (Cairo: Dar al-Shuruq, 2009).

al-Faytūrī, Aḥmad, *Sarib* (Cairo: Markaz al-Hadarah al-^c^Arabiyya, 2001).

al-Ghazāl, ^c^Abdallāh, *al-Saw^ʾ^a* (Sharjah: Da^ʾ^irat al-Thaqafa wa-l-I^c^lam, 2005), partially trans., Ethan Chorin, 'The Mute' in Ethan Chorin (ed.), *Translating Libya: In Search of the Libyan Short Story* (London: Darf Publishers, 2015), pp. 76-94

al-Ghazāl, ^c^Abdallāh, *al-Tabut* (Tripoli: Dar al-Farjani, 2004 (2009)); first published: Sharjah: Da^ʾ^irat al-Thaqafa wa-l-I^c^lam, 2004.

al-Ghazāl, ^c^Abdallāh, *Al-Khawf Abqani Hayyan* (Beirut: al-Intishar al-^c^Arabi, 2008).

al-Kiddī, ^c^Umar, 'al-Hayah al-Qasira al-^c^Ajiba li-l-Kalb Ramadan', *Majallat Nizwa*, 63 (2010), pp. 219–23; trans. Robin Moger, 'The wonderful short life of the dog Ramadan', *Banipal*, 40 (2011), pp. 49–60.

al-Kiddī, ^c^Umar, *Hurub Marish wa-Thawratuha al-Thalath* (Tripoli: Wizarat al-Thaqafah wa-l-Mujtama^c^ al-Madani, 2013).

al-Kūnī, Ibrāhīm, *Nazif al-Hajar* (Misrata: al-Dar al-Jamahiriyya li-l-Nashr wa-l-Tawzi^c^ wa-l-I^c^lan, 2005); first published: London: Riyad al-Rayyis li-l-Kutub wa-l-Nashr, 1990; trans. May Jayyusi and Christopher Tingley, *The Bleeding of the Stone* (Gloucestershire: Arris Books, 2003).

al-Kūnī, Ibrāhīm, *al-Tibr* (Misrata: al-Dar al-Jamahiriyya li-l-Nashr wa-l-Tawzi^c^ wa-l-I^c^lan, 2005); first published: London: Riyad al-Rayyis li-l-Kutub wa-l-Nashr, 1990; trans. Elliott Colla, *Gold Dust* (London: Arabia Books, 2008).

al-Kūnī, Ibrāhīm, *Diwan al-Nathr al-Barri* (Limassol: Dar al-Tanwir li-l-Tiba[c]a wa-l-Nashr, 1991).

al-Kūnī, Ibrāhīm, *Anubis* (Beirut: al-Mu'assasa al-[c]Arabiyya li-l-Dirasat wa-l-Nashr, 2002), trans. William Hutchins, *Anubis* (Cairo: American University in Cairo Press, 2005 (2014)).

Matar, Hisham, *In the Country of Men* (London: Penguin Books, 2006 (2012)).

Matar, Hisham, *Anatomy of Disappearance* (New York: Penguin Books, 2011).

Matar, Hisham, *The Return* (London: Penguin Books, 2017).

al-Minifī, Rajab Buḥwaysh, 'Ma bi Marad', in Kamal Ben Hameda (ed. and trans.) *Le livre du camp d'Aguila* (Tunis: Éditions Elyzad, 2014), pp. 21–51; trans. Khaled Mattawa, 'No Illness But This Place', *Jadaliyya*, 16 May 2011, http://www.jadaliyya.com/Details/23985/Rajab-Buhwaysh,-No-Illness-But-This-Place (last accessed 17 July 2019).

al-Na[c]ās, Muḥammad, 'Majnun Aghzala', in Khālid al-Maṭāwi[c] and Laylā Na[c]īm al-Maghrabī (eds.), *Shams [c]ala Nawafidh Mughlaqa* (London: Darf, 2017), pp. 464–84.

Naṣr, Aḥmad, *Wamid fi Jidar al-Layl* (Tripoli: Manshurat Dar Maktabat al-Fikr, 1974).

al-Nayhūm, al-Ṣādiq, *Min Qisas al-Atfal* (al-Maya: Tala li-l-Tiba[c]a wa-l-Nashr, 2002); first published: Benghazi: Dar al-Haqiqa, 1970.

al-Nayhūm, al-Ṣādiq, *Min Makka ila Huna* (Tripoli: Tala li-l-Tiba[c]a wa-l-Nashr, 2001); first published: Benghazi: Dar al-Haqiqa, 1970.

al-Nayhūm, al-Ṣādiq, *al-Hayawanat* (Benghazi: Maktabat al-Tumur li-l-Kitab, 2010); first published: Benghazi: Dar al-Haqiqa, 1975.

al-Nayhūm, al-Ṣādiq, *al-Qurud* (Benghazi: Maktabat al-Tumur li-l-Kitab, 2010); first published: Sirte: al-Dar al-Jamahiriyya li-l-Nashr wa-l-Tawzi[c] wa-l-I[c]lan, 1984.

al-Qadhdhāfī, Mu[c]ammar, *al-Qarya al-Qarya, al-Ard al-Ard wa-Intihar Ra'id al-Fada' ma[c]a Qisas Ukhra* (Sirte: al-Dar al-Jamahiriyya, 1993), trans. *Escape to Hell and Other Stories* (London: Blake Publishing, 1999).

al-Qammūdi, Muḥammad Ṣāliḥ, *Thalathun Yawman fi al-Qahira* (Tripoli: Manshurat Dar Maktabat al-Fikr, 1971).

Qanāw, Miftāḥ, *[c]Awdat al-Qaysar* (Benghazi: Majlis Tanmiyat al-Ibda[c] al-Thaqafi, 2004), partially trans., Ethan Chorin, 'Caesar's Return', in Ethan Chorin (ed.), *Translating Libya: In Search of the Libyan Short Story* (London: Darf Publishers, 2015), pp. 172–5.

al-Quwayrī, Yūsuf, *Min Mufakkira Rajul lam Yulad* (Tunis: Dar al-[c]Arabiyya li-l-Kitab, 1981), first published: Tripoli: Dar al-Fikr, 1972.

Spina, Alessandro, *I confini dell'ombra* (Brescia: Morcelliana, 2006), trans. André Naffis-Sahely, *The Confines of the Shadow* (London: Darf Publishers, 2015).

Siyāla, Muḥammad Farīd, *I^{c}tirafat Insan* (Alexandria: Dar al-Sharq al-Awsat li-l-Tiba^{c}a wa-l-Nashr, 1961).

al-^{c}Uraybī, ^{c}Abd al-Rasūl, *Abwāb al-Mawt al-Sab^{c}a* (Tripoli: Al-Dar al-Jamahiriyya li-l-Nashr wa-l-Tawzi^{c} wa-l-I^{c}lan, 1998).

Secondary Sources in Arabic

al-^{c}Abbār, Sālim ^{c}Alī, *Maqalat fi al-Turath al-Sha^{c}bi* (Tripoli: al-Munsha$^{\circ}$a al-^{c}Amma li-l-Nashr wa-l-Tawzi^{c} wa-l-I^{c}lan, 1982).

Abū Dīb, al-Ṣīd, *Mu^{c}jam al-Mu$^{\circ}$allafat al-Libiyya al-Matbu^{c}a fi al-Adab al-Hadith* (Sirte: Majlis al-Thaqafa al-^{c}Amm, 2006).

al-^{c}Amāmī, Muḥammad ^{c}Aqīla, *Qut^{c}an al-Kalimat al-Mudi$^{\circ}$a: ^{c}An al-^{c}Alaqa al-Adabiyya bayn al-Mubdi^{c}ayn Sadiq al-Nayhum wa-Khalifa al-Fakhiri* (Cairo: Markaz al-Hadara al-^{c}Arabiyya, 2003).

Amlūda, Maḥmūd Muḥammad, *Tamthilat al-Muthaqqaf fi al-Sard al-^{c}Arabi al-Hadith: al-Riwaya al-Libiyya Anamudhajan* (Irbid: ^{c}Alam al-Kutub al-Hadith, 2010).

al-Aṣfar, Muḥammad, 'Riwa$^{\circ}$i Yanhit ^{c}Awalimahu min Sakhr al-Mutakhayyal: al-Khawf Yubqi ^{c}Abdallah al-Ghazal Hayyan', *libya-al-mostakbal*, 29 April 2008, http://archive.libya-al-mostakbal.org/Thaqafa/April2008/mohammad_alasfar290408.htm (last accessed 27 June 2019).

al-Aṣfar, Muḥammad, '^{c}Ilkat Bushnaf Yata$^{\circ}$allam fi Afwahina', *middle-east-online*, 15 December 2008, https://middle-east-online.com/علكة-بوشناف-تتألم-في-أفواهنا (last accessed 18 September 2014).

al-Aṣfar, Muḥammad, 'Mansur Bushnaf: Bin Walid wa-Misrata Shakkalata Wijdani', *alwasat*, 17 September 2014, http://alwasat.ly/news/art-culture/34601 (last accessed 3 April 2019).

al-Aṣfar, Muḥammad, 'Mansur Bushnaf: ^{c}Ashriyya al-^{c}Ilka al-Libiyya', *alaraby aljadid*, 9 June 2015, https://www.alaraby.co.uk/culture/2015/1/9/العلكة-الليبي-منصور-بوشناف-عشرية- (last accessed 10 September 2018).

^{c}Aṭiyya, Aḥmad Muḥammad, *Fi al-Adab al-Libi al-Hadith* (Beirut: Dar al-Tadamun li-l-Tiba^{c}a wa-l-Nashr, 1973).

al-Awkalī, Sālim, 'Hiwar ma^{c}a al-Qass Ahmad Yusuf ^{c}Aqila', *al-Fusul al-Arba'a*, 93 (2000), pp. 174–8.

^{c}Ayyash, ^{c}Abdallāh, 'Athr Irnist Himinjway fi al-Riwaya al-^{c}Arabiyya', PhD Dissertation, Yarmouk University, 2010.

al-Barʿaṣī, Intiṣār, 'Ahmad Yusuf ʿAqila wa-Lughat al-Ashyaʾ al-Tazija', *al-Hayat*, 17 July 2014, http://www.alhayat.com/article/أحمد-يوسف-عقيلة-ولغة-الأشياء-الطازجة (last accessed 2 November 2018).

Bin Jumʿa, Būshūsha, *al-Riwaya al-Libiyya al-Muʿasara: Sayrurat al-Tahawwulat wa-Muʿjam al-Kuttab* (Casablanca: al-Magharabiyya li-l-Tibaʿa, 2007).

Burhāna, ʿAlī, 'al-Sukhriyya fi Riwayat Min Makka ila Huna', *al-Fusul al-Arbaʿa*, 96 (2001), pp. 6–20.

Burhāna, ʿAlī, 'al-Riwaya al-Libiyya: al-Nashʾa wa-l-Tatawwur', in *al-Mashhad al-Riwaʾi al-ʿArabi* (Cairo: al-Majlis al-Aʿla li-l-Thaqafa, 2008), pp. 349–76.

Būshnāf, Manṣūr, 'Bi-l-Yusra: Min Huna Ila Makka', *alwasat*, 2 February 2011 http://www.alwasat.ly/ar/news/kottab/2665/ (last accessed 3 May 2016).

al-Dalnasī, Yūsuf, 'Adab al-Qissa fi Libya', in Bashir al-Hashimi (ed.), *Khalfiyyat al-Qissa al-Libiyya al-Qasira* (Tripoli: al-Munshaʾa al-ʿAmma li-l-Nashr wa-l-Tawziʿ wa-l-Iʿlan, 1979), pp. 177–80.

Falḥī, Muḥammad, 'Darb al-Halazin: Bayn al-Bashar wa-l-Tabiʿa', *Middle East Online*, 25 June 2010, https://middle-east-online.com/درب-الحلازين-بين-البشر-والطبيعة (last accessed 11 July 2019).

Fanūsh, Yūnus ʿUmar, *al-Ibl fi al-Shiʿr al-Shaʿbi: Dirasa fi Surat al-Ibl Kama yaʿkisuha al-Shiʿr al-Shaʿbi fi Libya* (Sirte: Majlis al-Thaqafa al-ʿAmm, 2008).

al-Faqīh, Aḥmad Ibrāhīm, 'Sahib al-Nufudh', *al-Naqid*, 83 (1995), pp. 45–7.

al-Faqīh, Aḥmad Ibrāhīm, 'Sura Qalamiyya li-Sadiq al-Nayhum', *Watanona*, 18 July 2009, http://www.libya-watanona.com/adab/aalfagih/af18079a.htm (last accessed 27 April 2016).

al-Fayṣal, Samar Rūḥī, *Dirasat fi al-Riwaya al-Libiyya* (Tripoli: al-Munshaʾa al-ʿAmma li-l-Nashr wa-l-Tawziʿ wa-l-Iʿlan, 1983).

al-Fayṣal, Samar Rūḥī, *Nuhud al-Riwaya al-ʿArabiyya al-Libiyya* (Tripoli: al-Munshaʾa al-ʿAmma li-l-Nashr wa-l-Tawziʿ wa-l-Iʿlan, 1990).

al-Faytūrī, Aḥmad, 'Marthiyat al-Zawal: Qiraʾa Naqdiyya fi Riwayat al-Tibr', *al-Fusul al-Arbaʿa*, 104 (2003), pp. 40–7.

al-Faytūrī, Aḥmad, 'Kitab Hayati', *al-Hiwar al-Mutamaddin*, 3 July 2009, http://www.ahewar.org/debat/show.art.asp?aid=176526 (last accessed 11 October 2018).

al-Faytūrī, Aḥmad, 'al-Hibi wa-l-ʿAqid', *al-Jadid*, 1 January 2017, https://aljadeed-magazine.com/الهيبي%E2%80%AD-%E2%80%ACوالعقيد (last accessed 27 June 2019).

al-Faytūrī, Aḥmad, 'Shams ʿala Nawafidh Mughlaqa: Kitabat Shabba la-Kitabat Shabab', in Khālid al-Maṭāwiʿ and Laylā Naʿīm al-Maghrabī (eds), *Shams ʿala Nawafidh Mughlaqa* (London: Darf Publishing, 2017), pp. 33–68 al-Fiqhī, ᶜAbd al-Salām, 'al-Mashhad al-Thaqafi al-Libi ma baᶜd al-Qadhdhafi', *al-Sharq al-Awsat*, 26 February 2018, https://aawsat.com/home/article/1186766/المشهد-الثقافي-الليبي-ما-بعد-القذافي (last accessed 18 July 2019).

al-Ghānamī, Saᶜīd, *Malhamat al-Hudud al-Quswa: al-Mukhyal al-Sahrawi fi Adab Ibrahim al-Kuni* (Casablanca: Al-Markaz al-Thaqafi al-ᶜArabi, 2000).

al-Ghazāl, ᶜAbdallāh, 'al-Sufiyya fi al-Nass al-Riwaᵓi al-ᶜArabi: bayn Iltibas al-Mafhum wa-Ahliyyat al-Tahaqquq', *Muntada al-Qissa al-ᶜArabiyya*, 7 August 2006, http://www.arabicstory.net/forum/index.php?/topic/4748-الصوفية-في-النص-الروائي-العربي/ (last accessed 3 May 2019).

Ghazūl, Faryāl, 'al-Riwaya al-Sufiyya fi al-Adab al-Magharibi', *Alif: Journal of Comparative Poetics*, 17 (1997), pp. 28–53.

Ghazūl, Faryāl, 'Qisas al-Hayawan bayn Mawruthina al-Shaᶜbi wa-Turathina al-Falsafi', *Fusul*, 13: 3 (1994), pp. 134–52.

Hābīl, Sālim, 'Wāqiᶜ al-Riwaya al-Libiyya', *al-Fusul al-Arbaᶜa,* 78 (1994), pp. 35–9.

al-Ḥājī, Fāṭima, *Al-Zaman fi al-Riwaya al-Libiyya: Thulathiyyat Ahmad Ibrahim al-Faqih Namudhajan* (Misrata: al-Dar al-Jamahiriyya li-l-Nashr wa-l-Tawziᶜ wa-l-Iᶜlan, 2000).

Ḥasan, Anīs Zakī (trans.), *Lawhat Tasili* (Tripoli: Maktabat al-Farjani, 1967).

al-Hindāwī, Sālim, 'al-ᶜAᵓid ila Binghazi', *al-Naqid*, 83 (1995), pp. 38–40.

al-Hūnī, Abū Bakr, 'al-Tariq ila Inkar al-Dhat', in Sālim al-Kubtī (ed.), *Turuq Mughattah bi-l-Thalj: ᶜAn al-Sadiq al-Nayhum* (Beirut: Tala li-l-Tibaᶜa wa-l-Nashr 2001), pp. 47–52.

Ibn Manẓūr, *Lisan al-ᶜArab* (Beirut: Dar Sadir, 1992).

Ibn Qutayba, *Kitab al-Shiᶜr wa-l-Shuᶜaraᵓ: al-Juzᵓ al-Awwal* (Cairo: Dar al-Maᶜarif, 1958).

Ikhwān al-Ṣafāᵓ, *Epistles of the Brethren of Purity: the case of the animals versus man before the King of the Jinn; an Arabic critical edition and English translation of Epistle 22,* eds and trans. Lenn E. Goodman and Richard McGregor (Oxford: Oxford University Press in association with the Institute of Ismaili Studies, 2009).

Ishtaywī, al-Bahlūl, *Thaman al-Hurriyya: Libya wa-l-Sanawat al-ᶜIjaf* (Beirut: Muntada al-Maᶜarif, 2013).

Jamāzī, al-Ṭayyib, 'Qiraᵓa fi Majmuᶜa Darb al-Halazin li-Ahmad Yusuf ᶜAqila', *al-Kharawba*, 17 August 2010, http://alkarrobah.blogspot.com/2010/08/ (last accessed 9 April 2019).

Kashlāf, Sulaymān, *Kitabat Libiyya* (Tripoli: al-Sharika al-ᶜAmma li-l-Nashr wa-l-Tawziᶜ wa-l-Iᶜlan, 1977).

Khushaym, ᶜAlī Fahmī (trans.), *Tahawwulat al-Jahsh al-Dhahabi: Riwaya* (Tripoli: al-Munshaᵓa al-ᶜAmma li-l-Nashr wa-l-Tawziᶜ wa-l-Iᶜlan, 1980 (1984)).

al-Kiddī, ᶜUmar, 'al-Ghazala wa-l-Hasnaᵓ Tahruban min Tarabulus', *Hunasotak*, 11 May 2014, https://hunasotak.com/article/12896 (last accessed 14 June 2016).

al-Kubtī, Sālim (ed.), *Nawaris al-Shawq wa-l-Ghurba: Baᶜd min Rasaᵓil al-Sadiq al-Nayhum* (Beirut: Tala li-l-Tibaᶜa wa-l-Nashr, 2002).

al-Kubtī, Sālim (ed.), *Turuq Mughattah bi-l-Thalj: ᶜAn al-Sadiq al-Nayhum* (Beirut: Tala li-l-Tibaᶜa wa-l-Nashr, 2001)

al-Kūnī, Ibrāhīm, 'Wa-l-Shiᶜr Aydan Yaktub al-Nayhum', in Salim al-Kubti (ed.), *Turuq Mughattah bi-l-Thalj: ᶜAn al-Sadiq al-Nayhum* (Beirut: Tala li-l-Tibaᶜa wa-l-Nashr, 2001), pp. 71–88.

al-Kūnī, Ibrāhīm, *Watani Sahraᵓ Kubra* (Beirut: al-Muᵓassasa al-ᶜArabiyya li-l-Dirasat wa-l-Nashr, 2009).

al-Kūnī, Ibrāhīm, *ᶜUdus al-Sura: Ruh Umam fi Nazif Dhakira*, parts 1–4 (Beirut: al-Muᵓassasa al-ᶜArabiyya li-l-Dirasat wa-l-Nashr, 2012, 2013, 2015, 2016).

al-Kūnī, Ibrāhīm, *Bayan fi Lughat al-Lahut: Lughz al-Tawariq Yakshif Lughzay al-Faraᶜina wa-l-Sumar* (Beirut: Dar al-Multaqa, 2004).

al-Mālikī, ᶜAbd al-Ḥakīm Sulaymān, *Jamaliyyat al-Riwaya al-Libiyya: Min Sardiyyat al-Khitab ila Sardiyyat al-Hikaya* (Benghazi: Manshurat Jamiᶜa 7 Aktubar, 2008).

al-Maqhūr, Kāmil, 'Hawl al-Qissa al-Libiyya', in Aḥmad Ibrāhīm al-Faqīh, *Thalath Majmuᶜat Qisasiyya* (Tripoli: Qitaᶜ al-Kitab wa-l-Tawziᶜ wa-l-Iᶜlan, 1981), pp. 135–41.

al-Mismārī, Idrīs, *Dhakirat al-Kitaba: Qiraᵓat fi al-Qissa wa-l-Riwaya al-Libiyya* (Cairo: Maktabat al-Usra, 2006).

al-Miṣrātī, ᶜAlī Muṣṭafā, *al-Mujtamaᶜ al-Libi min Khilal Amthalihi al-Shaᶜbiyya* (Tripoli: Dar Maktabat al-Fikr, 1972).

Muḥammad, Farīḥa, 'al-Khawf Abqani Hayyan: al-Riwaya al-Libiyya al-Mamnuᶜa', *Tieob*, 31 October 2011, http://www.tieob.com/?p=2611 (last accessed 27 June 2019).

al-Nayhūm, al-Ṣādiq, *al-ᶜAwda al-Muhzina ila al-Bahr* (Beirut: Tala li-l-Tibaᶜa wa-l-Nashr, 2004).

al-Nayhūm, al-Ṣādiq, *Fursan bila Maᶜraka* (Tripoli: Tala li-l-Tibaᶜa wa-l-Nashr, 2001).

al-Nayhūm, al-Ṣādiq, *al-Kalima wa-l-Sura* (Tripoli: Tala li-l-Tibaᶜa wa-l-Nashr, 2003).

al-Nayhūm, al-Ṣādiq, *Niqash* (Tripoli: Tala li-l-Tibaᶜa wa-l-Nashr, 2001).

al-Nayhūm, al-Ṣādiq, *al-Ramz fi al-Qurᵓan* (Tripoli: Tala li-l-Tibaᶜa wa-l-Nashr, 2008).

al-Nayhūm, al-Ṣādiq, *Tahiyya Tayyiba wa-Baʿd* (Tripoli: Tala li-l-Tibaʿa wa-l-Nashr, 2001).

al-Nayhūm, al-Ṣādiq (ed.), *Tarikhuna*, parts 1–7 (Geneva: Dar al-Turath, 1976).

al-Riyāḥī, Kamāl, 'al-Riwaʾi al-Libi Muhammad al-Asfar: al-Hamishi Yudawwin Matn al-Riwaya al-Libiyya al-Muʿasira', *Tieob*, June 2014, https://www.tieob.com/?p=9834 (last accessed 27 June 2019).

Salām, Rafʿat, 'Zahira Adabiyya Libiyya Ismuha al-Kuni', *al-Fusul al-Arbaʿa*, 78 (1994), pp. 149–51.

Ṣāliḥ, Muḥammad al-Faqīh, *Fi al-Thaqafa al-Libiyya al-Muʿasira: Malamih wa-Mutabaʿat* (Dar al-Ruwwad, 2016).

Sāliḥ, Munā, 'al-Riwaʾi Kamal Bin Hamida: al-Qadhafi Saraqa al-Dhakira', *Deutsche Welle*, 7 October 2011, https://www.dw.com/ar/القذافي-سرق-الذاكرة-الليبية-الروائي-كمال-بن-حميدة/a-15436218 (last accessed 3 April 2019).

Shalqam, ʿAbd al-Raḥmān, *Hiwar maʿa al-Sadiq al-Nayhum* (Tripoli: Tala li-l-Tibaʿa wa-l-Nashr, 1999).

Shalqam, ʿAbd al-Rahman, *Ashkhas hawl al-Qadhafi* (Tripoli: Dar al-Farjani, 2012).

al-Shaylābī, Aḥmad, *al-Qadaya al-Ijtimaʿiyya fi al-Riwaya al-Libiyya* (Misrata: Dar wa-Maktabat al-Shaʿb, 2003).

al-Ṭaḥāwī, Mīrāl, *Muharramat Qabaliyya: al-Muqaddas wa-Takhayyulatuhu fi al-Mujtamaʿ al-Raʿwi Riwaʾiyyan* (Casablanca: al-Markaz al-Thaqafi al-ʿArabi, 2008).

Zaydān, Sulaymān Ḥasan, 'al-Qasida al-Shaʿbiyya fi Libya: Fann wa-Thaqafa wa-Taʾrikh', *al-Thaqafa al-Shaʿbiyya*, 20 (2013), pp. 54–71.

al-Zughaybī, ʿAbd al-Salām, 'Darih ʿUmar al-Mukhtar: Mata Yaʿud ila Makanihi al-Asli?', *Libya-al-mostakbal*, http://www.libya-al-mostakbal.org/95/26956/ضريح-عمر-المختار-متى-يعود-الى-مكانه-الاصلي.html (last accessed 11 July 2019).

Secondary Sources in Other Languages

Agamben, Giorgio, *Homo Sacer: Sovereign Power and Bare Life*, trans. Daniel Heller-Roazen (Stanford, CA: Stanford University Press, 1998).

Agamben, Giorgio, *The Open: Man and Animal* (Stanford, CA: Stanford University Press, 2002).

al-Ageli, Nahla, 'Interviewing Najwa Benshatwan', *Shubbak*, 2 July 2017, https://www.shubbak.co.uk/interviewing-najwa-benshatwan/ (last accessed 11 July 2019).

Ahmida, Ali Abdullatif, *Forgotten Voices: Power and Agency in Colonial and Postcolonial Libya* (London: Routledge, 2005).

Ahmida, Ali Abdullatif, 'Libya, Social Origins of Dictatorship, and the Challenge for Democracy', *Journal of the Middle East and Africa*, 3: 1 (2012), pp. 70–81.

Ahmida, Ali Abdullatif, 'Libya: State, Society, Culture, and Postcolonialism', in Waïl Hassan (ed.), *The Oxford Handbook of Arab Novelistic Traditions* (Oxford: Oxford University Press, 2017), pp. 311–24.

Ahmida, Ali Abdullatif, *The Making of Modern Libya: State Formation, Colonization and Resistance* (Albany, NY: SUNY Press, 2009).

Ahmidan, Ibrahim, 'The Libyan Novel', *Banipal*, 40 (2011), pp. 46–8.

Aitmatov, Chingiz, *The White Steamship*, trans. Tatyana Feifer and George Feifer (London: Hodder & Stoughton, 1972).

al-Asfar, Muhammad, 'Libya's Patient Revolutionaries', trans. Ghenwa Hayek, *New York Times*, 2 March 2011, http://www.nytimes.com/2011/03/03/opinion/03asfar.html?_r=0 (last accessed 6 June 2019).

Allen, Roger, 'A Different Voice: The Novels of Ibrahim al-Kawni', in Issa Boullata and Terri de Young (eds), *Tradition and Modernity in Modern Arabic Literature* (Fayetteville, AR: University of Arkansas Press, 1997), pp. 151–9.

Allen, Roger, 'Rewriting Literary History: The Case of the Arabic Novel', *Journal of Arabic Literature*, 38: 3 (2007), pp. 247–60.

Almond, Ian, *Sufism and Deconstruction* (London: Routledge, 2004).

Altaleb, Amal M., 'The Social and Economic History of Slavery in Libya: (1800–1950)', PhD Dissertation, University of Manchester, 2015.

Amnesty International, *Long Struggle for Truth: Enforced Disappearances in Libya* (London: Amnesty International, June 2010).

Anag, Giuma et al., 'Environment, Archaeology, and Oil: The Messak Settafet Rescue Operation', *African Archaeological Review*, 19: 2 (2002), pp. 67–73.

Anderson, Benedict, *Imagined Communities: Reflections on the Origin and Spread of Nationalism* (London: Verso, 2006).

Anderson, Lisa, *The State and Social Transformation in Tunisia and Libya, 1830–1980* (Princeton, NJ: Princeton University Press, 2014).

Ansell, Meredith O. and Massaud al-Arif, Ibrahim (eds), *The Libyan Revolution: A Sourcebook of Legal and Historical Documents, Vol. I: 1 September 1969 – 30 August 1970* (Wisconsin, WI: Oleander Press, 1972).

Armstrong, Philip, *What Animals Mean in the Fiction of Modernity* (Abingdon: Routledge, 2008).

Atkinson, David, 'Encountering Bare Life in Italian Libya and Colonial Amnesia in Agamben', in Marcelo Svirsky and Simone Bignall (eds), *Critical Connections:*

Agamben and Colonialism (Edinburgh: Edinburgh University Press, 2012), pp. 155–77.

Bachelard, Gaston, *The Poetics of Space*, trans. Maria Jolas (Boston: Beacon Press, 1958).

Baker, Steve, *Picturing the Beast: Animals, Identity and Representation* (Manchester: Manchester University Press, 1993).

Bakhtin, Mikhail, *The Dialogic Imagination: Four Essays*, trans. Caryl Emerson and Michael Holquist (Austin, TX: University of Texas Press, 1981).

Bakhtin, Mikhail, *Rabelais and His World* (Bloomington, IN: Indiana University Press, 1984).

Baldick, Chris, *The Oxford Dictionary of Literary Terms* (Oxford: Oxford University Press, 2008).

Baldinetti, Anna, *The Origins of the Libyan Nation: Colonial Legacy, Exile and the Emergence of a New Nation-state* (London: Routledge, 2010).

Bamia, Aida, 'The African Novel: Northern Africa', in Paul Schellinger (ed.), *Encyclopaedia of the Novel*, Vol. 1 (Chicago: Fitzroy Derborn, 1998), pp. 15–26.

Barthes, Roland, *Empire of Signs*, trans. Richard Howard (New York: Noonday Press, 1982).

Beaumont, Daniel, *Slave of Desire: Sex, Love and Death in the 1001 Nights* (London: Associated University Presses, 2002).

Ben Hameda, Kamal, 'Dans les sables Libyens', *Lignes*, 3: 36 (2011), pp. 48–50.

Ben Hameda, Kamal, *Le livre du camp d'Aguila* (Tunis: Éditions Elyzad, 2014).

Benjamin, Walter, *Illuminations*, trans. Harry Zohn (New York: Schocken Books, 1969).

Benjamin, Walter, *The Origin of German Tragic Drama*, trans. John Osborne (London: Verso, 1998).

Benjamin, Walter, 'Surrealism: The Last Snapshot of the European Intelligentsia', in Michael Jennings, Howard Eiland and Gary Smith (eds), *Walter Benjamin: Selected Writings, Volume 2, 1927–1934* (Cambridge, MA: Belknap Press of Harvard University Press, 1999), pp. 207–21.

Berger, John, *Why Look at Animals?* (London: Penguin, 2009).

Blundell, Geoffrey, 'African Rock Art of the Northern Zone', October 2001, *The Met: Heilbrunn Timeline of Art History*, https://www.metmuseum.org/toah/hd/nroc/hd_nroc.htm (last accessed 4 July 2019).

Bulughma, M. R., 'The Urban Geography of Benghazi', PhD Dissertation, University of Durham, 1964.

Calarco, Matthew, *Zoographies: The Question of the Animal from Heidegger to Derrida* (New York: Columbia University Press, 2008).

Casajus, Dominique, *La tente dans la solitude: la société et les morts chez les Touaregs Kel Ferwan* (Cambridge: Cambridge University Press, 1987).

Chittick, William, 'The Wisdom of Animals', *Journal of the Muhyiddin Ibn ᶜArabi Society* 46 (2009), http://www.ibnarabisociety.org/articles/wisdom-of-animals.html (last accessed 26 April 2016).

Chorin, Ethan, *Exit Gaddafi: The Hidden History of the Libyan Revolution* (London: Saqi Books, 2012).

Chorin, Ethan, 'Homeless Rats: A Parable for Postrevolution Libya', *Words without Borders*, 9 January 2012, http://www.wordswithoutborders.org/dispatches/article/homeless-rats-a-parable-for-postrevolution-libya (last accessed 27 April 2016).

Chorin, Ethan, (ed. and trans.), *Translating Libya: In Search of the Libyan Short Story* (London: Darf Publishers, 2015).

Claudot-Hawad, Hélène, *Éperonner le monde: nomadisme, cosmos et politique chez les Touaregs* (Aix-en-Provence: Edisud, 2001).

Clayton, Robert, 'Aesop, Aristotle and Animals: The Role of Fables in Human Life', *Humanitas*, 21: 1–2 (2008), pp. 179–200.

Coetzee, J. M., *Foe* (London: Penguin Books, 2015).

Colla, Elliott, 'Translating Ibrahim al-Koni', *Banipal*, 40 (2011), pp. 175–8.

Colla, Elliott, 'Ibrahim al-Koni's Atlas of the Sahara', in Ali Abdullatif Ahmida (ed.), *Bridges across the Sahara* (Newcastle: Cambridge Scholars, 2009), pp. 187–95.

Connor, Steven, *Fly* (London: Reaktion Books, 2006).

Cooke, Miriam, 'Magical Realism in Libya', *Journal of Arabic Literature*, 41 (2010), pp. 9–21.

Cooke, Miriam, *Dissident Syria: Making Oppositional Arts Official* (Durham, NC: Duke University Press, 2007).

Cowan, Benjamin, 'Walter Benjamin's Theory of Allegory', *New German Critique*, 22 (1981), pp. 109–22.

Davis, John, *Libyan Politics: Tribe and Revolution* (London: I. B. Tauris, 1987).

DeFilippo, Joseph G., 'Curiositas and the Platonism of Apuleius' Golden Ass', *American Journal of Philology*, 111: 4 (Winter, 1990), pp. 471–92.

Deheuvels, Luc-Willy, 'Le "lieu" de l'utopie dans l'oeuvre d'Ibrahim al-Kawni', in Boutros Hallaq, Robin Ostle and Stefan Wild (eds), *La poétique de l'espace dans la literature arabe moderne* (Paris: Presses Sorbonne Nouvelle, 2002), pp. 25–43.

DeLoughrey, Elizabeth and George B. Handley, 'Introduction: Toward an Aesthetics of the Earth', in Elizabeth DeLoughrey and George B. Handley (eds), *Postcolonial Ecologies: Literatures of the Environment* (Oxford: Oxford University Press, 2011).

Deleuze, Gilles and Guattari, Félix, 'What Is a Minor Literature?', trans. Robert Brinkley, *Mississippi Review*, 11: 3 (Winter/Spring, 1983), pp. 13–33.

Derrida, Jacques, 'The Law of Genre', trans. Avital Ronell, *Critical Inquiry,* 7: 1 (Autumn, 1980), pp. 55–81.

Derrida, Jacques, '"Eating Well" or the Calculation of the Subject', trans. Peggy Kamuf in Elisabeth Weber (ed.), *Points . . . Interviews, 1974–1994* (Stanford, CA: Stanford University Press, 1995), pp. 255–88.

Derrida, Jacques, *Of Hospitality*, trans. Rachel Bowlby (Stanford, CA: Stanford University Press, 2000).

Derrida, Jacques, 'The Animal That Therefore I Am (More to Follow)', trans. David Wills, *Critical Inquiry*, 28: 2 (2002), pp. 369–418.

Diamond, Cora, 'The Difficult of Reality and the Difficulty of Philosophy', in Stanley Cavell et al., *Philosophy and Animal Life* (New York: Columbia University Press, 2008), pp. 43–90.

Diana, Elvira, *La letteratura della Libia: Dall'epoca coloniale ai nostri giorni* (Rome: Carocci, 2008).

Diana, Elvira, 'Literary Springs in Libyan Literature: Contributions of Writers to the Country's Emancipation', *Middle East Critique*, 23:4 (2014), pp. 439–51.

Diana, Elvira, 'Libyan Narrative in the New Millennium: Features of Literature on Change', *La Rivista di Arablit*, 3: 5 (2013), pp. 25–40.

Dunton, Chris, 'Black Africans in Libya and Libyan Images of Black Africa', in René Lemarchand (ed.), *The Green and the Black: Qadhafi's Policies in Africa* (Bloomington, IN: Indiana University Press, 1988), pp. 150–66.

El-Ariss, Tarek, 'Return of the Beast: From Pre-Islamic Ode to Contemporary Novel', *Journal of Arabic Literature*, 47: 1–2 (2016), pp. 62–90.

El-Ariss, Tarek, *Trials of Arab Modernity: Literary Affects and the New Political* (New York: Fordham University Press, 2013).

El-Enany, Rasheed, *Arab Representations of the Occident: East–West Encounters in Arabic Fiction* (Abingdon: Routledge, 2006).

Elmarsafy, Ziad, *Sufism in the Contemporary Arabic Novel* (Edinburgh: Edinburgh University Press, 2012).

Elmarsafy, Ziad, 'Ibrahim al-Koni's Hybrid Aesthetic', *Canadian Review of Comparative Literature*, 39: 2 (2012), pp. 190–201.

Elmusa, Sharif, 'The Ecological Bedouin: Toward Environmental Principles for the Arab Region', *Alif: Journal of Comparative Poetics*, 33 (2013), pp. 9–35.

Elsadda, Hoda, *Gender, Nation, and the Arabic Novel: Egypt, 1892–2008* (Edinburgh: Edinburgh University Press, 2012).

El-Youssef, Samir, 'The Curse of Topicality', *New Statesman*, 31 July 2006, https://www.newstatesman.com/node/164938 (last accessed 8 April 2019).

El-Zein, Amira, 'Mythological Tuareg Gods in Ibrahim al-Koni's Work', *Alif: Journal of Comparative Poetics*, 35 (2015), pp. 200–16.

Fähndrich, Hartmut, 'Ibrahim al-Koni: Le désert e(s)t la vie', *Feuxcroisés*, 4 (2000), pp. 155–64.

Fähndrich, Hartmut, 'The Desert as Homeland and Metaphor', in Angelika Neuwirth, Andreas Pflitsch and Barbara Winckler (eds), *Arabic Literature: Postmodern Perspectives* (London: Saqi Books, 2010), pp. 331–41.

al-Faqīh, Aḥmad Ibrāhīm, 'The Libyan Short Story', PhD diss., University of Edinburgh, 1983.

al-Faqīh, Aḥmad Ibrāhīm, 'Foreword', in Ethan Chorin (ed.), *Translating Libya: In Search of the Libyan Short Story* (London: Darf Publishers, 2015), pp. v–ix.

al-Fārābī, Abū Naṣr, *On the Perfect State*, trans. Richard Walzer (Chicago: Great Books of the Islamic World, 1998).

Finkelpearl, Ellen, 'Marsyas the Satyr and Apuleius of Madauros', *Ramus* , 38: 1 (2009), pp. 7–42.

Foltz, Richard C., *Animals in Islamic Tradition and Muslim Cultures* (Oxford: Oneworld, 2006).

Fouad, Jehan Farouk and Alwakeel, Saeed, 'Representations of the Desert in Silko's *Ceremony* and Al-Koni's *The Bleeding of the Stone*', *Alif: Journal of Comparative Poetics*, 33 (2013), pp. 36–62.

Foucault, Michel, 'Of Other Spaces', trans. Jay Miskowiec, *Diacritics*, 16: 1 (1986), pp. 22–6.

Foucault, Michel, *Discipline and Punish: The Birth of the Prison*, trans. Alan Sheridan (London: Vintage Books, 1995).

Foucault, Michel, *The History of Sexuality, vol. 1, The Will to Knowledge*, trans. Robert Hurley (Harmondsworth: Penguin Books, 1998).

Fromm, Erich, *The Sane Society* (London: Routledge, 2002).

Fromm, Erich, *The Heart of Man: Its Genius for Good and Evil* (New York: Harper & Row, 1964).

Fudge, Bruce, 'Underworlds and Otherworlds in *The Thousand and One Nights*', *Middle Eastern Literatures,* 15:3 (2012), pp. 257–72.

Fudge, Erica, 'A Left-Handed Blow', in Nigel Rothfels (ed.), *Representing Animals* (Bloomington, IN: Indiana University Press, 2002).

Fudge, Erica, *Pets* (London: Routledge, 2008).

Gana, Nouri, 'An Interview with Hisham Matar', *Words without Borders,* August 2007, https://www.wordswithoutborders.org/article/an-interview-with-hisham-matar (last accessed 30 August 2018).

Gana, Nouri, 'Introduction: The Intellectual History and Contemporary Significance of the Arab Novel in English', in Nouri Gana (ed.), *The Edinburgh Companion to the Arab Novel in English* (Edinburgh: Edinburgh University Press, 2013), pp. 1–38.

al-Ghadeer, Moneera, *Desert Voices: Bedouin Women's Poetry in Saudi Arabia* (London: I. B. Tauris, 2009).

Ghazoul, Ferial, *Nocturnal Poetics: The Arabian Nights in Comparative Context* (Cairo: American University in Cairo Press, 1996).

Ghosh, Amitav, 'Petrofiction: The Oil Encounter and the Novel', in Imre Szeman and Dominic Boyer (eds), *Energy Humanities: An Anthology* (Baltimore, MD: Johns Hopkins University Press, 2017), pp. 431–40.

Gifford, Terry, 'Pastoral, Antipastoral, and Postpastoral as Reading Strategies', in Scott Slovic (ed.), *Critical Insights: Nature and the Environment* (Ipswich, MA: Salem Press, 2013), pp. 42–61.

Goodman, Lenn E., 'Introduction', in Lenn E. Goodman and Richard McGregor (eds and trans.), *The Case of the Animals versus Man before the King of the Jinn: An Arabic Critical Edition and English Translation of Epistle 22 of the Epistles of the Brethren of Purity* (Oxford: Oxford University Press, 2009), pp. 1–56.

Goodman, Lenn E. and Richard McGregor (trans.), *The Case of the Animals versus Man before the King of the Jinn: An Arabic Critical Edition and English Translation of Epistle 22 of the Epistles of the Brethren of Purity* (Oxford: Oxford University Press, 2009).

Gross, Aaron, 'Introduction and Overview: Animal Others and Animal Studies', in Aaron Gross and Jane Vallely (eds), *Animals and the Human Imagination: A Companion to Animal Studies* (New York: Columbia University Press, 2013), pp. 1–25.

Gunderson, Ryan, 'Erich Fromm's Ecological Messianism: The First Biophilia Hypothesis as Humanistic Social Theory', *Humanity & Society*, 38: 2 (2014), pp. 182–204.

Hafez, Sabry, 'Women's Narrative in Modern Arabic Literature: A Typology', in Roger Allan, Hilary Kilpatrick and Ed de Moor (eds), *Love and Sexuality in Modern Arabic Literature* (London: Saqi Books, 1995), pp. 154–74.

al-Hagi, Fatima, 'The Concept of Time in Five Libyan Novels', PhD Dissertation, Durham University, 2008.

Hamarneh, Walid, 'Welcome to the Desert of Not-Thinking', *Canadian Review of Comparative Literature* , 41: 1 (2014), pp. 86–98.

Hamza, Abdulmaula, 'Libya', in Paolo Casale and Dimitris Margaritoulis (eds), *Sea Turtles in the Mediterranean: Distribution, Threats and Conservation Priorities* (Gland, Switzerland: International Union for Conservation of Nature, 2010), pp. 157–69.

Hanssen, Beatrice, *Walter Benjamin's Other History: Of Stones, Animals, Human Beings and Angels* (Berkeley, CA: University of California Press, 2000).

Haraway, Donna, 'Primatology is Politics by Other Means', *Proceedings of the Biennial Meeting of the Philosophy of Science Association*, 2 (1984), pp. 489–524.

Haraway, Donna, *The Companion Species Manifesto: Dogs, People and Significant Otherness* (Chicago: Prickly Paradigm Press, 2003).

Harel, Naama, 'The Animal Voice Behind the Animal Fable', *Journal for Critical Animal Studies*, 7: 2 (2009), pp. 9–21.

Harlow, Barbara, 'From Flying Carpets to No-Fly Zones: Libya's Elusive Revolution(s), According to Ruth First, Hisham Matar, and the International Criminal Court', *Journal of Arabic Literature*, 43: 2/3 (2012), pp. 431–57.

Hashem, Noor, '"The Feast of the Ants": Agency, the Body, and Qur'anic Narrative in Hisham Matar's *In the Country of Men*', *Journal of Qur'anic Studies*, 16: 3 (2014), pp. 39–61.

Hassan, Waïl, *Immigrant Narratives: Orientalism and Cultural Translation in Arab American and Arab British Literature* (Oxford: Oxford University Press, 2011).

Hassan, Waïl, 'Toward a Theory of the Arabic Novel', in Waïl Hassan (ed.), *The Oxford Handbook of Arab Novelistic Traditions* (Abingdon: Oxford University Press, 2017), pp. 19–48.

Heath, Peter, 'Allegory in Islamic literatures', in Rita Copeland and Peter T. Struck (eds), *The Cambridge Companion to Allegory* (Cambridge: Cambridge University Press, 2010), pp. 83–101.

Herodotus, *The Histories*, trans. George Rawlinson (Ware, Herts: Wordsworth Editions, 1996).

Higgins, Benjamin Howard, *The Economic and Social Development of Libya* (New York: United Nations Technical Assistance Programme, 1953).

Higgins, Charlotte, 'How Gaddafi Toppled a Roman Emperor', *The Guardian Online*, 28 November 2011, https://www.theguardian.com/culture/charlottehiggins-blog/2011/nov/28/libya-muammar-gaddafi (last accessed 14 June 2016).

Hilsum, Lindsey, *Sandstorm: Libya from Gaddafi to Revolution* (London: Faber & Faber, 2013).

Hine, Alyn, 'Empty Spaces at the Heart of Ibrahim al-Kuni's Literary World', *Comparative Critical Studies* , 11, Issue Supplement (2014), pp. 29–43.

Hine, Alyn, 'Travelling Home: Ibrahim al-Kuni's *al-Tibr* (*Gold Dust*)', *Comparative Critical Studies*, 10, Issue Supplement (2013), pp. 13–26.

Huggan, Graham and Helen Tiffin, *Postcolonial Ecocriticism* (Abingdon: Routledge, 2014).

Hutchins, William, 'Ibrahim Al-Koni's Lost Oasis as Atlantis and His Demon as Typhon', in Edith Hall and Justine McConnell (eds), *Ancient Greek Myth in World Fiction since 1989* (London: Bloomsbury Academic, 2016), pp. 31–46.

Ibn al-ᶜArabi, *Tarjuman al-Ashwaq: A Collection of Mystical Odes*, trans. Reynold A. Nicholson (London: Royal Asiatic Society, 1911).

Ibn Khaldun, *The Muqaddima*, trans. Franz Rosenthal, ed. N. J. Dawood (Princeton, NJ: Princeton University Press, 1966).

Irwin, Robert, *Camel* (London: Reaktion Books, 2010).

Irwin, Robert, 'The Arabic Beast Fable', *Journal of the Warburg and Courtauld Institutes*, 55 (1992), pp. 36–50.

Jameson, Fredric, 'Third-World Literature in the Era of Multinational Capitalism', *Social Text*, 15 (1986), pp. 65–88.

Jameson, Fredric, *Postmodernism, or, The Cultural Logic of Late Capitalism* (London: Verso, 1991).

Kafka, Franz, *Franz Kafka: The Complete Stories*, trans. Martin Secker et al. (London: Vintage, 2018).

Kassam, Zayn, '*The Case of the Animals versus Man*: Toward an Ecology of Being', in Kimberley Patton and Paul Waldau (eds), *A Communion of Subjects: Animals in Religion, Science, and Ethics* (New York: Columbia University Press, 2006), pp. 160–9.

Kearney, John, 'Traumatised Narrators in Hisham Matar's Novels', *Journal of Literary Studies*, 30: 3 (2014), pp. 124–48.

Khan, Pasha, 'Nothing but Animals: The Hierarchy of Creatures in the *Ringstones of Wisdom*', *Journal of the Muhyiddin Ibn ᶜArabi Society*, 43 (2008), http://www.ibnarabisociety.org/articles/nothing-but-animals.html (last accessed 26 April 2016).

Kilito, Abdelfattah, *The Author and His Doubles: Essays on Classical Arabic Culture*, trans. Michael Cooperson (New York: Syracuse University Press, 2001).

Kilpatrick, Hilary, 'Arab Fiction in English: A Case of Dual Nationality', *New Comparison*, 13 (1992), pp. 46–55.

al-Kuni, Ibrahim, 'Le discours du desert (témoignage)', in Boutros Hallaq, Robin Ostle and Stefan Wild (eds), *La poétique de l'espace dans la literature arabe moderne* (Paris: Presses Sorbonne Nouvelle, 2002), pp. 95–102.

Kunzru, Hari, 'Hisham Matar: Libya's Reluctant Spokesman', *Guernica*, 15 October 2011, https://www.guernicamag.com/matar_kunzru_10_15_11/ (last accessed 8 April 2019).

Larkin, Philip, *Collected Poems* (London: Faber & Faber, 2003).

Le Guin, Ursula, *Buffalo Gals and Other Animal Presences* (Santa Barbara, CA: Capra Press, 1987).

Lejeune, Phillipe, *On Autobiography* (Minneapolis, MN: University of Minnesota Press, 1989).

Lhote, Henri, *A la découverte des fresques du Tassili* (Paris: Arthaud, 1973).

Lowenthal, David, *Possessed by the Past: The Heritage Crusade and the Spoils of History* (London: Viking, 1996).

Lowenthal, David, *The Past Is a Foreign Country* (Cambridge: Cambridge University Press, 1985).

Lynx-Qualey, Marcia, 'The Animals in Libyan Fiction', *Arablit*, 8 May 2011, https://arablit.org/2011/05/08/the-animals-in-libyan-fiction/ (last accessed 15 June 2016).

Al Maleh, Layla, 'Anglophone Arab Literature: An Overview' in Layla al Maleh (ed.), *Arab Voices in Diaspora: Critical Perspectives on Anglophone Arab Literature* (Amsterdam: Editions Rodopi, 2009), pp. 1–64.

Margoliouth, D. S., 'Abu'l-^{c}Alā al-Ma^{c}arri's Correspondence on Vegetarianism', *Royal Asiatic Society*, 34: 2 (1902), pp. 289–332.

Marzolph, Ulrich and van Leeuwen, Richard, *The Arabian Nights Encyclopaedia, Volume Two* (Oxford: ABC CLIO, 2004).

Matar, Hisham, 'Once Upon a Life: Hisham Matar', *The Guardian*, 20 February 2011, https://www.theguardian.com/lifeandstyle/2011/feb/20/hisham-matar-once-upon-a-life (last accessed 18 November 2019).

Matar Hisham, 'A Tree that Scarcely Fruits', review of *La compagnie des Tripolitaines* by Kamal Ben Hameda and *Chewing Gum* by Mansur Bushnaf, *Times Literary Supplement*, 16 January 2015, http://www.the-tls.co.uk/articles/private/a-tree-that-scarcely-fruits/ (last accessed 16 July 2019).

Matar, Hisham, 'Author Spotlight', *The O. Henry Prize Stories*, https://www.random-house.com/anchor/ohenry/spotlight/matar.html (last accessed 16 July 2019).

Mattawa, Khaled, 'Preface to the Libya Issue of Words Without Borders: The Magic Lanterns of Libyan Literature', *Words without Borders*, July 2006, http://www.wordswithoutborders.org/article/preface-to-the-libya-issue-of-words-without-borders-july-2006#ixzz48v1sS7db (last accessed 17 May 2016).

Mattawa, Khaled, 'Libya', in *Literature from the Axis of Evil: A Words without Borders Anthology* (New York: Words Without Borders, 2006), pp. 225–8.

Mattawa, Khaled, 'Dispatches from Benghazi', *PMLA*, 122: 1 (2007), pp. 264–70.

Mattawa, Khaled, 'Introduction', in Nouri Zarrugh, *The Leader* (Massachusetts Review Working Titles, 2017).

McHugh, Susan, 'Hybrid Species and Literatures: Ibrahim al-Koni's "Composite Apparition"', *Comparative Critical Studies*, 9: 3 (2012), pp. 285–302.

Metz, Helen Chapin, *Libya: A Country Study* (Washington, DC: Federal Research Division, 1987).

Micklethwait, Christopher, 'Zenga Zenga and Bunga Bunga: The Novels of Hisham Matar and a Critique of Gaddafi's Libya', in Nouri Gana (ed.), *The Edinburgh Companion to the Arab Novel in English* (Edinburgh: Edinburgh University Press, 2013), pp. 171–96.

Mikhail, Alan, 'The Fallow between Two Fields', in Alan Mikhail (ed.), *Water on Sand: Environmental Histories of the Middle East and North Africa* (Oxford: Oxford University Press, 2013), pp. 1–25.

Montgomery, James, *al-Jāḥiẓ: In Praise of Books* (Edinburgh: Edinburgh University Press, 2013).

Moretti, Franco, *The Way of the World: The Bildungsroman in European Culture* (London: Verso, 2000).

Nash, Geoffrey, 'Britain', in Waïl S. Hassan (ed.) *The Oxford Handbook of Arab Novelistic Traditions* (New York: Oxford University Press, 2017), pp. 557–74.

Nash, Geoffrey, *The Anglo-Arab Encounter: Fiction and Autobiography by Arab Writers in English* (Bern: Peter Lang, 2007).

Nixon, Rob, 'Environmentalism and Postcolonialism', in Ania Loomba et al., *Postcolonial Studies and Beyond* (Durham, NC: Duke University Press, 2005), pp. 233–51.

Nixon, Rob, *Slow Violence and the Environmentalism of the Poor* (Cambridge, MA: Harvard University Press, 2011).

Nora, Pierre, 'Between Memory and History: Les Lieux de Mémoire', *Representations*, 26, Special Issue: Memory and Counter-Memory (1989), pp. 7–24.

al-Nowaihi, Magda, M., 'Reenvisioning National Community in Salwa Bakr's "The Golden Chariot Does Not Ascend to Heaven"', *Arab Studies Journal*, 7/8: 2/1 (1999/2000), pp. 8–24.

Obeidi, Amal, *Political Culture in Libya* (Richmond, Surrey: RoutledgeCurzon, 2001).

O'Brien, Susie, 'Articulating a World of Difference: Ecocriticism, Postcolonialism and Globalization', *Nature/Culture: Special Issue of Canadian Literature*, 170–1 (2001), pp. 140–58.

Oerlemans, Onno, 'The Animal in Allegory: From Chaucer to Gray', *Interdisciplinary Studies in Literature and Environment*, 20: 2 (2013), pp. 297–317.

Ohrem, Dominik, 'Animating Creaturely Life', in Dominik Ohrem and Roman Bartosch (eds), *Beyond the Human–Animal Divide: Creaturely Lives in Literature and Culture* (New York: Palgrave Macmillan, 2017), pp. 3–20.

Olszok, Charis, 'Creaturely Encounters: Animals in the Libyan Literary Imaginary', PhD Dissertation, SOAS, 2016.

Olszok, Charis, 'The Litterscape and the Nude: History Escapes in Mansur Bushnaf's *al-ᶜIlka*', *International Journal of Middle East Studies*, 51 (2019), pp. 1–19.

Olszok, Charis, 'Creaturely Memory: Animal Tales and Deep History in Modern Libyan Fiction', *Middle Eastern Literatures*, 19: 3 (2016), pp. 260–77.

Omri, Mohamed-Salah, *Nationalism, Islam and World Literature: Sites of confluence in the writings of Mahmud al-Masᶜadi* (Oxford: Routledge, 2006).

Orafi, Senussi, 'Libya: Intentions and Realities', in Serra Kirdar (ed.), *Education in the Arab World* (London: Bloomsbury, 2017), pp. 307–26.

Ortiz-Robles, *Literature and Animal Studies* (London: Routledge, 2016).

O'Sullivan, Timothy M., 'Human and Asinine Postures in Apuleius' Golden Ass', *Classical Journal*, 112: 2 (2016–17), pp. 196–216.

Ouyang, Wen-chin, *Poetics of Love in the Arabic Novel: Nation-state, Modernity and Tradition* (Edinburgh: Edinburgh University Press, 2012).

Ouyang, Wen-chin, *Politics of Nostalgia in the Arabic Novel: Nation-state, Modernity and Tradition* (Edinburgh: Edinburgh University Press, 2013).

Patterson, Anabel, *Fables of Power: Aesopian Writing and Political History* (London: Duke University Press, 1991).

PEN International, 'Libya: Fears for Safety of Writers and Editors over New Literary Collection', 3 September 2017, https://www.pen-international.org/news/libya-fears-for-safety-of-writers-and-editors-over-new-literary-collection (last accessed 29 July 2019).

Pflitsch, Andreas, 'The End of Illusions: On Arab Postmodernism', in Angelika Neuwith, Andreas Pflitsch and Barbara Winkler (eds), *Arabic Literature: Postmodern Perspectives* (London: Saqi, 2009), pp. 25–50.

Phillips, Christina, *Religion in the Egyptian Novel* (Edinburgh: Edinburgh University Press, 2019).

Pick, Anat, *Creaturely Poetics: Animality and Vulnerability in Literature and Film* (New York: Columbia University Press, 2011).

Pinnault, David, *Story-Telling Techniques in the Arabian Nights* (Leiden: Brill, 1992).

al-Qadhafi, Muᶜammar, *The Green Book, Part One: The Solution of the Problem of Democracy* (London: Martin Brian & O'Keefe Reading, 1976).

Quinones, Ricardo, J., *The Changes of Cain: Violence and the Lost Brother in Cain and Abel Literature* (Princeton, NJ: Princeton University Press, 1991).

al-Qushayri, Abu-l-Qasim, *al-Qushayri's Epistle on Sufism*, trans. Alexander D. Knysh (Reading: Garnet Publishing, 2007).

Ramsay, Gail, 'Breaking the Silence of Nature in an Arabic Novel: *Nazif al-Hajar* by Ibrahim al-Kawni', in Tal Davidovich, Ablahad Lahdo and Torkel Lindquist (eds), *From Tur Abdin to Hadramawt: Festschrift in Honour of Bo Isaksson* (Wiesbaden: Harrasowitz Verlag, 2014), pp. 149–72.

Rasmussen, Susan, 'Animal Sacrifice and the Problem of Translation: The Construction of Meaning in Tuareg Sacrifice', *Journal of Ritual Studies*, 16: 2 (2002), pp. 141–64.

Rasmussen, Susan, 'The People of Solitude: Recalling and Reinventing *essuf* (the wild) in traditional and Emergent Tuareg Cultural Spaces', *Journal of the Royal Anthropological Institute*, 14 (2008), pp. 609–27.

Reeck, Laura, 'France: Historical and Cultural Relationships', in Waïl S. Hassan (ed.), *The Oxford Handbook of Arab Novelistic Traditions* (New York: Oxford University Press, 2017), pp. 603–22.

Ricoeur, Paul, 'Memory, History, Forgetting', *Iyyun: The Jerusalem Philosophical Quarterly*, 45 (1996), pp. 13–24.

Rooke, Tetz, '*Mahattat*: "Stations" on the Road to the Libyan Nation', in Elisabeth Özdalga and Daniella Kuzmanovic (eds), *Novel and Nation in the Muslim World: Literary Contributions and National Identities* (Basingstoke: Palgrave Macmillan, 2015), pp. 114–32.

Rooke, Tetz, *In My Childhood: A Study of Arabic Autobiography* (Stockholm: Stockholm University, 1997).

Roos, Bonnie and Hunt, Alex, 'Introduction: Narratives of Survival, Sustainability and Justice', in Bonnie Hunt, Alex Hunt and John Tallmadge (eds), *Postcolonial Green: Environmental Politics and World Narratives* (Charlottesville, VA: University of Virginia Press, 2010), pp. 1–13.

Rossetti, John Joseph Henry, 'Darkness in the Desert: Tradition and Transgression in Ibrahim al-Kuni's "*ᶜUshb al-Layl*"', *Journal of Arabic Literature*, 42 (2011), pp. 49–66.

Sakr, Rita, *'Anticipating' the 2011 Arab Uprisings: Revolutionary Literatures and Political Geographies* (New York: Palgrave Macmillan, 2013).

Saleh, Fakhri, 'Libya's Intellectuals under the Gaddafi Dictatorship', trans. John Bergeron, *Qantara*, 11 March 2011, https://en.qantara.de/content/libyas-intellectuals-under-the-gaddafi-dictatorship-suppression-at-home-flourishing-in-exile (last accessed 27 June 2019).

al-Samman, Hanadi, *Anxiety of Erasure: Trauma, Authorship, and the Diaspora in Arab Women's Writings* (New York: Syracuse University Press, 2015).

Santner, Eric L., *On Creaturely Life: Rilke, Benjamin, Sebald* (Chicago: University of Chicago Press, 2006).

Scanlan, Margaret, 'Migrating from Terror: The Postcolonial Novel after September 11', *Journal of Postcolonial Writing*, 46: 3–4 (2010), pp. 266–78.

Scholtmeijer, Marion, 'What is "Human"? Metaphysics and Zoontology in Flaubert and Kafka', in Jennifer Ham and Matthew Senior (eds), *Animal Acts: Configuring the Human in Western History* (Routledge: London, 1997), pp. 127–45.

Scholtmeijer, Marion, *Animal Victims in Modern Fiction: From Sanctity to Sacrifice* (Toronto: University of Toronto Press, 1993).

Selim, Samah, *The Novel and the Rural Imaginary in Egypt, 1880–1985* (Richmond, Surrey: Curzon Press, 2004).

Sells, Michael, 'The Muᶜallaqa of Tarafa', *Journal of Arabic Literature*, 17 (1986), pp. 21–33.

Sells, Michael, *Early Islamic Mysticism: Sufi, Qurᵓan, Miᶜraj, Poetic, and Theological Writings* (New York: Paulist Press, 1996).

Shamsie, Kamila, 'Where the Mulberries Grow', *Our Daily Read*, 29 July 2006, http://www.ourdailyread.com/2006/07/where-the-mulberries-grow/(accessed 8 April 2009).

Shepard, Paul, *The Others: How Animals Made us Human* (Washington, DC: Island Press, 1997).

Shryock, Andrew, 'Thinking about Hospitality, with Derrida, Kant, and the Balga Bedouin', *Anthropos*, 103: 2 (2008), pp. 405–21.

Shryock, Andrew and Smail, Daniel Lord, 'Introduction', in Andrew Shryock and Daniel Lord Smail (eds), *Deep History: The Architecture of Past and Present* (Berkeley, CA: University of California Press, 2011), pp. 3–21.

Sinno, Nadine, 'The Greening of Modern Arabic Literature: An Ecological Interpretation of Two Contemporary Arabic Novels', *Interdisciplinary Studies in Literature and Environment*, 20: 1 (2013), pp. 125–43.

Sleiman, Rima, 'Ville, oasis, desert: La négation de la Création', in Boutros Hallaq, Robin Ostle and Stefan Wild (eds), *La poétique de l'espace dans la literature arabe moderne* (Paris: Presses Sorbonne Nouvelle, 2002), pp. 43–55.

Smail, Daniel Lord, *On Deep History and the Brain* (Berkeley, CA: University of California Press, 2008).

Sperl, Stefan, '"The Lunar Eclipse": History, Myth and Magic in Ibrahim al-Kawni's First Novel', *Middle Eastern Literatures: incorporating Edebiyat*, 9: 3 (2006), pp. 237–55.

Sperl, Stefan, '"O City Set Up Thy Lament": Poetic Responses to the Trauma of War', in Hugh Kennedy (ed.), *Warfare and Poetry in the Middle East* (London: I. B. Tauris, 2013), pp. 1–38.

Stetkevych, Suzanne, *The Mute Immortals Speak: Pre-Islamic Poetry and the Poetics of Ritual* (New York: Cornell University Press, 1993).

Szeman, Imre and Boyer, Dominic, 'Introduction: On the Energy Humanities', in Imre Szeman and Dominic Boyer (eds), *Energy Humanities: An Anthology* (Baltimore, MD: Johns Hopkins University Press, 2017), pp. 1–14.

Taji-Farouki, Suha, 'Sadiq Nayhum: An Introduction to the Life and Works of a Contemporary Libyan Intellectual', *Maghreb Review*, 25 (2000), pp. 242–73.

Taji-Farouki, Suha, 'Modern Intellectuals, Islam, and the Qurʾan: The Example of Sadiq Nayhum', in Suha Taji-Farouki (ed.), *Modern Muslim Intellectuals and the Qurʾan* (London: Oxford University Press, 2006), pp. 297–332.

Talasek, J. D., *Imagining Deep Time* (Washington DC: National Academy of Sciences, 2014).

Tarbush, Susannah, 'That Last Summer in Tripoli', review of Hisham Matar, *In the Country of Men*, *Banipal*, 26 (Summer 2006), online, https://www.banipal.co.uk/book_reviews/20/%20in-the-country-of-men-by-hisham-matar/ (last accessed 16 July 2019).

Taylor, Chloë, 'Abnormal Appetites: Foucault, Atwood, and the Normalization of an Animal-Based Diet', *Journal of Critical Animal Studies*, 10: 4 (2012), pp. 130–48.

Thomas, Natalie and Nigam, Sumant, 'Twentieth-Century Climate Change over Africa: Seasonal Hydroclimate Trends and Sahara Desert Expansion', *Journal of Climate*, 31: 9 (2018), pp. 3349–70.

Tlili, Sarra, *Animals in the Qurʾan* (Cambridge: Cambridge University Press, 2012).

Tlili, Sarra, 'The Meaning of the Qurʾanic Word "dābba": "Animals" or "Nonhuman Animals"?', *Journal of Qurʾanic Studies*, 12: 1–2 (2012), pp. 167–87.

Tsing, Anna, *The Mushroom at the End of the World: On the Possibility of Life in Capitalist Ruins* (Princeton, NJ: Princeton University Press, 2015).

Vandewalle, Dirk, J., *A History of Modern Libya* (Cambridge: Cambridge University Press, 2012).

Van Gelder, Geert Jan, *Classical Arabic Literature: A Library of Arabic Literature Anthology* (New York: New York University Press, 2013).

Van Leeuwen, Richard, 'Cars in the Desert: Ibrahim al-Kawni, 'Abd al-Rahman al-Munif and André Citroën', *Oriente Moderno*, 77: 2/3 (1997), pp. 59–72.

Van Leeuwen, Richard, *The Thousand and One Nights and Twentieth-Century Fiction: Intertextual Readings* (Leiden: Brill, 2018).

Vermeulen, Pieter and Richter, Virginia, 'Introduction: Creaturely Constellations', *European Journal of English Studies*, 19: 1 (2015), pp. 1–9.

Vermeulen, Pieter, 'Creaturely Memory: Shakespeare, the Anthropocene and the New *Nomos* of the Earth', *Parallax*, 23: 4 (2017), pp. 384–97.

Wehr, Hans, *A Dictionary of Modern Written Arabic: Arabic–English*, 4th edn, ed. J. Milton Cowan (Urbana, IL: Spoken Language Services, 1994).

Weil, Kari, *Thinking Animals: Why Animal Studies Now?* (New York: Columbia University Press, 2012).

Weil, Kari, 'Matters of Memory and Creaturely Concerns: A Response to Pieter Vermeulen', *Parallax*, 23: 4 (2017), pp. 398–402.

Weisberg, Meg Furniss, 'Spiritual Symbolism in the Sahara: Ibrahim Al-Koni's *Nazif al-Hajar*', *Research in African Literatures*, 46: 3 (2015), pp. 46–67.

Wenzel, Jennifer, 'Petro-Magic-Realism: Toward a Political Ecology of Nigerian Literature', in Imre Szeman and Dominic Boyer (eds), *Energy Humanities: An Anthology* (Baltimore, MD: Johns Hopkins University Press, 2017), pp. 486–503.

Woodward, Wendy, *The Animal Gaze: Animal Subjectivities in Southern African Narratives* (Johannesburg: Wits University Press, 2008).

Woodward, Wendy and McHugh, Susan, 'Introduction', in Wendy Woodward and Susan McHugh (eds), *Indigenous Creatures, Native Knowledges, and the Arts: Animal Studies in Modern Worlds* (Cham, Switzerland: Palgrave Macmillan, 2017), pp. 1–10.

Woolf, Virginia, *A Room of One's Own* (London: Penguin Books, 2004).

Wright, John, *Libya, Chad and the Central Sahara* (London: Hurst & Co., 1989).

Wright, John, *The Trans-Saharan Slave Trade* (Abingdon: Routledge, 2007).

Wright, John, *A History of Libya* (New York: Columbia University Press, 2010).

Wright, Laura, *'Wilderness into Civilised Shapes': Reading the Postcolonial Environment* (London: University of Georgia Press, 2010).

Yaeger, Patricia, 'Literature in the Ages of Wood . . .', in Imre Szeman and Dominic Boyer (eds), *Energy Humanities: An Anthology* (Baltimore, MD: John Hopkins University Press, 2017), pp. 440–5.

Zipes, Jack, *Fairy Tales and the Art of Subversion* (Oxford: Routledge, 2012).

Index

al-ᶜAbbār, Sālim, 175
Abu Salim Prison massacre, 8, 130, 145, 205, 224
Adam and Eve, 41, 63, 65, 88, 191–2, 195–6, 210, 217
Aesop, 38
Agamben, Giorgio, 18
Ahmida, Ali, 174
Aitmatov, Chingiz, 57–8
alcohol, 84, 159, 206, 213
alienation, 14, 28, 72, 92, 131, 136, 196, 201, 252n
Almond, Ian, 97
al-ᶜAmāmī, Muḥammad, 173
Amazighs (Berbers), 7, 183, 202, 209–10
Amlūda, Maḥmūd, 77
Amnesty International, 8
Anderson, Lisa, 20
Animal Studies, 5–6, 18, 25, 38
animals, 26–7, 38, 50, 183
  and alienation, 28
  'animal collective' trope, 70
  anthropomorphism, 38–9, 52, 74
  '*becoming-animal*', 61
  centrality to human thought, 86–7
  communication with, 103–6
  companionship and coexistence with humans, 5, 27, 98–9, 101–8, 214–15
  death of, 116–17, 120, 180; by slaughter or sacrifice, 44–8, 60–1, 173–4, 179, 185, 207–8, 255n
  gaze, 19, 44–6, 57, 60–1, 86, 91, 117, 171, 211
  human subjugation of, 28, 184–5
  human versus animal societies, 20, 69–71
  human-animal forms, 122, 156
  hunting, 36, 59–60
  kinship with, 59–61
  as a means of rethinking hierarchies, 5
  as moral beings, 39
  as 'nations like you', 20, 37, 55
  as political allegory, 67, 70, 74
  self-sacrifice, 58–9
  shared vulnerability, 186
  as similes, 112, 207, 215–16, 220–1
  speaking, 36, 38, 39
  stray, 1–2, 113, 119, 126, 189, 233
  see also creatures/creatureliness
Ansar al-Sharia, 227
anthologies, 228
Anthropocene, 18
anthropomorphism, 38–9, 52, 74
ants, 183, 188, 218–19
anxiety, 6, 67, 109, 112, 136, 165, 207
Apuleius
  The Golden Ass, 29, 231–3, 235
ᶜAqila, Ahmad Yusuf, 16, 22
  al-Jirab: Hikayat al-Najᶜ (A Sack of Village Stories), 173, 175, 176–82
  life and career, 176–7
Arab British fiction, 199–203
Arab identity, 211
Arab Socialist Union, 68
Arab Spring, 5, 226–7

Arab unity, 136
Armstrong, Philip, 89
al-Asfar, Muhammad, 19–20, 129–30, 231
  on the 2011 uprising, 166
  Hajar Rashid (A Guiding Stone), 130
  al-Mudasa (The Crushed), 130
  Sharmula (Sharmula Salad), 127, 130, 144–56, 158
  Thuwwar Libya al-Sabirun (Libya's Patient Revolutionaries), 226
  word play and humour, 144
ᶜAṭiyya, Ahmad, 45
atomic bomb, 67, 69, 115
autobiography, 173–97
āya (sign/miracle/verse), 25–7, 96–7

Bachelard, Gaston, 119
Baker, Steve, 38
Balad al-Tuyub (https://tieob.com/), 9
Balbo, Italo, 44
Bamia, Aida, 12, 16
Barthes, Roland, 73, 95–6, 97, 124
BBC Arabic Service, 201
Bedouin rebellion, 193
'Bedouinisation' of Libya, 127
Begag, Azouz
  Le Gone du Chaâba (*Shantytown Kid*), 198
Ben Hameda, Kamal, 198
  La compagnie des Tripolitaines (*Under the Tripoli Sky*), 16, 198–200, 202–11, 215, 223–4
  life and career, 203
  on linguistic exile, 201
  La mémoire de l'absent (Memory of the Absent), 203–5, 211
Ben Jelloun, Tahar, 199
Benghazi, 127
  2006 protests, 129
  Arab Spring, 226–7
  backdrop of al-Fayturi's *Sarib*, 185, 187–8
  decay and oppression under al-Qadhafi, 144–5, 148, 175
  during and after the Second World War, 183, 185
  history, 144–5, 155
  HIV infection of children in hospital, 147–8
  al-Nayhum in, 15, 40
  literary depictions, 16, 41, 43, 130, 144–50, 189–90
  transformation into 'ghost town', 128
  vulnerability, 189–90
Benjamin, Walter, 18, 64, 68, 128, 138, 175, 178, 205
Berbers *see* Amazighs
Berger, John, 74, 82, 86, 108
Bildungsroman, 172–6, 182, 188, 191, 197–203
bilingualism, 91
Bin Lamin, Muhammad, 122–3
Bin Shatwan, Najwa, 16–17
  Madmun Burtuqali (Orange Content), 191
  Al-Malika (The Queen), 191
  Wabr al-Ahsina (The Horse's Hair), 17, 173, 176, 190–7
  Zaraʾib al-Abid (Slave Pens), 228
biopower, 18
birds, 46–7
birth, 4, 88, 167, 192, 195
black population of Libya, 7, 43, 227
Blair, Tony, 129
blood imagery, 54–5, 58, 62, 102
books
  banning and censorship, 7–9, 127, 204, 219
  burning, 8, 213, 219
British Military Administration (1943–51), 2
al-Buᶜīssī, Wafāʾ, 9
al-Bukhārī, Aḥmad
  Kashan, 228–9
al-Būrī, Wahbī, 3
Bushnaf, Mansur, 16, 129–30, 166
  al-ᶜIlka (*Chewing Gum*), 16, 127, 130–44
  imprisonment, 16
  al-Kalb al-Dhahabi (The Golden Dog), 230–4
  on Libya after al-Qadhafi, 227
  narrative structure, 131–2
  word play and humour, 144

Cain and Abel, 54–63, 115, 121
camels, 115, 115–18, 255n
as companion animals, 98–9
in literature, 99–103; in al-Kuni's *al-Tibr*, 101–8
piebald, 102–3, 105
cannibalism, 56
Case of the Animals Against Man, 39, 53
Catholicism, 200
cave art, 28
censorship, 2–4, 8–9, 11, 12, 95–6, 219
post-2011, 228–9
Chad, 16, 96, 98, 110
Chernobyl, 67
chewing/chewing gum, 134–7, 141–3, 167, 227, 231
childhood, 172
curtailed, 202–3
memoirs of, 176–98, 201–2
children, as narrators, 173–4
cholera, 189
Chorin, Ethan, 6, 8, 17, 53, 145, 147–8, 200
circumcision, 207
city, 126–9
depictions of, 119–24, 131, 145, 158, 164–6, 186–90
the 'ideal city' (*al-madīna al-fāḍila*), 80–1
al-Qadhafi's antipathy towards, 24, 128
Claudot-Hawad, Hélène, 57
climate change, 55
Cold War, 67, 75
Colla, Elliott, 86
colonialism, 11, 22, 96, 140, 199
concentration camps, 22
Connor, Steven, 114
consumerism, 14, 164
Cooke, Miriam, 61, 144
Cowan, Bernard, 205
cows, 180, 216, 219, 220
creatures/creatureliness, 4–6, 17–22
and animation, 21–2
'creaturely signs', 26, 114, 123, 132, 144, 140, 173, 205, 218, 224, 230, 232
in Anat Pick, 19
in Eric Santner, 18–19
in Walter Benjamin, 18
crucifixion, 61
Cultural Revolution, 4, 7–8
Cyrenaica, 3, 22, 30, 37, 64, 140

dābba (animal/beast), 186
Dalí, Salvador, 139
Darwinism, 41, 65, 86
social, 69
date palms, 120–1, 126
decapitation, 186
deconstruction, 97
deep time, 66
Deheuvels, Luc, 86
Deleuze, Gilles, 17, 61, 199
DeLoughrey, Elizabeth, 38
democracy, 6, 68, 69
depression, 80
Derrida, Jacques, 59
'The Animal that Therefore I am', 19, 171
desert journeys, 102, 105, 118
desert landscape, 24, 37, 67, 99, 103; *see also* Sahara
desire, 113, 140–2, 219
Diamond, Cora, 19, 118
Diana, Elvira, 11
diasporic Arab literature, 198–225
Djébar, Assia, 199
dogs, 113, 126, 178–81, 189, 216, 230–4
'journey home' genre, 1–2
trustworthiness, 27
drought, 172
drugs, 84

earthquakes, 12, 172, 189
ecocriticism, 5, 18, 25, 36, 38
education, 6, 174
Egyptian cinema, 132
Eid, animal slaughter during, 173–4, 179, 191, 207–8
El Maleh, Layla, 199
Elmarsafy, Ziad, 37, 61, 86, 91
El-Youssef, Samir, 200
environment
degradation and destruction of, 4, 42, 50, 95, 240n
and spiritual transformation, 40

environmentalism, 36, 54–5, 178
Ethiopia, 43–4, 47, 61
ethnic cleansing, 227
evolution, 41, 73
executions, 8, 22, 221
exile, 202, 213
existentialism, 41, 133
extinction, 12

fables, 36, 37–8, 46, 52, 54, 191, 241n
Fähndrich, Hartmut, 55, 85
al-Fākhirī, Khalīfa
  Mawsim al-Hikayat (Season of Stories), 173
Falḥi, Muḥammad, 177
fantasy, 13
al-Faqih, Ahmad Ibrahim, 14, 66–7, 70, 76–85, 77, 131
  as a diplomat, 77
  Hadaʾiq al-Layl (*Gardens of the Night*), 14, 66
  Fi Hijaʾ al-Bashar wa-Madih al-Bahaʾim wa-l-Hasharat (In Praise of Beasts and Censure of Humankind), 20
  Fiʾran bila Juhur (*Homeless Rats*), 14, 36–40, 49–55, 99
  Huqul al-Ramad (*Valley of Ashes*), 14
  'al-Jarad' ('The Locusts'), 50
  Kharaʾit al-Ruh (*Maps of the Soul*), 14
fascism, 22
al-Fayturi, Ahmad
  imprisonment, 182
  life and career, 182–3
  Sarib (A Long Story), 173, 175, 182–90
fear, 96, 97, 122–3
fertility, 234
Fezzan, 3
fidelity, 27
Finkelpearl, Ellen, 232
fishing, 44–8
flies, 71, 112, 114, 116, 209
  Le livre des mouches, 205–11
floods, 12, 40, 53, 179
folklore, 5, 10, 28, 50
food metaphors, 130, 146
football, 149–50
Foucault, Michel, 9, 18
Frankfurt School, 41
fratricide, 119
Freudianism, 41, 100, 142
Fromm, Erich, 41, 46
Fudge, Erica, 101

Gadhafi, Muᶜammar *see* al–Qadhafi, Muᶜammar
Gana, Nouri, 198
gazelles, 188–9
  in al-Asfar's *Sharmula*, 147–8, 150, 154–5
  in al-Kuni's *Nazif al-Hajar*, 56–60
  genocide, 3, 22
al-Ghadeer, Moneera, 26
al- Ghānamī, Said, 101
al-Ghazal, ᶜAbdallah, 95–100, 118–25
  al-Khawf Abqani Hayyan (Fear Kept Me Breathing), 16, 30, 95, 98, 118–25, 129, 138, 166
  al-Tabut (The Coffin), 109–18, 122, 124
Ghazoul, Ferial, 77
Gifford, Terry, 24
Girl and Gazelle statue, 21, 83, 126, 128, 140, 163, 229–31, 234–5
Goodman, Lenn E., 39
Government of National Accord, 227
Graziani, Rodolfo, 22
Green Book, 6, 8, 17, 67, 68, 145, 174, 201, 205
The Guardian, 224
Guattari, Félix, 17, 61, 73, 199

Hābīl, Sālim, 17
Ḥaftar, Khalīfa, 227
al-Hājī, Fāṭima, 11
  Surakh al-Tabiq al-Sufli (Screams from the Bottom Rung), 228
hallucinations, 45–6, 117, 189
al-Haqiqa, 13, 40, 127
Haraway, Donna, 101, 102, 105–6
Harel, Naama, 38
Harlow, Barbara, 214
Hemingway, Ernest, 40
  The Old Man and the Sea, 29, 43
heredity, 67
Herodotus, 205
Hine, Alyn, 91
Hiroshima, 115
HIV, Benghazi children infected, 147–8

homelessness, 126
housing, 6, 127–8
Huggan, Graham, 57
hunger, 9, 71, 72
al-Hūnī, Abū Bakr, 41
al-Hūnī, Rashād, 127
hunting, 36, 44, 59–60
Husseini, Khaled, 198

Ibn Khaldun, 64–5
Ibn al-Muqaffa[c], 27
Ibn Manẓūr, 68, 155
Ibn Mūsā, Husayn, 11
Ibn Tufayl, 27, 55
Idris al-Sanusi, King, 3, 190
incest, 119
intertextuality, 10
Iraq, 28
Irwin, Robert, 27
al-Islam, Sayf, 9, 129
Islamic State, 227
Islamist militias, 227
Italian colonisation, 2–3, 10, 22–3, 28, 35, 96, 120, 140, 174, 186
Italian gardens, 139

Jamahiriyya, 2, 6, 9, 14, 23, 65, 82, 92, 111, 150, 167, 194, 221
  censorship and oppression in, 106–8, 119, 151, 200
  intellectuals and writers in, 11, 30, 67, 75, 78, 151–2, 155, 205
  meaning/origin of term, 6, 21
Jameson, Fredric, 136–7
Jandouba, Battle of, 52
jerboas, 51–3
Jesus myth, 72
Jewish population, 7, 200, 209–10
Jonah and the whale, 48, 63

Kafka, Franz, 18, 29, 231
  'Metamorphosis', 68, 89
  'A Report for an Academy', 73
  'The Trial', 68
Kalila wa-Dimna tradition, 69
Kashlāf, Sulaymān, 12
Kearney, John, 222
al-Kiddi, [c]Umar
  Hurub Marish wa-Thawratuha al-Thalath (The Wars and Three Revolutions of Marish), 2, 228.
  'al-Hayah al-Qasira al-[c]Ajiba li-l-Kalb Ramadan' ('The Wonderful Short Life of the Dog Ramadan'), 1–2, 129, 231, 233
al-Kiklī, [c]Umar
  Sijjiniyyat (Prison Sketches), 228
Kilito, Abdelfattah, 91
Kilpatrick, Hilary, 198
The Kite Runner, 198
Klee, Paul, 138
al-Kuni, Ibrahim, 7, 11, 14–17, 24, 29, 69, 97–8, 108–9, 124, 153
  Anubis, 15, 67, 85–91
  autobiography, 105
  environmentalism, 54–5
  friendship with al-Nayhum, 15
  influence on al-Ghazal, 95–7
  Nazif al-Hajar (*The Bleeding of the Stone*), 15, 25, 54–62, 86, 97–8
  physical and mental crisis, 36–40
  al-Tibr (*Gold Dust*), 96–109, 111, 117, 124
  [c]*Udus al-Sura* (Night Wanderer), 15
  al-Waram (The Tumour), 253n

Lampedusa, 1
landmines, 118, 180, 188
language, 159
  linguistic exile, 105–6, 201
  retreat from, 214
Larkin, Philip
  'This Be the Verse', 191, 196
Laylā, Majnūn, 26
Le Guin, Ursula, 38
Lebanon, 28
Lejeune, Phillipe, 176
Leptis Magna, 21, 28, 141, 214, 219, 221, 235
libraries, 8, 204
Libya
  2011 uprising, 226–35
  diasporic writing, 198–225; 'representational burden', 200–1
  exile from, 202, 204

Independence (1951), 3
as seen by western media, 200–1
Libyan National Army, 227
Libyan Studies Centre, 174
Libyan Writers' Union, 11, 77, 145–6, 151–2
literacy, 3, 6, 223
litterscape, Tripoli as, 130–5, 143
Llote, Henri, 57
loss, 207
of innocence, 212
poetics of, 203
lucklessness, 35

McHugh, Susan, 54, 61, 87–8, 91, 101
madness, 140, 142
al-Maghrabi, Razzan Na^cim, 16–17, 129–30, 157
Nisa' al-Rih (Women of the Wind), 17, 127, 155–66
magical realism, 36
Maḥmūd, Fāṭima, 76
Maḥraz, Sīdī, 220
makhlūq (creature), 5, 18–19, 47, 58, 89
al-Mālikī, ᶜAbd al-Ḥakīm, 11
al-Maqhūr, Kāmil Ḥasan, 6, 10
marginalisation, 9
marriage, 102, 103, 113, 145, 192
martyrdom, 61
Marx, Karl, 204
al-Marzubān, Ibn, 27
maskh (transformation/metamorphosis/distortion/monster), 68, 82, 92, 231
Matar, Hisham, 7, 11, 17, 23, 198, 202–3
Anatomy of a Disappearance, 200, 223
In the Country of Men, 16, 173, 198–201, 203, 211–24
life and career, 199, 224
on linguistic exile, 201
The Return, 202–3, 223
Maṭar, Jāballāh
'In the Stillness of the Night: A Libyan Tale', 223–4
Mattawa, Khaled, 21, 149, 182, 200
meat eating, 27, 38, 43, 51–2, 55–60, 70, 185, 188, 255n
melancholy, 100–1
memory, 96, 113, 142, 177–9
of childhood, 172
and recording history, 174–5
metamorphosis, 61, 183, 230–2
Micklethwait, Christopher, 200, 212, 220
migrants, 1–2, 7, 43, 227
Mikhail, Alan, 99
al-Minifi, Rajab Buhwaysh
influence on Arab diasporic writing, 202–3
'Ma bi Marad . . .' ('No Illness But . . .'), 23, 202–3
Misrata, 98, 120, 127
Montgomery, James, 27
Moretti, Franco, 172, 174
Muḥammad, Fāṭima, 110
al-Muḥayshī, ᶜUmar, 7, 69
al-Mukhtar, ᶜUmar, 12, 22
mulberries, 217–19
Munif, ᶜAbd al-Rahman, 28
Muṣṭafā, Khalīfa Ḥusayn, 14
misogyny, 56

al-Naᶜās, Muḥammad, 'Majnun Ghazala', 229–30
al-Naᶜās, Marḍiyya, 16, 156–7
Nagasaki, 115
narrative mirroring, 142
National Transitional Council, 227
NATO, airstrikes on Libya, 227
nature, 178, 214–15
natureculture, 256n
al-Nayhum, al-Sadiq, 6, 7, 11, 15, 29, 39–49, 75, 91
al-ᶜAwda al-Muhzina ila al-Bahr (Sad Return to the Sea), 41–2
connections with al-Qadhafi, 68
exile from Libya, 68
fables as 'Libyan *Animal Farm*', 70
al-Hayawanat (The Animals), 13, 66–71, 74–5, 78, 127
house arrest, 41
journalism, 69
life and career, 40–1, 249n
Min Makka ila Huna (From Mecca to Here), 12–14, 29, 36, 52–5, 61, 69, 71–3, 75, 82, 229

al-Nayhum, al-Sadiq *(cont.)*
al-Qurud (The Primates), 13, 66–70, 74–5, 81
'al- Raja' min al-Hajj al-Zarruq' ('A Request from Hajj Zarruq'), 173
al-Ramz fi al-Qur'an (Symbolism in the Qur'an), 41
religious imagery, 72
short stories, 41
Tarikhuna (Our Past), 69
warning of al-Qadhafi regime's inhumanity, 69
Nixon, Rob, 24, 62
Nora, Pierre, 172, 174
al-Nuwayṣirī, Rāmiz, 146

Oedipus Rex, 57
Oerlemans, Onno, 38, 58
Ohrem, Dominik, 20, 22
oil/oil industry, 2–3, 5, 7, 12, 14, 23–4, 35, 98, 126, 129, 193, 227
and blood imagery, 54
as a symbol of environmental neglect and corruption, 40–2
Omri, Mohamed-Salah, 99–100, 108
oppression, naturalisation of, 71–2
oral history, 174, 177
origin, myths of, 203, 206
Ortiz-Robles, Mario, 70, 234
Orwell, George, 74
Animal Farm, 70
Ottoman Empire, 3, 140, 193, 195
Ouyang, Wen-chin, 77
Ovid, 29, 231

panoptic gaze, 9
parks, 139–40, 143
patriarchy, 139, 163, 200
peasant figure, 35
Pflitsch, Andreas, 137
Phillips, Christina, 42
phone tapping, 213
photographs, 137, 139
Pick, Anat, 19, 21, 64–5, 114, 118, 185, 191, 195, 232
poetry, 6, 137, 202, 212
modern, 242n
oral, 10, 99, 242n
political allegory, 65, 69, 70
pop culture, 135–6
postcolonial thought, 5, 36, 38
postmodernity, 136, 143
post-pastoral, 24
Potter, Beatrix, 38
power, iconography of, 36
pregnancy, 79, 81, 119, 160–1, 162, 176, 190–1, 193–6
primordiality, 65–6
prisons/imprisonment, 8–10, 16, 23, 30, 129, 137, 181–2, 193, 204, 225, 227–9
Abu Salim Prison massacre, 8, 130, 145, 205, 224
propaganda, 213
prostitution, 135, 142
proto-ethics, 19–20, 71
publishing
government-controlled, 13
self-publishing, 127
punishment, divine, 68
Pygmalion, 141

al-Qadhafi, Muᶜammar, 4, 6–9, 85, 96, 221
assumption of power, 3, 6, 12
as a character in fiction, 2
brutal regime, 49, 69
connections with al-Nayhum, 68
death and legacy, 227–35
dislike of sports gatherings, 149
environmental rhetoric, 24
Green Book, 6, 8, 17, 67, 68, 145, 174
labelling of people as 'rats' and 'cockroaches', 4, 49
loyalty to, 213
short stories, 8, 24, 128
Third Universal Theory, 67
Qadirbuh, Salih, 151–2
al-Qammūdī, Muḥammad Ṣāliḥ, 12
Qanāw, Miftāḥ, 21
al-Quddūs, Iḥsān ᶜAbd, 12, 132–3
al-Quwayrī, Yūsuf
Min Muffakira Rajul lam Yulad (Diaries of an Unborn Man), 12
Quinones, Ricardo, 55

Qur'an, 17, 20, 22, 41, 52, 98, 115–16, 178, 201, 204, 217, 232
on animals, 20, 25, 37, 39, 51, 55, 65, 186, 188–9, 193
concept of God's land (*arḍ Allāh*), 37, 53

rats, 46–7
Red Palace Museum, 140–1, 143
refugees, 227
repression, 136, 142
revelation, 96–7
Revolution (17th February 2011), 2–3
Revolutionary Command Council (RCC), 7, 68, 76, 233
failed coup, 74
Revolutionary Committees, 6–7, 203, 214, 217
Revolutionary Intellectuals Seminar, 69
Ricoeur, Paul, 174
rizq (sustenance), 37–8, 39, 46
Robinson Crusoe, 89
Rooke, Tetz, 10, 172
Roy, Arundhati, 5
The God of Small Things, 198
Russia, 108

al-Safa', Ikhwan
Case of the Animals Against Man, 27, 39, 52–3, 71–2, 184
Sahara, 59, 85, 96, 101, 246n
Sakr, Rita, 8, 49
Ṣāliḥ, Muḥammad al-Faqīh, 4
sandstorms, 12, 187
Santner, Eric, 18–19, 21, 66, 83, 98, 100, 114, 126, 134, 165, 173
al-Sanūsī, Ṣāliḥ, 228
Sarkozy, Nicolas, 129
Saro-Wiwa, Ken, 5
Satan, symbolising consumption, 42
satire, 1–2
Satfat, Massak, 28
Scanlan, Margaret, 201
Scholtmeijer, Marian, 73
sculpture, 140–1; *see also* statues
Second World War, 3, 35, 49, 175, 180, 183, 185–6
security forces, portrayed as animals, 71
self-harm, 84
Selim, Samah, 35
Sells, Michael, 100
Seminar on Revolutionary Thought, 7
Senusi Monarchy, 2–3, 15, 135, 139, 140
Septimius Severus statue, 21, 128, 141, 147, 214, 221, 231
sex, 78, 84, 133, 135, 145, 229
Shahrazad, 213
al-Shaylābī, Aḥmad, 11, 157
Shepherd, Paul, 178
Shukri, Muhammad, 145
Shwaysha, Raḍwān Abū, 76
sirr (secret), 26, 56–7, 96, 106
Sirte, 227
Siyāla, Muḥammad Farīd, 12
slavery, 43, 47, 227
Sleiman, Rima, 86
Smail, Daniel Lord, 65–6
Sophocles, 57
Soviet oppression, 97, 108
Spina, Alessandro
I confini dell'ombra (*The Confines of the Shadow*), 64
spiritual encounters, 48, 97, 102
starvation, 3, 49
statues, 131, 155–6
in Bushnaf's *al-ᶜIlka*, 140–1, 143
Girl and Gazelle, 21, 83, 126, 128, 140, 163, 229–31, 234–5
of Septimius Severus, 21, 128, 141, 147, 214, 221, 231
Stetkevych, Suzanne, 99
stories, bedtime, 213, 215
story, difficulty of, 3, 208
'Stray Dog' campaign, 2, 4, 7, 216, 227, 233
stuttering, 142
Sufism, 13, 25–6, 36, 96
concept of 'oneness', 38
and ecology, 25
imagery, 43, 103
mystical verse, 26
and openness, 97
as 'relational epistemology', 25
suicide, 135
sunglasses, 216, 222

surrealism, 140
surveillance, 6–7, 71, 203, 213, 216
al-Suwayḥilī, Ramaḍān, 11

Taji-Farouki, Suha, 8–9, 13, 68
Tala, Dar, 11
tasbīḥ (glorification of God), 25
Tawergha, 227
Tebu people, 7
al-Thanī, Ḥusām, 228
theatre, 74, 145
al-Tilisī, Khalīfa, 6
Tlili, Sarra, 25, 47
torture, 8, 71–2, 214, 217–18, 228
totalitarianism, impact on private lives, 224
tourism, 54
trafficking, of people, 227
translation, 178
trauma, 95–6
trials, 74
  televised, 8
Tripoli, 80
  in al-Maghrabi's *Nisaʾ al-Rih*, 157, 164–6
  'anxious' and 'enslaved' city, 204
  growth of, 127
  as litterscape, 130–5, 143
Tuareg people, 7, 11, 14, 55, 90–1, 101–3, 108, 238n
Ṭuraybshān, al-Jīlānī, 6, 204
turtles, 43–6

umamun amthālukum, 20, 37–8
Union of Libyan Writers, 8
universities, 182
uranium, 110
urbanisation, 4, 15, 172; undermining of, 127–30
al-Usbuᶜ al-Thaqafi, 77
al-ᶜUwaytī, Nādira, 16, 156–7

Van Leeuwen, Richard, 82
vegetarianism, 70–2
violence, 70, 139, 192
  slow, 62
vulnerability, 5, 17–22, 42, 61, 97, 181, 186, 188, 189, 201
  shared with animals, 18–20

waddān (mouflon), 36, 54, 59–62
waḥdat al-wujūd (the oneness of being), 25, 38, 62, 177
war, 103, 110
  depictions of, 96, 98
water, 53
  and spiritual transformation, 40
weapons of mass destruction (WMD), 9
Weil, Simone, 177
Wenzel, Jennifer, 40–1, 54
women
  blocks to creativity, 163–4
  disintegrating rights, 157, 228
  in fairy tales, 213
  friendships between, 159, 161
  in Libyan novels, 156
  as mythical warriors, 205–6, 210
  as national symbol, 156
  as writers, 16–17, 156–7, 176, 191–2
writers
  in al-Asfar's *Sharmula*, 151–6
  as characters in fiction, 159–63
  diasporic, 198–225
  imprisonment, 8, 16, 182, 204
  as intellectuals, 146–7
  from Libyan diaspora, 198–225
  online abuse, 229
  suppression, 7, 12, 66, 69, 127, 153, 204, 219; post-2011, 228–9
  women, 16–17, 156–7, 176, 191–2

Yaeger, Patricia, 23

Zarrugh, Nouri, 228
al-Zawāwī, Muḥammad, 24

EU representative:
Easy Access System Europe
Mustamäe tee 50, 10621 Tallinn, Estonia
Gpsr.requests@easproject.com

www.ingramcontent.com/pod-product-compliance
Lightning Source LLC
Chambersburg PA
CBHW071828230426
43672CB00013B/2788
* 9 7 8 1 4 7 4 4 5 7 4 6 0 *